Adolf Hitler
and
The Third Reich

Adolf Hitler and The Third Reich In American Magazines, 1923-1939

Michael Zalampas

Bowling Green State University Popular Press
Bowling Green, Ohio 43403

Acknowledgement

The author wishes to express his deepest appreciation to Dr. Joseph Slavin of the University of Louisville for his inspiration and encouragement; to Dr. Ron Horvath, President of Jefferson Community College, for his unqualified support; and Sherree Zalampas, his wife, for her sacrifice and devotion.

Contents

Chapter I
The Period of the *Parteikampf*, 1923-1932

"An extraordinary person," an "artist turned popular prophet and savior" was the way Ludwell Denny described Adolf Hitler in March, 1923. Denny, who had met Hitler privately, wrote that Hitler "seemed hardly normal; queer eyes, nervous hands, and a strange movement of the head." Hitler was an Austrian "locksmith" who, when temporarily blinded during the war was "subject to ecstatic visions of Victorious Germany." After the war, Hitler created the National Socialist Party dedicated to "reactionary aims and terrorist methods."

The ultimate goal of Hitler and his followers was "to destroy the present Germany, not to fight for their country but for their class." Their enemy was not France but an enemy "within" Germany—"the trade unions and Social-Democrats-'Reds', 'Jews'." Hitler proclaimed "Jews are Reds" and that "Jews are *Schiebers* (war profiteers)." In either case, Hitler believed "Jews caused Germany's present ruin." Hence, Hitler proclaimed that only *Volksgenosse* could be citizens and that no Jew could be a *Volksgenosse*. Bavarians greeted the message with enthusiasm as "Munich has never forgotten" the Jewish led communist regime of 1919. The "good people of Bavaria" openly sang "We'll hang a dirty Jew on every tree."

Hitler was determined to overthrow the hated Weimar government as the first step in the achievement of his aim of a united Greater Germany. The Bavarian government, led by von Kahr, shared his hatred of Berlin and so had provided his party with equipment from "the old German army" and the "active or passive support of the military." When Berlin demanded Bavaria declare martial law, von Kahr complied—and, after a few hours lifted the ban on the National Socialists while maintaining it on "the workers."

Hitler was well-financed by "three known sources". Von Kahr had turned over to Hitler funds from Berlin that were actually intended to disband local separatist organizations collectively named the "Orgesch." A second source of funds was provided by Munich capitalists led by Hulgeburg, general director of Krupp, and Kuhlo, president of the *Bayern Industrialen Verband*. Confidential circular appeals for funds sent out by Kuhlo had been uncovered and published. The third source of funds was France. Money from there, possibly official, possibly private, was channeled from banks in the Saar to the Deutsche Bank in Munich. France supported Hitler for the reason it supported other reactionary groups—to keep Germany weak and in an uproar.

1

Denny concluded, however, the Bavarian government and not Hitler was the real "menace to Europe." The Munich government "openly participated in sedition against the republic" and was determined to secede from Berlin. It was providing refuge for "the vicious elements of Europe." Hitler would probably fail personally as he had been unable to enlist the Bavarian peasants "despite generous sops" made to them in his platform. Hitler might, therefore, "make a revolution but cannot maintain a dictatorship."[1]

The same week, *The Literary Digest* reported the French occupation of the Ruhr had created a "frenzy of indignation" in Munich among the followers of the "German fascist Adolf Hitler." Of Hitler, it wrote, "his aim in life is to parallel in Bavaria the Mussolini triumph in Italy." Hitler's speeches were "tinged with anti-Semitism" and one result was the the Bavarian "atmosphere is laden with electricity and minor disturbances are the order of the day." Frenchmen, Belgians, and "Jewish-looking persons" were "maltreated in the streets" by Hitler's nationalists. When Bavarian Minister Schweyer "begged" Hitler to desist, Hitler saw the plea as "weakness" and "proceeded to bluster in his very best style." Hitler called upon his followers "to sweep away the Government." The authorities imposed martial law but quickly withdrew the ban on the National Socialists who were "not further interfered with."

Pre-war Munich, a "town of wide-spread toleration," had become anti-Semitic in reaction to the communist regime of 1919 which was led by "a few Jewish scribes." This "first wave of anti-Semitism" was thus a "justified revolt against a terrorism exercised by a handful of Semitic literates." The reactionary nationalists, who overthrew the communist regime, found their need for a war cry "easily supplied" by anti-Semitism. Hitler framed the "simple formula":

The world's capital is Jewish; Marxism is Jewish; Marxism and capitalism are responsible for the desperate straits the world is in. Therefore, Down with Jews! The world's salvation depends on the destruction of the Jews.

This cry was "taken up by the multitude."

Hitler, an "excited and muddle-brained Bohemian," was "devoid of solid convictions and incapable of a definite line of action." Like Mussolini, Hitler was a master of "opera effects." A "decorative painter by trade," Hitler employed "very effective" political placards and displays. Also like Mussolini, Hitler was an effective speaker because of his Viennese birth[sic], "his vivacious personality and ready dialectic." Any revolt led by Hitler would likely fail, however, as he was opposed by the "workers" of Bavaria.[2]

On November 3, 1923, *The Literary Digest* devoted its lead article to "the bleak prospect" of a "German Smash." The smash would occur if German unity was destroyed by monarchism in Bavaria, communism in Saxony and Thuringia, and republican separatism in the Rhineland. The chaotic situation was fostered and financed by Poincare of France, according to David Lloyd George of England and President Ebert of Germany. While Hitler was not mentioned in the text of the article, the article did include his photograph.

with the caption "the Grey-Shirt Leader" who expected "his National Socialists to be 'the sledge-hammer of Germany's resurrection'."[3]

Paul Gierasch, writing in the November, 1923, issue of *Current History*, described Hitler as a "man of little education, of the smaller middle class...a machinist by trade, who was by no means a good speaker." Gierasch, identified as a German publicist well acquainted with the Bavarian political scene, wrote the article in response to Hitler's attempted *putsch* in Munich. It is typical of the admixture of fact and fancy, perspicacity and prediction common to most early reports on the Nazi movement.

Gierasch asserted Hitler, a "street demagogue," had emerged as the most conspicuous of the reactionary leaders sponsored by the Bavarian state government of Gustav von Kahr as a bulwark against Bolshevism. Hitler's personal ideology was nationalistic, anti-socialist, militaristic, anti-Semitic, and "Wotan-worshipping." He was "more or less" subservient to the reactionaries led by von Kahr, whose intention was to establish a separatist federation of Bavarian, Hungarian, and Alpine lands under French tutelege. The Nazi movement was financed jointly by the "Kuhlo group of the Bavarian Industrial Association" and by France. France alone, according to Gierasch, had contributed "some thirty or forty million marks" to the Nazi party.

Hitler's "youthful party" was based on thousands of:

> ...the featherbrained, unbalanced types...students, clerks, mechanics, even plain hoodlums...purchasable for a few marks, a square meal and the prospect of a free fight with the odds on their side...a mixture of unbalanced visionaries and undisguised ruffians...alledged fugitives from the Ruhr.

Well-armed and well-equipped, "aided and abetted" by the Bavarian government, these Nazis were distinguishable from similar groups by their use of the swastika and the "open terrorism" against their opponents. They were held together only by "vaguely defined emotions and passions."

Although Hitler's attempted *putsch* was frustrated by the conservatism of the Bavarian peasants and a last-minute show of determination by the Bavarian government, Gierasch concluded that clearly "big events are brewing in the Bavarian witches cauldron." Only the future would reveal whether or not Hitler's defeat was temporary or permanent.[4]

Hitler and von Ludendorff were tried in February, 1924, for the leadership of the attempted *putsch*. The "outstanding event" of the trial, according to *The Independent*, was a speech by Hitler in which he "openly admitted" he sought to overthrow the Weimar government as it was "corrupt." Hitler argued that if he was guilty, then von Kahr and von Lossow were also guilty as his accomplices. If they were not guilty, then he was also not guilty and "the whole trial was a farce." Von Kahr and von Lossow, Hitler alleged, "wanted to overthrow the Government of the Reich, but lacked the moral courage to do so." *The Independent* reported Hitler's speech "made a powerful impression." Hitler spoke to the courtroom "as if he were addressing one of his mass meetings." Repeatedly, "the listeners showed signs of sympathy."[5]

The Review of Reviews believed Hitler's trial was interesting for what it revealed about the "extra-legal or secret societies with political aims" that had arisen in post-war Germany. These societies had certain "common aims" epitomized by Hitler: the revival of German nationalism, the elimination of Marxism in Germany, the "freeing" of Germany from "Jewish capitalism" and, for some, the "substitution of a crown in place of the presidency." The societies believed they alone could "preserve the basis of Western civilization" defined as "individualism and private property." Organizationally, they resembled "military associations" and could be mobilized in a moment. As a group, they owed their existence to "the Communist or 'Spartacist' rising of 1919" and, therefore, were similar to the "Italian Fascist associations." These associations were so numerous and so well-organized that they constituted an "invisible government in Germany."[6]

In March, 1924, *The Living Age* reprinted a letter by a Nazi named F. Goetz that had first appeared in the Berlin daily *Vorwärts*. Goetz, who participated in the *putsch* attempt, wrote the letter to explain its failure. According to Goetz, on the night before the *putsch* he personally led a Nazi company of 420 men to the Capuchin cloister. There he handed over a letter from von Kahr ordering the prior to supply them with hidden arms. The prior had them break into a sealed vault where they retrieved "8750 stands of arms in perfect condition." It took fourteen trucks to transport the arms. Goetz then took his company to the Dresden Bank where they picked up 3200 cases of ammunition and proceeded to the *Burgerbrau.*

Once there, Goetz "half-died laughing" at the sight of "fifty-eight Jews, mostly in their underwear and socks." "The dogs were raising a devil of a howl," so Goetz, "jokingly" drew his pistol and "the room instantly became as silent as the grave." Goetz left the *Burgerbrau* believing "our people would begin to shoot them in a few minutes."

The following morning Goetz led his company to the Louis Bridge where they disarmed a Security Police detachment without incident. He and his men were ordered to unload their weapons to avoid any mishap as they marched through cheering crowds in the streets. No one had "any hint of the scoundrelly betrayal that had meantime been arranged." At the moment when he entered Residenz Street, Goetz heard "wild shooting" lasting "some fifteen seconds." As his men took cover, Goetz saw "Hitler entering an automobile with an unconscious bleeding child in his arms." Goetz could not conceive "how the man escaped death" as "about one hundred dead and wounded" lay around him. He insisted no shots had been fired by Nazis as their weapons were empty. He and his men disappeared into the side streets and hid their arms and uniforms. Von Kahr and von Lossow had arranged "a cesspool of treason and betrayal" by their agreement to support Hitler while secretly ordering the Security Police and Reichswehr to fire on the Nazi columns. No one had the "slightest suspicion Lossow or Kahr or Seisser would betray us." *The Living Age* printed the letter without comment.[7]

Following these few articles, further mention of Hitler and the NSDAP is missing from our sample of magazines until the early fall of 1930. Hitler, after serving a brief period of imprisonment for his attempted *putsch,* slowly rebuilt the NSDAP into a national party. By the Reichstag election campaign of 1930, it had become a force to be reckoned with in German politics. Hitler once again attracted international press coverage. In the election of September 14, 1930, the NSDAP polled almost six and a half million votes and won 107 seats in the new Reichstag. Hitler leaped to prominence as leader of the second largest party in Germany.

American magazines were quick to conclude that Hitler was the key to any understanding of the Nazi movement and its goals. There was, however, little consistency in their description of him personally. *Time* saw him as a "demagog [sic]" and as an "oratorical, Jew-baiting terrorist." Hitler was "personally attractive for his 41 years, an orator comparable to Kerensky, Trotzky [sic] or Mussolini."[8] "Handsome Adolf" was described physically as a "medium-sized man with a small blond mustache, but hard, blue twinkling eyes."[9] *The Literary Digest* characterized him as a "slight, timid mannered man with a Charlie Chaplain mustache [who] grabs the world by the ear to roar about his plans." His speeches were "big talk" delivered with an "intense seriousness." It described Hitler as a "visionary" and a "madman," the most "fantastic figure" in post-war Europe. Beyond doubt, he ruled his party with an "iron hand."[10] Hitler was characterized as a "woman-hater" who denigrated them in his speeches. His "mental self-defense" for his own poor education was a "contempt for intellectuals." Hitler's ideas were formed during his years in Vienna where he began to "suffer from an inferiority complex."[11] To *The Reader's Digest,* Hitler was "completely unimpressive" physically and most resembled a "Moravian traveling salesman" with a "vacuous face" who had "grown fat." Hitler, a "German hypnotist," held people "spellbound" with his oratory as he was "consummately clever" although "nonsensical." "Anti-semitic and anti-foreign," he was indeed "anti-everything except the Dictatorship of Hitler."[12]

The same admixture of truth and fiction, ambiguity and confusion continued when biographical sketches were attempted. According to *The Literary Digest,* Hitler was the son of an Austrian railway employee and had fought against England as a volunteer in the Boer War. Reputedly he was the last man to leave Daspoort Fort when Lord Robert's troops marched into Pretoria. Following the war, Hitler worked as a house-painter in Munich until World War I, when he enlisted in the German army where he attained the rank of sergeant.[13] The very next week, *The Literary Digest* reported he had worked as an "architect's draftsman" prior to World War I.[14] In its biographical sketch, *Time* noted Hitler discouraged any reference to his early life as it, while not shameful, was "not sufficiently romantic for *Der Fuehrer.*" Correctly identifying his father as an Austrian customs inspector, *Time* proceeded to err in describing his pre-war occupation variously as "housepainting, carpentry, locksmithery, draughting." Hitler "served with distinction" in the German army where his was "once wounded and once gassed." In post-war "Catholic, reactionary Munich," Hitler entered politics with the moral and financial support of Ludendorff.[15]

Hitler's political goals were much more accurately delineated, as they were based mainly on direct reports of his speeches. *Time* summarized his "extraordinary program" as:

1) annulment of the Versailles and St. Germain treaties, 2) abandonment of reparation payments, 3) dissolution of the *Reichswehr* (voluntary army) and organization of a strong conscripted German army, 4) restoration of all colonies, 5) socialization of all basic industry, 6) disfrancisement of all Jews, 7) expulsion of all non-Germans who have immigrated since August 2, 1914.

Achievement of this program, *Time* concluded, would "ring the knell of the Republic."[16] *The Literary Digest* predicted the "guillotine scenes of the French revolution will be repeated when Hitler comes to power." It reported that if Hitler came to power "the lives of Socialists, proletarians and pacifist professors will be taken."[17] *The Nation* commented Hitler was "demanding policies and methods akin to those of a dictatorship."[18] On October 6, *Time* quoted Hitler's testimony before a Leipzig court, that, if he gained power the "November criminals of 1918" would soon have "their heads rolling in the sand." He would abrogate or revise the Treaty of Versailles with diplomacy if possible, or failing that, ignore or circumvent them with legal means. If necessary Hitler asserted he would use illegal means, for he was "answerable solely to the German people" for his actions.[19] *The Nation*, on October 8, informed its readers that in Germany "the whole principle of self-government through freely elected representatives is at stake." If Germany turns to a "dictatorship as its only hope in time of stress, the repercussions of its surrender will be worldwide."[20] On October 29, *The Nation* returned to this theme by stating Germany "stands in danger of an explosion that might readily be felt throughout the Western world."[21] *The Literary Digest* supported this view, noting that to give power to Hitler might not tame him for "gaining power legally, he would act illegally." The result "might bring about catastrophic upheaval not only in Germany but in all Europe."[22] *The Saturday Evening Post* characterized Hitler's political platform on November 1, 1930, as one of extreme Pan-German ideals which called for the unification of Germany and Austria, repudiation of the Young Plan, restoration of all German colonies, restoration of military parity, nationalization of trusts and socialization of industry and a nationwide campaign to remove Jews from the political and economic life of Germany.[23]

Varying explanations were given for the Nazi electoral gains in the Reichstag election of September 14, 1930. *The Literary Digest* initially attributed it to Hitler's appeal to female voters. It noted women provided a large part of the audience at his speeches and led "the fervent applause for handsome Adolf." They saw in him a "Siegfried and adulation by them is increased by his attitude toward them—one approaching contempt."[24] In a similar vein *Time* reported the large female support for Hitler, stating that when Hitler had recently appeared in Saxony "soprano voices cried *'Ach, der schone Adolf'* " and "pelted him with flowers." It attributed this support, at last in part, to the dislike of "thrifty German housewives" for the payment of reparations and the Young Plan—which Hitler insisted he would repudiate.[25] *The Saturday Evening Post* also attributed the Nazi vote to Hitler's ability as a "brilliant and forceful orator" which enabled him to make "a strong appeal to women."[26]

Alternative explanations stressed Hitler's appeal to Germany's "inflamed" youth and to the middle class. The young, it was stated, were attracted by Hitler's intention to repudiate the Young Plan as well as his willingness to employ physical force against communists on the streets. According to *The Literary Digest*, Hitler was able to exploit their youthful "lack of judgement" and "radicalism" as German sufferage law gave the vote to anyone twenty years old.[27] *The Nation* attributed the increase in Nazi strength to the support of the middle class whose fortunes were "swept away in the period of inflation."[28] *The Reader's Digest* agreed the middle class had provided Hitler with his victory but stressed this support was not due to the inflation of 1923 but to the current "hopeless economic distress," stating all he "needed for success was a good business depression." It asserted any alleviation of the depression would cause the Nazi movement to "die automatically."[29]

Even as they reported on the dangers of a possible Nazi dictatorship, American magazines in 1930 held out the hope it would be forestalled. *Time*, reporting on the election returns which gave a huge impetus to the Nazis and communists, predicted Bruening would either dissolve the Reichstag and rule by executive decree or would form a "Left Centre 'Grand Coalition' " with the aid of the socialist parties. In either case, both the "Reds and Browns" would be excluded and would therefore "remain merely blatant right and left 'lunatic fringes' on the garment of the government."[30] When Bruening did force through an adjournment of the Reichstag until the end of the year, *The Literary Digest* reported Bruening believed that neither the communists nor Nazis "will turn Germany upside down."[31] Both *Time* and *The Nation* stressed Hitler had renounced the concept of a *putsch* and intended to seek power legally. They quoted Hitler's statement that "ours is not a physical revolution but a revolution of the intellect "and concluded he would, at least for the moment, accept a continuation of the German constitution.[32] On October 8, *The Nation* argued it "appears reasonably certain that the parliamentary regime will not be immediately and violently destroyed" as Hindenburg would "make short work of any revolt." Further, any repudiation of the Young Plan would "automatically revive the punitive provisions of the Versailles Treaty."[33] *Time* took heart when the Reichstag met and re-elected Paul Lobe, the Socialist leader, as the President of the Reichstag for the tenth consecutive year. This "proved" Germany, "despite all the yelling, is not yet dominated by extremist parties." Bruening, all agreed, possessed the intelligence, determination, and political support necessary to forestall a Nazi victory.

Although Bruening was unable to gain Socialist support for a coalition government, with their aid he was able to secure passage by the Reichstag of an austerity budget based upon a $125,000,000 international loan. This was combined with financial and tax reforms along with an adjournment until December 1930. *Time* responded with an article entitled "Bruening Uber Alles."

It argued Bruening was decidedly "no fool" and was moving to obtain the largest possible reduction in reparations payments while, at the same time, restoring German prosperity coupled with its pre-war parity as a great power. Bruening even hinted a moratorium on payments might be forced upon the Allies by circumstances. If successful, he would pre-empt Hitler's position with the German people.[34] *The Nation* noted parliamentary "government in Germany has been given a six week's reprieve" and "may save the day."[35] *The Reader's Digest* closed out the year by predicting the "great majority of the people will never support such patent foolishness as Hitlerism." With prosperity regained, the Nazi movement would collapse. It saw the "real question for Germany" as continuation "of the status quo and the Gordian solution of communism." Hitler, it felt, could only "contribute to history by forcing the issue" as he was willing to employ terror as a political and psychological weapon.[36]

The systematic use of street terror by both the Nazis and the Red Front of Ernst Thaelmann was immediately reported by *Time* and *The Nation*. On August 25, 1930, in its first article on the Nazi movement, *Time* noted a pre-election debate at Nuremberg had "terminated in a free-for-all" between Nazis and communists in which "70 contestants" were injured before the police "dispersed the rioters with truncheons and fire hose." *Time* blamed the Nazis for the clash, noting Hitler had organized youthful members of his party into "clean-up gangs called 'storm-squads' " to confront the Red Front squads. On October 6, 1930, *Time* placed the odium on the Red Front for initiating a fray at Unterbermsgruen in Bavaria. There communists attacked a Nazi parade "with brick-bats" and injured "20 Facists, four critically." *Time* also reported that Viscount Rothermere, the "blatant 'Hearst of England,' " had cabled the *Daily Mail* from Munich that under "Herr Hitler's control, the youth of Germany will be effectively organized against the corruption of Communism."[37] *The Nation* noted on October 29, 1930, that "about 60 have died and perhaps as many as 800 have been wounded or injured since January 1" in the Nazi-Communist street-fighting. It commented the fighting could not "be explained away on the grounds of hoodlumism" for the "political background of the street battles has been everywhere apparent."[38] In December, *The Nation* re-interpreted the cause of the clashes when it stated they were increasingly assuming the "character of food riots rather than street-fighting between rival political gangs." The clashes were escalating to the point where civil war occurred daily in German towns and the ballot box was being replaced by the club.[39] Only alleviation of Germany's economic distress by its creditors could diminish the clashes and prevent a German dictatorship.[40]

The concurrent Nazi violence directed against Jews was also reported quite early by American magazines. *Time*'s initial article described Hitler as "Jew-baiting." It noted he intended the total disenfranchisement of the Jews from German political life. On September 29, 1930, *Time* reported Jewish "mother-instinct knew the meaning of Jew-baiter Adolf Hitler's election victory [a] fortnight ago" and so they were fleeing Germany with their children. Asking "what do German Jews face from Adolf Hitler," *Time* summarized Hitler's anti-Semitic program as one under which:

1) All Jews who have entered Germany since August 2, 1914 would be expelled; 2) the term 'Jew' would mean anyone whose ancestors practiced the Mosaic faith after March 11, 1852; 3) Jews would be banned from service in the German army or navy, would pay a special tax by reason of the 'exemption'; 4) Jews would not be admitted to schools of higher learning, either as teachers or instructors; 5) sales of land to Jews would be void; 6) Jewish-owned news organs would be compelled to state that fact in their front-page headline, printing under the symbolic *Mogen David* (Star of David).

On October 27, 1930, *Time* devoted a full column to "Plate Glass Riots." It stated that the previous week, Jewish-owned department stores in Berlin such as Wertheims, Gruenfelds, Behrendt, and Cords had their show windows shattered by stone-throwing gangs shouting "Heil Hitler". In addition, a number of shots were fired at windows on upper floors. Concurrently, "Jewish-owned cafes and banks suffered similar pane-smashes." Although Hitler issued a statement blaming the attack on "rowdies, plunderers and Communist provocateurs," *Time* observed Berlin chief of police Zorgiebel stated "virtually none but Fascists participated in the attacks."[41] *The Literary Digest* stressed that violence, especially that directed against Jews, was the "first thought of Hitlerites."[42] *The Reader's Digest* reported anti-Semitism was not only a theoretical premise of Hitler but a brutal Nazi reality occurring daily throughout Germany.[43] In no magazine, however, was editorial outrage coupled with a call for any action by the American public.

One further subject attracted the attention of *Time* and *The Nation* in the fall of 1930—the effect of Nazi election successes upon the holders of reparations and Young Plan bonds. At the end of September, *Time* reported German reparations bonds were being sold at an eleven percent discount in London. Further, Wall Street common stocks had dropped "some five points" when a rumor circulated that a German revolution had occurred but the news was being suppressed by censors. American, British and French bankers were anxiously seeking some reassurance from German bankers.[44] While expressing concern reparations might be "readjusted," *The Nation* argued "German financial standing is not yet imperiled."[45] When Hjalmar Schacht visited the United States at the beginning of October, *Time* devoted an entire article to his visit under the title "Schacht Shocks." The shock occurred when Schacht told the New York Board of Trade for German-American Commerce there was "no doubt that one day the moratorium provided in the Young Plan will be declared." Schacht pointed out Germany had borrowed since 1924 almost twice what it had paid in reparations—a situation that could not continue. He concluded "the Reparation problem must either be solved or disappear."[46]*The Nation*, commenting on Bruening's budget and tax reforms, asserted that without them, "Germany's credit standing would also have been severely shaken."[47]

Yet, so far did the Nazi threat to the German republic seem to wane in the early months of 1931, that *Time* chose to characterize the Nazi success at the polls as a "flash in the pan."[48] *The Literary Digest* also re-evaluated the Nazi electoral success and decided it represented a demand for a revision of Versailles but not an endorsement of "Hitler's program as a whole." If the treaty were revised, "Germans will not call for a tin hat and a bayonet but for lower taxation and competent administration."[49] *The Atlantic Monthly* agreed that the "ordinary German, the man in the street, gives little thought to the eastern frontiers of Germany" or to the question of the war guilt for he is "thinking of his job and his taxes."[50]

A number of additional factors seemed to preclude further Nazi success. Among these was the then perceived strength of Bruening, who was described as "modest, sincere, industrious and self-effacing" by *The Literary Digest*.[51] *The Saturday Evening Post* declared happily "the troubled Teutonic hour" had found its man in Bruening who overnight had reached "the front rank of European statesman."[52] When Hitler ordered the Nazi party to withdraw from the Reichstag in February, 1931, it was interpreted as a victory for Bruening as it was expected to strengthen his hand in the rump Reichstag.

It further seemed Hitler was losing control of the Nazi party. On March 28, Bruening issued an emergency decree designed to reduce the level of political violence. The decree provided that political rallies were banned unless the police had given permission twenty-four hours prior to a proposed meeting. When Hitler ordered his party to obey the decree, he precipitated an open revolt by Berlin SA leader Walter Stennes. *Time* regarded the incident as indicative of widespread discontent with Hitler among Nazi party members and noted there was a "great likelihood" that "many disgruntled Fascist gangsters" would "hire out to the Communist gangs." Hitler, it reported, was only able to suppress the revolt through his control of party funds.[53] *The Nation* interpreted the revolt as representative of a deep fissure within the Nazi party. Hitler's "most serious mistake" occurred when he trained the SA for "positive revolutionary action" but then failed to lead their expected revolution. Hitler's control of party funds, while it might save him, constituted his only hold on his party.[54]

Simultaneously, Hitler had received a further blow when the Socialists in the Thuringian Diet forced out of office the local Nazi Minister of the Interior, Wilhelm Frick. Taken together, these events were interpreted by *Time* and *The Nation* as signs Hitler's star was waning. According to *Time,* Hitler had decided to repudiate the idea of being a "political Al Capone" for he wished to maintain his party's twelve million votes rather than surrender to "his Gang" of only 150,000 members. His new intention was to "tone down his Gang, moderate his policies" and accept Nazi participation in the next German cabinet.[55] *The Saturday Evening Post* wrote the Nazi movement was "slightly bent" and that if German unemployment dropped, "Hitler is probably doomed."[56]

In 1931, as in the fall of 1930, American magazines devoted much attention to German finances. However, whereas in 1930 interest had been directed toward the question of reparations, in 1931 it centered on the depression that engulfed the German economy. It was increasingly recognized there was a clear connection between the decline of the German economy and the fortunes of Hitler and the Nazi party.

By January, 1931, it was quite apparent the German economy was in a serious slump. *Time* believed the drop directly attributable to Hitler's radicalism. It reported his "wild words" had caused $380,000,000 to flee Germany as Jews transferred their wealth to London, Paris and Amsterdam banks. The flow was staunched only when the Reichsbank raised its discount rate to five percent at a time when the rate was three percent in London and Paris.[57] On January 22, *Time* noted $100,000,000 in short-term credits had been recalled the previous week by American bankers who were frightened by the increasing political radicalism in Germany. The Berlin stock exchange had dropped sharply.[58]

The Nation attributed the German economic decline to the demand Germany continue to make reparations payments. It argued for a cancellation of reparations as the "bulk of the German people have reached the limit" in the reduction of their standard of living. It warned any further economic drop would probably lead to a Nazi dictatorship as millions of Germans saw it was the only party determined to terminate the Young Plan.[59] For the same reason, *The Atlantic Monthly* added its weight to the cause of cancellation in February, 1931. In the end, it was not enlightened statesmanship nor intelligent self-interest that resolved the reparations problem.

In need of a political victory and in an attempt to restore confidence in the German economy, Bruening proposed a joint customs union with Austria on March 21, 1931. The French government immediately protested the action while the Hague Court declared the proposal to be illegal. When Bruening showed no sign of withdrawing his proposal, French bankers withdrew their money from the Austrian Credit-Anstalt bank on May 11. This triggered a financial crisis which, in turn, ruined the Darmstadter and National Bank in Berlin and exposed the German government to bankruptcy. This crisis was so severe President Hoover proposed a one-year moratorium on the payment of intergovernmental debts on June 20.

On June 24, *The Nation* reported German bonds had dropped so precipitously in value that the Reichsbank had lost $250,000,000 of its reserves during the previous two weeks. Bruening was being widely described as the "hunger chancellor" by all classes of Germans.[60] *The Saturday Evening Post* the same week featured an article by Dorothy Thompson entitled "Something Must Happen" in which she asserted it was the economic crisis precipitated by Bruening that was driving German youth to the Nazi banner.[61]

It was not until July 6 that President Hoover was able to announce the acceptance, at least in principle, of the moratorium. For *The Literary Digest*, it was too little, too late. It predicted the coming winter would see revolution in Germany led either by the Red Front or by the Nazis. The desperate economic situation had produced a political climate in which the typical "Hitlerite" was driven by forces that were "emotional and irrational." Nazis were possessed by the feeling "Life has missed us! We will hit back"—at the government, capitalists, Jews and foreigners. In this sense, Hitlerism resembled a "religious movement" with qualities of "asceticism, renunciation, spirituality."[62] *Time* concurred with this prediction of imminent revolution, noting that France had announced it expected to continue to receive the Young Plan payments due her until Berlin agreed to a list of French demands. These demands included the abandonment of any customs union with Austria, abandonment of German naval construction, adoption of tighter credit restrictions and immediate dissolution of nationalist organizations. For any German government to accede to these demands, *Time* asserted, would precipitate immediate revolution— to reject them would lead to further French economic pressure and revolution. Castle, the Acting Secretary of State for the United States, faced with this attitude of France, announced that "Germany's salvation was up to the world's banks to settle privately."

Time reported France was withdrawing its on-demand credits from Germany. When a desperate Reichsbank requested a halt to all foreign withdrawals for a period of six months, it was Wall Street that "quibbled." German banks thereupon collapsed, major bankers committed suicide, and the bank clearing system "degenerated into pure anarchy." Bruening had been forced to institute "state capitalism" as the only alternative to total economic catastrophe. Nazi and Red Front Clashes were plunging the nation into a political chaos that paralleled its economic chaos.[63]

An emergency economic conference the last week of July had failed to budge France from its position. Indeed, France began to withdraw its on-demand credits from the Bank of England as a means of pressure on the British cabinet.[64] On one day alone, France withdrew $16,911,700 in bar gold—the single greatest drain the Bank of England had known in all its 237-year history. Over a period of three weeks, a total of $160,000,000 was withdrawn by Paris. The pound sterling dropped from $4.86 to $3.45 and was taken off the gold standard. The British government was forced to announce severe austerity cuts in its budget. Only a emergency loan of $243,000,000 arranged by the Federal Reserve Board of New York forestalled a collapse of the London Bank. When Dutch banks began to withdraw their gold from London, the result was a "severe flutter" felt world-wide. Albert H. Wiggen, Chairman of the Chase National Bank, announced his immediate departure for Europe for consulations, noting that American banks had a direct interest in the European financial situation.[65]

Even as the Red Front castigated Bruening from the left, *Time* reported a "mad-eyed, bristle-lipped" Hitler on the right was pledging to repudiate all foreign debts, had refused any fresh obligations to France and had succeeded in having a plebliscite called on representation in the Prussian Diet. Although Bruening won the plebliscite, *Time* noted Hitler regarded the political and economic chaos with "greatest glee." Hitler argued the eyes of the German people had finally been opened to "the unimaginable lies, trickeries and deceits of the Marxist swindlers of our nation."[66] *The Nation* stated "Herr Hitler" was "beginning to show signs of delusions of grandeur" by claiming to be the "last hope" of Germany. Though it labeled such talk "vain-glorious," *The Nation* insisted France was pursuing a "ruthless anti-German course" which would strengthen his appeal among Germans. Indeed, it wrote, "one wonders whether France is not deliberately planning for anarchy in Germany."[67]

This theme was echoed by *The Atlantic Monthly* which insisted the international economic crisis in general, and the German crisis in particular, was due to French intransigence on the question of reparations. Coupled to the "millstone" of reparations were fears the Nazis would, on achieving power, unilaterally repudiate German private debts. It pleaded for a permanent cancellation of reparations when the Hoover moratorium expired as a means of both reducing Hitler's appeal to the Germans and of stabilizing the international economic balance. Only the United States possessed the necessary moral force to overcome French opposition to cancellation. Without the aid and understanding of America, the moderate forces within Germany were doomed.[68] During October, Hitler seemed to move closer to the chancellorship while Bruening's control of events seemed to slip markedly. The moderate parties were defecting to extremist parties on the right with Hitler being the primary beneficiary of the move. At a meeting at Bad Harzburg, Hitler rallied the nationalist parties to his support. When Bruening survived a Nazi inspired vote in the Reichstag by only twenty votes, *Time* described him as a "German Eliza" able to continue only by leaping from one "ice floe" to another. Replying to criticism his followers had attacked communists in Berlin and Brunswick, Hitler replied that if the government members wanted law and order, they "must yield their place to those who alone have the will and ability" to keep the peace.[69] The banking system was further endangered by charges by Schacht that the Reichsbank had falsified the extent of its indebtedness and that fully half of its negotiable bonds were worthless. Hindenburg decided "during this critical hour" to encourage the Nazi party by meeting with Hitler even though Hitler had just ordered his followers to desert the Reichstag. *The Literary Digest* released a survey of the German press which revealed most editors believed the anticipated distress of the coming winter would bring Hitler to power.[70]

By November 18, *The Nation* was ready to declare there were only two ways out for Germany: "Hitler's nationalism" or "communism of the Russian brand." Under Bruening's leadership, taxes had been tripled, wages and land values had plummeted and, at the same time, the cost of living had soared 250 percent. "Young Germany" had "nothing to lose, and everything to gain, in an overthrow" of the government. French denial of international cooperation served only to increase "the validity of militant German nationalism." One could only "stand by in a horrible fascination for the moment the building will come down in a great roar."[71]

The same week *The New Republic* reported France was attempting to capitalize on the crisis in Germany with a demand Bruening acquiesce in the formation, under French financial auspices, of a confederacy of Austria, Hungary, Yugoslavia, Bulgaria, Rumania and Czechoslovakia. France had already "bought and paid for the Yugoslavian and Rumanian governments." For the moment, France was insisting Bruening agree to an Eastern Locarno— a move that would be "political suicide" for him. Some of Laval's entourage in France even felt it would be best for Hitler to take power at once as he would "rapidly discover he could not do without French support and, as dictator, he would be able to make far greater concessions than the Bruening cabinet."

Indeed, *The New Republic* believed Hitler and representatives of France had already held secret conversations. In a separate article in the same issue, *The New Republic* reported Germans of all classes were entangled in a web of fear—of suffering in the coming winter, of a Nazi or communist revolution, and of uncontrolled inflation. Conditions were so bad even the Nazis would have to think "twice before becoming captain of a waterlogged and probably sinking ship" as they had no "real program" while their "counsels are those of despair." Their philosophy "is madness, their mental horizon is that of the Ku Klux Klan" and yet, they were able to strike a "spark in the breast" of young Germans who were led by their fears rather than hope. Hitler's path to power was paved with these fears.[72]

In the belief Hitler would soon be in power, *The Literary Digest* began to print extracts of his speeches. On November 21, it quoted Hitler as saying:

...pre-war Germany belongs to history, Nazi Germany will be a new Germany, free of guilt for the war and free of having signed at Versailles....The new Germany will put down the Communists, restore the moral fiber of the German people, will repudiate reparations but will pay private debts....Nazi Germany does not intend to make war but peace in order to reconstruct Germany. Versailles should be revised and abrogated. Only the Nazi movement can restore faith in Germany.

Hitler further stated the United States had a "moral responsibility" to see the Versailles Treaty revised as American intervention on the side of the Allies and Wilson's treachery at Versailles had produced Germany's subsequent suffering. Hitler's speeches struck such a responsive chord among the Germans, according to *The Literary Digest*, that even the communist newspaper *Welt am Abend* believed he would soon attain power.[73]

On December 19, *The Literary Digest* reported Hitler's primary goals were the repudiation of reparations and the "destruction of the Communists." Hitler would adjure a revolution by force but, once in power, would impose a "stringent dictatorship." Although it might be difficult to accept Hitler as "a champion of legal and constitutional methods," in time the states of Europe would "learn to live with him." It noted "some in France think that coming to power will make him more responsible" as they detected elements of moderation in his recent speeches.[74]

By the first week of December 1931, it was daily anticipated Bruening would be replaced by Hitler. In municipal and provincial elections, the Nazi party continued to make impressive gains. The Prussian Diet, responding to the Nazi campaign against reparations as "tribute," overwhelmingly repudiated the Young Plan. When the Boxheim Document, a secret Nazi plan to forcibly prevent a communist coup in Hesse surfaced, the federal prosecutor refused the charge the Hesse Nazi with treason. *Time* interpreted this decision to mean it was possible for Nazis to plot "whatever they please anywhere in Germany without committing treason." In a move designed to both "throttle the spread" of Nazism and to convince the Young Committee he had done all that was possible to save the German economy, on December 8, Bruening issued a forty-six point emergency decree. The decree prohibited all political meetings for a month, placed injunctions on the possession of weapons and provided imprisonment for the defamation of public officials. The economic sections increased the sales tax, reduced the interest rate, restricted the flight of capital and reduced public salaries. Bruening further prohibited a broadcast by Hitler to the United States and was said to be considering Hitler's expulsion from Germany. *Time* interpreted these actions to mean "the Bruening Dictatorship was trying to out-Hitler Hitler." *Time* believed the decree might be too late to save the day.[75]

In the view of *The New Republic*, Bruening's "veiled dictatorship" was the only alternative to a dissolution of the Reichstag and new elections leading to an "open dictatorship" by Hitler. *The Nation* characterized the decree as "Bruening's Last Stand." Although *The Nation* acknowledged his courage in issuing the decree, it questioned the "wisdom and practicality" of the action and charged Bruening with "having set himself up as dictator of Germany." If the decree failed to limit the level of political violence it would precipitate an "explosive reaction" by the Nazis or Red Front. In any case, Hitler was not far from power. When a rumor reached New York that Hitler intended to take the mark off the gold standard on his assumption of the chancellorship, Young Plan bonds dropped from $84 to $25.50 and Manhatten bank stocks "dipped as much as 20 points"—the result was a "black afternoon" on Wall Street.[76]

The German economy suffered an even worse decline. The "flight from the mark" accelerated as large amounts of gold and silver were smuggled out of Germany. German securities were sold off abroad and any profits invested in foreign banks. Industrial goods were dumped overseas at any price. Bruening publicly acknowledged 4,600,000 men were out of work and privately speculated 7,000,000 would be unemployed by spring. In Berlin, artillery cassions were pressed into service to collect "old clothes for the destitute unemployed." "Is it any wonder," *The Nation* asked, "that the German people are saying to themselves, 'Better an end with terror than terror without an end,' and turning to the panaceas of Adolf Hitler as the only remaining solution?" It believed Hitler commanded the allegiance of most Germans and that the political violence he inspired "had ceased to constitute news."[77]

In December, 1931, the Young Plan Committee convened in Basle. Rather than addressing the old problem of the claims of reparations versus payment of war debts, it debated the claims of reparations as opposed to private debts owed by Germany. The German delegate Melchior, utilizing a study prepared by A.H. Wiggen of Manhatten Chase National Bank, insisted it was impossible for Germany to continue to pay reparations to the Young Plan. The United States delegate, W.W. Stewart of the New York firm of Case, Pomeroy and Company, supported Melchior's position. Charles Rist, representing France, insisted any reduction of cancellation of reparations had to be matched by a corresponding decision on war debts and so deadlocked the conference. Concurrently, *Time* reported Wiggen convened a "Banker's Committee" in Berlin to discuss the repayment of short-term private American loans to Germany. Wiggen's visit, it noted, "seemed to have been the signal for Herr

Hitler, long a bogeyman to bankers, suddenly to transform himself into the Banker's Friend." Never, it averred, was "the favor of U. S. bankers sought more openly." Hitler stated he rejected the expropriation of private property and stressed 5,500 Nazis had been killed or wounded the past year protecting the principle of private property against communists. While he repudiated reparations payments, Hitler affirmed he did accept the obligation for Germany to repay its private debts.[78]

On December 16, *The Nation* reported there were rumors Hitler had reached a private agreement with foreign financiers "anticipating his eventual rule." Germany would repudiate reparations but would repay private debts. These rumors, it noted, could explain the ominous "calm with which his frank plays" have been received by "foreign industrialists and financiers." *The Nation* editorialized "Hitler's rosy pledges, of which there is no guaranty, would be a dear price for the enslavement of the German people under a reactionary, bombastic, anti-Semitic, militaristic dictatorship."[79]

As 1931 drew to a close and 1932 was ushered in, speculation was still rife that Hitler would shortly come to power. *The Literary Digest* predicted there would be a "Great Hitler Upheaval" in February, 1932. Many Germans had come to regard Hitler as a "hero facing a world at arms against his race." Although he was expected to impose a "stringent dictatorship," there were signs he was becoming more moderate. For example, Hitler had adjured any attempt at a coup and was pledged to see power constitutionally. As chancellor, he would be more responsible and, in time, the states of Europe would "learn to live with him."[80]

A series of actions by Bruening, however, soon changed the tone of some American magazines. Bruening, taking advantage of the deadlock in the Young Committee between France, Britain and the United States, unilaterally announced that Germany would no longer pay reparations. Further, he succeeded in obtaining a moratorium of one year on Germany's short-term loans. Through a series of economic controls on the movement of capital, salaries, rents and prices, Bruening was able to restore a measure of prosperity in Germany. On February 6, *Collier's* lauded Bruening as the "Best Since Bismarck." It described him as "a scholar by training, a recluse by inclination" who was "one of the key men in world politics." Bruening's intelligence, combined with his deep religious convictions, provided him with "iron determination." Bruening was the perfect man for Germany as he realized "Hitlerism, when challenged, tends to resolve itself into bluster." He had repeatedly forced the Hitlerites to a showdown and each time had "held the winning hand." For these reasons, *Collier's* believed Bruening would be able to block the Nazi bid for power.[81]

This prediction seemed to be borne out as the presidential and Prussian Diet elections scheduled for May, 1932, drew near. Hindenburg had been elected to a seven-year term in 1925. Bruening, according to *Time*, fearing "his opponents the Hitlerites" would make enormous gains in the Diet election and even threaten Hindenburg's re-election, had put Hitler in a "tight position." Bruening had "summoned Fascist Hitler to Berlin" and appealed to Hitler to agree to a simple extension of Hindenburg's tenure so "the Fatherland could present a united front to the world." This placed Hitler in the position of either repudiating "Germany's idol" or being "diddled out of his great chance to seize the government legally." Further, he offered the Nazis two seats in the cabinet—a concession that, if accepted, would preclude a Nazi campaign against the government in the Diet elections.

The following week, *Time* reiterated its belief that Bruening had placed Hitler in "a tight position." It was sure "Handsome Adolf" would "think twice" before opposing Bruening and "four or five times" before campaigning against Hindenburg. Adding to Hitler's problems was a spontaneous statement by Wilhelm Frick, Nazi leader in the Reichstag, that the Nazi would oppose the re-election of Hindenburg. "Handsome Adolf's mustache wiggled convusively" before this possible rebellion in his own party which forced him to refuse the extension of the presidential term.[82]

The New Republic refused to believe there had been any decisive alteration in the German political scene. It wrote the same week that Bruening was "frantically seeking a way out of a desperate situation." Any extension of Hindenburg's presidency would at best produce a truce "more apparent than real" and would not reduce opposition to the government in the upcoming elections to the Prussian Diet. To abrogate the Diet elections, however, would possibly "provoke the much feared Fascist putsch" which, in turn, would "inevitably precipitate a retaliatory general strike of organized labor." Bruening's repudiation of reparations had clearly "come too late to recouncile the hostile camps in the German Republic." German voters were limited to a choice between Hitler's NSDAP and the Red Front.[83]

Several American magazines, believing a Hitler presidency to be likely, made an attempt to assess Nazi ideology and its appeal in early 1932. *The Reader's Digest* answered its own question "Who Are the German Fascists?" by identifying them as a diverse cluster of factions centered on a middle-class nucleus. This central nucleus was composed of merchants, artisans and minor capitalists devastated by monopolization. Various clusters represented former army officers, soldiers' widows, tradesmen and farmers unwilling to acknowledge a common interest with the proletariat. For economic reasons, these groups welcomed Nazi anti-Semitism. Allied to these were large numbers of university students "who want to rule the world." The real strength of the Nazi party lay in its youthfulness, enthusiasm, and promise of economic improvement. If the depression deepened, it was likely industrial leaders and the traditionally privileged would also come to see Hitler as the only alternative to a communist state. On that day, power would come to Hitler. In March and April, 1932, *The Atlantic Monthly* published two articles entitled "Hitler and Hitlerism." The March article, subtitled "A Man of Destiny," was an exposition of *Mein Kampf*, "the Bible of the National-Socialist movement." It identified the heart of Hitler's ideology: violent racial nationalism, violent animosity to Marxism, violent hatred of the Jews, concern for social betterment, contempt for the intelligence of the ordinary man and parliamentary democracy, insistence on the power of personality and on economic nationalism, and the strategic doctrine that Germany had to break France prior to conquering land in the East at the expense of Russia. It attributed his success at winning Germans to these ideas to his "egocentric mentality." As Hitler had a "poor grasp of abstract principles," he had to put "his faith in high feeling and strong emotion." His supreme goal was the extension of the German "tribe" of which he envisioned himself its "chief." In short, his political philosophy was "a kind of religion, based on pseudo-science and tribal psychology."

Hitler's domestic goals were described in a second article in April subtitled "Germany Under the Nazis." Hitler could be expected to institute a stringent dictatorship that would promote a competitive, nationalistic capitalism led by Aryans. Labor unions and Marxism, both "Jewish contrivances" in Hitler's mind, would be removed from German life. There would be strict eugenic measures designed to preserve "Aryan blood" for the future. Education would be reformed so as to develop character and determination rather than intelligence in German youth. All non-German cultural activities and movements would be suppressed. Hitler's ultimate goal would be the establishment of "an organic people's state," a folkish community, which would be devoted to gaining more living space at the expense of Russia. To obtain his ends, Hitler would do whatever was expedient at the moment without surrendering his ultimate intentions.[84]

To *The Nation*, the Nazi party was best described as a "Hitler cult." The cult centered on "a speaker of unquestionable hypnotic power, a leader of undoubted force and ability, a man utterly lacking in any sort of intelligence." Hitler was surrounded by a "strange collection of heavy doctrinaires and helpless neurotics" motivated by a "lurking sense of inferiority to the Jews" and a "continuing obsession of being persecuted." The Nazi party was "the haven of all the malcontents of Germany" apart from the communists. It especially attracted former army officers, monarchists and university students—all of whom spurn the German Republic. Nazism was "a rush of exploding political emotions" that "naturally appeals to the citizens of a country that is treading along the brink of collapse." In this sense, the party was "a mass of high-strung, nervous, and tragic young men" condemned to unemployment. As the traditional forces for good, epitomized by Goethe, had failed them, German youth were left with the desire to "hail some new Messiah."[85]

Even as these interpretations of the Nazi movement were being made, the German presidential election entered its closing days. *Time* believed Hindenburg's campaign represented a decision by him to "give his life for his country" as he was eighty-four and would be ninety-one if he lived to the end of a second term. Communist Ernst Thaelmann was expected to receive at least 6,000,000 votes out of 38,000,000 ballots. "Handsome Adolf" had done a "risky thing" in running in the election, because he might be struck from the ballot on the grounds that he was "no real citizen." In that event, the Nazis would be forced to vote for Hindenburg and so ensure his election on the first ballot. If allowed to run, Hitler was likely to force a run-off election.

The New Republic believed it likely Hitler would poll 10-12,000,000 votes and force a second election. It lamented the "tragic fate" of Germany in not having a democratic movement willing to defend the republic. The Social Democratic party had become "so panic-stricken in its fear of Fascism" it had pledged to support "Hindenburg, the embodiment of nationalism and militarism in Germany."

On March 2, *The Nation* reported Bruening had met with Hitler to request an extension of Hindenburg's presidency at the instigation of Wilhelm Groener, Minister of Defense and the Interior. Groener, who enjoyed the highest confidence of Hindenburg, represented "the highest type of German army officer" with the attendent "virtues and failings" of that class. While he would faithfully serve a legal Nazi government, he would equally oppose a Nazi *putsch*. It had been Hugenberg who had rejected Groener's ploy and thereby forced Hitler to concur, for "in the race for extremism" the Nazis could not afford to lag behind the Nationalists. Bruening had seized upon Groener's suggestion out of "the simplicity of a child or with Jesuitical cunning" as it placed Hitler in the position of having placed party politics above country. The election would be more of a referendum of Bruening than on Hindenburg.[86]

When the election was held on March 13, Hindenburg placed first with 18,661,000 votes to Hitler's second place vote of 11,328,000. The election results were hailed with cries of "Vive Hindenburg" in Paris. A run-off election was scheduled for April 10. *The New Republic* interpreted the result as a "great personal triumph" for Hindenburg but warned any assumption the Nazi threat had been removed was "an optimistic delusion" as Nazism could not "be conquered by popular elections." Indeed, it was certain the Nazis would win the elections for the Prussian Diet on April 24. *The Literary Digest* believed the election demonstrated Hitler had not been "scotched" as he had precluded a clear victory by Hindenburg. However, it predicted Hindenburg would win the second election and guarantee the continued security of American investments.[87]

In the run-off election, Hindenburg won with roughly 19,000,000 votes. Hitler increased his vote to 13,000,000 votes. *Time* believed Hindenburg's "personal victory" obscured the fact that "the brown tide" had become the foremost party in Germany. Hitler's bid for the presidency had been checked only by the opposition of all other German parties. He was certain to win 120 deputies in the elections for the Prussian Diet. Bruening imposed a ban on the SA to hinder Nazi campaigning in the elections. To maintain his pose of legality, Hitler acquiesced in the order but continued to personally campaign all over Prussia. *Harper's* reported the mere mention of Hitler's name "acted as a magnet" to unite Germans of all classes. *The Nation* warned that if the Nazis won the Prussian state elections, which was probable, Hitler would control two-thirds of the territory and three-fourths of the population of Germany.[88]

On May 2, *Time* commented "orderly Germans marched on toward a Fascist form of government last week." It reported Nazi pluralities in four out of five state elections—Hamburg, Anhalt, Wuertemberg, and Prussia. Only in Catholic Bavaria had the Nazis failed to win a plurality. In Prussia, they had increased the number of their deputies from six to 162. As Otto Braun, the Socialist premier of Prussian, was able to put together an equal-sized coalition of 162 votes, the Nazis were unable to immediately oust him. While the Nazi party could obstruct legislation, it would not be required to accept responsibility for enactment of a legislative program of its own. Hitler was sure to capitalize on the situation. *The Literary Digest* stressed Hitler's star was "still in ascendency."[89]

Hindenburg abruptly dismissed Bruening on May 30. *Time* attributed the dismissal to Nazi gains in the recent state elections and to Bruening's ban on the SA, "an act which the patriotic generals could not stomach." Additional factors were Bruening's projected plans to break up Junker estates and to raise taxes through yet another emergency decree. Hitler responded to Bruening's dismissal with a demand for a Nazi government. *Time* believed the stage was set either for a Hitler cabinet or a "dictatorship by military leaders." The latter prediction was fulfilled the following week when *The Nation* reported the "notorious spy" Fritz von Papen had been appointed to the chancellorship. The choice of von Papen was the work of "intriguer" General von Schleicher. Von Schleicher had reputedly told Hindenburg "the army could not be depended on in a crisis" as long as Bruening remained chancellor. Von Schleicher would actually exercise power in the new government as he reportedly was "completely dominating" von Papen. The first acts of the new reactionary "cabinet of monocles" were to repudiate "deliberate inflation" and to call for new Reichstag elections. It was rumored von Schleicher might attempt to form a "Junkers-Army-Fascist coalition."[90] In any event, it was expected the Nazis would experience large gains in the up-coming elections.

Although street brawls between the SA and communists had long been a staple of German life, the fighting erupted with an increased intensity with the Nazi success in the recent Prussian Diet elections. When the Diet met, anti-Nazi taunts by the Marxist Wilhelm Pieck provided the signal for a brawl in which "inkwells, water bottles, desk drawers, chairs, ledgers" and chair legs were used as weapons. The Nazis, who outnumbered the Marxists three to one, drove the communists from the chamber and then sang "roaring old war songs." Immediately, communists and "Hitlerites began punching each others' noses all over Germany." In Hamburg, Cologne, Remschied, Duesseldorf and Berlin, police were forced to fire on rioting communists. In Munich, the police attacked the SA. The fighting continued to escalate during the remainder of the summer. *Time* reported there was "knife work aplenty in German streets." In the suburbs of Berlin, there was a "welter of knifing, bludgeoning and wild shots" as Nazis invaded Marxist areas. The offices of the socialist paper *Vorwarts* saw Nazi attackers evicted only after a violent "pistol battle."[91]

By the middle of July, the violence "crept from proletariat to fashionable quarters" in Berlin when five hundred Nazi students rioted along the Unter den Linden before being dispersed by the police. To no avail, fourteen of Germany's seventeen states protested the removal of the ban on the SA. Hitler employed 6,000 SA to provoke a riot in "Red Altoona." The riot continued into the evening until police armored cars "blazed away ruthlessly" and police infantry moved in with "rifle, pistol, hand grenade" and tear gas. At Ketschdorff, the regular army was used to forestall a communist attack on Nazis. Serious fighting also occurred in Cologne and Munich.[92] *The Literary Digest* reported socialists were uniting with communists all over Germany to resist Nazi attacks. *The Nation* reported "gangs of young Nazis" were terrorizing "whole communities, destroying property, assaulting and even killing" their opponents.[93]

The period of terror continued unabated after the Reichstag elections on July 31. "Murder and terror" remained "the order of the day." Four people a day were being killed in the fighting while "hundreds of persons" were assaulted on the street, hand grenades were "thrown into scores of homes" and newspapers were wrecked by "gangs of hoodlums." *The Literary Digest* reported "twenty attacks with bombs, grenades and revolvers" in a single day in Silesia and East Prussia. When von Papen decreed special courts and the death penalty for terrorists, Hitler approved of the decree and blamed communists for the fighting. The Marxist *Welt am Abend* argued the decree was pro-Nazi and intended to prevent communists from defending themselves.[94]

The Nation says the fighting was a direct consequence of the suffering caused by the depression. *The Atlantic Monthly* concurred, stating the depression had created a "lost generation" of Germans dedicated to a "period of destructive work." German youth were now convinced their only salvation lay in the demise of the republic and "the end of the *status quo* in Europe." Their desperation had driven them into "the camp either of the Communists or of the Hitlerites." *Time* found a more immediate cause in the frustration felt by Germans due to the reactionary decrees imposed by von Papen and his "camarilla." He had instituted a salt tax, raised individual taxes five percent, extended the sales tax to small merchants and cut the dole by twenty-three percent even as he chose to rescue by state purchase the German coal, iron and steel trust of Friedrich Flick. He had also requisitioned all German radio stations for an hour each evening to promote the election campaign of his cabinet. Finally, instead of affirming Bruening's refusal to pay further reparations, von Papen had agreed at the Lausanne Conference to make at least token reparation payments. German frustration had, as a result, expended itself in violence.[95]

In the Reichstag elections of July 31, the NSDAP won 230 seats and so more than doubled its previous representation. Hitler overnight became the leader of the largest parliamentary block in the history of the Weimar Republic. However, even with the support of the other nationalist parties, he failed to achieve a governing majority. *The Nation* believed the very size of his victory would prove his undoing. His "party of action" expected the fruits of success and might quickly turn upon its "false messiah." Although the "Von Papen— von Schleicher regime" had no votes in the new Reichstag, it was expected to remain in power as von Schleicher meant "no less than Hitler" to rule Germany. *Time* interpreted the election as a victory for von Schleicher whose intention was to use "bristle-lipped Adolf Hitler" to attain his goals of restoring the monarchy and rebuilding the German army. Von Schleicher had held secret talks with Herriot and Blum of France and promised to "smother the German propaganda" against Poland, to "break Germany's close business and financial" ties to Russia, and agreed to "hold down Hitler." This provided him with the means of winning Hindenburg's approval for his "cabal."[96]

The following week, *Time* reported von Schleicher and Hitler had gone "to the mat." Von Schleicher offered Hitler the vice-chancellorship or the interior ministry and even suggested Hitler might have the chancellorship provided von Schleicher remained the defense minister. As part of this latter proposal, the SA would be enrolled in the army as unarmed labor battalions. Von Schleicher made the proposal knowing that Hindenburg, who secretly viewed Hitler as "a ne'er-do-well opportunist," would veto it. "Shy von Schleicher" thus proved himself to be a dictator with the velvet gloves of a Metternich or Machiavelli "for Hitler was now frozen out of power." *The Nation* commented Hitler had asked for "all or nothing" and had "received nothing" due to von Schleicher's machinations. If, in frustration, the Nazi attempted a *putsch*, there was now little doubt the government possessed the means and determination to suppress it. *The Literary Digest* believed "von Papen, not Hitler" would be the dictator of Germany as he was quickly "cutting down the German Fascist leader's hope of control." Von Papen had Hindenburg's assurance that the Reichstag would be dissolved if it attempted to oust him from the chancellorship.[97]

Of the magazines understudy, only *The Reader's Digest* insisted Hitler would "come to control at no distant date" as Germans had "succumbed to reaction." This was all the more regrettable as Hitler was not "a great leader" like Mussolini but "only a brilliant agitator" who headed:

> ...not a political party with fixed principles, but a mob united by an intricate mesh of passions and hatreds. His platform is the most extraordinary farrago of nonsense conceivable. His followers are held together by a common revolt against the existing order.

If Hitler attained power, even legally, his advent would deepen the depression in Germany by causing a "flight of the mark" and so accentuating its poverty. Further, he would reduce Europe to "the atmosphere of an armed camp" and end "international cooperation on the continent" for an indefinite period. France and its allies believed Hitler might precipitate a war as "a final gambler's throw" when his domestic policies failed—as they were certain to do.[98]

Time remained convinced, however, Hitler's bid for power had failed. On September 5, it reported the question was being asked if Hitler had "at last gone crazy" or if he was "really in a strait-jacket jittering in a Bavarian asylum?" The question arose when Hitler defended five Nazis convicted of political murder. While *Time* denied the report, it stated "Handsome Adolf" had "lost enormous influence in the Reich" as a result of the incident. Hindenburg responded by letting his associates know that "once and for all that he was through with Hitler." Von Schleicher agreed he could not offer to share power with Hitler.[99]

Hitler's position appeared to be further undercut by a series of "astoundingly provocative" acts by von Papen "plainly designed to steal" Hitler's platform. In September, von Papen raised the tariff on British goods 300 percent, informed France that Germany intended to re-arm, demanded the return of the Saar and former German colonies, and staged a review of 180,000 veterans at Tempelhofer field. To stabilize the German economy, he announced governmental wage cuts and state subsidies by tax remission certificates to employers. Von Papen took these acts to show the German people they "possess a government which can and does demand from the Allies every concession which 'Handsome Adolf' can think of—and possibly a few more.[100] Von Papen, under the guidance of von Schleicher, also partitioned Prussia into provinces ruled by federal sub-commissioners responsible only to him. This meant the Prussian Diet, dominated by the Nazis "could rave, rant and grow purple in the face" without threatening the republic.[101]

The first week of September, von Papen issued a decree over Hindenburg's signature which was designed to stimulate the German economy. It reduced corporate taxes, appropriated funds for new public works, raised the tariff and relaxed the minimum wage law for firms that hired new workers. In response, Marxist Ernst Torgler introduced in the Reichstag a vote of no confidence aimed at von Papen. When von Papen attempted to squash the vote with a presidential decree dissolving the Reichstag, "broad, big-boned and mighty-muscled" Goering, the Speaker of the Reichstag, "cut the figure of a squat ogre" and allowed the vote to continue. Marxists and Nazis united to pass the no confidence motion. Von Papen, however, did declare the Reichstag dissolved following the vote.[102]

In a national radio speech defending his dissolution of the Reichstag, von Papen, "is a voice tense with suppressed fury," declared his cabinet corresponded to the will of the German people. He predicted a "bitter disappointment" for the Nazi if they conducted "class warfare" against "the fine people, the Barons." He further stated the "system of formal democracy had broken down and is incapable of resurrection!" He served notice he intended to revise the constitution to prevent further Nazi electoral gains, perhaps by disenfranchising Hitler's youthful followers. He concluded by setting the new Reichstag elections for November 6. Hindenburg placed his prestige at the service of von Papen during the electoral campaign. As a result, for the "first time," Hindenburg was "openly and savagely attacked" personally by the "Brown-Shirt bands of Hitler" in their posters and newspapers. There was little violence during the campaign as Hitler ordered his followers to conduct themselves legally. Hitler predicted a Nazi victory and the "total collapse" of the government which would be replaced by a Nazi cabinet.[103] American magazines paid no attention to the events of the campaign itself.

In the election, the Nazis dropped from 230 to 195 seats—a net loss of thirty-five seats. The Socialists remained the second largest party while the Red Front became the third largest party with a gain of eleven seats. Support for von Papen's cabinet of Barons proved to be non-existent. Rumors in Berlin predicted von Schleicher would replace von Papen and rule by presidential decree. *Time* announced the results under the heading "Hitler Tamed." It believed if Hitler was drawn into the cabinet and "his blatancy toned down," Germany would be "on the highway back toward a representative government." If not, the alternative would be a continuing series of Reichstag dissolutions until Hindenburg died or some faction attempted a *putsch*. *The Literary Digest* interpreted the results to mean Hitler's "dream of dictatorship" had been shattered as his momentum had received "a fatal check." Its reading of London and Paris newspapers supported this view. To *The Nation*, the election demonstrated Nazi strength was "definitely waning" and German industrialists would not finance further Nazi campaigns. It was certain the government would have to call for a new election or else rule by dictatorship.[104]

The Nation, though believing the Nazi tide had passed its crest, insisted Nazism was a popular movement, "a *Volksbewegung*." Hitler reflected the misery of all classes which he knew how to express "in dramatic form." There was no "grievance that he does not visualize, not a wish that he does not promise to fulfill." The Germans, therefore, turned "to him who promises relief" and because things "couldn't be worse." The "weakness of the Hitler movement," however, was its "excesses" and the "numerous acts of terrorism committed by its members." If Germany were now provided with long-term loans, lower interest rates and a period of peace, "the Hitler movement will disappear" for the "Germans want no more war."[105]

Rumors of all types were rife in Berlin following Hindenburg's dismissal of von Papen. One was that German monarchists were merely waiting for the death of "85-year-old" Hindenburg prior to re-establishing a Hohenzollern as German regent. Another was that Hindenburg had asked Hitler to form a coalition government with a majority in the Reichstag. This later rumor caused a rise in the stocks listed in the Berlin exchange. Paul Lobe called for the unification of the socialist and communist parties which would ensure a "solid proletarian front" in the Reichstag. German newspapers representing "Biggest Business," such as the *Deutsche Allgemein Zeitung* and the *Rheinisch-Westfalische*, promptly switched "from hostility to support of Adolf Hitler." Finally, it was rumored Hindenburg would appoint von Schleicher as a presidential chancellor.[106]

When Hindenburg refused to allow "Leader Hitler" to form a government based upon presidential authority, the "Iron Man of German finance, brunt Dr. Hjalmar Schacht" announced he would henceforth support Hitler. Schacht thus lined up Berlin finance with "Biggest Business" behind Hitler. Schacht asserted Hitler would, under any circumstances, become chancellor within four months. Rumor continued to insist Hindenburg would establish "a military dictatorship with General von Schleicher as Chancellor." Such a dictatorship, *The Nation* asserted, would be preferable to giving Hitler power, for Hitler was "just a confused and weak demagogue in the process of being deflated."[107]

Under the necessity of selecting a new chancellor before the Reichstag met, Hindenburg finally appointed von Schleicher to the chancellorship. Von Schleicher continued efforts to include Hitler in his cabinet until the last possible moment. Hitler, on the advice of Goering and Goebbels, refused to join any cabinet which he did not lead. Von Schleicher was expected to continue his parallel efforts to undercut Hitler's appeal by expropriating the program of the Nazi party and making it his own. *The Literary Digest* reported von Schleicher's selection was greeted with "dismay and distrust." In addition to the chancellorship, von Schleicher held the portfolios of defense and commissioner of Prussia. This gave him control both of the German army and the bulk of the German police. He was further armed with permission from Hindenburg to dissolve the Reichstag if it showed "signs of getting out of hand." All in all, von Schleicher's government was highly militaristic and perhaps even a stalking horse for the restoration of the Hohenzollern monarchy.[108]

The Reichstag opened on a note of co-operation between von Schleicher and Hitler. Goering, elected speaker for a second time, followed a policy of toleration and abandoned his earlier declared intention of forcing a vote of no confidence in the government. Von Schleicher, in turn, allowed a Nazi bill to be passed which stated that, in the event of Hindenburg's death, he would be succeeded by the Chief Justice of the Supreme Court. This bill "cut both ways." It meant von Schleicher could not become president and then resign in favor of a Hohenzollern. It further removed Hindenburg's fear of a Hitler presidency if Hindenburg died while Hitler was chancellor. The Nazis, for their part, believed the bill would eliminate Hindenburg's last objections to a Hitler chancellorship. Debate on the bill's final reading led to a Nazi brawl with communists during which telephones and spittoons were used as weapons and the Reichstag's chandelier was smashed.[109]

Goering, at Hitler's direction, agreed to a suggestion by von Schleicher that the Reichstag adjourn for the holiday season. *Time* believed Hitler agreed to the truce due to an ominous split in the Nazi party engineered by von Schleicher. Von Schleicher had offered Gregor Strasser, the national organizing director of the Nazi party, the post of Reich Minister of the Interior with the authority to offer hundreds of unemployed Nazis steady jobs. When Hitler refused to allow any Nazi to join the cabinet unless he was chancellor, Strasser had abruptly resigned his party post in disgust. Gottfried Feder, Nazi party economic chairman, resigned as a sign of support of Strasser. *The Literary Digest* wrote that Hitler was "hard hit" by the defection. It attributed the break to Strasser's efforts to break into the "working-class front" and lead the party toward true socialism. Hitler, for his part, remained "in the hands of those who put money into the strong-box—the capitalists." The split in the party threatened to cost Hitler fifty of his 195 Reichstag deputies and he needed the adjournment to reunite his party. Once again, von Schleicher had demonstrated his capacity for political intrigue.[110]

Von Schleicher utilized the adjournment of the Reichstag to attempt to gain popular acceptance of his government. In a national radio address, he declared his foremost priority was the creation of jobs. He promised no further wage-cuts or increased taxes and an up-grading of the German army. Von Schleicher also approached trade union leaders with offers of concession to labor. He eased restrictions on the press and individuals, and declared there would be no further reductions in social welfare programs. Amnesty was granted to "more than 10,000 political jailbirds—mostly Communists and Fascists." With "the blessing" of Hans Luther of the Reichsbank, he announced his cabinet would spend $642,600,000 for public works.[111]

The Nation believed van Schleicher's efforts were meeting success and that monarchist sentiment was declining. It reported "there is growing confidence the worst period of collapse and misery had passed" in Germany. *Time*, on the contrary, argued von Schleicher's efforts were all in vain. In Berlin, a "blatant, blaring parade" by "miles of marching Reds" snarled traffic "for hours." "Shaking their fists" at the police, they shouted "Down with Hunger and Chancellor von Schleicher." The *Tagliche Rundschau*, the newspaper "closest" to von Schleicher, was quoted by *The Literary Digest* as reporting von Papen and Hitler had conferred for "an hour and a half" to hatch a plot to oust the chancellor. A massive Nazi rally held in Berlin for a slain SA youth was used to denounce von Schleicher and his cabinet.[112]

On January 30, 1933, Hindenburg abruptly dismissed von Schleicher and simultaneously appointed Hitler as chancellor of the Reich. *The Literary Digest* was caught flat-footed by the event. As late as February 4, it ran two articles on events in Germany—neither of them mentioned Hitler's appointment. One discussed the nationalistic and militaristic mood of Germany. A second reported a "Hitlerite Brown Shirt" named Hentsh had been murdered by fellow Nazis for refusing to accept a demotion in rank.[113]

The Nation interpreted Hitler's appointment as "a supreme personal triumph" but thought it "unlikely" that he would "rule unchecked." Hindenburg had "taken pains to prevent any real power from slipping" into Hitler's hands. Therefore, it appeared "improbable" that any major Nazi social or economic policies would be carried out. Von Papen would control the bulk of the German police as commissioner for Prussia. The appointment of von Neurath insured there would be "no flat repudiation" of the Versailles Treaty. There was "little doubt" von Papen would be "the real head of the Cabinet." Hitler's government might "survive for months" if the Center Party supported it—otherwise, it might "fall at once." Hitler seemed "destined to lose much of his following" unless he carried out some of his "blood-and-thunder promises." Yet, the possibility that his cabinet would carry out his promises was "entirely out of the question."[114]

To *The New Republic*, Hitler's appointment was the result of von Schleicher's "calculated endeavors" to reach and agreement with the German Trade Union Federation. These endeavors had "turned the big industrialists against him" and produced the "compromise" coalition of von Papen and Hitler. The negotiations for the coalition were conducted at the Cologne home of Baron von Schroeder, who was both a "prominent member" of the I. H. Stern banking firm and "closely connected" with the Steel Cartel. In this sense, Hitler's appointment represented "the last resort of the German reactionaries." The ministers of the new cabinet were "nationalistic to core," belonged to the "military caste" and were monarchists and reactionaries. Any promises that they would avoid unconstitutional policies had "to be taken with more than a grain of salt."

Time reported Hitler's appointment with the statement "this pudgy, stoop-shouldered, tooth-brush-mustached but magnetic little man" had just had "the biggest morning of his life." Von Schleicher lost the support of Hindenburg by requesting authority to dissolve the Reichstag. Von Papen had then convinced Hindenburg it was safe to make Hitler chancellor by surrounding him with "safeguards." These included making von Papen vice-chancellor and Reich Commissioner of Prussia, retaining von Neurath as Foreign Minister, appointing von Blomberg as Minister of Defense, and keeping von Krosigk at the Ministry of Finance. *Time* insisted that, not withstanding the "safeguards," Hitler had received "a handsome slice of power" provided he could secure support from "the Centre Parties." Such support was "not improbable," It was difficult to forecast Hitler's policies as the Nazi Party was "pledged to so many things that is is pledged to nothing." Nazism promised "the bulk of the German people whatever they wanted." *Time* noted the "best posted observers greeted the advent of Chancellor Hitler" with "equanimity." In Berlin, thousands of Nazis greeted the appointment with "guttural victory cheers" and shouts of "Heil Hitler! Deutschland erwache! Juda verrecke!"[115]

The twelve year history of the "Thousand Year Reich" had begun. The relative calmness of mind exhibited in American magazines at Hitler's appointment was rapidly replaced by an attitude of shock, horror, and opposition.

Chapter II

Gleichschaltung, 1933-1934

Hitler immediately dashed the hopes and expectations of those who anticipated he would moderate his policies on becoming chancellor. When the Catholic Center and Bavarian People's parties refused to support his cabinet, Hitler promptly dissolved the Reichstag and the Prussian Diet. New elections were scheduled for March 5. The machinery of repression was immediately set in motion. Communist and Catholic newspapers were suspended by the regime. Censorship of foreign books and periodicals was imposed. Communists were arrested and beaten without warrant or trial. *The Nation* reported "Nazi gangs" broke up "even informal groups of Socialists and Communists" while "murder and assaults" were the order of the day. It asserted Germany was "under worse than martial law" as it was "under mob law supported by all the powers of the reactionary centralized authority."[1]

The pace of suppression accelerated in the weeks that followed. All non-Nazi state governors, vice-presidents, and police chiefs were forced to resign and were replaced by Nazis. Liberal and pacifist authors were dismissed from university posts and from all literary societies. Goering instructed the Prussian police to use "utmost severity" against all Communists. They were to employ firearms at the least sign of resistance—failure to do so would constitute a "graver fault than errors made in action."[2] Catholics were no more secure than communists. At Kaiserlauten, Nazis turned a "Catholic parade into a bloody skirmish." At Krefeld and Muenster, Catholic rallies were converted into battlefields. As "bludgeons thudded, knives flashed and bullets whizzed," Hitler announced he would remain chancellor regardless of the outcome of the election as he was pledged to the "salvation" of Germany. For this reason, Hitler announced no communist deputies would be allowed to take their seats in the Reichstag even if elected on March 5. *Time* commented that "in less that two weeks Chancellor Hitler" had "reduced his opponents to a lower level of groveling fear" than Mussolini had achieved in his first two years of power.[3]

The burning of the Reichstag on February 27 triggered still another escalation in the level of violence. Goering, declaring the fire was the signal for a Marxist revolt, armed an additional force of 60,000 Nazis as auxiliary police and proceeded to use them to attack communist party buildings all over Germany. Communists were swept from the streets of Germany and housed in hastily improvised prisons. Three hundred and fifty Marxist deputies of the Reichstag, including Ernst Thaelmann, were among the first to be arrested. The Karl Leibknecht House in Berlin was first raided and them expropriated by the regime. The following day, at the request of Hitler, Hindenburg used his emergency powers to suspend all civil rights in Germany for an indefinite period. *Time* saw the true significance of the fire as an excuse for the Nazis to launch "a juggernaut of super-suppressive measure and decrees for which they needed an excuse."[4]

Given the level of violence and repression, the outcome of the election was anti-climatic. Hitler polled 17,000,000 votes which, with the 3,000,000 polled by the nationalist parties allied with him, gave him a majority in the Reichstag. The number of Nazi deputies climbed for 196 to 288— an increase of sixty eight percent. *The Nation* commented the election ensured Germany's "battle for democracy" was lost and that the spectacle of Germany is one to make the gods weep.[5]

Hitler's immediate post-election acts, as reported in American magazines, were relatively mild given the level of the pre-election violence. The national colors of the German flag were declared to be the old imperial black-white and red while the swastika was also to be regarded as a national banner. Hitler declared the creation of work to be the primary goal of his regime. Nudism was banned. Captain Ernst Roehm ousted the government of Bavaria and placed the state under Nazi control.

With Hitler firmly in power, speculation was rife about the role he could be expected to play in Germany and in Europe. *The Nation*, prior to the election, argued his anticipated victory ensured "only mean slavery of the worst conceivable sort" for the German people. Germans were to be "delivered into servitude for the greater glory and profit of the industrial and military rulers of Germany" for whom Hitler was a figurehead.[6] *The Reader's Digest*, on the other hand, believed Hitler's goal would be the creation of the most powerful army in Europe. It asserted every member of the German army was potential officer material and therefore, the army could be expanded overnight. *Newsweek* and *The New Republic* also saw Hitler primarily as a threat to the peace of Europe, predicting Germany would be rearmed and would press for the return of its territory lost in 1918. *The Literary Digest* wrote Hitler's election meant "the dreaded word 'War' is heard again throughout Europe" and insisted war was "an imminent possibility."[7]

Time found the true significance of Hitler's victory in what it presaged for German Jews. It believed "Hitlerism's most if not only definite tenet" was anti-Semitism. The "real pleasure" of the Storm Troopers was "Jew-baiting." It noted *The London Times* and *Daily Herald* reported rumors were circulating in Germany of "a massacre" being planned for Jews. *The Nation* insisted Nazis were anti-Semitic "to the exclusion of all other issues."[8]

By the middle of March, there were daily reports of attacks on Jews pouring out of Germany as "acts of bloody violence alternated with acts of bloody oppression." *Time* reported Jews were "beaten by the hundreds" while *Newsweek* stated a synagogue had been fire-bombed and that in Annaburg, Saxony, "every Jewish merchant had been arrested." Jewish refugees from

Germany told of "eyes gouged out, castor-oil poured down throats, [and] feet burned with red-hot coals" in addition to teeth being knocked out with pistol butts. The internationally renowned conductors Fritz Busch and Bruno Walter were forbidden to appear professionally. The novelist Lion Feuchtwanger and the physicist Albert Einstein had their homes raided prior to their exile. *The Nation* reported Jewish professors were driven from their classrooms while there was "a strong movement" developing to bar Jewish lawyers from the courts. It concluded "the pogrom is on" and the Nazi regime had "already forfeited the respect of decent-minded men and women everywhere."[9]

The reports of Nazi anti-Semitism produced anti-German demonstrations in Paris, London, Buenos Aires, and in Palestine. The British Opposition in Commons called for an official protest by the Foreign Office. Catholic prelates in London asked British Catholics to aid German Jews. In Paris, former premier Painleve organized a committee for Jewish aid. The Polish government lodged a formal protest with Berlin over the treatment of Polish Jews in Germany while Polish Jews organized a boycott of German goods.[10]

American Jews visiting Germany did not escape attack. At least seven were beaten on the street by Nazis. The correspondent of the Jewish *Daily Forward* was first arrested and then expelled from Germany, becoming the first journalist dismissed from the Third Reich. Woolworth's eighty-one German outlets were attacked or picketed. It was, however, not these specific incidents but Nazi anti-Semitism generally that attracted the condemnation of Germany by the American public. In some 300 American cities, protest meetings denounced Nazi Germany. In New York Bishop Manning and Alfred E. Smith led a protest with Rabbi Stephen Wise. Smith also joined Newton Baker and John W. Davis in an informal protest to the German embassy. The International Catholic Truth Society labeled the Nazi acts, official and unofficial, as "unjust, un-Christian and barbarous." Wholesalers, Gentile and Jewish, organized a boycott of German imports. German steamship lines were boycotted and passengers cancelled their bookings. Congressmen, Gentile and Jewish, called for a formal protest by the State Department to Berlin and were joined by the American Jewish Committee and the B'nai B'rith.[11]

Secretary of State Cordell Hull responded to the outcry in America by releasing a statement from the American embassy in Berlin which insisted "there was for a short time considerable physical mistreatment of Jews" but this "phase may by considered virtually terminated." Goering, responding on behalf of the German government, issued a statement summarized by *The New Republic* as:

a) that there has been no terror, b) that the terror is now over and c) that unless the foreign agitation is instantly stopped, they will begin a campaign of reprisals.

Hitler stated the foreign agitation "sharply affects every Jew in Germany" and announced there would be a boycott imposed on all Jewish goods and services in Germany. The *Frankfurter Zeitung* [sic] reported the Central Union of German Citizens of the Jewish Faith had denounced "distortions abroad" of

Nazi treatment of Jews—a statement *The Literary Digest* attributed to Nazi pressure.[12]

The anticipated Nazi boycott of Jewish stores was limited to just nine hours on one day, April 1, by a direct decree of Hitler. *Time* and *Newsweek* attributed the reduction to the severe economic pressures caused by the protests and boycotts in foreign countries. The Berlin stock market had dropped thirty points and there "were moments of panic selling." In response, Baron von Neurath threatened to resign if the boycott was realized and von Papen joined him in a protest to Hindenburg. Hindenburg then summoned Hitler, "like a naughty schoolboy," and "Handsome Adolf" backed down before threats Hindenburg would declare marital law and abolish the government. Hitler compromised for a single day of boycott and agreed that all but thirty five, one percent, of Berlin Jewish lawyers would be disbarred. Hindenburg further intervened to preserve the rights of all pre-War Jewish lawyers who had fought in the war, were not communists and whose fathers or sons had died in the war. This allowed 900 to continue practicing in the courts.[13]

The end of the official Nazi boycott and the reduction in the use of physical violence against Jews did not spell the demise of Nazi anti-Semitism. What did happen was that the Nazi regime moved to express its anti-Semitism in an official way through a veritable flood of decrees. All Jewish judges were ordered to resign and Jewish refugees were ordered to obtain a special police stamp on their passports. The kosher slaughtering of meat was forbidden throughout the Reich. The move to exclude Jews from the professions spread to medicine, education, and the arts. Jewish doctors were forbidden to practice in municipal and state hospitals while insurance companies were ordered to make no further payments to Jewish doctors. Jewish actors and musicians were banned from public performances while the state radio system was forbidden to play their music. Jewish children were barred from elementary public schools and Jewish enrollment in higher schools and universities was limited to one percent. The children of post-1914 Jewish immigrants were totally banned from the universities. All Jewish athletes were banned from participation in sports.[14] Jewish civil servants were forced from their jobs while Gentile bureaucrats were told to divorce their Jewish spouses or face dismissal. It was announced that shortly all Eastern Jews would be forced to leave Germany. The government-owned street public address systems blared the *Horst Wessel Lied* with emphasis on its words "When Jewish blood flows from the knife, things will go much better." *Time* noted ironically that dancing bears would henceforth be banned in Germany due to the inhumane treatment given the bears.[15]

Hitler responded to the continuing American demonstrations and boycott in a speech he made to the German Medical Federation. He asserted Americans had "the least excuse for such action" as they had been "the first to draw practical and political conclusions from differences among races and from the different value of different races." He pointed out that American immigration laws were used to prevent the entry of "so-called Jewish refugees from Germany." The same week Goebbels announced the German Student Corporation had set aside May 1 for the burning of all university library books written by Jews, Marxists, and pacifists.[16]

Foreign protests continued unabated against Nazi anti-Semitism. The wax model of Hitler in London's Tassuard Museum was splashed with red paint and labeled with a sign reading "Hitler the Murderer." A wreath laid by Alfred Rosenberg at the Cenotaph War Memorial was destroyed by J.E. Sears, a labor candidate, and Rosenberg was lambasted by Laborites in Commons. Franz Burnheim, a German Jewish refugee from Upper Silesia, presented an "expertly drawn" petition to the League Council. It asked the League to abrogate the Nazi anti-Semitic laws in Silesia on the ground they violated the Polish-German Convention of 1922. The Council agreed to discuss the petition over the protests of the German delegate.[17]

Anti-Nazi parades were staged in several American cities on May 10. Major General John F. O'Ryan and Mayor O'Brian led the parade in New York. Bainbridge Colby, a former Secretary of State, and former Congressman Fiorello La Guardia made extended speeches denouncing Hitler personally. The following day 600 representatives of 228 Jewish organizations met to institute a boycott of German imports. Twelve hundred clergymen, representing twenty six Protestant denominations, signed a protest prepared by George C. Steward, Episcopal Bishop of Chicago, and Harry E. Fosdick of Riverside Church in New York. The most violent anti-Nazi protests occurred in Poland. Protestors stoned the German consulate in Lodz. Windows in German Schools were smashed in a number of cities and German publications on public newstands were destroyed by irate Poles who also forced the closure of German cinemas. Berlin made two formal protests within four weeks to Warsaw about the incidents.[18]

Hitler was unmoved by the foreign protests against Nazi anti-Semitism. The remainder of 1933 witnessed a continual stream of official decrees aimed at further excluding Jews from German life. *Newsweek* reported more than 200 Jewish merchants in Nuremburg alone were arrested on charges of profiteering. *The New Republic* editorialized that Jews continued "to bear the brunt of Nazi venom" and reported they were banned from the movie industry, all stock exchanges and from the *Arbeiterfront. The Nation* simultaneously published a Nazi degree identifying Jews as those who had even one Jewish grandparent. It predicted an intensification of Jewish persecution for the future as "Terror" against Jews was "an organic part of the system."[19] In September, *Newsweek* reported Jews were compelled to appear in a film about Horst Wessel to identify them "with Communists in the popular mind." In October, Jewish jockeys were banned from German racetracks. In December, the ranks of noble orders in Germany were purged of all those who could not prove Aryan ancestry back to 1750.[20]

As it became apparent Hitler was determined to eliminate German Jews from the life of the Nazi state, two different counter-actions appeared. One was to intensify the boycott of German exports. The second was to assist Jews in emigrating from Germany. The leader in the boycott movement was the American attorney Samuel Untermeyer. In July, Jews from sixteen nations met in Amsterdam to establish the World Jewish Economic Federation as the clearing house for the boycott. Both *Time* and *The Nation* insisted the boycott was effective, particularly against the Hamburg-American and North German Lloyd steamship lines. Retailers were supporting the boycott in ever larger numbers. *The New Republic* argued that although boycotts were acts of war, injured both sides, and punished the innocent as well as the guilty, the boycott was justified "as a measure of self-defense."[21]

As the year wore on, disagreement developed over the effectiveness of the boycott. *The Nation* believed the boycott had produced a situation where "Hitlerism is Cracking." *Newsweek*, however, pointed out that German exports had reached greater heights than in 1932 and were increasing. The World Zionist Congress repudiated the concept of boycott entirely. The disagreement over the boycott led to a public confrontation between Samuel Untermeyer and Percy S. Straus, president of R.H. Macy and Company. Straus had ignored the boycott and continued to buy from Germany. When a customer objected, Straus defended his action with a full-page newspaper statement on October 2 defending Macy's purchase of German goods. Untermeyer responded with a half-page advertisement which he attempted to place with the *New York Times*, the *Herald Tribune*, and the *American*. All three refused to accept his statement as they felt it was a personal attack on Straus. The controversy ended, according to *The Nation*, "without any meeting of minds."[22] With this dispute, the subject of the boycott was largely dropped for the rest of the year by the American magazines of this study.

The World Zionist Congress rejected the concept of an international boycott of German goods. It did, however, provide impetus to a second effort to aid German Jewish emigration. *The Nation* had raised the question as early as April. It editorialized that it was "tragic" American immigration laws combined with the depression to prevent a "whole-hearted invitation to the victims of this new Old World tyranny to come to these shores." It called upon Washington to adopt "the most liberal and most humane interpretation" of the immigration statutes and permit the entry of refugees from Germany. *The Nation* noted the German quota of 25,000 immigrants per year had not been filled for years.[23]

In July, *The New Republic* also called for the increased immigration of German Jews to the United States though stressing the difficulty of emigration from Germany. Noting France and Holland had been generous with visas, it stressed there was "a limit to the number" they could absorb. It summarized the basic problems of immigrants as "What will they do? How will they live? There are no jobs. No one wants them." When the British government announced it was increasing the Jewish quota into Palestine from 6,700 in 1932 to 11,000 for 1933, "riots raged in the Holy Land." In Jaffa, Nablus, Haifa and Jerusalem, British troops opened fire upon rioters who were violently protesting the British decision. In Syria, Iraq and Transjordania, Arab mass meetings were held to show sympathy for the Palestinian Arabs. The British ordered two ships loaded with Jewish refugees to turn back because of the Arab protests. All further Jewish entry into Palestine was halted for the moment.[24]

In December, *The New Republic* wrote that the problem of Jewish emigration appeared insolvable. It concluded "the Jewish people are going to suffer [and] for those who are individually and innocently hurt, and who know not why, there can be no soothing words." Many articles defended German Jews on the ground of their cultural, intellectual and patriotic contributions to Germany. *Harper's* defended them on the most fundamental of all grounds— namely that they were human beings.[25]

In February and March, 1933, American magazines focused on Hitler's attacks on Marxists and Jews in Germany. At the beginning of April, they began to direct their primary attention to his *Gleichschaltung* or "Co-ordination" of all political, social, and economic power in Germany. *Gleichschaltung* was a double-pronged move to both concentrate all power in Hitler's hands and his use of that power against all possible centers of resistance. When the newly elected Reichstag met, "Hitler invited Parliament to legislate itself out of existence." Ignoring momentary shouts of protests by the Socialists, and in the absence of imprisoned Marxist deputies, Hitler secured passage of an Enabling Act which gave him dictatorial powers until April 1, 1937. By a vote of 441-94, the Reichstag ended the Weimar Republic. The act empowered Hitler to proclaim decrees by *fiat*, conclude treaties without further approval, announce an annual budget, borrow money, and to unilaterally amend the constitution.[26]

In the following weeks, Germany was "Hitlerized with breath-taking speed and thoroughness." Hitler promptly used the Enabling Act to abolish the traditional state governments and their parliaments. He announced henceforth the states would be administered by Nazi *Statthalters* who would be responsible only to him. A secret political police was established under Goering to "combat communism" and Franz Seldte's *Stalheim* was directed to join the Nazi party.[27] Goebbels was appointed to the cabinet and given authority to censor both the domestic press and the foreign correspondent's association. The directors of the Federation of German Industries, "the most influential organization in German industry," were forced to resign and were replaced by Nazis. The film industry ceased production until Nazis could be appointed to direct it. The North German Lloyd Line, the Tietz Department Corporation and the German Brewer's Federation were given Nazi directorates. The civil service was purged and placed under Nazi administrators. The People's Party was absorbed by the Nazi party while the Socialist Party was banned outright. The Masonic Order was "Aryanized" and forced to rename itself the "National Christian Order of Frederick the Great."[28]

Hitler also co-ordinated the few political parties that still existed. Alfred Hugenberg's "Battle Ringers" were dissolved by simple decree. Its leader, Herbert von Bismarck, was arrested and interogated before being finally released. Hugenberg himself was dismissed from the cabinet and retired to private life. Goebbels, proclaiming "political Catholicism must by uprooted," banned the Centrist party. By these actions, Hitler achieved his goal of a one-party state.[29]

Hitler decreed May 1 as a "Feast of Labor" glorifying the German worker. On May 2, he seized the property, funds, and leadership of the Social Democratic Federation to preclude "the possibility of a general strike" against the regime. The union of white collar workers was also seized and its property expropriated. On May 3, the Catholic Christian Unions and the Hirsch-Duncker Unions "placed themselves at the disposal of the government." Union affiliates, such as banks, insurance companies, and consumer's co-operatives, were expropriated. Hitler appointed Robert Ley, a Nazi Reichstag deputy, as Nazi Commissioner for labor. Hitler also used the occasion to announce a compulsory labor service for all Germans with emphasis on youthful workers.[30]

Within just a few months of Hitler's accession to power, American magazines realized they were reporting on a political phenomenon *sui generis*. *Time* reported as early as March 27 that Hitler had reduced his opponents to a level of "groveling fear." On March 29, *The Nation* editorialized Hitler had created a "Germany in which freedom and democracy dare not even ask to live." The same day *The New Republic* wrote the "dictatorship and the terror in Germany are now complete." *The Nation* stated in April that the Nazi regime stood "convicted of barbarism not seen since the Middle Ages" and incarnated a "tyranny without parallel in our time."[31] T.R. Ybarra wrote in *Collier's* that "brute force was in control" of Germany, its people were "living from day to day in peril" of their lives and that worse violence might overtake them "at any moment." In May, *Time* stressed the Nazi dictatorship was so complete "there is little more power for Adolf Hitler to seize." *The Nation*, however, predicted Hitler would not be content until he had co-opted the religious organizations in Germany—a prescient observation.[32]

Instead of directly "co-ordination" the Protestant churches by *fiat*, the regime authorized a meeting of "German Christians" in the Prussian Diet House in April, 1933. Alfred Rosenberg was invited to address the meeting as a representative of the new government. Rosenberg declared Nazism was "a new living mythology" and "a new religion" and received shouts of agreement and acclaim. The convention had no authority to re-organize the churches but it did issue a demand for the Nazification of all Evangelicals. It adopted a canon calling on the churches to stress "heroic piety" and to "glorify purity of race." All interracial marriages were to be forbidden. The Hebrew Bible was to be banned, the New Testament modernized and the Jewish prophets replaced with Germanic heroes. Plans were made to introduce a new constitution at a future meeting at Frankfurt which would abolish the Weimar church parliament. Following the meeting, a Nazi was appointed as church commissioner in Mecklenburg-Schwerin over the protests of the League of Protestant Churches.[33]

At a subsequent meeting of the combined Protestant churches held in Berlin in May, the Nazi wing nominated Ludwig Mueller, Hitler's former military chaplain, as Protestant Bishop for the entire Reich. Non-Nazis were, however, able to elect Fredrich von Bodelschwingh to the position. The dispute simmered through June only to be apparently ended when, in early July, the Prussian government appointed the Nazi August Jaeger as commissioner of the Protestant churches. Von Bodelschwingh promptly resigned rather than serve under the direction of Jaeger. Ludwig Mueller thereupon "assumed" the office and provoked a groundswell of denunciation. Hindenburg wrote Hitler a public letter asking the dispute be peacefully resolved but Mueller remained in office. *Newsweek* concluded the regime had won the struggle. *The Literary Digest,* however, insisted the issue remained undecided.[34]

On July 23, the regular annual elections to fill 400,000 Protestant lay church boards became a referendum on Mueller's tenure. Non-Nazis were barred from the use of the state radio while Hitler urged Germans to support the "German Christians." Nazi pressure forced approximately eighty percent of the Protestants to the polls and produced a resounding victory for the regime. *The New Republic* chose, however, to interpret the results to mean the non-Nazi faction had "stood its ground" by running "determined opposition candidates" and by refusing to accept the election results. Following the election, Mueller was elected as Reich Bishop by Nazi laymen while Goering assumed the former royal title of *Summus Episcopus* of the Prussian Protestant state church. Mueller's election was confirmed by a Lutheran synod which also chose "to bring the German Evangelical Churches under the *de facto* rule of the Nazi state." In response, ten bishops presented a protest signed by 2,000 pastors but the synod refused to accept the document.[35] Once again, the issue appeared to be settled in favor of the regime.

In November, 1933, the conflict erupted anew. Although the "German Christians" had succeeded in securing Mueller's appointment as bishop, the remaining planks of their platform remained in limbo. To remedy the situation, Berlin bishop Joachim Hossenfelder held a rally at the *Sportpalast,* to hear the Nazi Reinhold Krause. Krause again demanded the repudiation of the Jewish Bible and the revision of "palpably misrepresentative or superstitious" portions of the New Testament. Further, the crucifix was to be eliminated from all churches as were all non-Aryan Christians. There were immediate protests from all over Germany which continued to grow in tempo. Mueller, moving to quell the dispute, sided with the moderates. He denounced Krause's views as "intolerable" and suspended him. Mueller, further required all church officials to accept the Bible as authoritative and rescinded any church laws limiting church membership to Aryans. Not content with Mueller's actions, more than 3,000 pastors read a joint statement from their pulpits denouncing the doctrines of the "German Christians" in general and laws against non-Aryan Christian in particular. The Berlin Catholic newspaper *Germania* announced its support for the pastors and denounced "German Christianity" as an "anti-religious new heathenism."[36]

The dissenting pastors formed a Pastor's Emergency League to combat the Nazi German Christian movement. The League was so popular and influential it was able to enlist the aid of Hindenburg. Hindenburg for the second time asked Hitler to bring peace to the church. Mueller, possibly under the direction of Hitler, responded by resigning as "protector" of the German Christian Movement and by forcing the resignation of his church cabinet which they dominated. The replacement cabinet promptly forbade church political faction or group. *The Nation* hailed the event as the "first internal political defeat" for the Nazi regime.[37]

While reporting on the Protestant conflict with the regime, *The New Republic* also reported von Papen and Goering were in Rome to enlist the Vatican in a "great crusade against Communism." *The Nation* interpreted their visit as "the next logical step" in Hitler's control of the Catholic church. *Newsweek* insisted they were there simply to conclude a new concordat between Germany and the Vatican.[38]

The possibility of a concordat seemed unlikely due to Nazi attacks on Catholics. When the national meeting of Catholic journeymen was held in Munich, SA members forcibly prevented Cardinal Faulhaber from conducting mass in the convention hall and "then fists flew and clubs cracked skulls." A dozen Catholics were severely beaten while the stress caused the death of Prelate Zinser of Mainz. The convention was suppressed. Catholic bishops responded with a joint statement repudiating any notion of racism and of a Catholic church independent of Rome. At the beginning of July, Hitler dissolved the Catholic Swabian Guard and all Catholic workers clubs as they were "enemies of the state." The same week all Catholic political groups and parties were to "co-ordinate" with the regime and the Center Party voluntarily dissolved its units. No protest was made by the Vatican.[39]

The reason for the lack of a Vatican protest became clear the following week, when Berlin and Cardinal Pacelli jointly announced the signing of a concordat. The new concordat superseded the previous concordats between the Vatican and the separate German states. Both *Time* and *Newsweek* believed Hitler, who was a Catholic by birth and education, had made substantial concessions as he did not care to test Catholic opposition to his regime. Among these concessions was the right to the confidentiality of the confession, the right to Catholic educational institutions, the right of non-political Catholic organizations to continue to function and Catholic equality in Protestant German states. Hitler promptly ordered the release of all Catholic priests previously arrested on political charges. The Vatican, for its part, agreed priests would refrain from all political activity or opposition to the regime. *The Literary Digest,* to the contrary, interpreted the concordat not as a coup for the Vatican but as "a distinct moral victory for Hitler" as it gave him the *imprimateur* of the Pope upon his regime.[40] The subject of Catholic-Nazi state relations simply dropped out of the American magazines studied here for the remainder of 1933.

Hitler's domestic policies, major or trivial, met little or no internal opposition apart from the conflict with the Protestant churches. When Goebbels announced a purge of university libraries, more verbalized than real, the act was greeted with enthusiasm by most Germans. Hitler's announcement of compulsory labor service for all German youth on May 1 likewise received wide approval in a depression-racked Germany. In June, Hitler announced a popular unemployment relief plan administered by Schacht to be financed by gifts from industry as will as state funds.[41] The regime's efforts to return the German woman to the *volkish* role of *"Kinder, Kirche, und Küche"* were considered to be correct and proper. State loans of up to $300 in grants for furniture and household necessities, made to women who quit work to become brides of low-income husbands, were especially popular. When female make-up was banned as unbecoming of the natural beauty of German women, women enthusiastically hailed the ban. Compulsory sterilization of undesirable or unfit persons was widely accepted as, among other reasons, it was commonplace in Denmark and in half of the states in the United States.[42]

During the first half of 1933, Hitler directed his efforts almost exclusively to the consolidation of Nazi control over Germany. His initial moves in the area of foreign affairs were either a continuation of previously established German policies or responses to the initiatives of other nations.

A Disarmament Conference met at Geneva from February to July, 1932. Owing to French insistence that security considerations precede any discussion of disarmament, no progress was made and the negotiations were stillborn. At every point, the French proposals were met by a German demand for equality of arms. Bruening ended the deadlock by temporarily withdrawing from the conference. When the conference reconvened in February, 1933, Hitler, as anticipated, met the familiar French proposals with the continuing German insistence on arms equality. Once again the conference was deadlocked. Ramsey MacDonald of England, in an effort to breach the impasse, proposed all European armies be first reduced and then Germany be allowed arms equality with France. The conference was again blocked by Hitler's insistence the SA should not be included in the calculation of German troop strength. The conference recessed in June with only an agreement it would reconvene in October.[43]

From June to October, repeated efforts were made to discover a basis on which the conference could be resumed with a degree of hope. All participants felt pressure to reach some agreement. *The New Republic* believed "the German people demand action on the arms-equality issue" and that Hitler was under "constraint" to "make good" though "the odds" were against him. Roosevelt released a statement in June that declared the peoples of the world "demanded" immediate action "to save the world from chaos." Hitler replied in a speech that received wide acclaim. He stated Germany would disarm if other nations did, there should be a transition period of five years to implement disarmament and that he viewed MacDonald's proposal with favor. He repeatedly insisted Germany desired peace and abhorred war. His suggestion the United States serve as guarantor of such an agreement led to a swift "clarification" by Roosevelt. Roosevelt replied the United States would "not hinder" a disarmament plan but it could not serve as guarantor. *Time* reported Roosevelt was "very much pleased" with Hitler's reply—as were most major American newspapers. *The Literary Digest* wrote "Germany can and should insist on equality," adding "Hitler's speech is soothing to most observers." *The Nation*, after noting Hitler's speech had "evoked wide editorial praise," wrote it remained adamantly opposed to "any rearmament of Germany as long as the Nazis rule."[44]

Pressing forward on the impetus provided by Hitler's speech, Germany demanded the right to rearm. The German press uniformly insisted Germany be accorded "defensive" weapons at once. Goebbels stated Germany "must" have the right to rearm if other nations refused to mutually disarm. An air raid scare, undoubtedly staged by Nazis, underlined the defenseless position of Germany. Neurath issued a Wilhelmstrasse press release that declared an arms-equality agreement was a pre-condition of any further German participation in the disarmament conference. Most American newsmagazines chose to report these items without comment. *The Reader's Digest*, however, elected to reprint an article by Clifford Sharp from *Living Age* which supported German rearmament. Sharp interpreted the German demand for arms-equality, not as aggressive in intent, but as an understandable reaction to Versailles and French occupation of the Ruhr. Germany could be expected to remain at peace for the next ten to fifteen years as the Nazis intended to concentrate on internal affairs as a means of consolidating their new Reich. In the final analysis, Sharp asserted, "Hitlerism is the business of the Germans themselves."[45] In all these discussions, Hitler did little but continue previous German policy.

Hitler also chose to respond positively to the proposal by Mussolini for a Four-Power Pact of England, France, Italy, and Germany. Mussolini sought both to settle the most pressing European issues of the moment and to provide a means of resolving international disputes in the future. As originally proposed in March, the pact would have restored to Hungary territories with a solid Magyar population, restructured the German-Polish border to allow Germany a land bridge to East Prussia and established a four-power agreement to revise the Treaty of Versailles. Treaty revisions were to include equality of arms for Germany and cooperation regarding colonial matters. England objected to discussion of colonial matters while France and the Little Entente objected to territorial revision and German rearmament. After prolonged discussions, an agreement was finally reached which stated the signatories renounced the use of force to resolve disputes for ten years, renounced territorial revision without mutual agreement by all concerned parties, promised to maintain the integrity and independence of all League members against aggression and agreed to the rearmament of Germany after five years if the disarmament conference failed. The pact, while signed, was neither ratified nor applied by its signatories.[46]

American magazines were more outspoken on the Four-Power Pact than on the disarmament negotiations. *Time* hailed the pact as "this series of definite results" and later favorably quoted Franqui, the "friend" of King Albert of Belgium, as saying "the small nations will cluster about the sole statesman capable of leadership, Mussolini" and also that Mussolini was "fostering sensible ideas for united action while the Great Powers are doing nothing." *Newsweek*, noted, without approval or disapproval, that the Pact "signified recognition of Germany's claim to national equality." *The New Republic* denounced it as "the denatured Mussolini Four-Power Pact." The Pact was merely another part of the "transparent hypocrisy of 1919" which institutionalized collective intervention and so "prevented that reconciliation and appeasement" needed by Europe. *The New Republic* later editorialized "the most dangerous and significant aspect of Mussolini's Four-Power Pact" was that Hitler intended to transform it "into a capitalist coalition directed against Soviet Russia." Throughout the year *The Nation* continued to denounce Nazi foreign policy as aggressive and belligerent.[47]

In the latter half of 1933, American magazines began to recognize in Hitler's foreign policy a bellicose and aggressive attitude which threatened the peace of Europe. Two different aspects of his policy led to this recognition. One was his perceived threat to Austria and the other was his withdrawal from the League of Nations.

As early as June, 1933, *The Literary Digest* reported Hitler had aggressive designs on Austria. It defended Dolfuss' dictatorship as the only government capable of resisting a Nazi revolt. Beyond doubt, it argued, free elections would produce a Nazi victory. Later the same month, it approved of Dolfuss' arrest of 300 Austrian Nazis including Theodor Habricht, "the Nazi inspector for Austria." It insisted only Dolfuss and Mussolini stood between Hitler and Vienna. By August, *Time* also saw Hitler as a danger to Austria. Nazi subversion in Austria, it argued, was a violation both of the Versailles Treaty and the Four-Power Pact. It approved of the decision by England and France to extend a loan to Dolfuss who was "the sheet anchor of peace" in Europe. To *Time*, however, the major protector of Austria remained Mussolini. *The Literary Digest* foresaw an imminent Nazi attack on Austria in September with only Mussolini correctly positioned to preserve Austria.[48] War seemed a definite possibility.

On September 13, *The Nation* noted with approval that the "Allied Powers" had given Austria permission to increase its standing army by 8,000 men so that it could resist Nazi "terrorists." The action was necessary as Austria was in a "sad plight." *Newsweek* was reassured by the action as it demonstrated England, France, and Italy were committed to the preservation of Austria. *Time* reported Dolfuss had steadfastly rejected petitions to restore parliamentary government. He defended his authoritarianism by asserting it was the only possible defense against Hitler. He also issued a *Brown Book* detailing Nazi terrorism.[49] When Hitler did not militarily attack Austria, most of the magazines under study dropped the subject and turned their attention to other issues.

Only *The Literary Digest* asserted that Nazi designs on Austria remained unaltered. It believed Hitler was motivated by a desire to punish "his native land" for its rejection of him. Germany's unchanged policy of a "march to the East" required the annexation of Austria. A Nazi victory in Austria would therefore, represent the overthrow of the Versailles Settlement and the recognition that "after twenty years, Germany had won the war." It believed that, although "about thirty percent of Austrians are already Hitlerites," the remainder were united in their support of Dolfuss. With the support of France and Italy, Dolfuss had temporarily created a better climate for the continued independence of Austria.[50]

A second factor in the renewed interpretation of Hitler as a threat to peace was his re-militarization of Germany and his concurrent withdrawal from the League. In October, *The Literary Digest* insisted German re-militarization had introduced "a new and more ominous epoch" in Europe. Germans responded to Hitler with religious ecstasy and saw him as a "messiah." The external symbol of that "religious experience" was the re-arming of Germany. The same day, *Newsweek* reported Italy had gained important concessions from France and England. When the Disarmament Conference re-convened on October 16, Germany would be allowed "defensive weapons" under French supervision. To *The Nation*, these events demonstrated Hitler was "deepening the European political crisis" and so "leading the world to the verge of another war."[51]

When the Disarmament Conference re-convened, the Italian proposals were rejected outright by the delegates. *Newsweek* noted there was a "new climate" in international affairs due to general fear of Nazi intentions. Austria, Belgium, and Switzerland had increased their military budgets. Warsaw and Moscow had moved toward an unexpected rapproachment. Italy now feared for the Tyrol and England and France had vetoed even defensive weapons for Germany. France, with the support of England and the United States, proposed an arms limitation for four years, international supervision of the stand-still and discussion of German arms equality only at the end of the limitation period. Hitler thereupon recalled the German delegate, Rudolf Nadolny, to Berlin for consultation. The following day, Hitler announced Germany's withdrawal from the League as Germans could no longer accept "deliberate relegation" to an "inferior class." He also set November 12, the date for Reichstag elections, as the day for a concurrent plebiscite on his withdrawal from the League. He ended his announcement by stating he was ready to conduct bilateral negotiations with France on a non-aggression pact.[52]

According to *Time*, Hitler's announcement "rocked" the League and "shriveled" the Disarmament Conference. It noted Hitler's "technique of assault" consisted of "alternate hammer blows and conciliatory gestures." It predicted France would not conduct separate negotiations with Hitler, that the Conference would struggle on in a weakened condition and that Germans would approve withdrawal from the League. *Newsweek* also predicted an overwhelming Nazi victory in the November plebiscite. It had little hope for a continuation of the Conference as it would be a "Hamlet" and "Hamlet left out." The League was seriously weakened and there was little hope it could prevent German rearmament. The Four Power Pact was unreliable and unratified. It therefore concluded "none of the great powers" would henceforth "scrap a single cartridge." *The Nation* believed the "situation abroad is so grave as to be almost desperate." It called on Roosevelt to urge immediate disarmament, urge a revision of Versailles and to treat Germany as an equal in all negotiations. At the same time, it demanded "the moral opinion of this country must be ceaselessly alert" against Hitler and his government. It specifically repudiated the insistence of *The New Republic* that the United States withdraw from European affairs. *The Literary Digest* wrote that "today the question is no longer whether, but when" war would break out as only Germany's lack of arms prevented an immediate attack on its neighbors.[53]

As expected, on November 12, the German people elected a totally Nazi Reichstag and overwhelmingly endorsed Hitler's domestic and foreign policies. In the largest electoral turnout in German history, forty three of forty five million voters cast their ballots in support of Hitler. *Newsweek* reported that, although foreigners might consider the plebiscite a "farce," Germans, whipped by the entire police and propaganda resources of the Nazi regime, did give Hitler a striking mandate. *Time*, while echoing the charges of Nazi pressure in the balloting, agreed Hitler had been given a "blank check" by Germans. *The New Republic* accepted the election results as authentic, for all Germans were united in their support of Hitler's foreign policy. With prophetic insight it wrote "it may safely be predicted that Hitlerism will govern Germany at least until the closing phases of the next war." *The Literary Digest* reported sarcastically that ninety percent of the Oranienburg and Ostrazen concentration camp inmates had voted "ja" in the plebiscite. *Newsweek*, in the same vein, noted ninety seven percent of the inmates of "the dread prison camp in Brandenburg" had voted "ja". *Newsweek* believed the election result signaled the final achievement of a totalitarian state in Germany. Henceforth, the destiny of Hitler and Germany would be undissolvable.[54]

When the newly elected Reichstag met, it was a veritable sea of 661 Brown Shirted Nazis. For the first time since 1919 there were no female deputies. The Reichstag elected Goering as its president, authorized him to appoint all committees, to "dispose of all petitions and resolutions" and then adjourned after a session lasting only eight minutes. Foreign diplomats observing the meeting reportedly "snickered" at the charade but realized all legal or vocal opposition to the Nazi regime was silenced.[55]

One final theme of several American magazines in 1933 must be mentioned. On May 31, *The Nation* insisted Nazism aimed at "world dominance" and so constituted "a menace" to American institutions. Indeed, Nazism was "a direct challenge to every American basic principle." In July, it reiterated its warning, noting there was a definite pro-Nazi sympathy in the *Journal of Commerce*, the New York *Staats-Zeitung* and "other newspapers in this country." *The New Republic* reported in August that *The New York Evening Post* excused Nazi excesses and had written "if the world is to find Hitler a conservative force fighting against a revolutionary war, it may forgive him even his anti-Jewish insanities and offer a prayer for his success." In addition to these expressions of sympathy for Nazism, *The New Republic* reported in October that American fascist groups were being organized. The "first open and avowed movement for American fascism" was organized by one Art Smith of Philadelphia. Smith had formed the Khaki Shirts as the vanguard of "a march on Washington" to institute an American dictatorship. Smith, however, had come a "sad cropper" when the police raided his headquarters. Although Smith eluded arrest, scores of weapons had been confiscated and his movement quashed.[56]

In November, *Time* reported the activities of Heinz Spanknoebel. Spanknoebel, a Seventh Day Adventist minister who had lived in the United States for three years, had been appointed as the leader of American Nazis in 1932 by Ley of the Foreign Propaganda Bureau of Hamburg. When the bureau was dissolved in July, 1933, Spanknoebel became the leader of the New York based "Friends of Germany." He attempted to intimidate German-American newspaper editors and to re-orient New York's traditional "German Day" celebration to a "Hitler Day" celebration. Mayor Patrick O'Brien personally intervened to cancel the occasion when it also became apparent Spanknoebel had terrorized German-American societies in an effort to force out their Jewish members. The federal authorities thereupon issued a warrant for his arrest as an unregistered agent of a foreign government but Spanknoebel disappeared into the recesses of Manhatten's Yorkville and escaped arrest. Hitler responded to the action with a statement there was no authorized Nazi representative in the United States and any reports to the contrary were Jewish inventions. *Time* ended its article by quoting O'Brien's comment that a "secret invasion" by Nazis was underway.[57]

The Nation initially responded to the news of the warrant for Spanknoebel's arrest with a plea for the right of free speech even by Nazis. It noted Jews had protested the action of Mayor O'Brien on the principle that political suppression of the Nazi might establish a precedent for the future suppression of other unpopular or minority groups. It concluded Spanknoebel was entitled "to make an ass of himself in public" for there was "not the slightest reason to fear" Americans would follow him or adopt his views. The situation would be best met by adherence to the principles of free speech and liberty of assembly rather than resort to Nazi-type measures of suppression.[58]

Later in the same month, however, *The Nation* published a long exposé of Nazi propaganda in the United States. It refuted Hitler's statement there were no authorized German propagandists in America by carefully delineating the extent of that propaganda and the specific persons associated with it. It believed Hitler's statement was characteristic of his "accustomed policy of duplicity and deceit." It indicted the National Socialist German Labor Party led by Ernst Luedecke, a registered correspondent of the *Völkische Beobachter*, as subversive. It alledged Luedecke had influenced representatives MacFadden of Pennsylvania and Banton to make anti-Semitic speeches in Congress and, in MacFadden's case, an "impassioned defense of Hitler's regime." It further alledged there were Nazi organizations in all large northern cities directed by the German consulate in New York. Funds for these organizations were provided by the American branches of I.G. Farber, the Dornier Motor Works and the Hamburg-American Line.[59]

The Nation also indicted a number of Americans for being paid Nazi agents. Edwin Emerson, who had been a paid German propagandist from 1914 until 1917, was paid to represent the Nazi party in the United States. His assistant was the former American Consul General in Munich, T. St. John Gaffney. The New York public relations firm of Carl Byoir and Associates was being paid to place pro-Nazi material in the American press. George Sylvester Viereck and Carl D. Dickey were among Byoir's "associates" writing such press material. *The Nation* further alledged William D. Pelley's "Silver Shirts" had been co-opted by American Nazis. It concluded the principle of free speech had been used by Nazis to destroy the German Republic. There was no assurance that the same tactic would not also succeed in the United States—a lesson that "doctrinaires of 'pure democracy' " had yet to learn. An extended article in *Harper's* reviewed the nature of anti-Semitism in the United States and the native and German organizations that sought to exploit it. *Harper's* however, believed it was unlikely the groups would find a fertile soil in the United States.[60]

The New Republic agreed there was an indigenous fascist movement in the United States but defined its menace in a different manner. It identified a number of American fascist organizations: the Khaki Shirts, Silver Shirts, Order of '76, Crusaders for Economic Liberty and National Watchmen. All were, to a greater or lesser degree, anti-Semitic Nazi sympathizers. The real danger was that middle-class disillusionment, occasioned by the Depression, predisposed that class to radical, dictatorial political solutions. It concluded American fascists were "waiting in the wings" for a leader to unite them. Only an equal radical movement on the Left could forestall the fascists on the Right.[61]

In the summer of 1934, the Congressional Committee on Un-American Activities unearthed evidence of Nazi propaganda in the United States which incensed *The Nation* and *The New Republic*. In July, they reported Carl Byoir and Associates was receiving $6,000 a month to refurbish the Nazi image of Germany in America. Byoir, in turn, had hired George S. Viereck to propagandize for Germany at a fee of $1,750 a month. Viereck had also received $2,000 in cash directly from Otto Kiep, the German Consul in New York, as payment for advice on German publicity in the United States. Viereck declared the money had been paid in cash "to avoid spies among the professional Jews and bolsheviks." *The New Republic*, after recapitulating the above information, also revealed a number of writers had been paid to portray Germany in a favorable light. It specifically named Alexander Powell, Karl Kitchen, Helen Reed, James Aswelt and Allen Cleaton.[62]

Both magazines were especially angered by the revelation that Ivy L. Lee, the dean of public relations in the United States, was being paid $25,000 a year through the German Dye Trust for advice on German-American relations. *The New Republic* noted Lee had changed Rockerfellow's image "from ogre to Santa Claus and made America love the Pennsylvania Railroad." It saw great danger in having such skilled propagandist in the pay of "the most dangerous, depraved and bloody-handed government now to be found anywhere in the world."[63] This concern over "Hitlerism" in the United States subsided, however, after the congressional hearings and their attention returned to Hitler and his regime.

Newsweek elected to run a special article on the first anniversary of Hitler's rule. Primarily a recapitulation of the events of first year of Nazi power, it stated Hitler's "appearance suggests Charlie Chaplin" but his words "the fevered dream of a magalomaniac." Nevertheless, he inspired terror in opponents and blind loyalty in his supporters. Through the use of violence control of the media and superb showmanship, Hitler had "coordinated" all sources of power in his hands. Psychologically, the achievement was "prodigious" although the

German economic picture remained spotty. Certainly, Hitler had established the "greatest autocracy Germany had ever know.[64] *Time* took a different approach in several unique articles. One article detailed Hitler's personal financial assistance to a former wartime comrade named Ignatz Westenkirchner. Westenkirchner had emmigrated to Reading, Pennsylvania, after the war. Left unemployed by the depression, he appealed to Hitler for help. Hitler provided Westenkirchner and his family with return passage to Germany along with the promise of a job in the Munich Brown House. Hitler's bravery in the war was mentioned twice. Westenkirchner was quoted as saying Hitler was "a kind man" and that the reports of anti-Semitism were "not true." Hitler, he stated, was "for the poor" at a time when "the poor can't get along in America." The following week *Time* reported Hitler, upon meeting Westenkirchner, had warmly embraced him and asked for his "blessing." Westenkirchner was made superintendent of a Nazi building in Munich. According to Westenkirchner, Hitler was raising Germany's poor "without permitting the upper classes to be leveled down—which is real Socialism." In the same issue, *Time* printed a short paragraph, unrelated to any other article, in which it reported Hitler had stopped his Mercedes in "snow-covered Bavaria" to pick up two hikers on a lonely road. In addition to delivering them to their village, Hitler gave them both his coat and overcoat along with a gift of five marks apiece. In Germany, Hitler was referred to as "gentle Adolf" by growing numbers of its people. At the end of January, *Time* reported Hitler had repatriated a second German from America at his personal expense. Anton Karthausen of Brownville, Texas, wrote Hitler he was unable to find work and was desperate. Hitler had promptly responded with "Hitler tickets" for Karthausen and his family.[65]

In April both *Newsweek* and *Time* defined Hitler as a moderating force in the continued clash between church and regime in Germany. When Lutheran Archbishop Erling Eidem of Sweden intervened with Hitler on behalf of German Evangelical pastors, Hitler "roared" at Reich Bishop Ludwig Mueller "there must be peace in the German Protestant Church by May 1." *Newsweek*, after reporting several clashes between Catholics and zealous Nazis, asserted Hitler had intervened with "a conservative gesture" instead of troops and had suspended a number of Nazi Youth leaders. It concluded Hitler had elected to use a "gentle hand" to ease the religious conflict in Germany.[66]

By way of contrast, the men around Hitler were described as being more cynical and calloused in their attitude and conduct than their leader. In January, *Time* wrote that it was Goering who intended to "proceed violently" against the bishops opposed to the Nazification of the Evangelical Church. *The Reader's Digest* saw Goering as the "epitome of Prussianism", a man with a "cold, brutal" demeanor who was prone to react with violence in any situation. Ernst Roehm, commander of the SA, was the "Mailed Fist" of the regime who had organized the private army used to suppress civil liberties in Germany. Roehm, Hitler's former wartime commander, was the originator of Nazi militarism.[67] Goebbels was the "Hypnotist of Millions" and creator of the "greatest propaganda machine in history." He was "unquestionably the most intelligent and resourceful" member of the Nazi leadership. Although personally "un-Aryan looking," he was an anti-Semitic "fanatic." Hitler found this motley group individually and collectively useful, often found it difficult to control them, but stood apart from their excesses. Hitler was the Nazi who displayed "tact and courtesy" and "unquestionably" felt Goering was "steam-rolling" over Hitler's own moderation. The more Hitler veered away from violence the more likely there would soon be "a showdown between these two" on the role of violence in the Nazi state.[68]

Time also indulged in this speculation about potential divisions among the Nazi leadership. It reported "Berlin rocked at the news" that Hitler and Goering had refused to exchange New Year greetings. The "imp of discord" between the two was Goebbels who was scheming to abolish the Prussian state and thereby destroy Goering's base of power in the Nazi regime. It similarly reported Hitler had forestalled "that arrant Nazi queer" Roehm's ambition to lead the army by having Hindenburg appoint von Fritsch as commander of the Reichswehr.[69]

Even as Hitler was depicted personally in a more favorable light as a moderating force in the Nazi state, other news reports demonstrated his growing domination of Germany. At the end of January, Hitler laid to rest all speculation about a Hohenzollern restoration by assuming the title of *"Der Reichsführer"* and simultaneously announcing future *Reichsführers* would be chosen by a Nazi *"Führerrat."* Monarchists were denounced as "more dangerous than the Communists!" *Newsweek* quoted Hitler as warning monarchists "to keep their hands off" the German state. A monarchist restoration was henceforth not even to be discussed.[70] When the German Officer's League staged a "Kaiser's Geburtstag" festival, police reinforced by SA units "formally dissolved the meeting." The SA also broke up a monarchist birthday ball in Berlin and denuded "house fronts of the Imperial flag." Goering, who was about to publish a book entitled *I Am a Monarchist*, hastily changed it to *The Building of a Nation*.[71]

In February, Hitler abolished Germany's state diets and the *Reichsrat* and assumed the authority to promulgate a new constitution. The states were placed under Nazi viceroys who reported to "lean, fanatical" Wilhelm Frick.[72] In March, German industry was organized into twelve groups, each headed by a Hitler appointee. The groups were to prevent cutthroat competition and rationalize industrial production and labor. *Newsweek* announced the plan by writing that "having organized, reorganized, consolidated and reformed everything in sight," Hitler had now taken over "Big Business" and coordinated it into the Nazi state. At the same time, Hitler announced a new campaign against unemployment. Two billion marks were alloted to a plan designed to employ two million men during the next twelve months. Although Germany had a tremendous budget deficit, Hitler was compelled to adopt the program to fulfill his economic promises or risk his regime.[73] The expulsion of the Jewish community from German economic life had failed to either "boost" the German economy or to provide more jobs for Aryan Germans. Indeed, the anti-Semitism of 1933 had further depressed the economy.

The Nazi campaign against Jews continued unabated in 1934. Earlier expectations that Nazi anti-Semitism would ease with time were unfulfilled. *The New Republic* referred to the actions taken as a "cold pogrom" for, although Jews were no longer normally beaten on the streets, the entire legal apparatus of the state was used against them. An edict of January 1 forbade the employment of Jews for editorial or illustrative work in newspapers or magazines with the exception of those who had frontline service during the war. A similar edict by Rust, Minister of Education, gave Jewish university students in medicine and law the choice between keeping their German citizenship, which would eliminate them as Jews from state examinations and licenses, and relinquishing their citizenship. In the latter case, they could remain as "guests" and take their examinations but still be barred from practicing their profession. The same week it became apparent German Jews would be barred from participation in the 1936 Olympic Games.[74] In time, this ruling was to become a major issue in deciding where the games would be held.

Time reported the same week that Hitler had decreed a ban on the preparation of kosher meat in Germany. Although it could still be imported under drastic restrictions, a butcher from Wiesbaden named Ludwig Frohwein was given two months in prison for preparing kosher meat. In conjunction with the decree, Hans Frank, Commissioner for Justice, promised a new legal code based on "Teutonic law and culture" would soon be promulgated by the regime[75]

Following an SA demonstration at a film starring the blond Austrian-Jewish actress Elizabeth Bergner, Goebbels ordered the film withdrawn and also banned any other films featuring the actress.[76] Additionally, Goebbels banned the American film "The Prizefighter and the Lady" starring the half-Jewish boxer Max Baer because of the actor's race. *Time* reported Goebbels had also suppressed the venerable Berlin newspaper *Vossiche Zeitung*. The newspaper was only one of 600 Jewish newspapers similarly suppressed in the past few months.[76] Nazi anti-Semitism played a definite role in increasing the repulsion of Americans to Nazism.

One indication of the growing anti-Nazi feeling in the United States was the announcement by R.H. Macy's that its purchasing office in Berlin was to be closed as its orders for German goods had declined by ninety-eight percent in only six months. Gimbel's, Lord and Taylor, Bloomingdale's, Best, and Hearn also announced they were joining the boycott against German-produced goods.[77]

Another sign of this growing anti-Nazi attitude in the United States came when Elliott Cutler, marshal for the twenty-fifth anniversary reunion of the Harvard class of 1909, invited Ernst Hanfstaengl to be his aide at the reunion. Hanfstaengl had graduated from Harvard, returned to Germany and had become Hitler's "best personal friend, his liaison officer with the U.S. and British Press, his favorite piano player." Upon hearing of the invitation, Harvard alumni "instantly let out a loud squeal of rage." Telegrams poured into Washington asking that the visit be legally barred. Cutler was forced to call Hanfstaengl and withdraw the invitation. Hanfstaengl did, however, attend the reunion as an ordinary alumnus.[78] The anti-Nazi attitude of increasing numbers of Americans was also based, at least in part, on Hitler's continued assault on the German churches.

Church and state continued their conflict throughout 1934. The year 1933 had apparently ended with the victory of Evangelical pastors over the "German Christian" movement. However, the conflict between the regime and the Evangelical church now revolved around the issue of "co-ordination" of the organization of the church under Reichbishop Mueller and the extent to which Nazism would redefine the theology of the church. As presented by American magazines, the conflict resembled a see-saw battle with each side claiming victory at this or that point. Part of the confusion was the result of wishful thinking on the part of American editors. Another part of the confusion was occasioned by the ambiguous actions of Hitler himself.

As 1934 opened, a meeting of Lutheran bishops met at Halle for the avowed purpose of forcing Mueller's resignation. Hitler intervened by announcing his support for Mueller and by angrily denouncing the lack of unity in the church. When the bishops dispersed without action, the 6,000 member Pastor's Emergency Federation took to their pulpits to denounce Mueller. Mueller responded with a decree on January 1, which forbade the discussion of political issues, abolished self-government in the churches and prohibited Jewish converts from holding any church office. In Berlin, police broke up a parade of Sunday School Boys and subsequently dispersed Protestants who attempted to hold a recitation of the Lord's Prayer on the steps of the Berlin Cathedral. Martin Niemoeller reacted with a sermon urging resistance to the Reichsbishop. *The New Republic* believed these events demonstrated the church would "prove more difficult to handle than the 'Marxist mob' ".[79]

This prediction seemed to be borne out when Hindenburg twice intervened the following week to call Mueller "on the carpet" for "attempting to set up a religious dictatorship." Mueller responded with a request for an armistice with the Federation to consider their demand for a new church cabinet and Reichsbishop. At the same time, police seized membership lists of the Federation, whose leadership had been assumed by Niemoeller. In addition, Rosenberg was appointed by Hitler as "ideological supervisor" of all allied organizations of the state, including the church.[80]

In April, with a continued stalemate in the struggle, American readers were again told Hitler had intervened with a "gentle hand" and a "conservative gesture" instead of "calling out the troops." He demanded Mueller resolve the conflict and bring peace within the church. Hitler also suspended three Nazi Youth leaders who had directed an attack on a Christian Youth meeting. In Darmstadt, twenty-nine Bible students who had been arrested were ordered released. On the other hand, Mueller ordered Niemoeller deposed and replaced by a Dr. Scharfenberg. When Scharfenberg refused to accept the appointment, Niemoeller was allowed to continue as pastor of the Dahlem church. Further, a Berlin Court ruled Mueller had acted unconstitutionally in abolishing the Prussian church council. Mueller thereupon proclaimed an amnesty for the rebellious pastors, revoked his decree of January 1, surrendered his right to demote recalcitrant ministers and suspended his demand that Jewish converts be ousted from church positions.[81]

Heartened by their apparent successful resistance to the regime, the dissenting pastors met at Barmen in June to renounce Mueller's leadership. In addition to organizing a Reich Council of Elders, the pastors declared themselves to be the "right and lawful Protestant Church" and adopted a confession that explicitly rejected the Nazi doctrine of the state. *Newsweek* interpreted these actions as "a declaration of war" and a "courageous defiance of Hitler." No report of the reaction of the regime appeared in the magazines under study except for a brief report in *Time* near the end of July which stated Wilhelm Frick, Minister of Interior, had banned all discussion of church policies in groups of three or more persons or by written or printed words.[82]

In August, Mueller convened a virtually hand-picked National Synod and demanded its members pledge an oath of fealty to Hitler while also abdicating its legislative powers to his church council. Mueller's demands were adopted but opposition flared anew when the dissenting pastors, led by Niemoeller, read a manifesto from their pulpits denouncing both Mueller and the Synod. The manifesto also declared "obedience to this church regime means disobedience to God." In the following weeks Mueller proceeded to "co-ordinate" twenty-six out of the twenty-eight Evangelical church groups. Only the churches of Bavaria and Wuerttemberg held out against him. When, in September, Mueller declared he wanted to unite both Catholics and Protestants in one national church, recalcitrant pastors "hurled" a manifesto from their pulpits declaring the effort to found a national church "colored with Nordic Paganism" to be heretical.[83]

In Munich, 2,000 "irate" Protestants paraded before the Nazi Brown House singing hymns. At Bishop Meiser's residence, they pledged their support for his resistance to Mueller. In Nuremberg a "furious mob" rallied outside Streicher's newspaper to "bait" him for an attack on Meiser. *The Nation* hailed German Christians for being the first to "venture an open and organized opposition to Nazi tyranny."[84]

In the middle of October, Mueller suspended Meiser and placed him under house arrest. Meiser slipped out to his church and preached a sermon denouncing Mueller. The congregation then escorted him back to his home and "bellowed hymns" until police charged the crowd with sabers. The crowd reassembled the next evening before Meiser's home and marched to the Brown House where they paused "to spit on the pavement and denounce the dictator." *Time* reported Hitler was so concerned he "went quietly to Munich to watch developments." Hitler ordered the events be handled without violence, according to *Time*, but the police had gotten out of hand. *Time* also reported the crowd had spit on the pavement before the Brown House and "yelled defiance" at Hitler himself. The following Sunday 16,000 pastors described Mueller and Hitler to be "allied to Satan." *The Nation* believed the resistance would have "far-reaching repercussions" on the regime while to *The New Republic* it was clear Hitler had "lost" and that henceforth the issue would be settled by compromise.[85]

According to both *Time* and *Newsweek*, it seemed *The New Republic's* prediction of compromise was fulfilled. When Mueller requested an audience with Hitler to take his oath of loyalty as fully consecrated Reichbishop, Hitler twice refused to receive him, pleading he had a "toothache." Not only did Hitler publicly snub Mueller, but he also shortly ordered the dismissal of Mueller's chief advisor, one August Jaeger. Finally, the house arrest of Meiser and Theophil Wuerm of Wuerttemberg was cancelled. As the year ended, several American magazines generally predicted the conflict would continue until Mueller was ousted as Reichbishop and that ultimately the resistance of the church would succeed.[86]

Catholic conflict with the Nazi state received much less attention than the Protestant struggle. Reichbishop Mueller was a visible antagonist in the Protestant clash. Moreover, whereas the Lutherans had historically been a state church, the Catholic church was truly an international body. Finally, the 1933 concordat with the Vatican introduced a stabilizing factor into the situation. In January, 1934, *Newsweek* reported several priests had been arrested on a variety of offenses. Further, the Bishop of Mainz refused to allow Nazi flags to be flown by churches in his diocese. Cardinal Faulhaber, Archbishop of Munich, went so far as to openly denounce the anti-Semitic policies of the regime and its accompanying myths of "Teutonic Supremacy." In March, after Faulhaber's residence had been fired on by local Nazis acting on their own, Pope Pius XI extended diplomatic immunity to Faulhaber by designating him a Papal Legate.[87]

In April, *Newsweek* reported Hitler made a conciliatory gesture toward Catholics by suspending three Hitler youth leaders who had directed an attack on a Catholic youth group. At Wuerzburg, when a "shouting crowd of Nazis" forced their way into the bishop's residence to demand the transfer of a priest critical of the regime, an SA leader intervened to control the demonstrators. *Newsweek* interpreted these events to mean Hitler was using a "gentle hand" with the church. *The Literary Digest* reinforced this view by writing Hitler had launched an investigation into attacks on Catholics. However, Erich Klausener, a Catholic lay leader, was executed during the purge in June. This act served to stiffen the determination of Catholics to meet the regime with "stubborn resistance." Apart from these limited and unexpanded reference, the magazines under study made no further reference to Nazi-Catholic conflict in 1934.

The summer of 1934 saw a rapid series of events that, for a period of five weeks, fixed world attention on Germany and dominated the foreign news sections of the magazines under study. Von Papen flayed the Nazi regime in a public address, Hitler conducted a "blood purge" in Germany, Dolfuss was assassinated by Austrian Nazis and von Hindenburg died.

Von Papen's speech to the students of Marburg on June 17, 1934, was hailed by *Newsweek* as "Hitler's first great crisis." Von Papen, it averred, had delivered "the most scathing public attack on the Nazi regime ever made." *Time* wrote von Papen had "flayed" the Nazi regime "from stem to stern" for its "muzzling of the Press, its meddling with religion, its encouragement of fanaticism and the drift toward radicalism." Although Goebbels subsequently sought to censor it, the speech had slipped by the censors and made at least one edition of most papers in Germany before a lid was placed on the story.[89]

The American magazines were unanimous in their insistence von Papen spoke, not for himself alone, but for the reactionary industrialists and Junkers. The latter groups were incensed by the decline in Germany's foreign trade balance, lowering gold reserves and by Darre's attempts to redistribute the land of the Junker estates. This reactionary group was led by von Neurath, Kurt Schmitt and Hjalmar Schlacht. Behind them stood von Hindenburg, who "lost no time" in showing he "sided with his friend von Papen." Indeed, in Berlin, there were rumors the "speech was a preliminary to a military coup sponsored by von Hindenburg." The speech generally met with approval from the German people who were evidencing a "new Nazi-weariness."[90]

Goebbels reacted with anger to the speech, while Goering and Hess agreed there were certain justified criticisms to be made of Nazi rule. As for Hitler, *Newsweek* reported he "seemed eager to placate both extremists and reactionaries." While admitting there were faults in his regime, he "resented their public utterance." Above all, he wanted to avoid a "disastrous alienation of the industrialists without disappointing" his followers and so "write the end to his dictatorship." *Time* felt the event demonstrated Hitler was not a "real Dictator" or else he would have instantly "squelched" von Papen. To his cabinet, Hitler had shown himself to be a "Little Man" by inviting both von Papen and Goebbels to a tea party. Further, he declined to accept the proffered resignation of von Papen. *The Nation* believed the speech marked the "beginning of a battle" between the reactionaries and the Nazis which Hitler wished to avoid and in which he wanted to appear as a "moderate." The crisis would prove to be "a genuine test of Hitler's capacity as a statesman and fighter." *The New Republic* took the unique position that von Papen's speech was intended to "back up" Hitler and Goering in their struggle with the radicals led by Goebbels and Roehm. This explained Hitler's refusal to accept von Papen's resignation and his conciliatory visit with von Hindenburg. In the long run, the reactionaries would prevail and, with the support of the Junkers and the Reichwehr, move against the Nazis and establish a "military and industrial dictatorship" for Hitler could not play the role of moderator forever. Interest in von Papen's speech was almost immediately eclipsed by the news of Hitler's "blood purge" of the Nazi party. Except for some surprise von Papen was not killed in the purge,[91] no additional comment was made on his speech and its consequences.

Hitler's "Blood Purge" of the SA on June 30, 1934, generally took American magazines by surprise. Only an article by Augustus Bauer in the May 9 issue of *The New Republic* surmised Hitler might turn on the SA as a threat to his regime. Bauer argued the SA was "a very proletarian mass that beneath the surface boils with potential revolutionary movements" that might develop their own "brand of action." Bauer also correctly identified the SS as the group Hitler might use "to hold them in check."[92] Nevertheless, the actual event caught most magazines unawares.

The initial American magazine to reach print with the news of the purge was *The Literary Digest* on July 7. It wrote Hitler had chosen a "middle path" between the extremes of his party by executing "twenty or more persons" and arresting "hundreds." Effectively, this spelled the "end of the Nazi radicals" and was proof of Hitler's "manifest capitalistic sympathies." However, *The Literary Digest* believed that, in view of the economic difficulties of Germany, it was in question whether Hitler "could sustain himself without his radicals."[93]

Apart from minor discrepancies over the number of people shot and arrested, American newsmagazines were quite objective and accurate in their details of the purge and there is nothing revelatory in them in the light of present knowledge. What is more interesting is their interpretation of the motives behind the purge. *Time* believed Roehm had demanded Hitler dissolve the Stalhelm as an obscure SA leader had been stabbed in Pomerania by a Stalhelm member. When Hitler refused, "Berlin Storm Troop leaders were stupid enough to mutter openly" against Hitler. Hitler, in moving against his own followers, had forfeited the title of "the Gentle Dictator." *Newsweek* interpreted the purge as a decision by Hitler to remove both extremists on his left and the reactionaries on his right in order to further consolidate his power. It further suggested Hitler might also have used the situation to vent "a grudge" against von Schleicher. *The New Republic* found a wide variety of "certain fairly well defined" reasons for the purge. Roehm was caught planning a coup to "forestall a threatened nationalist-monarchist uprising." Again, Roehm was convinced Essen industrialists had persuaded Hitler to move strongly to the right economically and this the SA could not accept. If Roehm had succeeded, Hitler was to be forced to accede to "a two day reign of terror throughout Germany against radicals, Jews, nationalists, and monarchists." *The Nation* insisted the showdown was inevitable given Roehm's determination to ban the Stalhelm while simultaneously making the SA the military arm of Germany. Given the opposition of the army to Roehm's demands, Hitler aligned himself with the army. *The Literary Digest* wrote the purge was occasioned by malcontents in the SA who were unwilling to accept Hitler's "evolutionary" Nazism. These SA leaders were unable to accept the constraints of organic growth as they could not "adjust to normal life after the war."[94]

The varying interpretations of the probable consequences of the purge are also interesting. *The Literary Digest*, believing Hitler's power was already being undercut by the continued slump in the German economy, saw his position as "even more precarious." On the contrary, *Time* insisted Hitler "had at last proved himself a Strong Man" and so had "emerged with increased prestige." *The New Republic* initially concurred with this view. It later wrote Hitler had become "virtually the prisoner of the Reichswehr."[95] Later still, *The New Republic* believed Hitler had delivered himself into the hands of the industrialists who truly determined "Germany's destinies." To *The Saturday Evening Post*, it was obvious Hitler's power had become "more symbolic than actual" as he would be dominated by the Reichswehr. *The Atlantic Monthly* reported Hitler would retain visible power but, under the control of the Reichswehr, would cease to be a threat to the peace of Europe. *The Nation* predicted the purge was the precursor of a military dictatorship with "Hitler's position as tool and figurehead becoming more precarious." *Newsweek* wrote Hitler was faced with the choice of winning back the SA or relying on the Reichswehr— both of which "paths were stony." Only *Newsweek* accurately predicted the subsequent decline of the SA and the increasing importance of the SS and Heinrich Himmler in the Nazi state.[96] The assassination of Dolfuss of the Austrian Nazis quickly diverted attention away from the purge.

As 1934 opened, American magazines reported that both "overt and covert Nazi pressure on Austria was increasing daily." An Austrian Nazi Legion of 3,000 was poised in Germany along the Austrian border. Nazi bombs exploded in dozens of cities and it was public knowledge that Nazis had smuggled in large arms caches. Nazis reportedly spent between three and four million marks each month for bribes and propaganda. They had infiltrated the Austrian bureaucracy—even one member of Dolfuss' bodyguard was a Nazi. Dolfuss responded by establishing a dictatorship based on a united front formed upon a reactionary Catholicism, reactionary army, and reactionary Heimwehr.[97]

At the beginning of February, Dolfuss moved to protect his regime from the Nazi threat by announcing suspected Nazis would be arrested and held without trial. Further, he appealed to the League for aid and protection under the terms of Article XI of its charter. *Time* commented the League would, however, do little more than "send a commission and publish a book." It believed there would be no action as "Britain was too timorous, Italy dared not act alone, and France was far too deeply mired in her own political garbage."[98] Internally, instead of seeking to enlist the support of Austria's socialists in his opposition to the Nazis, Dolfuss chose to precipitate a crisis by destroying them as a political force.

Under the cover of a "conference" with Premier Goemboes of Hungary, "Millimetternich" Dolfuss went to Budapest. In his absence, governmental authority devolved upon Emil Fey, commander of the Heimwehr. Fey had instructions to "perform a few blunt maneuvers" for which Dolfuss "did not care to be directly responsible." Fey promptly attacked socialist centers all across Austria. In these assaults, police, army, and Heimwehr units utilized maximum force. When socialists in Vienna reacted with particularly strong resistance, Fey used artillery to destroy their strongholds. *Time* and *Newsweek* reported approximately 1,000 socialists, including women and children, were killed while some 5,000 socialists were arrested. On his return to Vienna, Dolfuss banned all socialist parties, dismissed the Austrian parliament and abolished the Austrian constitution. Rumors abounded both of a Habsburg restoration and a Nazi coup.[99]

In the event, neither rumor proved to be well-founded. Dolfuss quickly promulgated a new constitution that made him the *de facto* dictator of Austria. Having removed any threat from the left, Dolfuss also moved to forestall the possibility of a Nazi coup. The Austrian army and Heimwehr were sent to the German border to prevent a threatened incursion by Theodor Habricht and his Nazi Legion. Dolfuss enlisted the support of Mussolini, who mobilized the Italian army along Austria's southern border. France and Britain demanded

Germany respect Austrian independence. Hitler, facing reality, insisted he desired only peace and withdrew his support of the Austrian Nazi Legion. The immediate crisis receded.

Dolfuss' action against the socialists, and the international reaction to it, were reported in an objective manner by *Time* and *Newsweek*. *The New Republic* chose to excoriate Dolfuss as an "arch-fiend" whose "ignominity" was "exceeded by his folly" as "a tool of the suicidal tendency of capitalist imperialism." Dolfuss had precluded any possibility of an Austrian united front against Nazism and so had "handed that country to Hitler on a silver platter." John Gunther wrote in *The Nation* that Dolfuss' action was criminal. However, Dolfuss had not "been excommunicated by world opinion quite as Hitler was" as Dolfuss was perceived to be "the better of two bad alternatives." His bloodletting was moderate compared to that of Hitler in 1933.[100] Quiet descended upon Austria and international attention turned away for the next several months.

The apparent peace in Austria was shattered in July by a resurgence of the Nazi bombing campaign. Several factors sparked this renewed activity. One was the fear of Austrian Nazis that Hitler's promise to respect the independence of Austria, made to Mussolini in June, would preclude an Austrian Nazi state. There continued to be rumors of a possible Habsburg restoration and that Dolfuss and Mussolini were planning an alliance between their nations. Dolfuss, confident in the support of Mussolini, reacted with "a drastic ultimatum" that decreed the death penalty for any Nazi found to possess explosives. As tensions mounted, a major Austrian Nazi leader, Cornelius Zimmer, was shot to death on the streets of Vienna—an act laid at the feet of the police. Although the police vigorously denied any responsibility for the murder, Nazis refused to accept their disclaimer. Dolfuss, fearing for the safety of his family, dispatched them to Italy and placed them under the protection of Mussolini.[101]

Dolfuss' fears for his safety were fulfilled on July 25 when he was assassinated by Vienna Nazis who simultaneously seized the Chancellery and a radio station. The approximately 150 Nazis who attempted the coup represented only a small portion of the Nazi group in Vienna. There was no general Nazi attack across Austria. In Vienna, the revolt was quickly suppressed when Minister of Education Kurt Schuschnigg rallied the police and the Heimwehr. Sporadic fighting broke out across Austria, however, as Heimwehr units attacked Nazi groups. At times, the fighting was vicious. Surviving Nazis fled across the nearest border into surrounding nations. The limited nature of the coup seemed to indicate Hitler had not planned or ordered it but the perception existed he had created the conditions that lay behind it and that he might seek to utilize it for his purposes. War seemed inevitable when Habricht poised Austrian Nazis for a possible thrust toward Vienna and Mussolini again pledged to support Austrian independence. The spector of war caused Wall Street values to drop to their lowest level of 1934.[102]

The danger of war quickly receded when England and France issued statements supporting the independence of Austria and Mussolini's mobilization. Hitler quickly moved to cut his losses. Habricht was dismissed along with his Austrian Legion. The German ambassador Kurt Rieth was replaced by Catholic von Papen and the German border was closed to Nazis fleeing from the Hiemwehr. Hitler denounced the conspirators and sought to distance himself from the event.

Time, Newsweek, and *The Literary Digest* were content to simply report the coup attempt without speculation about its long-term effects. *The New Republic,* however, stressed the new chancellor, Schuschnigg, had inherited a situation even less promising than Dolfuss. He was supported only by a small minority in Austria and by the arms of Mussolini. The situation in central Europe was "disastrous and impossible." There existed only the probability of an "irrepressible conflict" whenever Hitler decided he was ready to precipitate it. *The Nation,* on the other hand, believed that the event had "destroyed the possibility of a Nazi victory over the Austrian people." Hitler had overreached himself and now Europe was united against him. John Gunther, writing for the same magazine, argued "the Hitlerite dreams of a Nazi Mitteleuropa are blasted into remote fatuity."[103]

Seldom has any political analyst been so wrong as Frank H. Simonds in an article for *The Atlantic Monthly.* He argued the attempted coup had been "the decisive episode for Hitler" as it revealed Hitler "had destroyed his own legend." It was evident Hitler no longer headed a united nation and was "on the defensive at home." Hitler was also "almost completely" in the hands of the Reichswehr. This was "one of the best guarantees of European peace" as the Reichswehr was opposed to another war. The conviction Hitler's regime was "impermanent" was now "general all over the world." Hitler would "not survive the winter" due to the economic disasters overtaking Germany. It was likely he would be followed by a Hohenzollern restoration. The danger of war seemed "remote and destined to diminish still further" as the nations of Europe were now united against him with Mussolini as their leader. The events of July 25 thus marked "the turn of the tide in Europe" as Hitler had "shot his bolt." Ironically, by his role in the coup, it might turn out that Hitler had "made the world safe for democracy."[104] Meantime, a new development in Germany had radically altered the domestic situation there.

Throughout 1934, von Hindenburg's health was problematical at best and there was speculation he was no longer in full charge of his faculties. In May, *The New Republic* wrote reports were circulating in Berlin that, upon the expected death of Hindenburg, Hitler would probably assume the additional duties and powers of the German presidency. Goering would then assume the position of second-in-command. Hitler would then face "the future with something facing equanimity."[105]

Throughout the late spring and early summer, von Hindenburg had visibly declined in health. He suffered from a degeneration of his prostrate gland, old age and a failing heart. On August 2, 1934, the aged president died quietly at his home in Neudeck. For several weeks prior to his death, all visitors except Hitler and the immediate family were barred from Neudeck. Immediately upon von Hindenburg's death, various officials of the regime issued a far-reaching series of decrees. Setting aside the Weimar Constitution, which provided for the Chief Justice of the Supreme Court to temporarily fill the presidency, Hitler announced he would assume the functions and powers of the office. Frick announced a plebiscite for August 19 to ratify Hitler's action. Minister of Defense von Blomberg ordered the armed forces to take a personal oath of allegiance to Hitler and they readily complied. Goebbels, ignoring the wishes of the Hindenburg family, announced the president would be buried at the Tanneburg Memorial. All females, including von Hindenburg's grand-daughters, were barred from the funeral. Hitler issued a series of moderate public statements, dealing with both foreign and domestic issues. Most surprisingly, Hitler decreed an amnesty for most minor political and criminal offenders. Only those charged with treason were specifically exempted from the amnesty. *The Literary Digest* believed approximately 10,000 persons would be freed.[106] Hitler delivered the eulogy at the funeral of the dead president and turned it into a propaganda event.

American magazines generally agreed von Hindenburg's death had strengthened the hand of the regime. There was less agreement on whether Hitler's own position had strengthened. There was a general assumption the army had agreed to Hitler as president as a *quid pro quo* for his purge of the SA. According to *The New Republic*, the agreement had been reached by Hitler and General von Fritsch. *The Nation* insisted General von Blomberg had negotiated for the Reichswehr. While *The New Republic* believed Hitler had agreed to surrender military policy to the General Staff and to resign as leader of the Nazi party, *The Nation* asserted the Reichswehr was bound by its oath to serve Hitler. *Newsweek* summarized the position of most magazines with its statement "no other dictator is invested with so much authority." *The Literary Digest* was insistent that only revolution could depose Hitler—and revolution was unlikely. It concluded there was "no longer a German Republic, a German constitution or a German government—there is only Hitler."[107]

The plebiscite to ratify Hitler's assumption of the presidency was held on August 19. Predictably, Goebbels pulled out all the stops in a brilliant propaganda campaign. All accounts of the plebiscite stressed it had been conducted "fairly" with "scrupulous respect for the secrecy of the ballot."[108] As expected, by a vote of thirty-eight to four million, the German voters approved of Hitler's action—a ratio of roughly nine and a half to one. *The New Republic* noted the opposition had doubled since the November, 1933, plebiscite. It believed this opposition would "continue to grow in arithmatical progression from election to election" if Hitler chose "ever again to invite such a demonstration of popular disapproval." More realistically, most magazines followed the lead of *The Nation* and interpreted the results to mean Hitler was solidly entrenched in power. As stated by *Newsweek*, Hitler "stood unchallenged" as "the world's most absolute dictator."[109]

In September, 1934, American magazines ran their first reports on the annual Nazi party rallies at Nuremburg. Reports on the 1934 rally, the sixth held by the party, were essentially narrative descriptions of the events of the seven day meeting. For the first time, there were Reichswehr units present. Attention was also directed to the SS units which were used to separate Hitler from the SA in particular and the crowd in general. *The New Republic* stressed the messianic tone of the rally and the enthusiasm of the 600,000 Nazis who attended. *Time* and *Newsweek* chose to stress the filming of the rally by the then twenty-seven year Leni Riefenstahl. She had first attracted Hitler's attention through her nature photography. No suggestion was made of any romance between them but much was made of her "orders" for Hitler to strike this or that pose. Generally, the rally and its events were treated quite satirically.[110] The rally portrayed a triumphant Germany which seemed to be master of its own fate. No one could have assumed from the film that Germany was considered to be virtually bankrupt.

As early as April, 1934, *The New Republic* reported the German economy was "in a critical state." The government faced a budget deficit of six billion marks for the year ending June 30. German gold reserves and foreign exports were dropping rapidly and, most likely, there would be an even greater deficit for the coming year. When Schacht announced German indebtedness had to "be regulated as speedily as possible," *The New Republic* interpreted his remarks to be the first step of "a point-blank refusal" to repay Germany's debts.[111]

The following month, *The New Republic* wrote that, just as Bruening had successfully repudiated reparations, Schacht was in the process of repudiating Germany's private debts. It noted Schacht had just made the "ingenious announcement" he regarded German private loans as "political obligations" which the government was "under no moral compulsion to pay." He argued Germany would "not sacrifice its credit" by such a repudiation as future creditors would only look at Germany's ability to repay any new loans it contracted. He pointed out to the Berlin American Chamber of Commerce that central and south American nations had repudiated their private loans a number of times without, however, being denied new loans. Schacht, it asserted, was deliberately depleting Germany's gold reserves to afford a plausible excuse for repudiation. He had recently halved Germany's gold reserves by paying out four million marks to the International Bank at Basel although no payment was yet due the bank.[112]

The Nation reported on May 23 that German gold reserves had dropped to "a record low" of "5.4 percent of its note issue." Early in June, Kurt Schmitt, Minister of Economics, and Hans Frick, Commissioner of Justice, made speeches denouncing the economic boycott of German goods, arguing the boycott made it impossible for Germany to repay its debts. Germany's balance of trade, according to *Time*, showed a deficit of 82,000,000 marks. Germany's gold reserves had, as a result, "dwindled to 4.6%." Schacht used the situation to demand a complete moratorium on the payment of all German debts except for the Dawes and Young Plan loans. He got Germany's creditors to accept the principle "that Germany wants to pay but cannot."[113] A new agreement was reached giving German creditors the choice of redeeming their loans at forty percent of their cash value or exchanging their loans for new long range bonds at face value. At the same time, various members of the regime called for the return of former German colonies if creditors wanted Germany to re-establish its ability to repay its loans.

On June 18, 1934, *Time* wrote "on the money markets of six continents plugs of pessimism were pulled" and "black warnings gushed out" that Germany was about to go off the gold standard. The *Reichsmark* dropped six percent in one day when Schacht announced German gold reserves had declined to "an ominous 3.4%." Fear that large British loans to Germany would be defaulted led to a "weakened confidence in sterling" and "quickened a nervous flight of capital to France." On one day, 100,000,000 francs poured into Paris and French gold reserves climbed "to near 79%." Max Winkler, President of the American Council of Foreign Bondholders, argued Schacht was only "staving off Germany's creditors with adroit panic statistics." *The Literary Digest* reported Germany still had thirty to thirty-five percent gold backing for its currency hidden away. However, fears for the mark continued to exist.[114]

Newsweek reported on June 23, that Germany had once again set "the world on its financial ear." Schacht had announced a six-month payment moratorium on all German loans—including the "sacred" Dawes and Young Plan loans. He asserted Germany was driven to this extreme by the drop in world trade, "enormous withdrawals" of foreign credit, the "reparation payments which Germany was forced to make," and by the "Boycott movements." Schacht also announced the mark would be kept stable and remain based on the gold standard although Germany's gold reserves had dropped to three percent. England and France "immediately threatened retaliatory measures" such as freezing German assets in their nations if Germany did not resume payments by July 1. *The Nation* reported that "Washington hopes to solve the problem by increased trade with the Reich."[115] In the event, retaliatory measures by England and France were not implemented. England gained special concessions from Schacht for repayment of its loans and British and French unity was broken.

On July 22, Frederick T. Birchall reported in the *New York Times* that American bankers were in Berlin to consider new loans for German industries. *The Nation* described the report as "little short of fantastic" considering Germany's default and the grave condition of its economy. As re-written by *The New Republic*, Birchall's despatch had reported "a number of America's outstanding bankers" were in Berlin "to devise ways of extending credit for raw materials" to German industries. The bankers included James H. Perkins of the National City Bank, Thomas W. Lamont of J. P. Morgan and Company, and George H. Harrison of the Federal Reserve Bank of New York. They represented short-term credits to German industry of three billion marks which had been "earning a fair profit" through "the financing of imports and exports." *Time* reported Montagu Norman, Governor of the Bank of England, had met with "American Bankers" in New York and speculated he might be "organizing a rescue party" for German industry.[116]

In the same article, *Time* also reported that German heavy industry was experiencing a "species of boom." The boom was fueled by lowered wages to workers and by governmental subsidies. As this boom was not reflected in statistics on German exports, *Time* wrote there was "the inevitable suspicion" that German iron and steel production was going "secretly into munitions."

This boom was continuing although German gold reserves had dropped to two percent of its currency issue, German exports were declining, and the government had drastically curtailed imports.[117]

On September 1, Schacht asserted Germany "was at the end of its tether" and that the "indeterminate moratorium" would have to be followed by a "general and generous reduction" of Germany's debts that it might be able to repay at "some future time." At the same time, Schacht continued his efforts "to interest an Anglo-American syndicate" in extending new loans to Germany. Although no report appeared in our magazines of the granting of such a direct loan, in October, *The New Republic* reported German representatives sent to America to arrange "extensive raw-material credits" had received a "favorable reception by important Wall Street firms." "Influential government officials" of the United States suggested "a trade agreement that would take the widest possible cognizance of Germany's needs." Samuel Untermyer protested Cordell Hull's "official support of Germany's wishes" and his "broadside against economic boycotts." Later the same month, *The New Republic* reported Germany had announced the cancellation of its most-favored-treaty with the United States. It had also announced that American holders of Dawes Plan bonds would receive "only 75 percent" of their interest payments although "several European countries will be paid in full."[118] Apart from reports the control of the German economy had been placed under Schacht's control by the firing of several Nazi economists, the subject of the German economy and loan payments disappeared from our magazines for the remainder of 1934. While Germany pleaded it could not pay its loans, it was able to pay for its rearming.

The Geneva Disarmament Conference met in June, 1934, in a less than hopeful atmosphere. On October 21, 1933, Germany had formally withdrawn from the League and the conference. On November 22, the conference adjourned without any progress except for an agreement to meet again in 1934. In the interim, Germany increased its army budget by forty percent and began to develop an air force. Proposals by Italy and Britain, which would have allowed limited increases in Germany arms, met with obdurate opposition from France. France refused to disarm "a single gun" as long as Germany was rearming. *Time* concluded, even before the conference met, that "disarmament was dead as Queen Anne" and a "great international race to rearm was well under way."[119]

The pace of the race, according to *Harper's*, was being set by Germany. In an extended article, *Harper's* insisted Germany was arming for a war of aggression in which mechanized columns, supported by airplanes, would make slashing attacks of up to 150 miles a day. The army would consist of highly trained professionals backed by less well-trained militia supplement. Germany actually had a advantage over its potential victims for they were burdened with massive amounts of obsolete equipment where as Germany was developing an entire new generation of weapons based upon the latest scientific technology. Siemans was producing 2,000 aircraft engines of the latest design, Daimler was turning out army trucks, Borsig was manufacturing shells, Bleichert was producing tanks, and Junkers was building aircraft. Lithuania, Holland and Switzerland were producing arms for Germany while even Creusot-Schneider of France was accused of accepting a German contract for 400 tanks. Germany, *Harper's* alleged, was also experimenting with poison gases and bacteriological weapons. In Germany, war had become "the end of statecraft" instead of "a measure for the protection of the state."[120]

American corporations were also engaged in supplying Germany with arms. *The Nation* reported Pratt and Whitney, Curtiss-Wright, and Douglas Aircraft were producing "bombing and fighting" planes for Germany. Their representatives in Berlin were "helping Germany to build up the best air fleet in Europe." Vickers and Armstrong were also fabricating aircraft components in England for Germany. Germany was paying for these products "in cash" and there was "plenty of money for such purposes." *Newsweek* detailed the volume of German aircraft purchases in America by writing that during January and February alone, Germany had transferred $650,000 to American airplane companies. Pratt and Whitney had also sold its patents to the Bavarian Motor Works. It was matched by the purchase by Fokker of patents for Curtiss-Wright engines. Boeing and Curtiss-Hawk were selling entire airframes to Germany. Germany was also concurrently making purchases from Britain and "even France."[121]

Time concluded these revelations meant the Disarmament Conference would "totter into its grave at Geneva." *Newsweek* referred to the conference as only an "orator's marathon." When the conference met, it was quickly derailed by a "Germany absent and rampant on rearmament" and a France that would "not have it." The United States stated it would not "participate in European political negotiations and settlements" and further, that it would "not make any commitment whatever to use its armed forces for the settlement of any dispute anywhere." *The Nation* concluded that the "statesmen of the world" had met at Geneva "to administer the last rites" to disarmament. *Newsweek* took the analogy one step further and wrote that the "corpse of the Disarmament Conference lies rotting on the shore of Lake Geneva, but nobody has the heart to bury it." The conference finally disbanded with only an agreement that individual governments would "angle for Germany's return" to future meetings of the conference. *The New Republic* believed the Disarmament Conference had been only a French charade to preserve the Versailles Treaty and to ensure American participation in any future war to maintain it.[122]

The Disarmament Conference met again in December. Its only agreement was one to submit an American proposal, to license arms manufacturers under international supervision, to their "home offices." The conference thereupon adjourned. Meanwhile, the European arms buildup continued and negotiations for alliances continued. Germany remained the focus of attention in the arms race. In October, *The Reader's Digest* reported Germany was preparing for war by staging gas drills and training gas teams in all its major cities. Berlin alone had appropriated eight million marks to make the city "gas-proof." *The Literary Digest* wrote that Winston Churchill was making a determined effort to persuade Parliament to build an air force to protect England against a Germany that was rapidly arming to the teeth. It was common knowledge Germany was planning an air force second to none.[123]

By the end of 1934, Hitler had firmly established his hold upon a "coordinated" Germany that was rapidly rearming. His regime was casting a long shadow of fear across Europe. As yet, Germany was contained within the boundaries established by the Versailles Treaty. The first opportunity to expand those boundaries was to come in 1935 with the Saar plebiscite scheduled for January, 1935.

Chapter III
Versailles *Kaputt*, 1935-1936

As early as June, 1934, *Newsweek* asserted Hitler was orchestrating a "violent campaign" to ensure "that all good Saarlanders" would vote for reunion with Germany in the plebiscite scheduled for January 13, 1935. In 1919, the Saar had been placed under a League Commissioner for fifteen years. Its mines, which produced thirty million tons of coal each year, had been given to France as a replacement for French mines destroyed during the war. Their estimated value in 1934 was $71,000,000 and, if returned to Germany, were to be redeemed in gold. According to *The Literary Digest*, the population of the Saar was ninety-nine percent German and "until Adolf Hitler became chancellor no one doubted the vote would be at least 90% for the Fatherland." *Newsweek* believed the plurality for a return to Germany had been cut "15 to 20 percent," however, by the Nazi attacks on socialists and Catholics and by refugees who had "overrun the region telling of atrocities" back in Germany. The Saar socialist, Max Braun, led an anti-Nazi rally at Saar-Bruecken which attracted 18,000 people.[1]

Throughout the summer of 1934, Nazi propaganda directed toward the return of the Saar grew steadily in its intensity. The campaign shifted into high gear in late August when Hitler, Goebbels, and other prominent Nazis began to hold massive rallies just outside the Saar border. To woo the Saarlanders, Hitler "set to work like a Tammany boss." He promised "Communists, Socialists, and Catholics forgiveness" if they voted for a return of the Saar to the Reich. Saarlanders were given free transportation to the rallies and provided with badges that proclaimed "The Saar is German." When Hitler spoke at Coblenz, relay runners brought torches from all over Germany to symbolize the unity of the Reich and the Saar.[2] At the Coblenz rally, Hitler spoke to more than 150,000 Saarlanders who made the trip to hear him speak. Appearing in his guise as "Peace Leader," Hitler insisted the separation of the Saar from Germany was due to "the injustice and unfairness of others" but that its return would lay "the groundwork for a lasting peace with France." Hitler asserted that a fair vote would see the Saar reunited with Germany.[3]

In September, Geoffrey Knox, League Commissioner for the Saar, requested that the League arrange for an extra two thousand German-speaking police to supervise the plebiscite and ensure a fair vote. He specifically requested they be recruited from nations that had no special interest in the balloting. Mussolini promptly offered to provide a special force recruited in the Southern

Tyrol and the League accepted his offer with alacrity. When rumors began to circulate in November that Hitler might seize the Saar by force to demonstrate his contempt for the League, Britain announced it would not use troops to prevent the action. France, on the other hand, pledged to intervene if requested to do so by the League. In time, the fear of a Hitler coup proved groundless and the subject of intervention was dropped. In the end, the League, for no stated reason, decided not to use Italians to police the Saar and, instead, declared the plebiscite would be supervised by British, Swedish, and Dutch military units. These contingents arrived none too early as the plebiscite campaign grew daily more intense.

At the beginning of January, *Time* interpreted the upcoming plebiscite as a vote upon the Nazi regime. It noted the Saarlanders were "racially and linguistically almost pure Germans." There was little doubt the Saar had desired union with Germany prior to Hitler's accession. Hitler's actions, however, had converted the vote into one on "the doctrine called Nazi and its works." Hitler himself realized this and was hard-pressed to achieve a *"ja* vote" to keep his promises to the Germans that he would openly "rupture the Treaty of Versailles." A negative vote would be a "titanic" blow to "Nazi prestige outside Germany." The importance of the vote to the Nazis was underlined by Goebbels's "feverish" propaganda campaign and Nazi violence directed against Catholic and communist rallies. To further insure the vote, Hitler had even arranged free steamship passage to the Saar for a "lumpy lot of Teuton farmers and workmen" from the United States so they could vote for reunion. *Time* ended by predicting the plebiscite would result in a Nazi victory.[4]

Newsweek also reported the Nazis were leaving no stone unturned in their efforts to guarantee their vote in the plebiscite. Money was spent freely, there were parades and rallies throughout the Saar, and there were scattered reports of Nazi intimidation. *Newsweek* reported Hitler had provided free transportation for 755 German-Americans and to thirty Germans from Chile so that they could return to the Saar and cast their vote for reunion with Germany. *The Nation* stated Hitler had imported 1,200 "qualified voters, rounded up from all the corners of Asia, South America, Africa, and Europe." It also remarked on the intensity of the Nazi campaign.[5]

The Nation agreed the Saar would vote to return to Germany, especially as Germany and France had reached a long-term repayment plan for the mines. It insisted, however, that an opposition vote of "not more than 30 percent of the total will be a moral defeat for Hitler" and "should have some influence on German public opinion." On the the other hand, the return of the Saar would "prove distinctly advantageous to Franco-German relations" and would be in the best interests of all concerned.[6]

On the day before the plebiscite, *Newsweek* reported hundreds had been injured and two people killed "in various battles throughout the turbulent territory" as Nazis clashed with communists. *The Nation* alleged "a few" opposition Saarlanders had been "kidnapped" and taken to Germany where they were "imprisoned and beaten." Social Democrats had been unable to find locations for their rallies due to Nazi pressure. Max Braun, their leader, was unable to find housing or even purchase a public meal. On the other hand, the Nazi financed German Front organization had "organized, propagandized, spoon-fed, and high-pressured" Saarlanders "in every conceivable manner." Five million dollars had been spent to entertain over 10,000 Saar youths in Germany.[7] To secure a favorable ballot, Hitler had even agreed not to arrest Saarlander communists and socialists for a period of three years and to not discriminate against the Saar's 5,000 Jews for at least a year. The proposed Gauleiter for the Saar, Josef Buerchel, promised no concentration camps would be established in the territory. *The New Republic* noted, however, that "emigrés from Germany have no guarantees whatever." Indeed, *Newsweek* reported Buerchel had "promised to turn German refugees over to the State for persecution."[8]

Even though a Nazi victory was anticipated, the extent of that victory came as a surprise. Hitler won a majority of 91.1 percent in the plebiscite that had drawn ninety-eight percent of the eligible voters to the polls. Only 2,033 out of the 522,702 who voted opted for union with France. *Newsweek* called it "this overwhelming German victory." *The Nation* described the results as "a severe shock" and "an overwhelming triumph" for Hitler. *The New Republic* believed the election had allowed Hitler "to make good on his promises" and had no doubt that "Hitler's prestige within Germany and in the European foreign offices" had been enhanced. *Time* saw the results as a "clear victory" for Hitler in the "world's most expensive" election. *The Literary Digest* expressed surprise the vote for Hitler was "equally overwhelming in every district" of the Saar. The League promptly announced the Saar would be placed under German jurisdiction on March 1, 1935.[9]

American magazines were divided in their interpretation of the events following the plebiscite. *Newsweek* reported Hitler was "elated" by the election results. In "a voice choked with emotion" Hitler had broadcast a speech thanking the Saar for its loyalty, expressing his appreciation to the League for its impartiality, and hinting that Germany might return to the League if given "equality of armaments." According to *Newsweek*, no reprisals against Jews and anti-Nazis had been taken although "Nazi joy" in the Saar "knew no bounds."[10]

Time, on the contrary, reported the Saar was in a turmoil. On January 28, *Time* reported Saarlanders were in "a mad rush" to export French francs to the Netherlands, Switzerland, and France. In one week, 1,650,000,000 francs were shipped out of the Saar to avoid their conversion into marks. *Time* also asserted "Saar Jews and other Saarlanders" were emigrating to France "at a rate of one every 30 seconds." Most of these refugees "told tales of terrorism which could not be checked" as all non-Nazi newspapers had ceased publication and the League's Saar commission "dared not respond to incessant pleas for protection." Thirty non-Nazi Saar policemen had been arrested and "seemed destined for Nazi concentrations camps." *The Literary Digest* reported there had already been numerous arrests and forced detention of Saarlanders by the pro-Nazi police.[11] Other events, such as the Franco-Italian accord and the Anglo-

French suggestion of an "Eastern Locarno," captured the attention of American editors.

It is of interest to note that American magazines believed the return of the Saar represented only another turn in Hitler's fortune and not the fulfillment of his ambitions. *Newsweek* observed the Nazi press had immediately begun a clamor for the return of Memel to Germany and believed he had turned his eyes eastward. *The Nation*, however, believed "Hitler's next objective" would be Austria as this would erect "in Central Europe the greatest German power ever witnessed." *The New Republic* suggested Hitler would attempt to reach an accord with Poland for the return of Silesia and Danzig by offering Warsaw the Nieman Corridor and Lithuania. *Time* wrote that Hitler, after accepting "his Saar plebiscite victory," would press on to his next objective which would be "to force the Great Powers to recognize and assert to the Fatherland's rearmament in violation of the Treaty of Versailles."[12] In the event, *Time's* prediction proved to be correct.

The first two months of 1935 witnessed a flurry of feverish diplomacy on the continent. At the instigation of Laval, Mussolini and Laval met in Rome on January 7 to sign an agreement that resolved their differences in North Africa, insisted on Austrian independence, and paved the way for Franco-Italian cooperation in the event of German aggression. While *Time* felt the reapproachment qualified Laval and Mussolini as candidates for the Nobel Peace Prize, *The New Republic* believed the agreement was only "temporary" at best and quite unlikely to deter Hitler.[13] Having accomplished his purpose in Rome, Laval, who had eased the admission of Russian into the League in late 1934, next attempted to bring England into discussions aimed at deterring German aggression.

Laval net with British Prime Minister MacDonald and Foreign Secretary John Simon in London during the first week of February. Their conversations produced a joint communique that provided Hitler with the "opportunity for a face-saving return to Geneva." Germany would be "legally" allowed to rearm in return for a commitment to "active membership" in the League. The communique also proposed a reciprocal accord under which the signatories would unite their air forces to aid contracting party that became a victim of "unprovoked aerial aggression." England promised its support for the Franco-Italian agreement of the previous month. Finally, the communique proposed new security pacts to "assure mutual assistance in eastern Europe." Under the proposed "Eastern Locarno" pacts, Russia would "defend Germany against attacks on her eastern frontier, and aid France in case of German aggression."[14]

Time felt it summarized the "popular and press reaction" as being "now everything is up to Hitler." If Hitler was "sincere in his professions of peace and non-aggression," this was his opportunity to gain legal recognition of Germany's rearmament, receive a guarantee of his frontiers, and preclude the possibility of an air attack on the Reich. *The Nation* believed the proposals came "years too late to remedy the situation," but yet hoped that the proposal of an "Eastern Locarno" would prove "beneficial." If the proposals were not taken up by Germany, the world would "be back precisely where it was in

1914." *Newsweek* wrote Hitler "faced a poser," especially when Mussolini quickly accepted the London proposals "in principle." Hitler, "temperamentally adverse to quick decision," had to retire for "some heavy thinking" about the future.[15] Both *The Literary Digest* and *Time* felt Hitler would be slow to respond as he would have to examine all facets of the proposals and consult with his advisors.[16]

In the event, however, Hitler responded quite rapidly to the proposals on February 15. His response was mixed in tone and substance and was overshadowed by reports that Mussolini had mobilized Italy's reserves as a "precaution" against "attacks by Abyssinian tribes" on Italian Somalialand.[17] According to *Newsweek*, the proposals had "proved too bitter a pill" for Hitler to swallow and so he had "licked off the sugar and spat out the medicine." Hitler agreed to "consider" the various proposals but pointedly ignored the suggestion that Germany rejoin the League. He caustically blamed the Allied Powers for causing the arms race by their own refusal to disarm. However, he requested private talks with London on the proposed air pact. *Time* reported Hitler had "virtually invited" Simon to come to Berlin for the talks. *The New Republic* believed "little comfort" could be derived from Hitler's reply as it was obvious he had adopted a policy of "divide and conquer" and was attempting to drive a wedge between Britain and France. *The Nation* saw Hitler's reply as a "master piece of skillful diplomacy." He had gained "tacit recognition of Germany's air force" but had no been compelled to accept an "Eastern Locarno." Hitler had successfully "snubbed France" and gotten away with it when Simon agreed to meet with him in Berlin.[18]

Initially, Hitler had agreed to meet with Simon in Berlin to discuss only the air pact. However, when Maisky, Soviet ambassador to Britain, issued a public statement that a fair interference of Hitler's opposition to an Eastern Locarno was that he was contemplating aggression in the East, Hitler quickly agreed to discuss all the London proposals with Simon. The talks were delayed, in the event, when Hitler developed a "diplomatic cold" in reaction to a British White Paper that announced a large increase in British arms procurement. Hitler was "stunned and then wild with anger" as the increase was attributed to German rearmament. The "cold," according to *Time* and *Newsweek*, quickly improved when Simon announced Anthony Eden was leaving for talks with Warsaw and Moscow. Hitler promptly agreed once again to receive Simon. *The New Republic*, although it accepted Hitler's explanation of "a malady of the larynx," believed he had to act immediately to prevent the addition of Poland and Russia to the Anglo-French Entente. *The Nation* insisted that the Soviet attitude was the "decisive" factor in Hitler's willingness to talk with Simon and perhaps accept the London proposals in their entirety. It later stated the major significance of these events was Hitler's inability to sever Britain from the rest of Europe.[18]

Discussion of Simon's impending visit to Berlin was cut short by Hitler's announcement on March 16, 1935, that Germany would institute universal military conscription to develop an army of 500,000 men organized into thirty-six divisions and twelve corps. Just the week before, Hitler had announced that all commercial and sports aircraft would be subject to the orders of the Reichswehr with Goering as their immediate commander. *Newsweek's* front cover showed German army units on parade with the caption "More Goose-Steppers." It reported Hitler had decided to "scrap" the Treaty of Versailles because he had received a "a series of jolts." The Red Army had been increased to 940,000 men. Mussolini had recently boasted of having 7,000,000 reservists, and Britain had decided to rearm. The final jolt came when France announced it would extend its compulsory military service period from one to two years. Rather than reducing their armaments as agreed in the Treaty of Versailles, they were arming while denying armaments to Germany. According to *Newsweek*, the announcement of German rearmament had made the Germans "delirious," the Russians had "screamed," and French diplomats had "suggested an immediate military alliance with the Reds."[19]

Time reviewed much of the same information in its issue two days later. It wrote that Europe felt the shock of a husband who knew his wife was cuckolding him "when she finally not only admits all but earnestly explains how pure, how inevitable her acts have been." Hitler's decision had place "into the cuckold class" Flandin of France, MacDonald of England, Mussolini of Italy, and "even President Roosevelt." Hitler had finally "torn up the diplomatic pack of cards and reached for the jackpot." Simon had responded with a formal protest which, in effect asked if "the Nazi are mad dogs or gentlemanly players of a gentleman's game."[20]

The New Republic wrote that "the dogs of war that have been baying faintly in the distance for so long are coming nearer with terrifying rapidity." It described Simon's protest as "a weak futile gesture," noting Hitler had only taken by a *fait accompli* what Simon intended to give after negotiations. Now, even if Germany entered the League, Hitler would fix his eyes on "further conquests." Only the threat of "overwhelming" Allied force could "maintain the status quo."[21] *The Nation* editorialized Hitler had only "officially announced what everyone knew" was happening in Germany. He had thereby destroyed "the world of illusion" in which the Allies had been living. The "little and weak men" who led Britain, France, and Italy now had to encircle Germany "with an iron ring" or take measures short of war that might well lead to war. Certainly, if they accepted German rearmament it would "inevitably" lead to a "war our civilization could not survive." *The Literary Digest* simply stated Hitler had finally achieved his avowed purpose of making "the Treaty of Versailles just another scrap of paper." No act by Hitler had so stirred Europe.[22]

France, Britain, Italy, and Poland delivered formal protests condemning German rearmament. Their notes were, however, "bluntly dismissed" by von Neurath. When France called for an emergency meeting of the "decrepit League" Council, Hitler did not bother to take notice. Roosevelt declined to protest, issuing a statement that the United States only wished to be a "good neighbor." The European arms race immediately intensified. France moved 30,000 men to the Maginot Line and increased its military budget, Mussolini called up 250,000 reserves and extended Italian military service to two years, and Britain voted to strengthen its air force. Russia announced an expansion of the Red army, while Austria, Hungary, and Bulgaria stated they intended to rearm. Even Turkey hinted it would re-militarize the Straits.[23]

Prior to their trip to Berlin, Simon and Eden consulted with Paris and Rome and agreed they would meet again at Stresa in Italy on April 11. At Berlin they were received by a burst of "compelling gutterals and animal magnetism" from Hitler. Hitler "got the jump on them" by demanding Austrians be allowed to vote on union with Germany. He further treated them to a "tirade" in which he defended German rearmament as necessary to save Europe from "Bolshevism." Hitler informed them he intended to have an army as large as France possessed, and a navy "30% as large" as Britain's. *Newsweek* added that Hitler had caused Simon and Eden's smiles to "vanish." In addition to the above demands, it stated he demanded the "return of the Versailles-snatched colonies, the Polish Corridor, and German areas in Czechoslovakia." Simon was particularly shocked and dismayed by Hitler's statements and behavior.[24]

When Simon returned to London, Eden continued to Moscow where he was cordially received. The Soviet leadership expressed their support for the Eastern Locarno pacts and their fears of a rearmed Germany. At Warsaw, Eden met a quiet but negative rebuff from the Poles, who did not wish to antagonize Berlin. While Eden was traveling, France placed an embargo on "raw materials essential to the national defense." For his part, Hitler extended Moscow $80,000,000 in private credits and offered to sell Abyssinia 300 armored cars on credit.[25]

The New Republic interpreted the events of the past weeks to mean that Europe was balanced "on the dividing line between peace and war" and insisted, if the reports of Hitler's comments to Simon were confirmed, "the situation is indeed about as bad as it could be." Hitler, it averred, seemed "still determined" on a policy that neither France nor Russia could possibly accept. *The Nation* argued "the powers" were uncertain how to meet "Hitler's bold challenge." It felt there were only three possible choices open to the powers: preventive war, to encircle Germany with a *cordon sanitaire*, or to establish "a system of European security based on full equality for the Reich." The first was impossible due to British and French public opinion, the second was unlikely as Britain distrusted entangling alliances. If the Nazis were bent on expansion, the third possibility was unlikely to avert war. It concluded that "from the path that leads to war there is no turning." *The Literary Digest*, to the contrary, believed allied solidarity would be strengthened at Stresa and there was yet hope the "progressive deterioration" of the European scene could be arrested.[26]

In early April, there was a minor flare-up in the Baltic when Lithuanian judges sentenced four Nazis to death for the murder of a fellow Nazi who informed Memel authorities of a planned putsch. Eighty-four other Nazis were given prison sentences collectively totaling 1400 years. "Nazidom," wrote Newsweek, "took the verdict as a slap in the face." Nazi mobs attacked the Lithuanian legation in Berlin and rioted in Tilsit. Lithuania then appealed to "the Versailles signatories for support." Hitler demanded with "passionate insistence" that England intervene. Simon, fearful a German invasion of Memel would "menace the whole territorial fabric of the Versailles Treaty," secured the agreement of France and Italy to a note informing Lithuania "its duty was to bring to an end without delay" any provocation to the Reich. Anti-Nazi Poles demonstrated along the frontier to protest German pressure on Lithuania, while anti-Lithuanian Poles rioted along the border with Memel. The issue quickly died down when the death sentences were commuted to life imprisonment.[27] Hitler then sought "to appear as a hero of peace" and so offered to sign a series of non-aggression pacts that would bind Germany to its borders for ten years.[28]

Even as diplomatic interest turned toward Stresa and Hitler's offer of the non-aggression pacts was placed on hold, Hitler received a set-back in Danzig. Danzig, under the supervision of the League, held its biennial Diet elections in early April. Earlier, in 1933, the Nazis had polled fifty-two percent of the vote. Hitler, desirous of repeating his Saar victory, sent in Hess, Goering, Goebbels, and Streicher to support the local Nazis. A Nazi majority of two-thirds would permit the re-writing of the Danzig constitution and the establishment of a Nazi state. However, the Nazis received only 59.9 percent of the vote. *Newsweek* called it a "rude surprise" and a "shock" to Nazis "from Hitler down." *Time* interpreted the election as the greatest "moral setback" Hitler had received "since the Blood Purge." No prominent Nazi commented on the election. *The Nation* believed the election results had destroyed the Nazi "myth of invincibility" and revealed an "unsuspected weakness" in the Nazi regime that foreign diplomats were sure to exploit.[29]

During early April, 1935, the attention of Europe was riveted on the upcoming conference of Britain, France, and Italy at Stresa. Generally, in Europe an aura of hope seemed to settle on the meeting. It is noteworthy, however, that American magazines did not share that optimism. *Time*, for example, reported Eden's diplomatic efforts had exhausted him. largely because he realized the "international peace effort" was "cracking up." As one result, the "virility" Eden had injected into British diplomacy "oozed away" when he was replaced at Stresa by the "temporizing and indecisive" Simon. Simon and MacDonald had no policy except a "vague notion" they could "mediate" between Germany and the rest of Europe. Paris saw this as a British "reluctance to take sides for or against Nazidom." Mussolini, alert to the "nuances" of the situation, warned that "no castles of illusions" should be erected about the Stresa meeting.[30]

The Nation believed Mussolini was striving to erect a "three-power action" to replace his former "four-power pact." But his hopes were doomed as this would be "impossible"for Britain to accept. *The New Republic* frankly expressed its pessimism. It wrote the British were "badly frightened" and their fright caused them to "simultaneously seek a balance of power with themselves as "arbiters" and to hope for the preservation of the "status quo by recourse to the machinery of the League." This was "a frail boat on the stormy sea" and would preclude definite action at Stresa.[31]

Newsweek reported Simon's review to Parliament of his conversations with Hitler had "dampened British enthusiasm for the conference." "Suspicious colleagues" of Simon "demanded" he not "commit the nation to any pledges or alliances without consulting Parliament." Such "British caution" caused Paris and to Rome to sniff "audibly" and "a mist of mutual distrust" settled on the conference.[32]

At Stresa, the delegates talked for three days. When the conference ended it issued, as *The Nation* had predicted, a "ringing communique" that said little or nothing.[33] Correspondents, however, reported Britain had indeed been "evasive." Simon simply had no "desire to line up against the Reich" even though Mussolini had repeatedly attempted to get "down to brass tacks." Simon had marked time "with an agility meant to look like walking." When Mussolini and Flandin urged "direct action" against Germany, Simon pleaded that Germany should not be mentioned "by name." Further, Simon refused to join in an "iron-clad guarantee to support Austria." Von Neurath "lifted some of the gloom" at Stresa when he announced Germany was willing to sign non-aggression pacts with its neighbors provided the pacts did not include guarantees of collective action. The conference ended with agreements that France alone assume "the duty" of arraigning Germany before the League for treaty violations, that approval of the air pact he pursued, and that they would invite "Germany and Central European Powers" to Rome in May to negotiate pacts guaranteeing Austria's independence.[34] England had, as predicted, precluded a strong, united front at Stresa.

The New Republic joined *Time* and *Newsweek* in their criticism of the Stresa Conference. It believed Stresa was "a triumph for Hitler." Hitler had gambled "boldly" in defying the Allies and had "won." *The Nation*, to the contrary, believed the conference had "ended on a note of optimism." The result was "distinctly to the credit of the diplomacy of the three powers." It interpreted the conference results to mean the allies were "definitely committed to a program of concerted action" if Germany continued its treaty violations. It did recognize, however, "that most of the spade work" of collective security "remained to be done." *The Nation's* self-deception was most-telling revealed in its statement that no one could yet pass "final judgment on the sincerity of Hitler's pledge of non-aggression."[35]

No sooner had the Stresa Conference concluded on April 13, than Laval asked the League Council on April 17 to condemn Germany for its rearmament in defiance of the Versailles Treaty. He had attempted to have "some neutral council member" sponsor the resolution. All declined, however, when Berlin warned it "would resent subservience to the three big powers." As the council could only act by unanimous action, the resolution for a time seemed headed for defeat when Denmark and Poland initially refused to assent to it. When the vote came, Poland decided to support it although Denmark ended by abstaining out of fear of German reaction. As finally adopted, the resolution condemned Germany for its "unilateral repudiation of international obligations," "invited" the Stresa powers to pursue the London Proposals of February, and proposed the appointment of a committee to "fix economic and financial reprisals" against any nation that violated "its international obligations" in the future.[36]

Hitler reacted to the council's action by informing Simon he resented Britain's failure to act as an honest broker in the League council. In a note to the council, Hitler repudiated its action as only another attempt at new discrimination against Germany. Germany would, therefore, reserve its freedom of action. While *Time* reported Hitler's reaction without comment, *Newsweek* wrote Hitler had told the council it could "go jump in Lake Geneva!" *The New Republic* interpreted Hitler's handling of the situation as "a tremendous diplomatic victory" for Germany. Although he was "a fanatic, not a diplomat," Hitler had achieved his goals without the penalty of reprisals. It noted he "intimated" any hope of Germany returning to the League was dashed forever. Hitler had further added insult to injury by concurrently announcing that in "any future war," German "pacifists" would "be subjected to the death penalty."[37] Laval, however, was still determined to achieve some type of collective European security.

At the beginning of May, Laval of France and Potemkin of Russia signed a pact providing for mutual military assistance and invited all eastern European nations, including Germany, to sign the treaty. The pact pledged mutual "aid and assistance" if any signatory was confronted by "unprovoked aggression." This pact was quickly followed by one between Russia and Czechoslovakia modeled on the Franco-Russian pact. Germany, by its actions, was the architect of a renewed encirclement similar to that of the pre-1914 period.[38] Hitler was placed on the defensive by the new pacts and their implications and so proceeded to mount a peace offensive.

On May 11, *The Literary Digest* printed a major article on an interview Hitler had given to its correspondent E. P. Bell. Throughout the interview, Hitler's voice was "quick and blunt." As light fell on "his violet-tinged eyes and rugged features," Hitler insisted to Bell that Germany had proven its desire for peace by accepting the Locarno Pact in the West and arranging the German-Polish Pact in the East. He also agreed to the Briand-Kellogg Pact which outlawed war as an instrument of national policy. Hitler asserted he intended to honor these pledges as his greatest concern was for peace once Germany's equality among nations was accepted. Europe was no longer "big enough for the terrible wars" that would be unleashed by modern "mechanized armies." As for Russia, Hitler ridiculed any idea of a German attack as they had no common frontier. His rejection of the mutual security pacts, however, did represent his refusal to "fight for the Bolsheviks." Hitler further rejected a German demand for colonies unless they were freely offered by the League. Actually, he was opposed to the inclusion of non-Germans in the new Reich. The League had ceased to matter as an international body and apparently the United States and Japan agreed with Germany on this point by their absence from it. Hitler concluded the interview by reiterating Germany's desire for a peace based on honor and equality.[39]

Many of these same themes were repeated in a major address by Hitler to the Reichstag the last week of May. In a speech lasting two and a half hours, Hitler again stressed his desire for peace. Hence, he was ready to participate in a multilateral air agreement, to conclude non-aggression pacts with neighboring states and to enter a general disarmament pact. He would honor the Locarno Pact and even the prohibitions against the re-militarization of the Rhineland. There was no plan to further enlarge the German army and he would agree to any naval limitations reached by mutual consent. Hitler stated he would even agree to the outlawing of offensive weapons such as heavy artillery, tanks, submarines, and weapons aimed at non-combatants. Germany, he averred, was opposed to the inclusion of non-Germans in its Reich and so had no territorial ambitions at the expense of surrounding states. Although he denounced Bolshevism, Hitler stated he would only attack Bolshevists in Germany and had no aggressive designs on Russia. Germany needed and wanted peace so that National Socialism could achieve its domestic goals during "the next ten or 20 years."[40] On the whole, the speech was vintage Hitler in his guise of responsible statesman.

The response of the German public was predictably positive. *Newsweek* reported "Britons found the speech reassuring" while the French and Italians "sniffed." The Russians simply "damned it as an effort to hoodwink Europe." For itself, *Newsweek* saw in it a number of "conciliatory points." *Time* interpreted the speech as a "strategic retreat" by Hitler in the face of reapproachment between France and Italy and between France and Russia. *The Literary Digest* noted Britain found the speech "a step toward peace," as did Italy, but that France was "disappointed." It reported American press comment "ranged from outright approval to flat rejection." *The Nation* found the speech "far more conciliatory than anyone had been led to expect." It revealed Hitler was "definitely on the defensive." However, it felt there was an air of insincerity in the speech and that Hitler's peaceful intentions would have to be tested against his actions. *The New Republic* concluded the speech "was on the whole pacific in character if he meant what he said—a highly important 'if.' " It agreed his words would need to be tested by his behavior.[41]

The British interpretation of the speech as "reassuring" was due, at least in part, to a favorable reference by Hitler to the Anglo-German naval talks already underway in London. At the beginning of May, Hitler had announced his intention to construct "twelve small 250-ton submarines." *The New Republic* responded by alleging Germany intended to build "every other type of war vessel" and was preparing "with desperate energy for war."[42] The British cabinet, already being frightened by German parity in the air, reacted by suggesting bilateral negotiations on naval limitation. Hitler demanded the right to build up to thirty-five percent of the total tonnage of the British fleet. Britain, fearing the tonnage would be devoted totally to submarines, insisted on a limit of thirty-five percent in each category of naval construction. As finally negotiated, the pact limited Germany to thirty-five percent of British tonnage in each category but one—submarines. A stunning concession by London granted Hitler parity in submarines if Germany deemed it "necessary" in the future. The bargain was quickly struck on June 14. *Time* noted the pact was cynically presented to the British public as a limit upon Hitler while Germans were told Hitler had pressured London into the pact.[43]

The agreement, according to *Newsweek*, hit Paris and Rome as "a studied affront" that not only violated the Versailles Treaty and the 1922 Washington Naval Treaty but also smashed the Stresa Front. Italy announced it would use the pact as "a bargaining point" in discussion of an Italian protectorate over Abyssinia. *The Literary Digest* noted France was "resentful and sullen" and that the French press was calling of closer ties to Italy and "smiles for his venture into Ethiopia." The American press, it wrote, displayed "no great furor either way" over the pact. *The Nation* felt the pact represented the "tacit sanction" by Britain of Hitler's unilateral abrogations of the Versailles Treaty. London "had capitulated completely to Hitler" and possibly had decided to "play an independent role in Europe" and abandon the Stresa accords.[44]

Time believed the naval pact also represented the conquest by Hitler of the British press. Whereas Fleet Street had previously attacked "Nazidom and all its stands for," it had now decided with "characteristic clannishness" to take "a pro-Hitler tact" and was "openly admitting this about-face." The London *Times, Daily Mail, Daily Telegraph, News Chronicle*, and *Daily Herald* were now praising Hitler. "British Press Tycoon" Viscount Rothermere "rapsodized" over Hitler, calling him the "most prominent figure in the world today." Rothermere insisted Britons would increasingly appreciate Hitler's greatness and that "the future" of Britain was bound with him. *Time* found it significant that Edward, Prince of Wales, "whose royal ear is never far from the ground," had called upon British veterans to "stretch forth the hand of friendship to the Germans."[45]

The frenzied diplomatic activity of the first half of 1935 that centered around Germany came to a virtual halt at the end of June. Although Hitler had regained the Saar and abrogated the military provisions of the Versailles Treaty, the construction of a united front against him had proved impossible. As interpreted by American magazines, French efforts to form such a front, led by Laval, had a policy of appeasement. Britain was unfortunate in having a government that was unable to perceive that, with Hitler, all the old rules of diplomacy had become obsolete. British leaders were so fearful they were unable to see that the time for appeasement had ended once Hitler became chancellor.

Hitler himself had gained increased prestige at home and had created a fluid international situation through his adroit maneuvering. In early July, he paused to consolidate his gains and, for a period, retired from public view. Concurrently other international events attracted the attention of the magazines in this study. For the remainder of the year, their primary attention focused on Japan's renewed assault on China and, even more extensively, Mussolini's Abyssinian adventure.[46] News reports about Germany were shortened and were run in secondary positions.

Although Hitler's international maneuvers dominated the attention of our magazines in early 1935, there continued to be occasional articles on domestic events within the Third Reich. One subject that attracted increasing attention as the year wore on was the continued tragedy of German Jews. On February 13, *The Nation* asserted the condition of German Jews was "worse than ever." It insisted the diminished number of reports on their situation was due only to the "diabolical technique" of censorship imposed by Goebbels and not to any reduction of Nazi anti-Semitism. *The Nation* reported 85,000 Jews had been driven from Germany while 8,000 Jewish doctors and lawyers had been barred from practicing their profession. Another 800 Jews had been expelled from their university posts. Over 1,200 journalists and some 2,000 entertainers had been barred from employment. Approximately 125,000 workers and shopkeepers had been economically reduced to applying to the German Jewish Central Committee. *The Nation* concluded that Nazi protestations of fair treatment for Jews were an "obvious and malign falsity."[47]

At the end of February, a Nazi official admitted for the first time that the international Jewish boycott was hurting the German economy. At the instigation of Schacht, Julius Lippert, State Commissioner for Berlin, addressed the American Chamber of Commerce club in Berlin. He asserted Jews still had "equal economic rights" in Germany and that the boycott was "contrary to all American interests." Lippert ended with threats of retaliation if the boycott continued. *The Literary Digest* noted German-American trade had declined by one-sixth in the past year. When German Jews, under Nazi pressure, labeled the boycott useless, they drew the ire of Jews world-wide. In New York, Fiorello La Guardia responded by defending the boycott as a protest against "an arrogant, bigoted, cruel government."[48]

German Jews immediately felt Nazi retaliation. Jews were banned from the Leipzig Trade Fair, customers were photographed as they left Jewish shops, and restaurants put up "Jews not wanted" placards. Jews could attend theaters, movies, or the opera only at the risk of insult or beatings. The worst anti-Semitic behavior took place in Streicher's Franconia. Only Schacht, the president of the Reichsbank, was able to protect Jews—and then only those in the employ of the Reichsbank.[49] In March, *The Nation* printed an article filed from London by William Zukerman. Zukerman wrote that a wave of optimism had appeared among German Jews at the end of 1934. The optimism had been generated by Nazi moderation prior to the Saar vote, by a rising "disgust" with Streicher's "vulgarity and sadistic brutality," and by the refusal of the regular German courts to enforce the Aryan codes against private employees. According to Zukerman, this optimism was dashed immediately after the Saar vote. Streicher unleashed a new anti-Semitic drive and the boycott against Jews was revived. "Racial science" directed against the Jews had been made "a compulsory course in all the public schools of Germany." Frick, the Prussian Minister of the Interior, had announced a projected Nazi constitution which would deprive Jews of all their remaining civil protection. Zukerman concluded the Jewish "pathetic hope had ended in tragedy" and that "until the Nazi system is ended" there could be no hope for German Jews.[50]

Zukerman's article had hardly reached the newsstands than *Time* reported that, in Franconian Fuerth and Zirndory, posters had appeared stating if Hitler was "shot," "we will kill all Jews and Free Masons." "Fist-shaking mobs" had "surged in the streets" and new posters had appeared with the words "Kill the Jews!" By midnight, when it seemed "Nazidom's first avowed pogrom was ready to burst," Streicher had belatedly resorted order and blamed the incident upon the zeal of a subordinate.[51]

On July 15, an anti-Semitic riot broke out in Berlin when Jewish movie patrons booed the Swedish film "Petterson and Bendel" which portrayed a Jewish lawyer as a villain. "Organized gangs" of Nazis first attacked Jews leaving the theater and then "roamed" the Kurfuerstendamm hurling "Jewish-looking patrons into the street." The police "looked on calmly" while "mobs pursued terrified Jews down the street." *Newsweek* attributed the riot to a newspaper circulation drive by Streicher and to a governmental decision to distract attention from a recent rise in food prices. It noted the riot also coincided with renewed Nazi persecution of Catholics, Marxists, and the Stalheim. *The Nation* saw the riot as the "result" of a power struggle between the "conservative Nazi anti-Semitics" led by Goering and the Nazi "radicals" led by Goebbels.[52] The government attributed the riot to "agents provocateurs" and moved quickly to quell the attacks. Count von Helldorf, a "renowned pogrom-engineer," replaced the former police chief and Hans Hinkel, Cultural Chamber director, was placed "in charge of Jewish intellectual activities." Hitler issued a statement forbidding "individual enterprise" against Jews, adding the "State has its own movement for fighting Jews by other means."[53]

What these "other means" were was partially revealed over the next few weeks as "mixed" marriages were forbidden in many areas of Germany. Jews were barred from public swimming pools, and even forbidden to sell ice-cream after seven in the evening in Berlin. *Newsweek* featured Streicher on its front-cover of August 3 along with the caption "Jew-baiter." Within the magazine a brief biography identified him as an "old crony of Hitler" whose hatred of Jews was "an obsession." Streicher demanded still harsher laws against Jews.[54]

American outrage at the Nazi "purification" campaign was quickly expressed by both Jews and Gentiles. Senator William H. King of Utah demanded the United States sever diplomatic relations with Germany. Representatives Cellar and Dickstein of New York demanded an official boycott of German goods. Dickstein read a statement into the *Congressional Record* that called Hitler "a madman, a murderer, and the protagonist of an insane theory of government." Mayor LaGuardia announced that German citizens would no longer be able to obtain business licenses in New York City. He specifically denied a license to one Paul Krass, a masseur. President Green of the A. F. of L. issued a statement supporting both Dickstein and LaGuardia. Governor Curley of Massachusetts supported the passage by his state legislature of a resolution condemning the religious persecution by Nazis of both Jews and Catholics.[55]

The most dramatic protest occurred in New York on July 26. "Nearly 2,000" people demonstrated on the Hapag Lloyd pier as the *Bremen* prepared to sail. "Men and women milled" around shouting "Death to the Nazis" while "policemen's fists thudded."[56] Dozens had to be taken away in ambulances. Four to six boarded the liner and trampled the swastika before throwing it into the sea. When the men were brought before New York Magistrate Louis Brodsky on a charge of unlawful assembly, he released them for lack of evidence.

Brodsky referred to the swastika as "a gratuitously brazen flaunting of an emblem which symbolizes all that is antithetical to American ideals" and an ensign of "an atavistic throwback to pre-medieval, if not barbaric, social and political conditions." By coincidence, the same day the Hapag Lloyd Line gave the detective Matthew Solomon $150 to cover the injuries he received in trying to protect the swastika. When Hans Luther, the German Ambassador, protested Brodsky's remarks, Cordell Hull lectured him on the freedom of speech accorded to American judges.[57]

Foreign reaction to the anti-Semitic riots and decrees caused General von Blomberg and Goering to visit Hitler to insist "the more rabid" Nazis be "put in leash" before the German economy collapsed and the rearmament program was endangered.[58] The most vocal and public protest was made by Schacht after Jewish merchants at Stettin complained of the boycott against them and the destruction of their property. In a speech at the Reichsbank, Schacht gave the Nazi extremists a "sharp admonition" to avoid disruption of the economy. At an East Prussian trade fair, Schacht declared "Nazi extremism is damned dangerous!" He compared extremism to "sand in a machine" that would ruin the machine. Goebbels ordered the speech censored. *The Literary Digest* reported the two directly "clashed over the issue on August 21." Streicher, the S.A., and the Hitler Youth responded with "noisy street demonstrations" that demanded Schacht's dismissal.[59]

The Nazi extremists, instead of retreating, intensified their attack on Jews. At Stettin, 30,000 Germans marched through the streets to intimidate the Jews who had complained to Schacht. Jews were forbidden to immigrate to Berlin to escape the even worst persecution in provincial towns. All Jewish organizations were told to "coordinate themselves under government supervision" by August 31. Storm Troopers began to shave the hair and tar the bodies of Aryan women who remained friends with Jews. An "official Nazi legal journal demanded" that Jews be "shut up in ghettos." Streicher held a rally attended by 50,000 Berliners at which he declared Nazism's goal to be the "total suppression of Judaism," adding "the heaviest work has just begun!"[60] Hitler made no public pronouncements or appearances during the summer of 1935. However, as fall approached he left Bavaria and returned to Berlin to prepare for the annual party congress.

When the party congress met, Hitler quickly demonstrated where his sympathies lay in the struggle between the conservatives and extremists in the Nazi party. In his major speech, Hitler assailed Jews eight times, "invariably linking them with communists." He warned the conservatives it would be "the gravest mistake" for them to believe their protests would prevent the regime from dealing with the "Jewish problems."[61] In a series of decrees, Hitler excluded Jews from citizenship in the Nazi state and redefined them as mere "members" of the state. In a decree entitled the "Law for the Protection of German Blood and German Honor," Hitler prohibited Jews from displaying the German flag, barred them from marrying Aryans, made sex relations between Jews and Aryans a crime, and prohibited Jews from employing Aryan female servants under the age of forty-five. Hitler also stated that if the state was unable to "solve" the Jewish "problems," then they would "be solved by the Nazi movement." *The Nation* concluded that, while the church might also be under attack, the "Jews are still the main targets for Nazi oppression."[62]

It was at this congress that Hitler responded to the attack on the swastika flag of the *Bremen* by making it the official emblem of the Nazi state. The swastika, according to Goering, would henceforth be "the anti-Jewish symbol of the world" and "a holy symbol."[63]

Although some anticipated the new decrees depriving Jews of their citizenship would lead to an overt pogrom on the streets of every German city, most American magazines were heartened over the next few weeks. *Newsweek* noted Jewish businesses were not expropriated as expected. Schacht pleaded for Germans to patronize Jewish shops and asked Jews to "resume commercial dealings with citizens." He warned that "Jew-baiting hurts business." Dietrich von Jason, S.A. commander in Berlin, issued a statement reading "I forbid every violence against Jews" and "every unauthorized action whatever."[64] Hitler ordered all Jews still holding state jobs pensioned off—but with full salary for the rest of their life. The term "Aryan" was formally ordered dropped and replaced by the term "German." General von Blomberg had already ordered "half-Jews" were to be accepted into the army and given the protection of the *Reichswehr* uniform. *The Nation* interpreted this to mean that "mixed Jews" were "admitted into the fold."[65] It was speculated that Hitler's moderation was due to the anti-Nazi agitation against the Olympic Games to be held in Berlin in 1936.

As early as August 21, *The Nation* joined with the Catholic *Commonweal* and the Catholic *Christian Century* in a demand for a "widespread boycott" of the upcoming Olympic Games. Mass meetings in Boston and New York "unanimously adopted resolutions" urging the Amateur Athletic Union to refuse to certify American participants for the games. Jeremiah T. Mahoney, head of the A.A.U., supported the resolutions. However, Avery Brundage, chairman of the American Olympic Committee, refused to be affected by the resolutions.[66] In October, *The Nation* reported George G. Battle and Henry S. Leiper had formed a "committee on Fair Play in Sports" to protest American participation in the games and that the A.F. of L. convention had joined in the protest. When General Charles H. Sherrill, an American representative on the International Olympic Committee, announced that Helene Mayer, a German Jewess and the world's champion female fencer, would be on the German team, he also added "What Germany does to the Jews in Germany is no more my business than what it done to the Negroes in the South or to the Japanese in California." *The Nation* believed his attitude made American participation "impossible."[67]

In November, *The New Republic* also called for an American boycott of the Olympics. It noted the National Council of Methodist Youth, the American Youth Congress, and the Catholic War Veterans had joined in the call for a boycott. Governor Earle of Pennsylvania, New York Court Justice Pecora, Heywood Brown, and Congressman Emanuel Cellar had issued statements condemning American participation. *The New Republic* documented case after case of Nazi attacks on Jewish athletes and pointed out that Holland intended to boycott the Olympics. It argued that Spain, Belgium, Norway, Denmark, and Sweden might withdraw if given an American example. However, it also reported Brundage was unmoved and still intended for American teams to participate in the Winter Olympics beginning on February 6, 1936. On December 18, *The New Republic* reported the A.A.U. had finally voted to approve American participation in the games.[68]

At the same time that Villard, editor of *The Nation*, joined the movement to boycott the Olympics, he published a unique article. Villard noted the Nazis were making "a most determined effort to drive" Jews from Germany "or to shut them up like lepers." There was, therefore, "a challenge to the whole world" to find room for 400,000 immigrants. At the very moment the "Christian churches," with the exception of the Quakers, had "failed to contribute to the relief of this desperate need," the "wicked and godless Soviets" offered "to set aside" the entire province of Biro-Bidjan for Jewish immigrants. While immigrants would not have "liberty as we understand it," it offered them "a chance to live, to exist"— which the Third Reich did not. He concluded it was a "magnificent deed and history will so proclaim it."[69]

The final public protest of 1935 against the inhumane treatment of German Jews came from the Anglican General Assembly in London. The Archbishop of Canterbury opened the protest meeting but the loudest and most prolonged "cheering" came when the Bishop of Durham called Nazi racial ideas "sheer hallucination" and utterly "preposterous." He ended by crying "We loathe and detest this attitude obtaining in Germany and protest!" No suggestion was made, however, about a course of action to remedy the situation.[70]

Time reported there was bitter controversy in Germany over the new anti-Semitic decrees. The Nazi extremists, led by Streicher, argued they did not go far enough. Gerhard Wagner, head of the German Physicians' Association, drafted a note decreeing that "all who had ever been intimate with Jews should be counted in with Jews." The German "Old Guard" of Schacht, von Neurath, and von Blomberg opposed further anti-Semitic action. In the face of their opposition, Hitler "threw up his hands" and allowed the decrees to stand in their "original form" and rejected Wagner's draft. *Time* noted, however, that the following day Schacht banned all Jewish floor brokers from the stock exchanges of Germany.[71]

Hitler responded to the Soviet offer of Biro-Bidjan for Jewish immigrants and to the London bishops by arguing his fight against the Jews was an effort to "save civilization from bolshevism" and the world should understand it as such. *The Nation* called this a "monstrous misrepresentation."[72]

In 1935, the Nazi attack on the Christian churches of Germany continued unabated. In March, Bishop Niemoeller and "many other" pastors read from their pulpits a "manifesto" of the Confessional Synod's Brotherhood Council. The manifesto called for an "active Christianity" that would denounce Rosenburg's *Myth of the Twentieth Century* as "pure idolatry of a race and blood" and, as such, was "anti-Christ." The following Sunday Niemoeller and 500 Confessional Synod pastors were arrested. Streicher then suggested that the church-state struggle could be solved if Hitler, a Catholic, were made head Protestant bishop and a "partnership of Christ and Hitler" consummated. To avoid linking Hitler with a Jewish Christ, Streicher declared Jesus to be "just as un-Jewish as is Hitler!" Although the suggestion was not adopted by Hitler, Hitler did elect to support efforts to wean German youth from the church. At Easter, pagan "German Faith" rallies, "with vague but impassioned rites," were held across Germany. Under a "Viking flag," thousands of German young people swore allegiance to "the new Germany" and "denounced alien gods."[73] Twelve thousand professed pagans cheered" in Berlin as speakers denounced Christianity as "unworthy of heroic Germans." Hitler was called a "Messiah" through whom God spoke to the German people. *Newsweek* reported the rally had "the unexpected support of Hitler" and so led Bishop Mueller to hurry to Berlin to persuade Hitler to "end his flirtation with the heathen." The same week *The New Republic* wrote that Protestants and Catholics were barred from public rallies in the future. No such ban was placed on the pagan rallies.[74]

Catholics, as well as Protestants, were imprisoned by the regime. However, the attack took a different form and, at least in part, was the result of a Catholic refusal to abide by the currency regulations. *Time* reported on April 8 that the secret police had raided Carmelite monasteries and cloisters in Westphalia and the Rhineland and arrested "batches of Carmelites" for smuggling some 2,500,000 marks out of Germany. In May, a Sister Wernera of the Order of St. Vincent confessed to a Berlin court that she had smuggled 252,000 marks into Belgium. This was "only part" of more than $1,900,000 smuggled by Catholics out of Germany. The nun was fined and imprisoned while the Order of St. Vincent was given a fine of 252,000 marks. One result was that Nazi bands attacked Catholic charity collectors on the streets while police confiscated their money boxes. In early June, *Time* noted there were an additional fifty-two currency cases pending against monks and nuns. Two nuns had just confessed to smuggling 200,000 marks out of Germany. These revelations, according to *Time*, especially angered Nazis as it demonstrated in such a "worldly matter as money," that Catholic loyalty lay with their "international" organization and not the German nation.[75]

At the end of July, concurrently with the anti-Semitic riots, Hitler appointed Hans Kerrl, a "party radical," as Under Secretary for Church Affairs with "supreme authority." Kerrl, in accepting the post, declared "Hitler is the Holy Ghost." Goering simultaneously opened an attack on "political Catholicism" with a statement secret police would "eavesdrop at every church" to ensure priests did not "call upon God against the State." At Badan and Aachen, the Catholic *Deutsche Jugendkraft* was dissolved. A priest at Hanan was imprisoned for saying "Human life is worthless in the new Germany." *Newsweek* surmised the anti-Catholic moves were linked to a renewed "drive for sterilization" by the regime and to distract German minds off rising food prices.[76] *The Literary Digest* believed the moves were simply due to Hitler's hatred of the Center Party's role in the Weimar Republic. When the Berlin diocesan paper insisted the "aim of this battle is to dislodge Christianity," all Catholic papers were ordered dissolved. Pope Pius XI reacted with formal protest to Berlin and urged "Catholics to remain firm."[77]

In early November, Emil Lengyel wrote in *The Nation* that German "Catholics are in revolt against the Third Reich" and wanted it placed under an interdict and an international Catholic boycott. The College of German Bishops meeting at Fulda demanded Catholics "obey God rather than men!" They had reached the conclusion it was "their religious and patriotic duty to resist the Hitler regime"— which they regarded as "anti-Christ." Although Cardinal Pacelli was "pro-German," Pius XI was "anti-German" and supported Cardinal von Faulhaber of Munich, who led the Catholic "march into battle." Catholics met in underground groups, attacked Hitler Youth groups in the Rhineland, and tore down Nazi posters. Lengyel believed Nazi hatred of Catholics was inspired by the papacy's role in the division of medieval Germany, by the Roman culture of the church, and by Catholic support of the Weimar Republic. However, it concluded "the Vatican has built up an iron ring around the Reich" and "it would be surprising if Hitler succeeded" where Bismarck had failed.[78]

Lengyel's prediction seemed to be borne out within a week. Hitler issued a statement that he intended to "lead the party along the path of positive Christianity" and not the "false path of anti-Christian doctrine." Catholic Bishop von Preysing of Berlin was personally assured that the paganism of Rosenberg would be stopped at once. Both *The Literary Digest* and *Newsweek* attributed the shift to the intervention of Schacht who "insisted the 'new heathenism' did not pay" and the persecution of Catholics was strangling the economy of Germany.[79]

Protestants fared less well under Hitler's new church minister Kerrl. At the end of September, the opposition pastor's Prussian Confessional Synod met in Berlin to consider resolutions condemning the regime for excluding Christian children with Jewish blood from the Christian schools, demanding the release of imprisoned pastors, opposing the transfer of Confessional funds to the government church administration, and establishing two new independent theological schools banned by the state. Kerrl responded by arresting yet another pastor and by offering an "olive branch." He agreed to dismiss Reichbishop Mueller and appoint von Bodelschwingh to his post. Further, he offered to let the Synod nominate a majority of the members of a new church directorate. The Synod returned a flat and unanimous 'No' as they believed it only "a trap" and that Kerrl would dismiss the directorate when it suited his purposes. Hitler responded by issuing a decree giving Kerrl "absolute dictatorial powers over all Protestant churches in Germany."[80]

Kerrl proceeded to appoint a directorate "entirely from the ranks of his opposition." However, the opposition rejected his authority to appoint any church authorities and Kerrl ended by establishing another board which promptly "backed the Nazis." The opposition "retorted" Kerrl's earlier, conciliatory gesture was "a cowardly measure" designed to "put the Church back to sleep." In December, Kerrl "struck hard at the rebels." The opposition pastors were forbidden to hold synods, ordain new pastors, or to collect church taxes. They were also forbidden to read manifestoes or hold parish assemblies. The next Sunday Niemoeller led twenty ministers to the altar of his Dahlem church and ordained five new pastors. The following day 180 Synod delegates met in Berlin and "voted unanimously against making any compromises with Kerrl." Kerrl then ordered Otto Zaenker, Bishop of Breslau, expelled from the church. As the year ended, *Newsweek* concluded "the two rivals" waited "in opposite corners" for "the next round."[81]

In 1935, a number of Americans continued to run afoul of Nazi law. *Time* reported in January that Elsa Sittell, a naturalized American citizen visiting Germany, had, with more courage than discretion, told a customs official that Hitler was Jewish and not Gentile. She had also described Nazi uniforms as "awful." Promptly arrested for slander, Sittell was jailed for ten days before being expelled. An American music student in Germany, Isobel Steele, was held for four months before being expelled from Germany for being an acquaintance of a Polish spy named Sosnowski. On February 11, *Time* reported another naturalized American citizen, Richard Roiderer, had been charged with betraying state secrets the previous June and held without trial or legal counsel. Roiderer's crime was to describe the S.A. and S.S. as "military" units in his private notebook. *Time* subsequently noted Roiderer had surprisingly been acquitted by a Nazi court but told to leave Germany.[82]

Harper's, The Atlantic, The Saturday Evening Post and, to a lesser extent *Collier's,* decreased their coverage of Nazi Germany in 1935. Those articles they did run are best described as "deep-background material" and were not immediately related to given events. For this reason, they are included here as a group.

In February, *The Atlantic* published an article by Barbara S. Morgan that characterized Nazism as an "uprising" of the German middle class that idealized the concept of "the organic society" and so rejected democracy and its corollary of political equality. This uprising was fostered by German defeat in the World War, by the desire for order in society and by the feeling they were "ruled, in politics, in finance, in art and literature and learning," by an "alien race." The middle class protest took the path of an "agricultural-authoritarian as against urban-democratic" movement and was best defined as "a vitalistic school of thought." The resultant Nazi *leitmotifs* stressed loyalty rather than justice, duty above self-interest, ties of blood and race, obedience and paternalism, and sacrifice for the ideal. The land codes, penal codes, and labor laws of the Nazi state increasingly embodied these *leitmotifs.* In this sense, Nazism was "a crusade, a religion" applied to society "with brutality, sometimes savagery." A "mystical romantic core" lay at the heart of Nazism which, beneath its "tyranny and childishness," sought to "deliver man from the machine" of the modern economic state.[83]

In the same issue of *The Atlantic,* Bertrand Russell described Nazism as a "revolt against reason." According to Russell, Kant laid its groundwork by launching a "revolt against *reasoning*" in reaction to Hume's rationalism and skepticism. Kant had not only criticized "pure reason" but had also praised "practical reason" as a way to undercut Hume. "Practical reason," as defined by Kant, was thus an appeal to "something" beyond reason and so, safe from attack. Fichte, Carlyle, Mazzini, and Nietzsche adopted this "practical reason" as the foundation of their systems. They were, in turn, followed by secondary figures such as Treitschke, Kipling, Bergson and Houston Chamberlain. They sought "the good in *will*" rather than in cognition and feeling. They also valued power above happiness, force above argument, war above peace, aristocracy above democracy, and propaganda above impartiality. In time, a simplistic Social Darwinism was added to their brew. Reaction to industrialism and the war made these concepts popular to large groups in "the mood for pragmatic self-assertion." In Germany, these groups included those bourgeois afraid of egalitarian socialism, military men and arms-makers. They provided the "sane elements" of Nazism that politically enlisted those that could be "dazzled by the vision of glory, heroism and self-sacrifice." The "psychopathology of Nazism" was directly attributable to this mixture of goals and aims. Their hopes could only achieved by the "ruin of civilization." However, this did not make them "irrational, but only satanic."[84]

Anne McCormick, writing in *The Saturday Evening Post*, argued the Saar plebiscite and the rearmament of Germany marked the end of "war illusions" and the post-war organization of Europe. Hitler had "cut loose" from the treaty and closed a chapter in European history. Thus, "at least the first twenty years of the war are over." After Versailles, European leaders had multiplied "pacts and more pacts all signed in hope and despair—but never on faith." Hitler had, however, finally compelled neighboring states to conduct serious negotiations in good faith. Further, a new generation of leader had arisen who were unconnected with either Versailles or Locarno. They were spurred into action by "the danger of disintegration" in Europe occasioned by Hitler and by the "popular response" to Roosevelt's new "policy of action." These leaders felt it was better to "make mistakes than do nothing" and so, had given a new cast to European diplomacy. While armed or arming to the teeth, no European nation, including Germany was ready for war in 1935. Hitler's militant nationalism constituted the greatest future threat to peace as it was a "suction pump" pulling severed German minorities in neighboring states back to Germany. How the new diplomats handled this nationalism would determine the question of war or peace in Europe in the coming years.[85]

An article by Frank Simonds in the May issue of *Harper's* insisted the murder of Dolfuss had shocked most European leaders into resolving their differences in the spring of 1935. France, Italy, and Russia had proceeded to construct a "Continental circle" around Germany by discarding "the technic of Geneva" for the "old practice of coalition." The result included the Locarno Pact in the west, a coalition of France, Russian, and Czechoslovakia in the east, and Italy, France and the Littler Entente on the Danube. Italy and France wanted to cement these regional pacts into "one general alliance" by the inclusion of Britain. Britain, for its part, sought to avoid entangling alliances and wanted to mediate between Germany and the coalition. In the process, Europe had moved from "crisis to conversation" as even Hitler had been pulled into the conversations. Hitler would certainly try to placate Britain, keep "the

Austrian issue" confused, and exploit the "Western distrust of Communism"—but would talk rather than create a continual stream of crises. For the moment, "a time of truce had arrived" and now even "the most pessimistic prophets" saw "conflict postponed until 1937 or even 1940" although there might be minor problems in the meantime.[86]

According to Alfred Vagts, the question of war depended upon the intention of the *Reichswehr* and not upon Hitler. The *Reichswehr* had never accepted the Weimar Republic and merely bidded its time until Hindenburg became president and the depression had created a fluid political situation. After attempts to rule through Papen and Schleicher, the *Reichswehr* aided Hitler's rise to power as a means of remilitarizing Germany. In the "Blood Purge" of 1934, the army demonstrated its strength and now "the reign of the Party is over." The officer caste was thereafter "freed from even the slightest influence" and was directing "the economic and psychological as well as the technical mobilization" of Germany. The *Reichswehr* accepted Hitler's redefinition of Russia rather than Poland as Germany's major foe, but otherwise, its power as "assured." For the moment, it was concerned with "its own aggrandizement" and "the remilization of the popular mind." Toward this end, the *Reichswehr* had mobilized "every organ of education and public opinion." Its future goals remained undefined at the moment and until fully developed, peace was assured in Europe.[87]

T.R. Ybarra, the perennial foreign commentator for *Collier's*, insisted to the contrary that Hitler and not the *Reichswehr* would control the future destiny of Germany. His thesis was that six million young people were "being trained by the Nazis of today to be the Nazis of tomorrow." With Hitler's authority, twenty-eight year old Baldur von Schirach had absorbed the most foreign youth organizations of Germany—only Catholic youth groups had mustered the courage to resist Schirach. Special schools were training "youth to lead youth" in the acceptance of the Nazi *Weltanschauung*. They were taught to be self-reliant, physically and mentally hard, and racially pure. The Nazi method was to "get them young, treat them rough and tell them nothing but Nazi gospel." The result would be "a vast army" of youth that guaranteed Hitler's hold on the destiny of Germany in the future.[88]

As 1935 ended, two final substantive stories came out of Germany. At the 1935 party rally, Hitler attacked Lithuania for its alleged mistreatment of Germans in the city of Memel. Memel, which had been awarded to Lithuania by the Versailles Treaty, was scheduled to hold elections on September 29. Hitler's speech proved to be the opening gun in "a violent Nazi campaign" to influence the elections. *The Literary Digest* noted the British press generally took the attitude Versailles had performed "bad surgery in the Baltic" and that Lithuania was "continually infringing or frustrating" the rights of Germans in Memel. When the vote was finally announced in October, the Nazis elected twenty-four delegates to the Memel Council. Lithuania elected only five delegates. However, Hitler was angry as the Nazi vote was the same as in 1933. It was predicted that Memel would be the coming European trouble spot in 1936.[89]

On October 28, *Time* announced Hitler had formally reinstituted the German General Staff that had been banned by Article 160 of the Versailles Treaty. In accepting appointment as its chief, General Ludwig Beck revealed the General Staff had never been dissolved and during the Weimar period had been trained by von Seeckt in secret under the title "Troop Office." On November 1, the new conscript German army reported to training camps. 170,000 professional soldiers embarked on the expansion of the Germany army to 500,000 highly trained, highly mobilized troops. Germany had not only regained power, it was regarded as the major military power on the continent.[90]

In the final months of 1935 and the first two months of 1936, there was a plethora of international events that diverted the attention of American magazines away from Germany. Italy invaded Ethiopia and ultimately came so close to war with Britain that Britain stationed a battle fleet at Alexandria, canvassed the Balkans for allies, and voted money for a desert railroad from Egypt to Ethiopia.[91] The League branded Italy as an aggressor and voted limited economic sanctions against Italy— which the United States chose to ignore. It debated further sanctions on oil, steel, and coal. A Japanese demand for naval parity was rejected by the London Naval Conference and the Japanese withdrew in a huff. There was a clash between Japanese and Soviet troops on the Mongolian border that threatened to erupt into a major conflict. For a period, France seemed to be on the verge of civil war even as its lower chamber debated and finally approved a military alliance with Russia. Britain adopted its largest ever peacetime military budget against the opposition of the Labor party. In Japan, army officers attempted an armed uprising and installed a cabinet dominated by the military. For his part, Hitler remained quiet and precipitated no major domestic or international crisis before March, 1936, when he remilitarized the Rhineland.

At the beginning of 1936, John Gunther drew a profile of Hitler's personality that has generally stood the tests of time and scholarship. Gunther described Hitler as "a character of great complexity" who was simultaneously "a montebank, a demagogue, a frustrated hysteric, a lucky misfit." Hitler was "purely political" and was therefore socially "awkward and ill-at-ease" with "no poise." He cared nothing for exercise, books, clothes, friends, food or drink. Hitler's only relaxation was music which he needed "as if it were a drug" and was "obsessed by Wagner." He had no friends and was "almost oblivious of ordinary personal contacts." Women to him were only of value as housewives, potential mothers for Germany or as sexual outlets for males. His personal life was asexual. Religiously Hitler was an atheist. His war against religious groups was not theologically motivated but was occasioned by his demand that Germany be purged of all international religious ties and non-state loyalties. Hitler's anti-Semitism was so deep and broad that it was almost inconceivable if it had not been actualized.

Hitler's strengths were "his single-mindedness," his stamina, and his determination. His political sense, though largely based upon passion and intuition, was "highly developed and acute." Hitler's oratorical skills were likewise based upon his passion and instinct. His power was unchallenged within Germany while daily increasing in Europe.[90]

Although Hitler ordered the more obvious anti-Semitic signs, posters, and harassment muted due to the Olympic Games, the plight of German Jews continued to deteriorate in 1936. Adding to the plight of German Jews was the unwillingness of other nations to offer them refuge. On January 4, *Newsweek* reported Britain had proposed a Palestinian Legislative Council to advise the British Commissioner of Palestinian matters. Noting that the Council would give the Arabs a two to one majority over Palestinian Jews, Dr. Chaim Weizmann objected as the Council would surely suggest further restrictions on Jewish immigration. Britain brushed aside his protest and proceed with the proposal in spite of Jewish pleas and objections.[91]

Time reported the same week the "the Nemesis of Nazis," James McDonald, had resigned as the League's High Commissioner for Refugees from Germany. McDonald declared "he was sick at heart and discouraged at the unwillingness of the Great Powers to do anything" to assist German Jews. In a 20,000 word final report "excoriating the German Government" McDonald pleaded for action by "the Great Powers" to aid emigrating Jews. *The New Republic* described his report as the most "crushing indictment of Hitlerism ever published." The following week *The New Republic* argued private agencies were "simply not adequate to take care of the refugees" that would leave Germany if given the opportunity. It pleaded for easement of immigration regulations by all nations to rescue the German Jews.[92]

The Atlantic Monthly reacted to McDonald's resignation with an article by Ludwig Lewisohn. Lewisohn argued German Jews had become "pariahs, the great majority are already paupers, tomorrow they will all be." The problem, however, was not confined to Germany. Of three million Jews in Poland, "two million are ravaged by perpetual famine punctuated by suicide and assassination." In Lithuania, Latvia, Rumania, and Austria, Jews saw "the same terror approaching" but did not have "the wherewithal to flee." Even those who could flee found "the gates of the Western world are closed against them"—"the merciless knife comes nearer and nearer; the dreadful walls close in." Lewisohn concluded the "only avenue of hope left" was "the restoration of Palestine" as a Jewish homeland."[93]

The New Republic devoted a major article to the Jewish tragedy unfolding in Germany. It noted the Nuremberg Laws had disbarred Jews from citizenship, restricted their freedom of movement, barred them from owning property, segregated them from German life, and placed them in "a veritable ghetto." Worse was predicted. Streicher was demanding "the sterilization of Aryan women who had sexual relations with Jews, and signs had appeared demanding the "blood" of Jews. While 100,000 Jews had fled Germany, 550,000 remained, unable to flee and certain to suffer yet worse harm.[94]

The same week *Time* reported in Hanover it had become illegal to sing Christian hymns that included Hebrew words such as "Jerusalem," "Zion," or the derivative "Jehovah." Only the "most strenuous remonstrance" by Schacht had prevented Minister of Interior Wilhelm Frick from revoking the licenses of all Jewish salesmen. *The Nation* ran an article shortly thereafter that asserted "the Ghetto has now been established in Germany." It noted a number of German towns had prohibited "the sale of food to Jews, of milk to Jewish children, and of medicines to Jewish sick." "Hundreds" of German cities had banned Jews from their territory while "hundreds of other cities" had banned Jews from all "public places." It concluded the "hunt of the Jew had not been called off; the beast had only been declared fair game for all, and the hunt has been made legal national sport"—"On with the hunt!" The only hope was emigration but that hope was forlorn unless other nations revised their visa policies.[95]

Jews able to leave Germany in 1936 with an emigration visa had to pay a twenty-five percent "refugee tax." A number of proposals were made in the opening months of 1936 to meet this expropriation. One scheme would have allowed "wealthy Jews" to dispose of their property at sixty-five percent of its value, the proceeds to be paid through foreign trustees over thirteen years at four percent accrued interest. Another plan, proposed by Max Warburg of Hamburg, would have allowed "Jewish capitalists" to expatriate their wealth in the form of German export goods. These goods would be sold on the international market so they could recover their wealth. Schacht agreed to this plan with minor reservations.[96] These proposals, abhorrent to most Jewish leaders as a boost to the Nazi economy at the expense of its victims, were countered by a Jewish suggestion. British Jewish leaders led by Sir Herbert Samuel, Viscount Bearsted of Shell Oil, and Simon Marks, met with American Jews in St. Louis and Washington to urge the raising of $15,000,000 to finance the   emigration of 100,000 young Jews in four years from Germany. This plan had the virtue of allowing the boycott to be continued against German exports. Several American magazines lauded the idea as a desperate but necessary evil but felt the real problem was where the emmigrating Jews would find a haven.[97]

Beginning in January, 1936, *The Saturday Evening Post* published a series of four articles by Raymond G. Carroll calling for the restriction of immigration into the United States. The first article argued America was "carrying a heavy ballast of foreign nationals" who largely ended up the relief rolls. They not only raided the Treasury but, in effect, deprived needy Americans of aid. These indigent aliens were "synthetic citizens" who were "biting the hand that feeds them." Carroll used massive arrays of statistics to buttress his case. A second article stressed that aliens stole jobs from decent American nationals ravaged by the depression. Although gainfully employed, these immigrants were "Americans in name only" as they created their own enclaves of "Towers of Babel" and resisted assimilation. The third article argued Soviet Russia utilized America's immigration policies to slip communist aliens of all nationalities into the United States. These Communist agents were especially active in the ranks of organized labor. In the fourth and final article, Carroll stated "the American way" called "for the drastic exclusion of all new immigrant labor" and "the forthright exclusion of those aliens illegally here." He then noted there had "recently" been an effort to lower barriers to assist immigrants from

Germany. Although he felt "deep and sincere sympathy" for the refugees, "the time" had "come when the United States can be no longer an asylum for Europe." It was unjust to ask American "to clean up foreign blunders and problems." Those refugees who did not take away jobs from Americans would "of necessity go upon private and public relief." He concluded it was "hardly time to abandon wise and strong immigration restriction" as "genuine hardship cases" had always received "relief" on an individual basis from Congress."[98] In none of these articles were refugee German Jews singled out in particular. However, taken together, these articles were one more salvo in the battle to keep up American immigration barriers against all refugees. Thus, even those Jews able to quit Germany had little hope of finding refuge in the United States. Carroll covered each of the major objections that were to be endlessly raised by those opposed to providing a haven for German Jews—even in the case of children.

At one point, it appeared Britain might allow large numbers of German Jews to immigrate to Palestine.[99] However, Moslem opposition to British rule was growing and was fueled, at least in part, by rumors Britain was planning to assist Jews in the establishment of a homeland in Palestine. Anti-British riots erupted in Egypt, Jerusalem and even Zanzibar in British East Africa.[100] Jewish hopes of British assistance were ultimately to be dashed by this growing tide of Moslem opposition and unrest.

In early February, a young Croatian Jew assassinated Wilhelm Gustloff, "the chief Nazi agent in Switzerland," in the town of Davos. Frankfurter told police he wanted to "what little I could to avenge my brethren in Germany" and that his bullets "should have struck down Hitler." The incident gave "Europe war-fear cramps" as it was feared Hitler might invade Switzerland to prepare a staging area for a future attack on France. Or again, it might provide Hitler with an excuse to invade Switzerland and claim its 3,000,000 Germans for a greater Reich. In Germany, the assassination "made all good Brownshirts cry for blood." Streicher called it "another in a long series of Jewish murders." While it was momentarily expected a blood-bath would occur in Germany, Hitler intervened and "ordered: No violence" as he did not want to disrupt the opening of the Olympic Games. In Poland, where there were "no sportsloving foreigners to be shocked—Naziphile elements renewed persecution of Jews" and Jews across the country were attacked and beaten.[101]

Frankfurter was sentenced to prison for the shooting as Switzerland did not have a death penalty for political murders. Gustloff's body was returned to Germany and given a huge Nazi funeral at which Hitler eulogized Gustloff as a "martyr" of the German people and Nazi party. Gustloff, according to *Time*, was an early Nazi and the head of the Nazi movement among Swiss Germans.[102]

As early as August, 1935, *The New Republic* insisted Hitler had extended "Nazi parties into every country in Europe" that contained either ethnic Germans or "kindred" Aryan races. At that time, the magazine alleged, Switzerland was "infested by fantastic variety of Nazi parties, which it would be impossible fully to enumerate." This "Brown Army" was engaged in a "Jew-baiting campaign" but, in the event of war, would form "armed gangs" in the rear of armies opposing Germany. In early February, 1936, *The Nation* stressed strong pro-Nazi groups were being formed in every European nation where there were ethnic German enclaves. "Magnificently organized," these parties were set to stage a "cleverly launched attack" if war broke out.[103] Switzerland confounded Hitler when Gustloff was assassinated by ordering, not measures against Jews or Jewish organizations, but against its Nazi and German organizations. The Swiss Federal Council "ordered the suppression" of all such organizations and instructed its Justice and Police Departments to investigate "foreign political organizations" in the nation. Apart from a few purely pro-formal objections, Hitler accepted the Swiss action without demurrer.[104]

Speculation was rife in our magazines about Hitler's anticipated next moves in January and February, 1936. Attention focused primarily on an apparent growing demand by Hitler for Germany's lost colonies. In late December, 1935, he reportedly told the British ambassador to Berlin, Sir Eric Phipps, that the proposed air pact between Britain and Germany was dependent on the return of colonies to Germany. In January, Goebbels linked German food shortages and precarious economic situation to the lack of colonies and stated "the time is coming when we must demand colonies."[105] In February, Joachim von Ribbentrop, "special roving Ambassador and confidant of Chancellor Hitler," stated Germany had only "temporarily" relinquished its colonies and their return was a precondition for "Germany's reentrance into the League of Nations."[106]

An article by Louis Fischer in *The Nation* argued Hitler wanted to annex Austria as a first step toward the establishment of a German empire in eastern Europe. Until he could proceed openly against Austria, Hitler was arming as rapidly as possible and was using Austrian Nazis to subvert the Austrian state. In another article in the same issue, *The Nation* insisted Hitler was "busy sharpening the cutting edge of the fanatic knife with which he hopes to carve out a Nazi empire." Europe therefore demonstrated "all the symptoms of being locked in a house with an armed madman." Fischer reiterated this theme in an article on March 11. He wrote Germany would reach the height of its military production in 1936. Hitler was prevented from starting war only by the need to train his conscript army. "Foreign countries obligingly" helped Hitler arm. The American Socony Vacuum Company, for example, was building an aviation lubricants refinery for Hitler.[107] Such aid to Hitler's economy was also noticed by *Newsweek*. It asserted Harvey D. Gibson, president of Manufacturers Trust Bank, and Joseph C. Rovensky, president of Chase National Bank, had originated a "travel mark." American banks would sell the new mark to Americans traveling to Germany and apply the money to German debts in the United States. The money thus freed cost Germany nothing in export exchange which, in turn, could be used to finance German armaments.[108]

Yet another suggestion was that Hitler would next move to remilitarize the Rhineland. While in London for the funeral of George V on January 28, the French Foreign Minister told British Foreign Secretary Eden there were diplomatic rumors Hitler intended to send troops into the demilitarized

Rhineland. Flandin wanted to send Hitler a joint French, British, and Belgium note that such action would not be tolerated. Eden sounded out German Foreign Minister von Neurath about the rumors and received von Neurath's assurance the rumors were groundless. Eden then reassured Flandin. The rumors were revitalized when Goering visited Poland and informed Warsaw the Rhineland would shortly be remilitarized. The rumors became general public knowledge when the German press warned that if France ratified the Franco-Russian Pact, Germany "would consider it a violation of the Locarno Pact" and would take action to defend its western frontier.[109] There was much dismay and diplomatic furor, but little surprise therefore, when Hitler remilitarized the Rhineland on March 7, 1936.

Hitler chose to make his announcement of the remilitarization of the Rhineland during a dramatic speech to the Reichstag—which went wild with delirium. He ended by asserting "the fight for Germany's freedom was won" and by offering a series of diplomatic proposals. These included the establishment of a demilitarized zone on both sides of Germany's border with France and Belgium, non-aggression pacts with Belgium and France in the west and Lithuania in the east, a western air pact, and the reentry of Germany into the League provided the League was disassociated from the Versailles Treaty. He scheduled a general election for the Reichstag on March 29, asserting it would be a plebiscite on his actions. American news magazines carried long extracts from his speech to the Reichstag.[110]

The delirium of the Reichstag was surpassed by that of the Rhinelanders who met the entering troops with shouts, wine, and the singing of "The Watch on the Rhine." In France, "terror hit a new post-war high." Premier Sarraut rushed 50,000 troops to the French frontier, dispatched an immediate note to the League, and asked the signatories of the Locarno Pact, minus Germany, to meet at the Quai d'Orsay. What Sarraut did not do was order the French army into the Rhineland. The French General Staff stated it was unprepared to march, the French elections were approaching, and, most importantly, Britain urged caution and consultation.[111]

In Britain, Prime Minister Baldwin declined to call a cabinet meeting to consider Hitler's action and chose instead to refer the problem to Eden, the Foreign Secretary. Eden pledged British military assistance to France if it were attacked but left no doubt he regarded the reoccupation of the Rhineland as an accomplished fact. According to our magazines, the "new Eden diplomacy" was based on several considerations: the cabinet was divided between "appeasers" and Francophiles, the British public was verbally pacifistic and pro-German, while financial circles in the City wanted to continue making loans to Germany.[112] Most importantly, Eden was still embroiled in the dispute over the imposition of oil sanctions on Italy. While Germany was a potential menace to Britain, Italy was a more immediate danger as its invasion of Ethiopia had placed it on the Nile—Britain's "lifeline" to its empire. Parliament was content to allow Eden free reign while it "enjoyed a brief Silly Season" and awaited a "White Paper" from him.[113] Eden ended by choosing to see if Hitler's new offers of cooperation could be used to rebuild a general European peace structure.

He called for a meeting of the League Council in London—a move "obviously intended to flatter the Fuehrer."[114]

The American magazines utilized in this study took varying attitudes toward the reoccupation of the Rhineland. *The Atlantic Monthly, The Saturday Evening Post, The Reader's Digest,* and *Collier's* failed to react in any manner. *Time, Newsweek,* and *The Literary Digest* reported the event and the subsequent diplomatic maneuvering without comment. *The Nation, The New Republic,* and *Harper's* were quite direct in their comments.

The Nation wrote Hitler had "precipitated a crisis far graver in its implications" than anything he had done thus far. By his action, he had forestalled the possibility of further sanctions against Italy and made "a deliberate attempt to destroy the foundations of international organization." Hitler and Mussolini were now in a position to "play the powers against one another." France was willing to make concessions to Mussolini for Italian support while Britain was willing to woo Hitler to "assure a firm stand against Italy." In the end, "these measures are bound to lead to war." The following week *The Nation* asserted Hitler's actions belied "his claim to pacific intentions." He had finally exhausted the "possibilities for international histrionics" which did not impinge on neighboring states. His next steps had to violate international borders, probably those to his east. As a preventive war or sanctions against him were unlikely, the powers would likely fall back on a traditional system of alliances. In any event, there could be "no compromise with lawlessness." By April 1, when the crisis had largely passed, *The Nation* concluded that "the neglect of the Eastern problem must ultimately mean collapse of all efforts to restrain Hitler" and this "must open the West as well as the East to the threat of Nazi aggression." The powers should insist Hitler join an eastern security pact. If he refused, then he meant war "and it would be folly to give way to him."

John Gunther, writing in the same issue, believed Hitler could "claim almost complete victory" in the Rhineland crisis as the League Council condemnation of him was only "an academic gesture." The victory was awarded to him by "the pro-German faction of the British cabinet" which had torpedoed Locarno in exchange for a new set of peace proposals from Hitler. This was the height of folly for Hitler always prefaced "a request for new treaties by tearing up old ones." Simply put, "as a truth-teller he is a bad risk." Any peace structure "built on the sand of Hitler's plan" would put all "cards in the fist of the potential aggressor."[115]

The New Republic argued peace was now "almost impossible no matter what the existing governments may want to do." Nazi "protestations of pacifism are just words in the wind—the wind on which the Valkyries ride." The conflict would probably begin in eastern Europe as Hitler's "references to Soviet Russia were full of unreasoning, hysterical hatred." It was likely Hitler did desire peace with Britain and France. Yet, paradoxically, a new Locarno "would be no guarantor of peace." Assured peace in the west would only free Hitler to move eastward against Czechoslovakia and Russia.[116]

Nathaniel Peffer, writing in *Harper's*, agreed with *The New Republic* that Hitler's action had likely made a European war only a matter of time—perhaps "even before the end of the month." The "illusion" of the "so-called peace structure" had finally been toppled. Hence, for diplomats to talk of the League, of collective security, or of any international order was a "waste of energy and enthusiasm." Concessions to, and appeasement of, Germany had "little prospect of success." In this situation, "America can do nothing for peace" as it "cannot help establish a peace system." Nothing could be done "to soften Europe's tragedy" but American could "save itself from sharing Europe's fate to no purpose." Therefore, it should remain absolutely neutral, embargo the sale of all goods to the belligerents, and remain a "free agent."[117]

The League Council met in London on March 14. Most of its members were determined to avoid any drastic measures as the Locarno signatories themselves had taken no action and as most took the view Germans had merely moved about on German territory. Other, seemingly equally important events diverted their attention. War between Russia and Japan appeared likely while Spain was on the verge of civil war. Italy was nearing the end of its conquest of Ethiopia. Instead of agreeing to Flandin's demand for sanctions, the Council followed the lead of Eden and invited Hitler to send representatives to meet with the Council. *Newsweek* noted Eden and Neville Chamberlain, Chancellor of the Exchequer, were "harried by financiers who want to avert sanctions and lend Germany money."[118] Hitler sent von Ribbentrop to meet with the Council but von Ribbentrop merely reiterated Hitler's Reichstag charges and proposals. The Council then voted Germany was guilty of a treaty violation but dispersed without taking any further action. Eden subsequently made several half-hearted proposals which Hitler rejected out of hand. Events in Spain replaced the Rhineland as the leading news story in American magazines and news items on Germany became second-page stories after the plebiscite.

In the same speech in which he announced the reoccupation of the Rhineland, Hitler set March 29 as the date for new elections to the Reichstag. The elections were to constitute a plebiscite on his actions and were intended to impress foreigners, not Germans. The election campaign was described in perjorative terms by our news magazines. According to *Time,* Hitler was "howling his head off" in a "bellowing frenzy" at "monster Nazi campaign rallies all over the Reich." He was "in full swing" with the campaign although he had not announced the candidates for "they are all human blanks, der Fuehrer's stooges, and their names do not matter." *Newsweek* wrote the campaign theme was "come to the aid of the Fuehrer (Or else-)." It asserted "police will help non-Nazis, if any" to the polls so the result would be "40,000,000 or more" for Hitler and "Against Hitler - 0."[119] *Time* noted the ballots had only one circle marked "Ja" so it would be impossible "to cast any other vote." Ballots marked "Nein" or left blank were to be voided. Police had been ordered to carry "the sick and aged" to the polls on stretchers and to insure that criminals voted correctly. *The Literary Digest* asserted Jews and those married to Jews were barred from voting.[120] The entire Nazi leadership was active in the thousands of rallies but Hitler's speeches were the ones reported in American magazines. Hitler, in a Hamburg speech, had declared if European statesmen "could look ahead through the next decade they would be frightened!" Goebbels had censored the remark but only after correspondents had reported it. *The Literary Digest* thought it significant Hitler's climactic speech of the campaign was made at the Krupp munition works in Essen. All Germans were required to stop work and listen as 100,000 public loudspeakers and untold radios carried Hitler's speech. Insisting the election "marked the high point in the Nazis' mastery of mob-psychology," *The Nation* wrote Germans "were openly threatened if they failed to cast their ballots" on election day. *The New Republic* reported Nazis dragged "the German electorate to the polls practically at the sword's point."[121]

Hitler received a "ja" vote of 98.79 percent in the election. Out of 44,952,476 ballots only 542,953 were either negative or blank and so declared void. American magazines were unimpressed by the results and *The New Republic* summarized their attitude when it stated "the vote was meaningless, having been obtained by force" and only the "muddled minds" of the Nazis saw any value in it.[122]

Following the Nazi plebiscite, Hitler ceased being the center of news reporting for sometime. Spain moved rapidly into the chaos of its civil war, in May Mussolini realized his conquest of Ethiopia, the Russians and Japanese continued to clash on the Manchurian border, France went through one of its perennial domestic crises, and an anti-Jewish war erupted in Palestine. Hitler seemed to be directly or indirectly involved only in this latter crisis.

Arab resistance to Jewish immigration into Palestine once again flared into violence in mid-April. Young Arabs had organized gangs of "Holy Martyrs to kill all Jews and Britons in Palestine." One gang attacked a Jewish car killing one Israel Hazan and wounding two other Jews. A German in the car was released unhurt by the gang for "Hitler's sake." At Hazan's funeral in Tel Aviv, "furious Hebrews" began to riot. British police moved in, wounding four Jews, beating some thirty more, and arresting a large number. The police then invaded "scores of Jewish homes," arresting their residents on "riot charges."[123]

When two Arabs were subsequently killed by Jews, "Arab mobs ran riot in Jaffa" and "murdered Jews in the streets." The riots spread to Tel Aviv, Nablus and "other places." Palestine was swept with a "rampage of fire and assassination." "Arab urchins" tossed gasoline torches into Jewish homes and stores "all over Palestine." The Mufti Haj Amin el Husseini declared a general strike which spread into Transjordan while Arabs in Lebanon, Syria, and Iraq pledged their support for the Palestinian Jews. Tel Aviv had to be "ringed with barbed wire to keep out blood-thirsty Arabs."[124] *The Nation* felt the situation could only be called a "private war which the Arabs are waging against the Jews."[125]

At the end of May, youthful Arab gangs, equipped with explosives and "new rifles," began to snipe at British troops, cut telegraph lines, interdict highway traffic, and blow up British and Jewish buildings. The British government rushed another army battalion to Palestine, instituted collective guilt for Arab villages where sniping occurred, and promised the establishment of yet another royal commission of inquiry. At the same time, it issued 2,000 immigration visas to Jews.[126]

Arab leaders reacted by converting the general strike in the Transjordan into overt attacks on Jews and promoting anti-Jewish riots in the French mandate of Syria. By the middle of June, the violence had escalated to the point where Britain felt compelled to send in four more battalions, station five cruisers off the coast, establish detention camps for Arab leaders, interdict the Jordan with armed boats, and establish press censorship. When in July Transjordan Arab leaders decided to "offer 100,000 wild-riding desert horsemen to their beleaguered brethren" in Palestine, Britain closed the frontier. A French proposal to withdraw from its Syrian mandate produced Arab demands that Britain withdraw from Palestine.[127]

Moslem leaders in the French colony of Algeria, incited by the conflict in Palestine, launched attacks on Jews in Bou Saada, Algiers, Oran, and Constantine. When the French police attempted "to stop looting of Jewish stores," the Arabs turned on the police and the French army had to be called in to stop the riots. Arab leaders also expressed their support for the anti-Semitic parties of the extreme French Right.[128]

By the middle of August, Britain had built up its Palestinian Corps to 15,000 men, "yet even this army failed to keep Arab nationalists from killing Jews." *Newsweek* reported that in one August weekend alone, Arabs had killed "eleven Israelites." A British curfew on Jews, imposed to protect them, reminded Jews of the "Central European ghettos they had left."[129] The British High Commissioner, Sir Authur Wauchope, also welcomed the "mediation" of Nuri as Said, the Foreign Minister of Iraq. Nuri as Said thereupon "sent up a trial balloon to test Christian public opinion" by announcing the British were considering "a new policy of 'No More Jews,' temporarily at least." Pressure from London Jews, however, shot down the balloon and led to a decision in September to dispatch the British First Division to "squelch the Arabs and in due time make Palestine a real 'Jewish Homeland'." By the end of October, *Time* reported the Arab general strike and riots had been ended by "British might."[130]

The apparent peace was broken once again in early November when "Arab terrorists raided villages, looted stores, and fired on Jews and Britons." The British government reacted by sending a royal commission to Palestine and by making "its first retreat in Arab-Jewish quarrel" with an announcement of a "sharp reduction" of Jewish immigration. The Colonial Office attributed this reduction to "a conservative view" of "Palestinian resources." *Newsweek*, however, insisted it was due to British fear "that unappeased Arab militance" would threaten British military bases and oil pipelines in the Near East. Arab leaders decided to boycott the commission until Britain "completely" halted Jewish immigration. *Newsweek* also reported Palestinian Jews were breaking up into "political factions" over continued Jewish immigration and that earlier Jewish residents "now openly support the Arabs."[131]

Our magazines attributed the new Arab violence to a number of factors. One was Arab resentment over the increased immigration of Jews to Palestine and growing Jewish influence in its economy. Another was the perception that Britain had been weakened by the Ethiopian crisis and was no longer determined to maintain its empire. Arabs were also systematically incited by Italian broadcasts from Bari which, although not anti-Semitic in themselves, promoted Arab nationalism. Ultimately these magazines identified Hitler's anti-Semitism as the cause of the revolt. Not only had he intensified the issue of Jewish immigration, he had made anti-Semitism the hallmark of a great European nation, and perhaps, even provided financial assistance to the Arabs.[132]

The Nation and *The New Republic* attempted to place the Palestinian anti-Jewish war in a larger context. Albert Viton saw little hope for a peaceful resolution of the conflict as "revolutionary changes" were "taking place in the Arab world" as Arab religious identity was being replaced by "the new social force, nationalism" The "standard bearers of the nationalist crusade" were youthful and constituted "the most important phenomenon in the Near East." This new Arab generation represented "a complete break with the Arab past." Opposed "to them stand the Zionists." Led by Ben Guyron [sic], the Zionists defined Palestine as a "permanent" war zone where the conflict, usually fought on economic and social battlefields, occasionally became "a real war." Arab nationalists saw in Zionists a "mortal enemy who comes to rob him of his homeland." Zionists saw Arabs as "unnecessary obstacles to his homeland dream." Therefore, blood was inevitable and would "flow in the future until one side emerges victorious."[133]

Benjamin Stolberg argued the term "Jew" did not denote a physical race but a "culture," a "state of mind." This was a paradox for even as Jews came to physically resemble the peoples where they lived, this resemblance could not become identity. The Jew was "psychologically unassimilable" by word for giving it "the Christ who disapproves of what it is doing between Monday and Saturday and of its hypocrisy on Sundays and holidays." Where class domination was the strongest, there one found "anti-Semitism at its darkest" because of social guilt over the domination. When non-Jews attacked Jews, one result was to make the Jews "psychologically separate" although they were physically inseparable from their neighbors. The resultant "maladjustment" led to a gentile "psychosis" in which the Jews became the enemy alien that needed suppression.[134]

The New Republic attributed the Palestinian violence, directly and indirectly to Hitler—directly because he had created the Jewish refuge crisis and indirectly because he had given a semblance of respectability to anti-Semitism by institutionalizing it in a European nation. When the Jews sought refuge in a Palestinian homeland, their numbers and economic accomplishments antagonized Arabs. The Arabs, whose economic well-being had been neglected by the British, hated the Jew for the very prosperity which was beginning to aid Arabs and saw in it only a threat. Only an end to Arab economic misery would end the Palestinian violence—and this could best be done by allowing

Jewish immigrants into Palestine. There they would continue to raise the level of farming and industry.[135]

"Hitler's spirit similarly" directed attacks on Jews in Poland. There "mob attacks on Jews" had multiplied under a government that verbally deprecated anti-Semitism while doing "little to prevent or punish it." The "source of the infection" was Germany, which "should be forced to post on its door a sign reading, 'Unclean'." *The Literary Digest* reported that in Galicia peasants had "for months been raiding and pillaging Jewish stores" and boycotting and terrorizing Jews in Warsaw, Cracow, Zagrow, and Przytyk. Warsaw dailies called the "Jewish problem" a "boil for which the whole family must be operated on." In Hungary, there were growing demands for "a race of pure Magyar ideology." Behind all these movements appeared the hand of Hitler and his followers.[136]

As 1936 drew to a close, *The New Republic* asserted there was a rising flood of anti-Semitism in Europe inspired by the example of Nazi Germany. In Germany, "modern hatred of Jews" had been "erected into a program of expropriation and eventually of extermination." Hitler had made the Jews a "helpless instrument" for organizing Germany as a compact fighting mass," for overcompensating for the "feeling of inferiority and impotence of a defeated people," and for re-structuring of the German economy by expropriation of Jewish goods and businesses. Hitler further employed anti-Semitism as "a means of penetrating" and of "dividing and undermining" the nations of Europe as part of his "military-political scheme" to conquer Europe. The success of his tactic was real for the "same actual physical warfare conducted against the Jews of Poland goes on too against the Jews of Rumania" while if an *Anschluss* with Austria occurred, "the fate Austrian Jews would be sealed." Even in England, France, Holland, and Italy, anti-Semitic groups "financed 'from abroad' " had appeared. This Nazi-inspired anti-Semitism made the Jewish "plight a claim upon the humanity of the civilized world," particularly "lands of tolerance and freedom."[137]

Yet, where were European Jews to find a haven? Viton, who had earlier suggested increased Jewish immigration into Palestine, reversed his position in late December. Although he noted "eight million Jews will eventually be forced to leave Europe" by Hitler, Viton argued "Palestine" could offer "no haven for all these millions." Simply put, the limited Palestinian economy could not absorb them, the cost of their re-settlement would be too great, and the Arabs could not permit it. The only possible answer was for civilized nations to open their doors to the expected refugees. Palestine should be neutralized under international control and no group allowed to dominate its affairs.[138]

Even as Jews were being attacked in Palestine and anti-Semitism was washing across Europe, Germany hosted the 1936 Olympic Games. Most of our magazines simply noted the Nazi effort to remove the more obvious signs of German anti-Semitism and went on to report on the games. *The Nation*, however, took delight in the expectation three "American Negroes," Jesse Owens, Cornelius Johnston, and David Albritton, would win gold medals in the Games for "in Nazi Germany the only animal which is lower than a Jew is a Negro." One of the "gravest counts against the Jew" in "prevalent German racial theory" was that the Jew treated the Negro as a human being. *Newsweek* reported "the first question asked by German newspaper men on the arrival of the American team was how many Negroes are there on your team?"[139]

Although Avery Brundage, president of the American Olympic Committee, lauded Germany for capturing "the true Olympic spirit." *The Nation* insisted that in Germany "death" had only taken "a holiday." When "the Great Farce" of the games was over, Jews were likely to have their papers confiscated, be made "prisoners," be economically disenfranchised, and be the subject of " 'sporadic' riots and pillaging." On August 8, *The Nation* described the Olympic program as an "official pogrom" due to the absence of Jews on the German team. It also noted that *Der Stürmer* had printed a cover showing a Jew enviously watching a "noble-looking German" be crowned with Olympic laurels—the same week *The New Yorker* depicted "the converse on its cover." *The Nation* found it "extremely humorous, as well as entirely satisfactory" that Negro Americans had won their laurels "in the presence of Adolf Hitler, the leader of spurious Aryanism."[140] *The New Republic* found it ironic that Goebbels attributed American success in the Olympics to its "black auxiliaries" even as he attempted to stress the superiority of Aryan athletes. *Time* reported on August 31, in its final Olympic article, that "Jewish-blooded Captain Wolfgang Fuertsner, the Army officer responsible" for the construction of the Olympic village, had committed suicide as he had subsequently been cashiered due to his racial background.[141]

The staunch anti-Nazi attitude of *The Nation* and *The New Republic*, so apparent in their comments on the Olympic Games, was also apparent in their reports on the five-hundred-and-fiftieth anniversary celebration of the University of Heidelberg. In this instance, they were openly joined by *The Literary Digest*. On July 4, *The Literary Digest* reported "many outstanding universities had blackballed rites" honoring Heidelberg, as the ceremony was "sponsored by the avowed and shameless enemies of intellectual freedom." It noted that, in a university which had promised Spinoza "the utmost freedom of philosophizing," Jewish professors had been dismissed along with Jewish students, "Jewish mathematics" had been banned, and the student corps had been "Nazified." It applauded the "blunt rejections" sent to the Heidelberg committee by the universities of Stockholm, Oslo, Oxford, and Cambridge. It was critical, however, of the American colleges and universities, including Harvard, John Hopkins, and Yale, that accepted their invitations to send representatives to the ceremony. When Nicholas Butler accepted for Columbia, students burned "several of his masterpieces—'The Meaning of Education', 'The Faith of a Liberal'—on a bonfire."[142]

The Nation asserted "insanity was the order of the day" when "official or unofficial" representatives of twenty American colleges and universities participated "at least passively" in the Heidelberg ceremony. It wrote "it irks us a bit when our compatriots humor" Nazi "delusions" and attend "an orgiastic celebration over the dead body of German culture." *The New Republic*, in a similar vein, criticized American universities for sending "representatives to

Heidelberg to celebrate its destruction" by the "Nazi state." It noted "the statue of Athena, goddess of wisdom," an American gift to the university, had been replaced by a swastika and eagle. It reported with glee in October, 1936, that German universities had refused to attend Harvard's tercentenary celebration.[143]

In July, Hitler once again took advantage of international events to launch several dramatic diplomatic moves. The League had reveled its ineffectiveness in the Ethiopian crisis and was, in effect observably dead. The Locarno collective security system was a memory. Skirmishing between fascists and royalists had begun in Spain while Japan renewed its attack on China. Mussolini had visibly moved toward Germany while England quietly and without fanfare dropped all thought of sanctions against Italy. The United States was pre-occupied with the 1936 election campaign between Landon and Roosevelt.

Hitler began by sending the German cruiser *Leipzig* to Danzig both to support local Nazis and to flaunt the League's authority over the port. He also sent Arthur Karl Greiser, president of Danzig's Nazi Senate, to Geneva to demand the withdrawal of the League's commissioner from the city. At Geneva, Greiser literally "thumbed his nose" at the audience and the press-box, gave the Nazi salute, and left the rostrum. On his return to Danzig, Greiser convened a Senate meeting which banned all opposition political parties, voted to ignore the presence of the League commissioner, and instituted laws to make Danzig a Nazi police state.[144] Poland blustered but did nothing except begin desultory military staff talks with France, while the League quietly reassigned its commissioner to Geneva. By the end of the year Danzig was "under the Terror" of a Nazi state.[145]

The same week Hitler sent the cruiser *Leipzig* to Danzig, he also announced Helgoland and several other islands, "supposedly demilitarized forever" by Versailles, would be rearmed. Although the islands had once been "a pistol pointed at Britain's heart," the announcement "caused hardly a murmur in the House of Commons."[146]

The major event of the week, however, was the signing of a Berlin-Vienna Pact engineered by Hitler through Fritz von Papen, German ambassador to Austria. The pact was a *tour de force* for Hitler as it removed the chief obstacle to a close friendship between Italy and Germany. The effect of the pact was felt immediately when, on the same day, Mussolini announced Italy would not participate in an upcoming Locarno signatory conference on the remilitarization of the Rhineland. In anticipation of the pact, Mussolini had shortly before refused Italian participation in the Dardanelles session at Montreux. Further evidence of the awakening friendship between Italy and Germany was the visit of Mussolini's daughter and air force chief to Berlin. At the conclusion of the visit, Hitler closed the German consulate in Ethiopia and transferred its personnel and functions to Rome. He thus became the first foreign leader to recognize the Italian conquest of Ethiopia.[147]

Under the terms of the pact, Hitler agreed to respect Austrian independence and to refrain from interference in Austrian internal affairs. Schuschnigg agreed to release Nazi prisoners, accept a Nazi into his cabinet, to relax Austrian cordons against Nazi migration and literature, and to recognize Austria was a "Germanic state" by conducting a pro-German foreign policy.

It was predicted "Germany and Italy" would "get together," that Mussolini would be in a stronger position to bargain with England and France, that Hungary would slowly move toward support of Germany, and that "non-Nazi Austrians" would be politically paralyzed.[148] *The Literary Digest* felt the pact meant Jews "would soon face the repressive treatment their brothers receive in the Reich." *The New Republic* interpreted the pact to mean Britain and France had made "a cardinal error" in relying upon Mussolini as a check to Hitler and by their appeasement of the dictators.[149]

The major international event of the summer of 1936 was the outbreak of the Spanish Civil War. The war, according to *Newsweek*, was internationally recognized as a "test case" between the "ideals of Fascism and Marxism." The Blum cabinet, under intense pressure from the French left and right to intervene, officially compromised and called for an international policy of non-intervention. Privately it allowed French communists to open a recruiting station for volunteers in Paris and "surreptitiously" provided the loyalists with fifteen pursuit planes. Mussolini despatched a squadron of planes, several of which crashed in French North Africa, to aid the fascists in Spanish Morocco. Moscow announced a grant of $2,400,000 to the loyalist cause.[150] From Ireland, 2,000 volunteers sailed to assist the fascists. Hitler's initial action was to order a pocket-battleship, the *Deutschland,* to Ceuta to protect German citizens from loyalist attack while Argentina despatched a battleship to rescue its ambassador from the loyalists. Meanwhile Britain ordered the H. M. S. *Repulse* to lift a loyalist blockade of fascist ports.[151]

The Nation and *The New Republic* immediately attacked Hitler and Mussolini for supplying men and material to the Spanish fascists. *The Nation* believed these "gangsters" and "irresponsible megalomaniacs" had decided to aid Franco as a *quid pro quo* for naval bases in the Canary and Balearic Islands. Hitler and Mussolini had become "drunk with the successes" handed them by the "democratic states" and had reached the point where "they think they can get away with anything." *The Nation* called upon these "democratic states" to adopt a policy of "more than mere passive neutrality" and to bring pressure on Hitler and Mussolini to withdraw from Spain. *The New Republic* asserted "the fascist dictatorships" had followed "their usual course of acting first and talking afterward" and, in return for a promise of naval bases, had sent Franco massive aid. It insisted "rebel troops are wearing German helmets" and that "German planes and aviators" were already active in Spain. The civil war might ignite a world war if France and Britain did not immediately support the republican loyalists.[152] Both magazines praised Moscow for its pledge of aid to the loyalists.

After these initial reports of foreign intervention, news reporting on the Spanish conflict settled down to a recitation of battles, retreats, and casualties. By the middle of September, all the major European powers had officially assented to the French call for non-intervention. By September 23, *The New Republic* could write "all Europe is neutral today" due to "the elderly indifference of the Foreign Offices that prevailed in the end." It alleged a British refusal to support France, based on a "fear of war," had paralyzed the democracies and likely given fascism another easy success in Spain. True, Hitler had agreed to the call for non-intervention, but only because he still hoped "to win the sympathy of England" and to separate "Paris from Moscow." He had already sent all the aid the Spanish fascists could effectively use while Lisbon could be used to send more if needed. The threat to peace posed by fascism had not been reduced and would remain until "an international People's Front" had joined Britain, France, and Russia in "a firm defensive alliance." *The Nation* agreed a "present unequal 'neutrality' " had been imposed by the powers but only because "all the democracies" had failed once again to resist fascism.[153]

When Hitler and Mussolini continued to supply France, Moscow took the occasion of a London meeting of the twenty-seven nations pledged to non-intervention to accuse "Italy, Germany, and their little fascist ally, Portugal" of sending aid to the Spanish fascists. Russia announced that, if the aid was not stopped, it would "forswear its neutrality pledge and start shipping war materials" to the loyalists. *Newsweek* reported no one took the threat seriously given the distances involved. It believed the real import of the charge was that Russia "stood ready to make trouble if left out of Western European councils." Italy, Germany, and Portugal angrily denied the Russian charges while *Newsweek* noted "the conferees agreed by silent majority that Russia's action had been ill-advised." Mussolini promptly announced an increased Italian military budget.[154] Hitler accused Russia of threatening to invade the West and avowed resistance. In a hurriedly convened meeting, the non-intervention committee, under the leadership of Britain, absolved Italy of guilt in supplying the fascists while simultaneously "rebuking" Russia for its aid to the loyalists.[155]

Of much greater import was the signing on October 25 of the German-Italian Pact that came to be known as the Berlin-Rome Axis. *Time, Newsweek* and *The New Republic* saw the pact as the direct result of the Spanish civil war and Russian intervention in it. Under the terms of the pact, Hitler formally recognized the Italian conquest of Ethiopia and received trade concessions there, agreed Germany and Italy would pursue a common policy toward the League, pledged to recognize Franco as ruler of Spain when he captured Madrid, and, most importantly, agreed to form a solid front against the spread of communism. They agreed they would advocate a security pact for Europe that would exclude Russia from its signatories. There was no immediate reaction by Britain and France to the pact. However, it led Portugal to break diplomatic relations with the loyalist government, Yugoslavia to seek an understanding with Italy, while Belgium, responding to impending rumors of the pact, abandoned its military alliance with France.[156] On November 14, Hitler, taking advantage of the confused diplomatic scene, denounced the international control of her rivers established by the Treaty of Versailles. Only France, Czechoslovakia, and Yugoslavia bothered to protest.

In the middle of November, with Franco clearly gaining against the loyalists, Hitler and Mussolini formally recognized him as the ruler of Spain. This gave them the right, under international law, to legally and openly supply him with military assistance. Franco thereupon announced a blockade of Barcelona in open defiance of Britain's earlier announced determination to keep all Spanish ports open.[157] Eden, attacked in Commons for Britain's "do-nothing" Spanish policy and for acceptance of the Barcelona blockade, asserted Britain's policy in Spain was motivated by the desire to avoid a larger war and that Moscow "categorically" was "more to blame than Italy and Germany" for the conflict. More importantly, there were rumors that Hitler, with the support of Mussolini, intended to conclude a "military alliance" with Japan "designed to crush the Soviet Union."[158]

Rumor became reality on November 25 when Ribbentrop, nominally ambassador to Britain, signed a German-Japanese agreement provided for the future adherence of non-communist nations. Italy promptly signed a similar agreement with Japan. *Time* asserted Hitler had "outsmarted" Japan for Japan had now "made a red-hot enemy" of Russia while it was in a war with China and unable to match Russian strength in Asia. It noted there were rumors Hitler intended to seize Leningrad in the spring of 1937. When this toppled the Boshevik leaders, Hitler would then annex the Baltic and Ukrainian areas of Russia. A preliminary Nazi move would be "the attempt to nip off" the Suedetenland of Czechoslovakia.[159]

As might be expected, Moscow was incensed by the anti-Comintern pacts. Its Foreign Secretary, Litvinov, denounced the signatories as "asses" and Hitler, in particular, as "a pig." He alleged a new "Holy Alliance" had been formed to attack Russa and precipitate another "Great War." Litvinov pledged Russia would protect itself with massive production corresponding to its massive manpower.[160] Blum of France declined adherence to the pact for, although France had an army second only to that of Russia, it did not want to add to the possibility of a major war. He pledged French support to Britain if it were attacked and predicted "Russian would fight by their side." Baldwin, highly offended by the rumor of an assurance by Ribbentrop to Hitler Britons were cowardly and would only "fight for their soil," had Eden pledge the defense of Belgium.[161] However, like most Britons, Baldwin was distracted by the monarchical crisis over the relationship between King Edward and Mrs. Simpson.[162]

Most of our magazines were content to simply report these unfolding events. *The Nation*, however, interpreted the pacts to mean "the fascist powers" had "thrown away the last pretense of legality." They were "brazenly defiant of all laws and conventions" developed by "civilized nations." It was "no longer possible" for the democracies to "find pretexts for refusing to face reality" and they were compelled to recognize "fascism" was the "greatest immediate threat to world peace." *The New Republic* defined the pacts as a "Holy Alliance against democracy" for they signified "an intention" and "excuse" for the fascists to intervene anywhere they chose to combat communism. Hitler also intended to enlist the sympathy of French and British conservatives on Germany's behalf with an anti-communist crusade. However, this was "a serious miscalculation" for he had revealed himself as never before as a danger to their interests.[163] As the year ended, *The New Republic* argued "Nazi morale" was beginning "to crack" due to the economic strains created by Hitler's military production and because "more level heads" in Germany were alarmed by his foreign policy.[164]

As 1936 ended, there were a variety of speculations about Hitler's intentions in the coming months. For some time, various Nazi leaders had been demanding the return of the colonies taken from Germany by the Treaty of Versailles and one interpretation insisted Hitler would move to reclaim them in 1937.[165] Another rumor was that Hitler intended to "nip off" the Suedetenland in 1937 prior to an attack to the east.[165] A variant of this view insisted Hitler intended a major attack in eastern Europe as a means of acquiring "continental colonies."[167] It was realized that Hitler generally chose the spring to make a major move. Hence, Europe braced itself for his next move as 1937 opened.

Chapter IV
Sturm Und Drang, 1937

As 1937 opened, Europe braced itself for another spring "Hitler surprise" similar to his announcement of rearmament in 1935 and the reoccupation of the Rhineland in 1936. On January 2, *Newsweek* reported Hitler was at Berchtesgaden pondering whether to plunge Europe "into the long-feared second world war," thus making the "world hold its breath." *The New Republic* wrote on January 6 that Hitler was "sitting alone at his mountain retreat at Berchtesgaden deciding the issue of war or peace for almost the entire world." The Paris Stock Exchange announced it would remain closed on Saturdays due to "Hitler's unsettling habit of hurling political bombs on weekends."[1] Any new moves by Hitler, it was recognized, would involve the violation of the territory of a neighboring state and possibly result in war.[2]

Newsweek believed there was general agreement in Europe that Hitler favored an immediate war and was restrained only because von Blomberg and von Fritsch "bluntly told Hitler the army wasn't ready." A number of reasons were believed to lie behind Hitler's desire for war. Domestically, a critical economic situation and severe food shortage "threatened to cause dangerous unrest in the masses." Foreign visitors "detected symptoms of dangerous unrest."[3] Food rationing, food price fixing, and the use of *ersatz* materials were failing to alleviate Germany's desperate situation. *Harper's* asserted Germany had moved to a war economy but was still failing to resolve its crisis. "Economic retribution" for Hitler's faulty economic planning was "close behind" and would "not give him much margin" over the next months. Either Hitler would have to dramatically revise his policies or there would be war— an "alternative" that was "scarcely to be contemplated by sane men in this year 1937." *The New Republic* noted "the dictators' handbook recommends a foreign war when things get as critical" as Germany's distress.[4]

Yet, internationally, Hitler seemed to be on the defensive. The Spanish Civil War had placed him "in a difficult position" for, although Franco was insisting only German reinforcements could prevent a fascist defeat, Britain and France had delivered identical notes warning Hitler against increased intervention at the risk of war. Hitler's dilemma was further heightened as loyalists had just seized the German merchant ship *Palos*. To regain it, he would have to commit additional German naval forces to the war. If he did not, he would have to "back down and suffer a disastrous loss of face."[5]

In addition, Hitler's understanding with Mussolini was seemingly coming apart at the seams. Britain finally had succeeded in reaching a "gentleman's agreement" that appeared likely to pull Italy closer to the West. Mussolini agreed to stop inciting Moslems against Britain with his radio station at Bari, to reduce his forces in Spain, and to abandon his air and naval bases in the Balearic Islands. Britain accepted the *status quo* in the Mediterranean, including the Italian conquest of Ethiopia, a fascist victory in Spain, and an end to the building of additional fortifications in the Mediterranean. British understandings with Balkan states formed the previous year were to be nullified. It was rumored the agreement had been accompanied by a pledge of British loans from the City to aid the Italian development of Ethiopia.[6] *Time* asserted this agreement of "appeasement and concord" meant "the Eagle of Fascism had made peace with the British Lion."[7] Britain and France promptly reduced their Ethiopian embassies to the status of consulates.[8] Further, "British public opinion" would "now be educated" to see "Fascism as a movement Conservative in the British sense." The "catcalls of Communists," *Time* sarcastically concluded, would not be allowed "to frighten British investors in Glorious Ethiopia Ltd."[9]

Sir Arthur Willert, a former member of the British delegation to the Disarmament Conference, defended the British policy of appeasement toward the dictators. Writing in the January issue of *The Atlantic Monthly*, he argued Britain had only two courses of action pending completion of its rearmament program. One was to form an alliance with France to safeguard "the Rhineland frontier." This, however, would mean that "Nazi penetration in Central and Eastern Europe would proceed apace" and Britain and France would be reduced to the status of secondary powers. The alternative or "collectivist approach" was for Britain to make further efforts to redress legitimate grievances, re-establish the League, solidify world opinion against aggressive powers, and attack the "economic nationalism" spreading across Europe. The effort might well fail and war result. Peace, even for a few years, would, however, mean the liberal powers would be in a stronger position. Given the isolationism of the New World in general, and the Untied States in particular, Britain was "the one Great Power" able to lead the forces of liberalism and preserve the hopes of the peoples of the world. It could not, therefore, afford hasty and ill-conceived actions.[10]

John Gunther defined British policy as one of "stall and arm." This policy was adopted as a result of the Ethiopian crisis when Whitehall discovered that, "in a world of fists," its fist "wasn't big enough." Diplomacy had become ineffectual "in a world full of wrestling champions" who employed the "insurgent shouts of illegalistic cavemen." Britain awoke one morning to find that "through carelessness or overconfidence or pacifism" it had fallen behind in the arms race initiated by Hitler. British rearmament had, moreover, to face formidable opposition from the "powerful pro-German sentiment" held by a portion of the ruling class. Some were simply "afraid of Germany" while others were quite "sincere pacifists and idealists who believe in Hitler's promises." Many had "a pervasive dislike of France and the French accompanied by a "sentimental feeling of compassion and companionship with Germany, the beaten enemy." Yet others shared the "belief that Nazi Germany prevents the spread of Socialism or Bolshevism in Europe." The City was motivated by its faith in "the abilities of Dr. Schacht" and feared losing the "very large sums invested in his hands." Given the opposed factions, the cabinet had henceforth chosen to "stall and arm." While Britain would fight to protect France, this same discord made it "extremely doubtful" Britain would fight for Czechoslovakia or the Ukraine.[11]

In this situation, Hitler reverted, as *The Nation* predicted he would, to playing "both sides of the game."[12] He conciliated Britain and France by declaring he agreed, in principle, to an end of all foreign intervention in Spain although this would "favor only the Bolshevist party." He further agreed to forego reprisals against Madrid for the seizure of the *Palos*.[13] At the same time, he landed several hundred technicians in Spanish Morocco to work the Melilia iron mines for Franco. He further ordered the battleship *Graf Spee* to seize the loyalist merchant ship *Aragon* until the *Palos* was released. Britain and France immediately dispatched large naval forces to the area while France placed its French Moroccan garrison on the alert. This precipitated what *The New Republic* labeled "The Moroccan Crisis."[14] War seemed a distinct possibility.

Hitler moved quickly to resolve the crisis and exploit Anglo-French differences. In a "two minute earnest conversation" with the French ambassador Hitler pledged Germany had no territorial ambitions in Spanish Morocco and would not land troops there. France announced it was satisfied with the pledge but would still seek a nonintervention agreement by the parties involved in the Spanish conflict. Hitler also announced he had reached an agreement with Portuguese dictator Salazar settling their financial differences and opening up Portuguese colonies to German cooperation and "exploitation." The true significance of the treaty, according to *Time*, was that Hitler had severed Portugal's historic ties to Britain—a goal long also sought by the French.[15] Goering visited Rome and secured a German-Italian note stating the dictators were willing to accept British leadership in the establishment of a nonintervention policy toward Spain. Until the agreement was reached, however, they retained their freedom of action. Britain and France promptly agreed to imprison their nationals who volunteered for service in Spain.[16] They were, however, unable to reach agreement on the joint deployment of their naval forces in the Mediterranean.

Newsweek and *Time* insisted there were deep divisions between London and Paris. *Newsweek* asserted "Stanley Baldwin and his Conservatives want Franco to win." Their problem was "how to block Nazi aggression and still allow enough aid to slip through to guarantee Franco's success." After he won, they believed a British loan would "buy the impoverished Fascist's favor." *Time* more bluntly wrote "His Majesty's Government are now in cahoots against the Spanish Reds with Hitler and Mussolini.[17] The French cabinet, on the contrary, wanted "Franco to lose." Its problem was to ensure his defeat while "ostensibly cooperating with London's nonintervention policy."[17] *Newsweek* reported the British cabinet was severely divided over the issue of risking its battleships and "prestige" in Spanish waters.[18]

With the Moroccan crisis resolved, the Spanish Civil War continued unabated while Britain and France worked to reach agreement on a policy of nonintervention acceptable to all concerned parties. The attention of Europe turned to Hitler when he announced he would address the Reichstag on January 30 to mark the end of his fourth year of rule. The major European stock exchanges declared they would remain closed in the event Hitler gave them a "Saturday Surprise." *Time* noted there was a "scramble" by statesmen "to make speeches of appeasement, conciliation and even flattery" in anticipation of Hitler's speech. Hitler was now seen "by all Europe as a portentous figure, no longer an upstart but a German Chancellor of almost Bismarckian stature."[19]

The Reichstag, labeled the "best paid male chorus in the world" by *The Literary Digest* and "a parliament of soldiers" by *Time*, took less than five minutes to re-elect Goering as its speaker and to extend the Enabling Act for four years. Hitler then spoke for two hours. Although Hitler bitterly attacked Bolshevism and the League as anticipated, *The Literary Digest* found his speech to be "conciliatory" and wrote that the European press "generally found it good."[20] Hitler declared "the era of the so-called Surprises has been concluded" and pledged Germany would "henceforth do her share" in solving the problems of Europe. He insisted there was "no humanly thinkable cause for a quarrel" between Germany and its western neighbors. While Germany sought the return of its colonies as simple justice and as a way to ease its economic problems, they were not something for which he was prepared to fight. He insisted Germany had no territorial ambitions in Spain and only aided Franco to prevent the spread of Bolshevism. The Reichstag cheered the speech for almost thirty minutes.[21] *The New Republic* was unimpressed by the speech. It wrote that the European situation had not been changed by the address and that, significantly, "he did not promise to refrain from attacking Czechoslovakia and Soviet Russia." All in all, it believed his remarks would be "entirely comic" if they did not reveal his "diseased and twisted mentality." *The Nation* simply called it "the least successful" speech Hitler had ever made. It merely repeated old slogans and so told the Germans nothing. By referring to colonies, Hitler was sure to anger the British Foreign Office even though it was uncertain he meant overseas colonies.[22]

Henry C. Wolfe, writing in *The Atlantic Monthly*, agreed with the attitude of *The New Republic*. He insisted Nazis did not "necessarily mean overseas possessions" when they mentioned colonies. Rather, the Nazis looked to the east and south for redress of the "opportunities that are denied them at home." This meant "the acquisition of Polish, Lithuanian, Czechoslovak, or Russian territory." By his *coup de main* remilitarizing the Rhineland, Hitler was not so much threatening France as protecting his back when he began his move to the east. To achieve his purposes in the east, Hitler intended to annex Austria, peaceably if possible, but by war if necessary. This would, in turn, lead to the conquest of Czechoslovakia and the "partitioning of its territory among Germany, Hungary, and Poland." Hitler would be aided by the ethnic German minorities scattered across eastern Europe while the Balkan states, all revisionist and ambitious, were beginning to perceive the advantages of being on the side of the potential winner in the coming struggle. The time was coming when Hitler's opponents would "be compelled to resist his aggressive tactics or give way to him completely." Wolfe had already written that the German minorities in eastern Europe constituted the nucleus for a German colonial drive to the East.[23]

According to *Time*, Britain obviously understood Hitler's demand for colonies to mean the former pre-war German territories or substitutes for them form British colonial areas. The Opposition Labor Party leader, Clement Attlee, proposed in a Paris lecture that Britain "Share the Empire." *Time* called this "an obvious attempt to butter Germany."[24] The British Cabinet twice discussed in February the return of British mandate colonies in Africa to Germany. A "source close" to Eden stated the transfer could be made provided Germany agreed to "a general settlement of the European muddle." Failing such an agreement, Britain would veto colonial revision. Ribbentrop was eager to reach the agreement to recoup the standing he had just lost by greeting the king with the Nazi salute at a royal reception. An agreement with Britain over Spain, he hoped, would facilitate British cooperation over the colonial question.[25]

There were a number of new developments in the Spanish Civil War in the middle of February. The British Foreign Office dispelled "the last pretense of nonintervention" by placing the number of German "volunteers" at approximately 20,000 while insisting the Italian contingent was much larger. It noted 26,000 Italians had landed in Spain in the last two months. Further, with the fascist capture of Malaga, "Europe's master diplomats" conceded "Dictator-designate Francisco Franco had victory in the bag." As one result, Germany and Russia had "noticeably backed out of the war." British official opinion remained concerned over Hitler's ambitions even if the Spanish situation was resolved.[26]

The same week, therefore, although stressing Britain still desired a general European settlement, especially a new Locarno Pact, Neville Chamberlain asserted "we can do nothing but set our teeth" and asked Commons for $2,000,000,000 for the Royal Navy and a total of $7,500,000,000 for British rearmament. He insisted Britain would build the world's largest navy and would lay down five battleship keels during 1937. By this action, *Newsweek* wrote, Chamberlain signaled Hitler that Britain would fight if pushed too far.[27]

The most important development, however, was the announcement by the international Nonintervention Committee that it had finally reached agreement to halt the movement of foreign troops and munitions into Spain. By March 6, it expected to have 300 neutral observers along Spain's French and Portuguese borders. The French, British, Russian, German, Italian, and Portuguese navies were to establish a picket line off the Spanish coasts to detect violators.[28] Sir Robert Vansittart was given primary credit for the accord, but, as *Newsweek* noted, it was the assent of Hitler and Mussolini that made the agreement possible at last. They had decided they "had sent General Franco enough men to win the war." Moscow agreed because it was "tired of supporting anarchists and

Trotskyists" and had been cutting back its aid to the loyalist cause. It had already withdrawn its ambassador. Portugal assented as it had become convinced Franco would win. When Vansittart received Franco's assurance "British interests would be protected" and that no German or Italian bases would be allowed in Spain, he persuaded France to accept the inevitable.[29]

Time believed Britain's Spanish policy, largely determined at this point by Vansittart and Baldwin, was based entirely on crass and cynical motives. Baldwin knew "that many of his best friends" felt he had "bumbled in not getting Britain in on the Italian conquest of Ethiopia." He was determined not to miss out on "a similar opportunity in Spain" for "after all, the Empire is an imperialist Democracy." Baldwin had, therefore, worked to convince Blum it would be "disastrous" for Franco's victory to be considered a victory for Hitler and Mussolini "without also being a victory for Britain and France." *Newsweek* noted "many thought" British policy was so strongly tilted toward appeasement that Hitler was only awaiting word from Britain that it would not intervene before using "force to secure the 'rights' of Czechoslovakia's 3,250,000 Germans."[30]

Following the announcement by the Nonintervention Committee of the quarantining of the Spanish Civil War, the magazines under study turned their attention to other matters and devoted only minor columns to Spain during March. The coronations of the new king, George VI, occupied much of their primary interest from March to May. As was usual when Hitler was not at the center of the international stage, our magazines turned to reports of German domestic events. For example, on March 1, *Time* ran five short articles under the heading "Germany." One reported Hitler had hosted an international war veterans meeting and expressed his desire for peace. A second mentioned Goering's efforts to prevent the smuggling of currency out of Germany. Magda Goebbels gave birth to her fourth child, while Rosenberg referred to Hitler as Germany's "Son of God." Finally, Hitler hosted the eleventh annual Berlin auto show.[31]

In March, our magazines gave extended coverage to the mutual exchange of insults between Fiorello La Guardia and the German press. Before the incident was closed, Washington and Berlin exchanged brisk diplomatic notes and the German ambassador was replaced. The exchange began when La Guardia, speaking to 1,000 women of the American Jewish Congress, extemporaneously commented there was "a brown-shirted fanatic" suited to be "the climax" in any "Chamber of Horrors" projected for the 1939 New York World's Fair. The remark "provoked an instant protest from the Wilhelmstrasse" to Washington. Cordell Hull responded by expressing his regrets for the incident while defending the principle of free speech in America.[32]

The Nazi press replied by branding La Guardia "an impertinent Jewish lout," "a Jewish boob," "a dirty Talmud Jew," and a "master New York gangster" linked to "Jews in Moscow." It recommended he be placed "either in an insane asylum or in prison." Guardia retorted that, while his mother undoubtedly had some Jewish blood, "I never thought I had enough Jewish blood to justify boasting of it." Nazi news organs also alleged Washington was too fearful of "the Jewish lout" to "curb procurers" and "gangsters." When Rabbi Stephen Wise defended La Guardia, stating "National Socialism represents a threat to civilization," the "Goebbels organs" described America as a "civilization of gangsters," a "haven of kidnappers," and the "home of jazzing Negro women" that had only "a culture of lynch law." American women were called "prostitutes." When Mrs. Stephen Wise objected to Cordell Hull about the German press in a public letter, Hull delivered an "emphatic" note of protest to Berlin. Von Neurath replied with an "explanation" but declined to apologize or to express regret for the abuse. He then declared the incident closed.[34]

Representative Samuel Dickstein of New York, however, refused to allow the incident to pass. He charged "Nazi rats, spies and agents" were recruiting and drilling armed units in New York, Pennsylvania, Ohio, Illinois, and Michigan. He asserted "2,500 Hitlerites" drilled each Sunday at Camp Upton on Long Island. Dickstein identified Fritz Kuhn, a chemist for the Ford Motor Company, as the leader of American Nazis. Kuhn countercharged Dickstein, "a Jew born in Russia," was a Soviet spy.[35]

La Guardia, for his part, refused to be repressed. Speaking to a New York anti-Nazi rally attended by 20,000 people, including General Hugh Johnson and John L. Lewis, La Guardia declared Hitler was "not *satisfaktionsfaehig*— a person so low in social standing that gentlemen could have no dealings with him." Berlin once again protested to Hull. Hull expressed his "official regrets" but appealed for a truce in "the transatlantic word war." Goebbel's *Der Angriff* demanded Roosevelt "intervene" to prevent "Jewish vulgarisms." The *Berliner Nachtausgabe* alleged that speakers at the rally had been "bribed by Jewish banks." Although these "outbursts vanished" from later editions of the papers, "in the United States resentment continued." Rabbi Wise charged "our country is full of Nazi cells" while Julius Hochfelder, "anti-Nazi league counsel," complained to Attorney General Cummings that Kuhn led a secret organization that had "sworn allegiance to...the Germany army."[36] These charges and counter-charges continued to erupt on both sides of the Atlantic.

Hans Luther, the "non-Nazi" ambassador to the United States, consistently counseled Berlin against continuing the exchanges. He reputedly was ultimately told "to take orders, not give them." When he "bluntly informed Adolf Hitler" once too often that the "recent Nazi phillipics against Jewry and American womanhood had soured German-American relations," he was dismissed and summoned home. He was replaced by the "amiable, roundish" Hans Dieckhoff, who was expected to accept Berlin's instructions more whole-heartedly.[37] *The Nation*, while acknowledging Dieckhoff was not a member of the NSDAP, noted he was Ribbentrop's brother-in-law and his arrival would surely mark "the beginning of a new era in fascist propaganda in America."[38]

Berlin could not forego continued blasts at La Guardia and, in April, noted "the notorious Talmud Jew La Guardia" had not attended "an anti-Red rally" held in New York. It also announced that because of "his continued blasts at Hitler," all gatherings of more than four Jews were banned for sixty days in Berlin.[39]

According to *Newsweek*, with this incident "German-American relations touched a postwar low." An additional irritant was the publication by Nazi newspapers of an address supposedly made by Benjamin Franklin to the Constitutional Convention in which he pleaded for the exclusion of Jews from the United States. Charles A. Beard, the prominent American historian, not only demonstrated the alleged speech was a "barefaced forgery" but also that Franklin had actually feared "the influx of Germans" as they did not "know how to make modest use" of liberty. *The Literary Digest* wrote that "Americans generally were more amused than incensed" by the incident. Its fear was the incident had been contrived in Berlin as part of a massive campaign to demonstrate that "world Jews have been organizing a great crusade against Germany." *The New Republic* believed the result would be "a greatly increased chance for the reelection of Mayor La Guardia" but noted it had also "increased the unpopularity of the German regime throughout this country."[40]

Newsweek also reported in March that Putzi Hanfstaengl, "Nazi court jester," had disappeared from Germany after warning his friends he feared for his life. Long out of favor with Hitler for unspecified reasons, he had lost his former job of Nazi contact with foreign correspondents to Goebbels. After receiving orders to go to Spain on a mysterious mission Hanfstaengl fled first to Switzerland and then to London. From Claridge's Hotel, he announced he would remain permanently in London and that he had deposited his memoirs with a British publisher "in case I should meet sudden death." In August, *Newsweek* was finally able to discover the reason for Hanfstaengl's flight. Hanfstaengl "possessed a fiendish wit" and had "made one crack too many." Not only had he baited Goebbels, but he habitually referred to Ribbentrop as *"Brickendrop"*—"a dropper of diplomatic bricks." When he called Franco's Moors "the new friends of Aryan culture," Goebbels put him on a plane to Spain so he could be parachuted to his "bolshevik friends." Hanfstaengl, however, escaped from the plane as it refueled in Munich and fled to Switzerland.[41]

In June, another "friend" of Hitler ran afoul of Goebbel's anger. Leni Riefenstahl, who had directed *Triumph of the Will* and filmed the 1936 Olympics, had refused to submit to Goebbel's control of German films. Aroused by her resistance, Goebbel's accused her of not being an Aryan and refused to remain at a reception where she was present. On returning that evening to her apartment, she found it barred by Brownshirts and had to seek temporary shelter in a near-by hotel. Yet, in October, *Newsweek* reported Leni was on prominent display when Mussolini visited Hitler. No explanation was given for her rehabilitation.[42]

For some months, our magazines had given little attention to the continued persecution of Jews in Germany. In January, however, *Time* reported Heinz Weidemann, Evangelical bishop of Bremen, had published an anti-Semitic translation of *The Gospel of John*. Weidemann translated Judea as "Jewland," "then said the Jews" became "the Jews jeered and said," while throughout the new translation it was "implied that Christ and His disciples were not Jews." German booksellers did a "roaring business" with the translation. The

Negro play *Green Pastures*, which had opened in Berlin, was described by the Nazi press as "an instrument of Jewish propaganda" calculated "to twist the Jewish question into a Negro question."[43]

In February, *Time* reported Arnold Bernstein, owner of the Red Star, Palestine, and Bernstein shipping lines, had been "collared" by the Gestapo and thrown into a Hamburg jail along with two of his Jewish colleagues. Although Hitler had previously "paternally patted" Bernstein on the head for his contributions to the German economy and for providing Jews transportation to Palestine, Hitler now charged him with currency violations. Currency violation was "a crime punishable," if one was a Jew, "by death." Further, the regime had assumed operation of the Bernstein lines pending the trial. In November, 1937, *Time* reported Bernstein's case had finally gone to trial but the death penalty was not expected.[44] Meanwhile, the Nazi regime kept finding new ways to strike at Jews.

At the end of April, Hitler destroyed yet another element of the infrastructure of the German Jewish community. He dissolved the B'nai B'rith lodges and seized their funds and property on the pretext that one of its 14,000 members had "engaged in communist propaganda." This was a heavy blow to the system of hospitals, orphanages, and retirement homes that served German Jews. The Berlin press also again alleged La Guardia was a Jew and "selected" George Harvey of Queens as its preferred mayoral candidate in the fall New York elections, asserting Harvey would clear New York streets of communists.[45]

Julius Streicher published a new "Mother Goose" book by Elvira Bauer, a Nazi kindergarten teacher who had "a rare insight into the souls of children" according to Nazi critics. Forty-two pages of text and pictures showed "brute-faced Jews cheating, seducing, poisoning, and betraying handsome Nordics." The title of the book was *Trust Not the Fox by Field or Pond, Nor Any Jew Upon His Bond. The Nation* characterized the message of the book as "the Jew is a new sort of monster, combining all the classic qualities of the old witch, the boody man, the big bad wolf, and the wicked ogre." In every illustration, the Jew was "pictured with parrot-beaked nose, puffy pig eyes, unshaven jowls, and thick lascivious lips." The German was depicted as either a "dragon-killer" or "fairy prince." One picture showed Aryan children shouting names, sticking out their tongues, and thumbing their noses at "little Jewish children"—the caption read "Away with the Jewish brood." The last page pictured a German boy playing an accordion while sulking Jews marched down a road with a signpost reading "One-Way Street to Palestine." The book sold 50,000 copies the first month it was released.[46]

Time reported in August that Goebbels was constantly urging Germans to "Aryanize" their communities. Only certain park benches were available to Jews, Jewish booksellers were limited to selling only Jewish books, Jewish stores had been expropriated, and there had even been an edict issued stating husbands were not liable for their wive's debts with Jews. A young Jew, who had asked an Aryan girl for a date, was imprisoned for a year.[47]

In October, Philip S. Bernstein summarized the status of the German Jewish Community. He noted there were few scenes of anti-Semitic violence on the streets and that Jewish names still appeared on stores and restaurants. On closer examination, one found "that appearances belie the realities." The businesses had been "Aryanized" although they retained their former names. For every Jewish doctor still working, ten had been expelled from practice or had fled the country. Most professions were already *"Judenfrei"* or would soon be totally Aryanized. Jews were unable to attend concerts, lectures, exhibits, or the movies. Jewish children had been forced out of public schools either by "edict or by constant abuse and vilification." In small towns, life had "become literally impossible for Jews." In these towns, Jews could not buy "milk or bread or meat." Undertakers refused to "sell coffins or render burial services for Jews." In public parks, Jews were only allowed to sit on a few designated benches. Bernstein concluded the Nazi assault on Jews was moving "from segregation to pauperization, to emigration, to annihilation." For German Jews, the only choice was "between emigration and death."[48]

In February, *The Literary Digest* published several articles on the plight of Jews across Europe. It eulogized France for its historical willingness to provide a haven for all types of refugees although it had imposed a heavy financial burden upon France. Now, France had not only opened its borders to 35,000 Jewish refugees but had also refused "to extradite them for any reason whatsoever" due to fear "trumped up" charges would place them in "the tortures of a concentration camp." The United States, by contrast, had only accepted 7,500 refugees and continued to extradite those charged with crimes. French policy was fortunate, for "the victims of twentieth century barbarism have no place else to go."[49]

On February 20, *The Literary Digest* called attention to "the terror of anti-Semitism" stalking Polish Jews. Jews in Poland had been made "a race apart" and were being systematically starved. Young Jewish women "look like skeletons," children were "rickety," and only one Jew in three had a job. Boycotts had been organized by the extremely nationalistic National Democrats, *Endeks*, who had also revoked the business licenses of Jews and resorted to overt violence at times. More than 1,000 Jews had been wounded and forty killed in anti-Semitic riots. Jews had been banned from government jobs and *The Manchester Guardian* reported that, "in all of Poland," there was "not a single Jewish postman or cab driver." Jews had been banned from the wholesale meat trade and were being ousted from the professions. It noted Foreign Minister Joseph Beck had suggested all Polish Jews be "evacuated" and placed in League of Nation mandated colonies. *The Literary Digest* attributed the Polish anti-Semitic activities to the depression and to Poland having fallen "under the influence of Nazi Germany."[50]

The Nation also reported in May anti-Jewish riots had broken out across Poland, resulting in the death of fifty-three Jews. Market stalls belonging to Jews were daily being destroyed and Jews were being "forcefully ejected" from cafes and restaurants. Jews could no longer bid on government contracts or place orders for soft goods. Polish universities were expelling all Jewish students.

Tragically, Polish Jews had been made "the object of a systematic terror comparable to that in Nazi Germany."[51]

The virus of anti-Semitism was not unfortunately, confined to central and eastern Europe. *Time* reported Mussolini had published "a rousing anti-Jewish article" in his personal newspaper *Il Popolo d'Italia* in spite of the presence of "many prominent Italian Jews" in "responsible Government posts." It believed Mussolini had sought thereby to appease Hitler and also to attack the "scum Blum" of France. *The Literary Digest* returned to this subject in the same issue in which it praised France for its refugee policy. It reviewed the role many Jews had played in the Fascist movement in Italy. One of *"Il Duces's* closest friends and admirers" was the "fiery Socialist" Donna Sarfatti, "the author of his biography." Guido Jung had served as Fascist Minister of Finance and subsequently led 6,000 men in Ethiopia. Libyan Jews had contributed 1,000,000 lire to Mussolini's Ethiopian war chest and recruited troops for the "Jewish Volunteer Battalion" organized by their "47,485 brethren in peninsular Italy." Yet, Mussolini now "accused them of pushing aside other races and trampling their rights." Further, Libyan Jews were being forced to violate the Sabbath by keeping their stores open and two had been recently flogged in public. *The Literary Digest* wrote "Jews linked" the sudden outburst incident with *Il Duce's* recent close cooperation with their Nazi persecutors." Many Italian Jews "wondered if the centuries-long thread of happiness had been cut by the Nazi sword."[52]

The Literary Digest reported leaders of the American Jewish community believed anti-Semitism was also increasing in the United States due to the depression and as a result of "Nazi propaganda, fascist tendencies and the 'racial-superiority myth'." This discrimination was most obvious in business and education but was also apparent in social life. Father Coughlin and Gerald Smith were only the widest known representatives of the vulgar anti-Semitic fanatics in the United States. Anti-Semitism, *The Literary Digest* warned, was "the spear-head of the attack against democracy." Yet, if anti-Semitism was "increasing, so was also American dislike of Hitler and his Nazis."[53]

Some idea of the extent of growing anti-Nazi feeling in the United States in 1937 can be gained from American reaction to the bi-centennial celebration of Gottingen University. In 1936, fifty-three representatives attended the Heidelberg anniversary meeting. In 1937, only five attended The Gottingen celebration—and one of these was already residing in Germany. Both *The New Republic* and *The Literary Digest* attributed the change to an increasing American disdain for Nazi Germany. British and Dutch universities bluntly declined their invitations and, in effect, led a virtual boycott of the festivities by European universities. *The Nation* alleged Harvard had declined only after the Harvard Corporation had overruled its President Conant. The members of the corporation were offended by the very extension of the Nazi invitation to them. Earlier, Thomas Mann had been deprived of his honorary doctorate by Frederick-William University because he had surrendered his German citizenship. The Harvard faculty had then voted a degree to replace the one he had lost. In an open letter to the rector of Frederick-William University,

Mann contrasted the actions and accused Hitler of having destroyed the great tradition of the German universities.[54]

Some Americans, however, did find the German-American Bund seductive. *The Nation* placed its membership at the exaggerated figure of 100,000 in March, 1937, when it demanded Congress pass laws banning "uniformed organizations of any sort aiming to ferment social unrest." Ludwig Lore asserted the Bund had "more than one hundred branches and tens of thousands of members in this country." The Bund, he insisted, was directly assisted by Goebbels. Nazis were being sent to America to address the Bund while Nazi money was used to subsidize a movie chain that played only Nazi movies. Lore provided, in great detail, the names of American individuals and firms that supported the Bund. He feared the Bund, utilizing this vast assistance was a real and present danger to American institutions.[55] On July 31, Fritz Kuhn, leader of the Bund, reviewed 6,000 Bund members at Andover, New Jersey. In September, he paraded 25,000 German-American, White Russian, and Italian-American members at Camp Siegfried, the Bund's Long Island center.[56] *The New Republic* insisted the Bundists were influential all out of proportion to their size as their anti-Semitic and anti-communist propaganda struck a responsive cord among many Americans. Yet, it could not be denied the Bund was growing. *The Nation* alleged the Bund had recently decided to offer its "gangs" to American employers for use against the C.I.O. and the trade unions. Plans had been made for "Nazi intervention" on Henry Ford's behalf in Detroit by Kuhn.[57]

The Reader's Digest reported in October Kuhn had organized thirty-eight camps for the German-American Bund across the United States. In addition to the central camp on Long Island, Bundists were drilling with rifles at camps in Detroit, Chicago, Newark, Philadelphia, Houston, and Rochester. A captain of the New York 71st National Guard regiment provided rifles for one unit in New York. In 1936, 15,000 Bundist children attended a summer camp where they drilled with wooden guns, practiced the goose step, and "learned to admire Adolf Hitler." The activities of the Bund were financed by the German-American Business League which published a directory of German-American firms. The fee for a listing in the directory was pro-rated according to the firm's business volume. This income was "estimated in the millions." Kuhn even presented "a large sum" in person to Hitler in 1936. The Bund was pledged to racial purity in preparation "for the coming struggle with communism and Jews" in America.[58]

Hitler's conflict with the Catholic Church, muted for some time, erupted anew in April. Although the Hitler-Vatican Concordat of 1933 had guaranteed the church the right to continue its schools and social activities, the regime had systematically curtailed church organizations and pressured Catholic youths into the *Hitler Jugend*. A "campaign of terror" had forced many Catholic communities to close their parochial schools. Pope Pius XI replied in a Palm Sunday letter read from every Catholic pulpit that charged Hitler "had broken another treaty—the Concordat."[59] The letter stated those who had even a vestige "of love for truth" would attest the Church had kept the treaty but that the Nazi regime had repeatedly violated it. The Nazis had used "pressure, veiled and open, with intimidation, with promises of economic, professional, civil and other advantages" to attack the Church as Catholics were subjected to "violence as illegal as it is inhuman." Pius XI ended by pledging defense of the Church's "rights and liberties in the name of the Omnipotent." How the letter was smuggled into Germany and subsequently distributed was a matter of speculation but it was believed it had been first delivered to "that old warrior, Michael Cardinal von Faulhaber" of Munich.[60]

The Nazi press promptly charged Pius XI with interference in Germany's internal affairs. The SS magazine, under the banner "It Stinks to Heaven" editorialized that "conditions in church circles...from perjury to incest and sex murder...are the pestilential breath of a dying world." Some Nazis hinted Hitler might denounce the treaty openly and completely.[61] Protestants benefited from the incident, however, when Hitler, "who planned to deal with his former correligionists first," gave them permission to maintain their *status quo* indefinitely.[62]

Hitler indirectly continued the attack on the Church by meeting with General Ludendorff for two hours before granting him the title of "Der Feldherr" or "Field Lord." For some years, Ludendorff and his wife had been promoting the revival of "Germany's 'Old Gods' such as Wotan" by publishing "tracts against the Jews and especially Christians." Following the award, prominent press space was given to Ludendorff's statement "I am not only an opponent of Christianity but really anti-Christian and a heathen, and I am proud of it!" Germans would hopefully henceforth free themselves from "the teachings of Christianity" by following the example of Ludendorff.[63]

Hitler had also "long been lining up" charges that German Catholic monasteries "were hotbeds of immorality." In May, "more than 1,000 lay brothers and numerous priests" were arrested and charged with immorality. Fifty-three had already been convicted. A seminary in Thuringia was closed for sexual excesses. Chicago Archbishop Cardinal Mundelein attacked Hitler personally by stating it was difficult to understand how "a nation of 60,000,000" could "submit in fear and servitude to an alien, an Austrian paperhanger, and a poor one at that." American Catholics applauded the attack while the Vatican declared the Cardinal "had every right to speak his mind." German ambassador Dieckhoff lodged an "informal" protest with the State Department which declined to reply. The German press was whipped into "a lather of fury" against the Cardinal in particular and the Church in general. Additionally, it attacked the morality of New York City schools by alleging that under "Jew La Guardia there is wholesale bootlegging of contraceptives and unheard things." Berlin rumor was that Hitler, "somewhat alarmed" at the "Catholic batteries ranged against him," might replace the German ambassador to the Vatican with Catholic von Papen and seek peace.[64]

The rumor Hitler would make peace with the Church proved to be unfounded. Goebbels threatened publicly to "seize high members of the German Catholic clergy as hostages." He called upon the German people to "throw out" and to "lynch" erring clergy as the Nazi party had purged itself in July, 1934. Public opinion in Berlin was so aroused that clergy were told by their bishop to appear on the streets in non-clerical dress. The trials of the accused lay brothers and priests continued unabated. In Munich, groups of *Hitler Jugend* hurled stones at Catholic churches while at one church fist-fights broke out and ten priests were arrested for disturbing the peace.[65] Cardinal Faulhaber demanded the release of the priests in a letter to Kerrl, Reich Minister of Churches, which was read from every pulpit in Munich. He further demanded the arrests of priests be stopped and no further curbs be placed on sermons. The "Protestant Opposition" took heart from the Cardinal's stand. When Ribbentrop sought to "win favor with London's devout Anglicans" by seeking Episcopalian membership, the Anglican bishops referred him to "his ex-pastor" Niemoeller. Niemoeller declined to act until he was convinced Ribbentrop was prompted by religious conviction and not political considerations. The Confessional Synod warned its pastors against the regime's efforts to "de-Christianize the youth of the German nation."[66]

Adolf Wagner, Bavarian Minister of the Interior, acted "on the Fuehrer's orders" and closed every Catholic public school in Bavaria.[67] Pope Pius XI, who was gravely ill, reportedly stated a diplomatic breach with Nazi Germany could not be avoided. For his part, "delirious Jew-baiting" Streicher demanded immoral priests be beheaded. Protestants were subjected "to fresh raids, arrests, and browbeating" while Niemoeller was temporarily detained for questioning. Once again in his pulpit, he returned to his attacks on the government.[68] He was promptly arrested along with Dr. Frederick Dibelius. Dibelius was charged with accusing Kerrl, Reich Church Minister, of denying the divinity of Christ. Surprisingly, Dibelius was acquitted, perhaps to "show that the Nazi state was not interfering with matters of faith." Niemoeller's trial was postponed "following an unprecedented mass demonstration in his behalf" but he was kept in prison.[69]

Noting Niemoeller had become the most widely known "opponent of everything the rest of the world stigmatizes as Hitlerism," Paul Hutchisson attempted to place him in proper perspective. Niemoeller, he alleged, remained unrepentant for having sunk 17,000 tons of allied shipping in the war as even a casual reader of Niemoeller's *From U-Boat to Pulpit* was aware. After the war, Niemoeller led one of the three columns that moved into Berlin to suppress the Spartacist revolt and "gave every evidence of having had the time of his life while putting down reds." Niemoeller then tried farming before entering the ministry and rapidly rising to become pastor of the conservative and wealthy Dalhem congregation. Niemoeller "never disguised his scorn for the Wiemar republic" and, as "a fanatical German nationalist, voted for Hitler" and the Nazi party. Niemoeller even joined the Nazi party, seeing in it "an instrument approved by God for the revival of the German soul and as a bar to the further westward advance of a godless communism." He spoke "with almost unrestrained enthusiasm" for a regime that "protected and confirmed the alliance between the fate of the nation and the fate of the church." Theologically, Niemoeller had "a narrow, medieval faith" and gave complete allegiance to a literal interpretation of the Bible and the sixteenth century creedal statements of Luther. He therefore did not rebel against Nazi policy when it attacked

Jews and communists or remilitarized Germany. Niemoeller had applauded Hitler's "coordination" of German life and institutions until Hitler had moved to coordinate the Protestant churches under Bishop Mueller. Only then had Niemoeller moved to oppose the regime. American religious leaders, however, tended to ignore the real Niemoeller "for the sake of Niemoeller's fight against the Nazis." In point of fact, Germany could no more "go forward" with Niemoeller "than through Hitler."[70] News reports of Nazi conflict with the church ended in our magazines for 1937 with this article.

The Spanish Civil War, supposedly capped by the international naval blockade established in March, once again threatened on May 29 to ignite a general European war. On that day, loyalist bombers and the German battleship *Deutschland* exchanged attacks while the ship was refueling in the fascist-held port of Iviza in the Balearic Islands. The *Deutschland* was hit and set on fire with twenty-four dead and eighty-three wounded. As it slowly steamed toward Gibralter, Hitler cancelled all military leaves, placed the German fleet "on war basis," and dispatched additional naval units to Spain. He announced they had orders to fire on sight at loyalist aircraft and that Germany was withdrawing from the Nonintervention Committee. Five German ships, led by the battleship *Admiral Scheer*, bombarded the "fortified Red harbor" of Almeria for several hours on May 31. Mussolini declared his complete support of Hitler and ordered the Italian navy to stop and search all Russian ships in Spanish waters.[71] The Nonintervention Committee met in emergency session, France ordered its Toulon fleet to sea, and Blum hurriedly met with the British and Russian ambassadors to coordinate their actions. *The Nation* felt it was "impossible to exaggerate the danger" of a general war.[72]

For forty-eight hours, "all war scares of the past four years faded into insignificance" and the "world's stock market broke." Eden, now under the leadership of Neville Chamberlain, rushed "to the rescue."[73] He told Ribbentrop any further action might destroy the last hope of containing the war in Spain and encouraged Blum to override "the confident belligerence of the French general staff." Eden also promised Hitler and Mussolini "collective action" would be taken by the combined fleets if there were any further "incidents." A British Foreign Office "spokesman" accused the loyalists of "gross stupidity or blood malice" and insisted "Russia had always wanted to throw a spanner in the works." When Hitler stated he considered the incident closed, Chamberlain "blurted out" "Germany has not a more sincere or useful friend than Great Britain" and that "we have full understanding of Germany's great mission in the world." Mussolini thereupon announced "there will be no war." When twenty-nine Congressmen demanded an embargo on American arm shipments to Germany and Italy, Hull refused their plea. *The Nation* had predicted this would be Hull's attitude as early as January 9.[74]

A second incident on June 15 again threatened to bring on a general war. Hitler alleged the German cruiser *Leipzig*, steaming off Oran, had detected torpedoes fired at it. It was subsequently side-swiped by an unknown submarine. Hitler demanded an international reprisal against loyalist Valencia and canceled a visit of von Neurath to London. Failing an international reprisal, he threatened to unilaterally bombard the city. *Time* remarked Hitler "had one of his better tantrums" and "put the fear of Wotan" into British statesmen. George VI had Eden report constantly and personally to him on the situation.[75] Chamberlain thereupon "busied himself to caress the short hairs of the Prussian neck" and "pour oil on the water." He praised Hitler's "restraint" and promised closer supervision of the war. Eden stated "the Fascist powers are not the only offenders in Spain" and criticized Russian aid to the loyalists. He also met with the Italian, German, and French ambassadors to defuse the situation. *Newsweek* felt, failing their agreement, "the Four Horsemen of the Apocalypse might well ride out again over Europe." Eden insisted Britain's policy was "peace at almost any price." With that attitude, *Time* believed he might get it.[76]

Time suggested Britain was seeking to appease Hitler, Mussolini, and Franco because of its need for Basque iron ore held by the fascists and because of the Moscow treason trials that had weakened Russia.[77] Following this incident, the Spanish conflict settled again into a routine of attacks and counterattacks. For a period it ceased to be the major diplomatic problem. There remained, however, a plethora of other issues and problems that threatened to erupt into open conflict.

There was, for example, the threat of renewed Arab-Jewish-British warfare in Palestine. It had only been after Britain had moved in 17,000 troops, several air squadrons, and stationed a large naval force off Palestine that the Arab-Jewish clashes of 1936 had been suppressed. As part of its pacification campaign, London established a commission headed by Earl Peel to recommend a permanent solution for Palestine. The commission's report was awaited anxiously as it was feared the growing animosity of Arabs, fanned by Nazi propaganda, would produce a new explosion of violence.[78]

The Literary Digest attributed "the recent recrudescence of Pan-Arabism," with its attendant anti-Semitic violence, to Italy's anti-British radio campaign during the Ethiopian war and to the "no less virulent" work "of Nazi agents" who fermented "discontent in the Near East and North African lands." In Algeria, in particular, there was a "distinct Moslem weakness for Hitler, for his having crushingly trodden on the Jew." It was not uncommon to "come upon the swastika painted on the walls of farmhouses." It found all the more surprising then, the recent decree of Hikmet Bey Suleiman, ruler of Iraq, that Christians, Moslems, and Jews be regarded as equals. Suleiman was attempting to develop an alternative Pan-Arab policy on the Turkish model that would treat all minorities in Arab lands as equals to the Moslem majority.[79]

In May, 1937, Peel delivered his 400 page report to Whitehall. Its release was held up for two months due to the coronation of George VI but, in July, 1937, it was finally made public. The Peel report recommended the partition of Palestine as the national aspirations of the Arabs and Jews were irreconcilable. The proposed Jewish state was to consist of 2,500 square miles along the sea from the Syrian border to twenty miles below Jaffa. Arabs were to receive 7,500 square miles, including the Dead Sea and the Jordan Valley, and be joined to a Trans-Jordan kingdom under the rule of Emir Adullah. To totally evacuate the 225,000 Moslems from the proposed Jewish state, Jews were to contribute to a $10,000,000 British grant to the Arabs. Britain was to retain a belt of territory running from Jaffa to Jerusalem and including Bethlehem.[80]

Newsweek commented the proposed partition revealed Britain had decided "might makes right" and had "unsheathed a bayonet" to "cut the Gordian knot of the Palestine problem." *Time* pointed out that not only Parliament, but also the League of Nations and the United States had to approve the proposal before it could go into effect. The United States was involved because of nineteenth century treaty rights recognized by the League. *Time* predicted it would take at least "two years of negotiation and adjustment" to put the proposal into practice. *The New Republic* took the position that the partition was both impossible and improbable given the state of Arab-Jewish relations.[81]

Anticipating the report would precipitate renewed rioting, Britain moved its battleships *Hood* and *Repulse* to Haifa. It also announced Sir Arthur Wauchope would be replaced as High Commissioner by Sir John Anderson, "the efficiently ruthless sahib" renowned for his suppression of terrorism while Governor of Bengal. Eden again requested Mussolini to prevent the Bari radio from discussing the partition plan and inciting the Arabs.[82]

Philip S. Bernstein argued in *The Nation* that Britain should support the Zionist movement as it was "indispensable to the welfare of European Jewry and of the Arabs of Palestine." According to Bernstein, the Jews of Rumania and Poland were sitting "in the midst of their desolation...without hope" while "the Jews in Germany are doomed." Emigration to democratic states was closed by economic conditions and "intensified nationalism." Hitler had created a situation in which Zionism was the only answer for the Jews of Europe. It was, also, the only possible solution for the economic improvement of Palestinian Arabs. Britain, he hoped, would be convinced its proper course would be to honor the Balfour Declaration.[83]

The Nation, although it printed Bernstein's article, profoundly disagreed with him. Palestine's problems were insolvable by Zionists and, "in fact, not likely to be solved at all." The problems were "basically insolvable." Arabs obviously intended to resist "literally to the death" any Jewish domination of Palestine. Similarly, the Jews were determined "to stay in Palestine." For Britain to withdraw was a "hopeless suggestion" as Jews and Arab would immediately be at one another's throats. Zionists, therefore, "must be content with less than most of them want, less than the Jewish masses of Europe need." The best that could be expected of Britain was "enlightened muddling."[84]

Reaction to the proposal was mixed in all quarters. Emir Adullah of Trans-Jordan was pleased as the suggested partition would greatly expand his authority and revenues. The Grand Mufti Husseini of Jerusalem appealed for armed resistance to the proposal by all Arabs and vowed a fight to the death. Ibn Saud of Arabia declined any comment on the plan.[85] Some Zionists opposed the partition as they hoped to settle all of Palestine. Herbert Solow, writing in *The Nation*, asserted the plan placed Zionism "in extremis" as it meant the sun would set on Palestine "without setting on the British Empire" and would place European Jews in a hopeless position. Hitler, who encouraged Zionists and Arabs alike, was likely to be the only one to benefit from the situation. Certainly Zionism would undergo "the most extensive surgical operation in its rich clinical experience." Solow predicted Arabs would never abandon hope of "the liquidation" of any Jewish national homeland.[86] Rabbi Stephen Wise agreed, accusing Britain of betraying a sacred trust. He insisted Palestine must be organized to "absorb 200,000 Fascist-baited Jews by 1940." Wise believed American Jews could raise $175,000,000 to support these anticipated settlers. Interestingly, the Nazi press approved the proposal, claiming it was worthy of Solomon.[87]

Not all Jews believed Palestine was the answer to Jewish efforts to find a refuge. Pierre Crabites, writing in the July issue of *The Atlantic Monthly*, asserted there was a tremendous "Storm Rising in Palestine." American Jews, he insisted, were "entirely unconscious of the martyrdom that is awaiting their brethren in Palestine," and, in short, were "living in a fool's paradise." They believed an improvement in the economy of Palestine, including higher wages for Arabs, would eventually bring peace to the area. What they failed to understand was the frustrated nationalism and deeply religious devotion to Jerusalem of the average Arab, Moslem or Christian. The Arab saw Britain, correctly or incorrectly, as the great betrayer of Arab aspirations ironically encouraged in the Great War by Britain. Repeatedly Crabites stressed a bloody struggle between the Arab and the Jew was inevitable. Arab knives were "sharpened to cut Jewish throats," Arab guns would be used "to snipe every Jew they can," Moslems were "determined to kill every Jew who crosses their path," and they were "itching to shoot down every Jew." Crabites could foresee no answer to the problem as eventually Britain would withdraw and the real struggle would begin. He concluded the problem was heightened because "Hitler is driving Jews out of Germany" and they were "being brought into Palestine surreptitiously.[88]

However, when the World Zionist Congress met in Zurich in August, Dr. Chaim Weizmann argued for the British proposal as it was better than nothing. The Congress, after bitter debate, approved the partition plan by a vote of 300 to 158. H.N. Brailsford, writing in *The New Republic*, believed the Zionist vote meaningless as the Arabs would never agree to partition. He noted Winston Churchill had attempted to keep Commons from accepting the proposal as it not only was a "confession of defeat" but was "too little, too late." To coerce the Arabs into the partition would be difficult, particularly since Syria and Iraq had just been granted independence. To make further concessions to the Arabs was impossible as they were dedicated to the destruction of any Jewish homeland in Palestine.[89]

It is best to take the tragic story to its conclusion in 1937 at this point. By October, Palestinian Moslems were primed to revolt. The British army, aiming "to nip the movement," arrested "300 or more troublemakers" and exiled some to the Seychelles Islands. Grand Mufti Husseini took refuge in the Mosque of Omar and gave the signal to his "henchmen" for revolt.[90] Terrorism thereupon "burst afresh throughout the land." Snipers fired on British barracks, trains were sabotaged with explosives, Jewish settlements were attacked, and bombs were exploded in Jerusalem. The British Commissioner for Galilee, Andrews, was assassinated. Although the remaining members of the Arab High Committee were arrested, the terror continued while Husseini escaped to Syria.[91]

With Husseini gone, local direction of the revolt passed to Fawzi Bey. Under his leadership, Arabs ambushed British units, "wrecked the Near East's largest airdrome," bombed bridges, cut telephone lines, and cut the Mosul oil pipe line. In Jerusalem, his followers sniped at "soldiers, Jews, and policemen." In November, *Newsweek* reported terrorism had "cut a bloody swath through the Mohammedan crescent of North Africa and the Near East" as the revolt spread. Legionnaires had to use machine-guns to protect the city of Fez in French Morocco while Ibn Saud warned Emir Abdullah of Trans-Jordan against concessions to the British. More than 100 Jews and Arabs had been killed in battles in Palestine. Jews cooperated with, and enlisted in, the British army to suppress the terrorism.[92] The British army, hard put to put an end to the terrorism, hanged a prominent Arab leader, Faran al Sadi, for the possession of arms. The hanging, however, only served to escalate the level of Arab terrorism. Philip S. Bernstein ended reports on Palestine by our magazines for the year 1937 by asserting the violence had become a pogrom and that partition was the only hope for Palestine. Hitler's propaganda, he wrote, lay behind the Arab revolt as it had intensified Arab nationalism and anti-Semitism while, at the same time, driving Zionists to ever more desperate efforts to find a refuge.[93]

The desperate search for refuge was intensifying among Jews all over the world. Here, in America, *The New Republic* continued its campaign to open the United States as a haven for Jews. In November, it pointed with respect and pride to the distinguished refugees who had entered the United States. Mentioning dozens by name and attainment, it pleaded for help for those who had fled due to their conflict "with the fanatics and gangsters" in control of Germany. These refugees had "contributed notably to the advancement of our civilization" but, even more importantly, indicated "great promise that stretches forward through the years." For their very presence, "we owe a debt of gratitude to the Fuehrer." The tragedy was that, for others, "European immigration to the United States stopped more than a decade ago." This policy, it pleaded, had to be revised.[94]

In December, *The New Republic* argued the condition of Jews across Europe was an affront to civilization. Indeed, the future of civilization was tied to the future of the Jews as the decline of sanity and humanness in Europe was proportional to the rise of anti-Semitism. In Poland, the ghetto had reappeared. In Rumania, the "Jewish Question" had become "the one paramount issue in national elections." In Latvia, "the exclusion and elimination of Jews" was daily growing. In Hungary and Yugoslavia, anti-Semitism had become government policy. In the Balkans as a whole, only in Greece were the Jews "strongly defended by public men and sections of the press." The Jews, with a courage that had "much of fatalism and something of profound faith," were standing their ground wherever possible. There was no doubt the "Hitler disease" was spreading. The "Nazi International" fanned anti-Semitism as a means of penetration for Nazi propaganda. "Christian Civilization" was bound indissolubly to the fate of European Jews. It ended with a plea the American government take some action to assist European Jews.[95]

Domestically, the middle of 1937 saw the United States plagued by labor strife at a moment when the New Deal had seemingly run its course and the depression was returning. Roosevelt's efforts to alter the Supreme Court had created dissention in the Democratic party, particularly among senators. There were already hints of a presidential purge in the elections of 1938. The passage of a neutrality bill to replace the temporary bill of August, 1936, was increasing the level and volume of debate over American foreign policy. There were administration hints the United States should rearm. The great fear was not that the United States would be attacked, but that it might be drawn into a European war because of economic factors.

Ernest K. Lindley noted eight billion dollars had been invested in the United States between 1933 and 1936. Over half of this investment had come from France, Britain, and commonwealth nations of the British empire. Lindley argued this investment was "a potential chest." In the event of war in Europe, it would be "withdrawn in the form of American raw materials and manufactured products." This had drawn America into war in 1917 or "at least," created economic conditions which made "it extremely difficult for us to remain aloof." To avoid being drawn into the conflict by these investments again, he urged enactment of legislation that would "sterilize" this investment by requiring it be withdrawn in gold rather than war materials. Such legislation would support the present determination of the American people "to have no part in any war abroad." War profits, or the prospect of them, could not be allowed to drag Americans into the European mire of constant conflict.[96]

Henry Cabot Lodge, Jr., then senator from Massachusetts, argued the neutrality laws just enacted did not go far enough to prevent American involvement in a European war. Congress should be given a primary role in any decision to embargo goods to a belligerent or to implement a "cash and carry policy." Further, the defenses of the United States should be strengthened and American economic independence guaranteed. Only such action would meet the "desire" of the American people "to stay at peace in a war-torn world."[97]

Internationally, diplomatic coverage centered on Anglo-French efforts to secure the withdrawal of Italy from the Spanish Civil War—a war in which Germany increasingly played a minor role. In July, renewed skirmishes between Japanese and Russian forces along the Amur River threatened to break into a major war. By the middle of the month, Japan initiated a new assault on China, long a special interest of the American people in Asia. The Chinese War attracted a large and continuous amount of coverage thereafter. Americans were moved about the war in a way they did not feel for Europe. For example, when Roosevelt made his Chicago Quarantine Speech in October, *Newsweek* asserted Japan was the object of his remarks. In that same month, *Time* initiated periodic reports in special small boxes on the amount of Chinese territory conquered by the Japanese.[98] Japanese-American relations continued to deteriorate in 1937, particularly after the bombing and rape of Nanking, and the sinking of the American gunboat *Panay* at the end of the year. The coverage of Europe was proportionally reduced. What material there was, was often disparate and disjointed. The focus was Britain's efforts at appeasement and not Hitler or Nazi Germany.

Collier's, for example, ran only three articles, essentially biographical and anecdotal, on Germany during all of 1937. All by the same author, T.R. Ybarra, they rehashed old material and offered the reader no new insights. One, devoted to Goering, described his apparent joviality, fondness for lion cubs, and interest in uniforms. His role in the Nazi economy and his anti-Semitism were only briefly mentioned. A second depicted Udet, the Air Minister, as a flying ace interested in encouraging Germany boys to build model planes and enroll in glider clubs. The article "Hitler on High" described, from second-hand sources, Hitler's home and life at Brechtesgaden.[99]

There was, in some of our magazines, speculation about Hitler's future plans and ambitions. These speculations centered on a Nazi move against either Austria or Czechoslovakia. Renewed fears about Austria were fueled when Mussolini met with Schuschnigg in Rome as early as April. Mussolini reportedly told Schuschnigg Italy would not fight to preserve Austria "even if the Nazis invaded it."[100] He also cautioned Schuschnigg against making an alliance with Czechoslovakia. Rather, he counseled Schuschnigg to reach an agreement with Hitler and admit a Nazi to the Austrian cabinet. Schuschnigg not only rejected this advice but, on his return to Vienna, ordered the arrest of twenty prominent Nazis.

Schuschnigg's visit to Mussolini was quickly followed by one from Goering. Rumors circulated Mussolini had promised to support "eventual Nazi domination in Austria." Goering supposedly pledged to help Italy achieve economic independence.[101] *Time* commented it looked as though "an egg of unusual size were being hatched in the fascist incubator."[102] These rumors were reinforced by subsequent visits of von Neurath and Blomberg to Rome and by Mussolini's announcement that Italy's annual maneuvers would not be held as usual on the Austrian border, but in Sicily.

A move by Hitler against Czechoslovakia was considered an alternative possibility. In April, Henry Wolfe noted in *The New Republic* that Hitler was "waging an increasingly violent campaign" against Prague. Nazi papers charged Benes was creating a base in Prague "for Comintern activities," building airfields for Russian planes, and integrating Russian officers into the Czech army. These charges had been picked up and repeated by J.L. Garvin in his *London Observer*. Wolfe asserted, after a private interview with Benes, that Prague feared Britain would be "unwilling" to "involve the Empire in war to defend a cause in central Europe." France, Benes thought, would not make any major international move without British support. Wolfe therefore believed "to stop a Nazi *Putsch* in Bohemia, once it is under way, will be almost impossible." On May 1, *Newsweek* described Czechoslovakia as "the country which at present most fears a German invasion."[103]

George Slocombe had no doubt Czechoslovakia would be "Europe's Next Battleground." Not only was Hitler firmly committed to the traditional German policy of *Drang mach Osten*, but he also needed to seize the Moravian Gap to link up with Hungary and capture the Rumanian oilfields. Only Rumanian oil could provide him with the means to someday attack Russia. If forced to defend itself, Czechoslovakia had to receive aid from France and Russia within two weeks to survive. While France remained publicly committed to its pact with Prague, in actuality its policy in the event would certainly be determined by Britain. As British policy remained in doubt, the "fate of Czechoslovakia remains in doubt."[104]

Robert Dell argued the real "struggle for Czecho-Slovakia" was internal— the Czech government had to knit its "mixture of races" and their economic inequalities into a viable nation. If the efforts were successful there was hope Czechoslovakia could survive with the assistance of Britain, France, and Russia. Yet, if the effort failed, no amount of foreign support could maintain the integrity of the nation. Dell ended by writing the issue remained in doubt as he went to press.[105]

Elmer Davis agreed with Dell that Czechoslovakia was facing a difficult time due to its racial mix and economic problems. However, Davis was optimistic Prague would be able to weld the nation together. The *Sudetenland* Germans were, as a result of Nazi propaganda, the most dissatisfied. However, the government was moving to alleviate their grievances by reducing German unemployment, awarding them government contracts, and providing greater relief funds for German areas. Politically, Prague had agreed to allow the use of the German language in the government offices and courts of the *Sudetenland*.

Davis, however, believed the basic problem of Czechoslovakia was the attitude of Britain. There was no doubt Hitler wanted to either dominate or annex Czechoslovakia. Russia was physically separated from Prague and undergoing severe internal strains. Italy did not extend its interest in Austria to Czechoslovakia. France was allowing itself to be guided by Britain. The question was thus, what would Britain do? Undoubtedly, some British leaders would like to reach "agreement with Germany by sacrificing Czechoslovakia." They felt "if you could thus bribe the Germans to let western Europe alone (which is highly doubtful) it would be cheap at the price." As "a last resort," the Czechs might prefer to "become Germany's bridge to the southeast" if they found Britain unwilling to support them. Britain had only a year or two to decide whether Czechoslovakia would be a "bridge or a barricade" to Nazi ambitions. At the end of that time, Hitler would be ready to march.[106]

Willson Woodside was much more optimistic. He believed Hitler had missed his great opportunity by failing to march into *"mittel-Europe"* in 1936. With his delay, accompanied by threatening noises, Hitler had provided time for Britain, France, and Poland to pull together. Now, time was against him. In the east stood the Russian army, the largest and strongest in Europe and one growing stronger by the month. Hitler therefore needed, if he were to move east, "a hard-and-fast alliance with Italy and a secure rear" in the west. The key to the situation was Britain. British public opinion, formerly pro-German, was steadily being alienated by the Nazi attacks on churches, Hitler's involvement in Spain, and his "forcing on Britain of a vast armaments program." With Britain leading France in arming to the teeth, "the chance for a successful stroke in the west seems to have eluded Germany." Woodside concluded, therefore, the odds against a successful German attack were "lengthening month by month" as Britain mobilized Europe.[107]

Newsweek agreed Britain held the Key to Europe's future and asserted the key to future British policy was held by Robert Vansittart. Vansittart, an "autocrat of the secret service," was a diplomatic "genius" for whom "Britain's business and political leaders could be thankful." He had prevented the Bolshevist control of Spain's "iron, tin, copper, and mercury." At the same time, he had also prevented the acquisition by Italy or Germany of Spanish military and naval bases. If Hitler's intention was to neutralize Holland and Belgium and to enclose the remaining French frontiers with fascist bases, he had been stymied. Vansittart had arranged matters so that Germany had withdrawn from Spain to preserve its resources while Italy was allowed "to wear itself out supporting the wavering white cause." Vansittart had demonstrated, while keeping Britain out of war, the British intention to defend "its natural interests in the Mediterranean." Either by "implication, if not actually by a secret agreement," Vansittart had placated Hitler with a free hand in the east whenever Germany was ready to move. Yet, if the Germans did move, Vansittart had arranged things so "it will be a long time before they can become a danger to the Empire."[108] Chamberlain, who had replaced Baldwin as Prime Minister in June, was thought to be in complete agreement with Vansittart and Baldwin's policy.

The Nation also attributed to Vansittart the crafting of the British policy of appeasement. It asserted he believed, however regretfully, in "the necessity of leaving Hitler a free hand in Central and Eastern Europe." This attitude he shared with many in the House of Lords, the City, and "the English ruling classes generally." Vansittart had convinced Chamberlain Britain should not fight except for its empire, certainly not for any country east of the Rhine. It followed France must be urged to adopt the same policy. Hitler could be allowed to become a continental power, even a dominant power, but he must never be allowed "to become a world power." By the time Hitler "made himself master of the Continent east of the Rhine," Britain would be so strong it could arrange its relations with Germany "on its own terms." A final aspect of Vansittart's policy was "hostility to Soviet Russia." This "above all" had "rallied" the English ruling classes to the idea of an understanding with Germany.[109]

Anglo-German relations momentarily took a turn for the worst in August. Whitehall expelled three German journalists for intimidating Germans who lived in England into promoting Nazism and attacking Jews. Goebbels retaliated by expelling Norman Ebbut of *The London Times*. Both Ebbut and *The Times* had maintained "a pro-Nazi policy" while "Ebbut's reporting" had "given Adolf Hitler all the breaks."[110] When von Neurath proposed the journalist's replacement by three "cultural attaches," both Whitehall and *The Times* vehemently rejected the idea. *The Times* demanded Ebbut be allowed to remain in Germany. Failing such permission, it asserted his post would be left vacant. *The Times* accused the Nazis of the lack of "civilized courtesies" and altered its former pro-German policy. The British public was expected to follow suit and become anti-Nazi.[111]

An incident arising out of the Spanish Civil War again threatened the peace of Europe in September. Numbers of British, French, and Russian merchant ships had been torpedoed and two British destroyers attacked. Although the fiction was that the submarines belonged to Franco, it was an open secret they were Italian. Russia threatened war unless the attacks were stopped. Euphemistically describing the submarines as "pirates," Vansittart and Eden quickly had the "piracy" condemned by an international conference at Noyon and established a line of British and French naval ships to suppress the submarine attacks.[112] The crisis quickly passed when Mussolini realized the determination of Britain and France to fire on the "pirates." Not a single "mystery" submarine attack was reported during the following month. The agreement, however, did nothing to dispel the fear of war.

Sir Arthur Willert insisted the outlook for Europe in September was "as uncertain as ever." The political situation was "fundamentally rotten" with international trade down, the arms race up, and international strains increasing. There was an "ominous return of the pre-war alignment of the great nations," the "continual discomfiture" of Britain and France by Hitler and Mussolini and "the defeat of those" in the British cabinet who wanted "a collective system of security for Europe." Chamberlain, believing British public opinion would not support a strong British commitment in eastern Europe, remained wedded to an "empire and western Europe only" policy. Eden believed being ground between "the millstones of Fascism and Communism" represented a greater danger to Britain and France than the "power politics" of the dictators. Hence, he was seeking to keep the peace until Britain rearmed and the situation clarified itself. The only bright spot was that the German army leadership was opposed to war and was still thought to be very influential.[113]

It was thought Hitler might provide some indication of his plans at the annual Nazi party meeting. Yet, the 1937 Nazi Party Congress at Nuremburg in September produced no major drama or significant news either by Hitler or his henchmen. Correspondents were reduced to dispatches detailing its theatrical aspects and the amount of food consumed in the thirteen tent cities set up to house the million Nazis assembled for the occasion. The major news out of Germany focused on the state visit of Mussolini to meet with Hitler. *Time* and *Newsweek* asserted Mussolini was anxious for the meeting as he and Franco were locked in desperate conflict with the Spanish loyalists. With no end in sight in Spain, Franco was pleading he needed more Italian troops and poison gas if victory was to be won.[114] However, France was threatening to open the Pyrenees and pour unlimited aid through to the red cause if Mussolini landed any more troops or munitions in Spain. Mussolini had to either secure Hitler's support or reach a bargain with Chamberlain. The price for Hitler's support was a free hand for Germany in Austria. The price for Chamberlain's support was the abrogation of the Rome-Berlin axis. As there was little hard information coming out of the meeting, news reports were padded out with details of the pomp and circumstance attendant to the meeting.[115]

Immediate reports did little to clarify the reason for the meeting or its outcome. *Newsweek* commented there was little foreign interest in the meeting for "shrewd diplomats guessed there was nothing to announce." *Time* interpreted the meeting to mean "Hitler and Mussolini had now linked themselves" and were obviously "bidding jointly" for "close and peaceful relations with Britain and France" while excluding Russia and a leftist Spain from Europe's future. The "whole show was a $1,000,000 Fascist way" of telling the western democracies "You agree to our joining up with you—OR ELSE!"[116] The actual result was the adherence of Italy on November 6 to the anti-communist pact between Germany and Japan which "dramatically transformed the Rome-Berlin axis into a written alliance." Mussolini also "granted the Fuehrer his coveted free hand in Central Europe." *The New Republic* asserted Mussolini and Hitler were untrustworthy and would have no qualms about betraying anyone—including one another.[117] As for Britain, it was likewise untrustworthy as it would gladly sacrifice Russia if it could only secure "a firm basis of peace in Western Europe."[118]

As a result of this meeting, Emil Ludwig drew contrasting portraits of Hitler and Mussolini. Mussolini undoubtedly came off best. Hitler was described as a youthful "idler" who finally gained power "by his one genuine gift—that of oratory." His speeches were punctuated with egoism and hysteria. Hitler acted like "the strong man because of his inherent weakness" and neuroticisms. He desired war, not for colonies or the Ukraine, but simply for power—if war came, it would be "Hitler's war." Mussolini, by contrast, had worked hard all his life and had a self-confidence totally lacking in Hitler. Mussolini was "a man in every respect," who worked hard and played hard. He was cultured, learned from visitors, and was superior to the officials in his government. Mussolini planned no European war but, as a "realistic and cynical" Italian diplomat, would "wait and go with the winner." If anyone drew profit out of the next war, it would be Mussolini.[119]

The visit of Mussolini to Berlin was followed by that of the Duke and Duchess of Windsor. The obstensible purpose of the visit was for the Duke to review housing conditions in Germany. If there were any serious discussions, these went unmentioned. The Windsors were scheduled next to visit the United States. It was later reported Hitler spent only twenty minutes with the Windsors.[120]

In October, there were continuing reports Chamberlain was "engineering a deal" with Hitler about eastern Europe over the objections of Eden. In return, Chamberlain expected an agreement that would "leave Britain free to control Mussolini by force or bribery." Hitler seemed to respond positively to Chamberlain when, in October, he sent a surprise note to Belgium promising to respect Belgium neutrality if ever war did erupt. By this note, he reassured Britain, which was fearful of Belgium falling into hostile hands. Hitler also put out feelers for a four-power pact to include Britain, France, Italy, and Germany. As "additional bait for London," Hitler intimated he might desert Mussolini and support British policy in Spain, provided, of course, he received colonies.[121] *The New Republic* believed it was common knowledge Britain would gladly strike an agreement with Hitler if only he could be trusted. The problem for Whitehall was to decide if an Anglo-German accord would indeed be honored. Clearly, the "second world war" had begun with fascists acting as the aggressors. Yet, the British cabinet temporized as the British ruling class was still divided about the Nazis as some believed in Hitler's anti-bolshevik crusade. These same ideas were repeated by H.N. Brailsford later in October.[122]

At the beginning of November, *Newsweek* wrote British policy toward Germany remained "conciliatory" and Chamberlain "seemed on the point of throwing meat to the wolves." Rumor was that he was considering recognition of the Italian conquest of Ethiopia, a loan to Mussolini, and the granting of trading rights in Spain to Italy. For Germany, there would be colonial concessions, a new loan, and "support in Central Europe." Henry C. Wolfe predicted the same week that Hitler was becoming impatient and would not long delay beginning his march to the east. He hoped for an accord with Britain and would work to secure it but, with or without an agreement, he was determined to act. Wolfe thought the growing demands and agitation by the *Sudetenland* Nazis indicated Czechoslovakia was therefore "the first objective of the Nazi *Drang Nach Osten.*"[123]

There was little surprise then, when Chamberlain, ignoring Eden and Paris, announced the despatch of "pro-Nazi" Lord Halifax to Berchtesgaden to confer with Hitler. Eden had not been consulted about the visit and threatened to resign but was dissuaded from doing so by Chamberlain. Nevertheless, Eden remained at home with "a chill" and had his family newspaper, *The Yorkshire Post*, attack the meeting as a possible sell-out to Hitler. According to *The Yorkshire Post*, "a certain number of people," including Halifax, were "prepared to welcome" German expansion into Austria, Czechoslovakia, and Russia in return for a pledge to drop any German demand for colonies.[124] *Newsweek* asserted Halifax was to tell Hitler that should Germany make any move "short of actual war" against Austria, Britain would prevent France, and thereby Czechoslovakia and Russia, "from taking action." In the House of Lords, *Time* reported, "prominent Jewish and Labor peers surprisingly outdid themselves in speeches calculated to dispose Adolf Hitler favorably" toward Halifax. Viscount Samuel, "one of Britain's top Jews," urged Germany be cleared of "war guilt" for 1914, that its former colonies be returned, and the Treaty of Versailles be detached from the League. He was seconded by the Laborite Lord Allen, the Liberal Lord Crewe, and the Conservative Lord Plymouth.[125] Lord Cecil, the winner of the 1937 Nobel Peace Prize for his work with the League and known for his "weakness for the Nazis," issued a statement from the New York home of Morgan partner Thomas W. Lamont in support of the Halifax visit.[126]

The New Republic castigated "the pro-German school of thought" in Britain that included Lord Halifax, Lord Lothian, Sir John Simon, Sir Samuel Hoare, Sir Kingsley Wood, and Sir Montagu Norman of the City. Major leadership for this group came from the Astors and their family papers, *The London Times* and *The Sunday Observer*. They believed if Germany were given central Europe, it "would have before her an open road to the Soviet Ukraine" and would cease to vex Europe. *The Sunday Observer* argued that, since Britain would never fight for Austria or Czechoslovakia, it should go ahead and give "positive assent" to German action and receive the advantages this would bring London. *The Times* suggested "the consideration" of German political and economic claims in Europe. Britain, after all, had its empire. *The New Republic* believed, in the end, the "pro-German" clique would not "explicitly" give Hitler "a free hand"—but neither would it oppose any move he made. It reiterated its earlier prediction that, given this British attitude, Hitler was "sure to push ahead toward, as a minimum, the annexation of Austria and the German-speaking part of Czechoslovakia."[127]

Reports on Halifax's conversations quickly surfaced. They asserted Hitler had demanded Britain remain quiet if he annexed Austria by removing or reaching a bargain with Schuschnigg. He further wanted autonomy on the Swiss model for Czechoslovakia's *Sudetenland* Germans. Halifax and the cabinet were shocked by the demands but Chamberlain did agree to invite French Premier Chautemps and Foreign Minister Delbos to London to consider the demands. *The Nation* predicted there would be "no immediate agreement" between London and Berlin but, as the appeasers were continuing to gain ground in Britain, the attempt would be made to meet his demands as it was "cheaper to buy him off than fight a major war." Anglo-French policy would gradually be oriented to an accommodation with Hitler that would allow him the *Sudetenland. The Nation* subsequently wrote that appeasement was a popular policy in Britain and was opposed only by elements in the Labor and Liberal parties. The appeasement "clique," if it could not persuade France to accept its lead, could be expected to work "for a program that would leave France wholly isolated."[128] France reportedly disagreed with British policy, but felt it could not allow itself to be estranged from Britain.

The Saturday Evening Post attributed the subordination of French foreign policy to that of Whitehall to the decline of the French economy. The franc had "gone through crisis after crisis" and had "been nearly wiped out" as it dropped from "18.4 cents" on the dollar in 1918 to "below 4 cents" in 1937. Reparations, designed at Versailles to keep Germany weak and to rebuild the destruction of World War I, had proved to be uncollectable by Poincare, then suspended by Hoover, and, finally, repudiated by Hitler. France rebuilt itself with its own funds. When successive premiers were unwilling or unable to reduce the interest paid to bondholders, to reduce the bloated bureaucracy, or to properly collect taxes, the franc was destroyed. Any premier who threatened the *status quo* was repudiated "on flimsy pretexts" by the numerous special interest parties in the Chamber of Deputies. France could, therefore, only "stagger from crisis to crisis" in its foreign policy. Paris had ended by becoming dependent on London which, in effect, became the arbiter of French foreign policy. It could be anticipated this situation would continue into the forseeable future.[129]

Delbos visited Rumania, Poland, Yugoslavia, and Czechoslovakia at the end of the year in an effort to reinforce their ties to France. He found all of them, except Czechoslovakia, wavering in their determination to resist Hitler.

In Prague, he reputedly informed Benes that Chamberlain's strategy was to allow Germany to annex Austria. This would precipitate an economic rivalry between Italy and Germany for central Europe and ultimately destroy the Rome-Berlin Axis. This was all the more likely as Schacht had been ousted from his post as Minister of Economic by Goering. Goering, it was believed, was less likely to be able to keep the Nazi economy on a smooth course.[130] Britain would then be able to play the dictators off against one another. Benes informed Delbos Prague stood by its French alliance and was constructing a railway line across a small strip of Rumania that could provide access to Czechoslovakia for the Russian army. Benes, according to the reports, was determined to resist Hitler. While Delbos was making his rounds, Mussolini announced Italy's withdrawal from the League.[131] On this note, the stresses and strains of 1937 ended.

1937 had opened with the general expectation of a "Hitler surprise" including the possibility of a general European war. Although no such major surprise had materialized in 1937, it was realized Hitler had not exhausted his ambitions and that 1938 would be a crucial year for Europe. Hitler and Mussolini had tightened their bond while Chamberlain had defined his policy of appeasement and drawn France into acceptance of that policy. It was generally anticipated Hitler would take advantage of the "permission" given him by Chamberlain and would annex Austria at the earliest opportunity and go on to pressure Czechoslovakia for the return of the *Sudetenland*. In the minds of many Europeans then, the real question was not whether Hitler would reach across the borders of the Third Reich but whether his ambitions could be met without war.

Chapter V

Drang Nach Osten, 1938

The initial issue of *Newsweek* for 1938 carried a number of articles that presaged the types of reports on anti-Semitism and Hitler that would appear in our magazines in the next weeks and months. Anti-Semitism inspired by the Nazi regime increased where it already existed and appeared in several new areas. In that first issue of 1938, for example, *Newsweek* reported Arab attacks on Jews and British troops had led to a pitched battle after 400 Arabs ambushed a British patrol in Galilee. Forty-three Arabs were killed in the "worst battle in Palestine since the World War." *Time* noted on January 17 that this battle had produced a lull in the Palestinian conflict. Britain, however, reacted by announcing the "partition plan would not be forced through and might even be abandoned." A "technical commission" was sent to Palestine with authority to "alter the scheme in any way it sees fit."[1]

Nazi-inspired anti-Semitism also appeared in Rumania when King Carol dismissed Premier Tatarescu and replaced him with "violently anti-Semitic and pro-Nazi" Octavian Goga.[2] Many Jews, including the King's Jewish mistress, Magda Lupescu, immediately "fled the country." Goga announced he wanted to evict "more than 500,000 Jews" out of Rumania's 1,000,000 Jewish population. King Carol asserted "250,000 Galician and Russian Jews," who were not "a good element," had to be expelled so the remaining Jews could "be saved." It was immediately made an offense for Jews to employ "non-Jewish female servants under 40 years of age" and Jewish newspapers were suppressed.[3] Health insurance companies were told to discharge Jewish doctors on their boards, Jews were forbidden to sell salt, gasoline, and liquors, and industrial firms were told their employees had to be ninety percent Gentile. All Jews, who had entered Rumania after 1918, lost their right to vote even if naturalized. Subsequently, Jews were forbidden to speak Yiddish, prepare kosher meat, or marry Gentiles. Jewish lawyers were beaten out of a Budapest courtroom and the National Theater announced "a gala production" of the anti-Semitic play, "The Village Bloodsucker." Goga officially asked the League "to see that 500,000 (Jews) be removed." He also stated he wanted a treaty of friendship with Germany.[5] Minister Alexander Cuza officially announced "it is for the world to find a residence for the world's Jews! Madagascar seems a suitable place!" In a one sentence note, *The Nation* reported Nazi subsidized propaganda had succeeded "in driving the last Jewish representative out of the parliament at Belgrade."[6]

Governmental anti-Semitism appeared in South America when President Enriquez of Ecuador decreed all Jewish aliens who were not farmers had to begin farming or leave Ecuador within thirty days. In Mexico City, merchants requested the government to ban Jews from certain types of business.[7]

Not to be outdone, Hitler announced that by September 1, German Jews had to "sell or liquidate their businesses and retire from all corporations." Arnold Bernstein, whose trial for alleged currency violations had finally ended, was sentenced to two and a half years in prison and all his shipping interests were expropriated in lieu of a $400,000 fine. The Erie Railroad and the United States Chemical Bank and Trust Company, which had loaned him $3,000,000 stood to have their money tied up for years. Streicher blasted the regime for allowing emigrating Jews to take any money out of Germany. When local Nazis banned his paper for the criticism, Hitler overruled them and Streicher's paper was on the streets again within two days.[8]

Another thread that appeared in *Newsweek* was the continued conflict between the Church and the Nazi regime. Pius XI, near death from asthma and old age, "delivered the most vigorous" attack yet on Hitler's violation of the concordat. He accused Hitler of religious "persecution that lacks neither the brutality of violence nor the pressure of threats nor the deceits of cunning and falsehood." He asserted German Catholics were experiencing a martyrdom analogous to that of the early Church. When Nazi and Italian newspapers failed to print his statement, the Vatican newspaper attacked them. Although 120 Evangelical ministers had been released from concentration camps and "protective custody" at Christmas, Niemoeller remained in jail awaiting trial. At Christmas, the neo-pagan movement conducted winter solstice festivals all across Germany. SA units were especially visible as hosts for the Hitler Youth groups participating in the ceremonies. Traditional nativity scenes were, however, displayed in many public Christmas celebrations.[9]

Roosevelt's "Quarantine Speech" at Chicago on October 5, 1937, triggered a debate between American isolationists and "internationalists." When Congress convened on November 15, Senators Clark, Clapper, and La Follette each introduced bills providing for a national referendum if the question of war should arise. In the House, there was an effort to bring the Ludlow amendment to the floor. The amendment provided for a national ballot before any declaration of war except in the event of an invasion. On January 10, 1938, the House responded to massive White House lobbying by defeating the effort by a vote of 209 to 188—that only eleven votes would have reversed the decision gives an indication of the nature of the debate. On January 28, 1938, Roosevelt asked Congress to vote a twenty percent increase in the Navy.[10] These actions led to a prolonged debate in our magazines.

Collier's, in its editorial columns, defended Roosevelt's plea for "the biggest navy ever assembled under the Stars and Stripes." This would signal the aggressor nations "we do not intend to be pushed around." However, Americans were certainly unable to make the world safe for democracy and should realize this fact. Rearmament would allow them to uphold their "essential rights without the last resort of a decision by war." *Collier's* subsequently added the United States was safe "from the predatory ambitions of the dictators because two oceans" safeguarded it. These oceans should be defended but there was "little reason to think that another world war" would "bring safety or freedom or any lasting good to Europe or to the world." Let Americans rest behind their oceans, therefore, without interweaving their "destiny with that of any part of Europe, however much solicitude we feel for a people unjustly attacked." It refused to modify this attitude even though it asserted Hitler had the "delusion that he is God." This "insanity" made Hitler "the number-one problem of the European world" but it did not make him an American problem.[11]

The Saturday Evening Post maintained a staunch isolationist policy. Writing for the *Post*, George F. Eliot argued Americans loved a cause and "a crusade" with "the very best intentions." Yet, he insisted, "the United States ought to stay out of other nations' wars" and avoid even the appearance of sanctions or boycott against the aggressor nations. These actions in themselves were acts of war and "it was time to face the facts" and realize they would "step by step" lure America "into the abyss of another war to make the world safe for democracy." If Americans did fight, they would win. Yet, "what possible gain could we derive from such a victory that would be worth the price?" War would mean the "loss of the best of our youth," a "crushing load of debt" with attendant "domestic troubles," and perhaps even "the destruction of our institutions." America's only hope was to avoid the call to a "crusade." Stanley High insisted Americans wanted peace and that "the peace movement in the United States" was "better organized and more militant than ever before." There were "a minimum of sixty organizations devoted, in whole or in part, to the business of peace...unquestionably the largest number of organizations devoted to a single reform in the whole history of moral uplift." Their combined anti-war budget came to "more than $2,000,000" a year. One organization, World Peaceways, would run 25,000,000 paid and free pro-peace ads in 1938 alone. In the first five months of 1937 local radio stations had broadcast "1054 peace programs." The result was that the peace movement had made "a considerable dent on the American mind" and "on the American conscience." The government would do well to heed the voice of the American people represented by the peace movement.[12]

The Saturday Evening Post also supported the cause of isolationism in its editorial columns. It insisted even if it were "impossible to keep out of the next war," what was "wrong with keeping out of it as long as we can?" Therefore, Americans should mind their own business and "keep out of everybody's wars" like a "sane man."[13]

Writing in *Harper's*, Elmer Davis argued the United States owed the rest of the world some cooperation and leadership in the maintenance of peace. Isolationism, he insisted, was ultimately not only impossible but morally bankrupt and likely to create more danger for the American people than it would solve. A refusal to cooperate with "the peaceful powers," Britain and France, made "a world war more probable" and, in the event of war, would "make a Fascist victory more probable." Fascism and Nazism could not be appeased for they had "become religions, ends in themselves" and therefore, had no rational policies that were susceptible to compromise and negotiation. Hitler, for example, was motivated "less by economic needs than by faith in the manifest destiny of the German people"—and could not negotiate that destiny as he defined it. A preferable policy to isolationism would be the proper cooperation that would deter the dictators from beginning a war for, in the next war, all would lose in some way to a greater or lesser degree.[14]

Hubert Herring delineated the nature and trend of the debate between isolationists and internationalists in an extended article in the May issue of *Harper's.* After impartially spelling out the argument of each camp of the debate, he argued Roosevelt had wavered between the two camps until October 5 and his Chicago speech. From that time, however, "the crusade was on." Roosevelt had crossed the Rubicon and moved into the camp of the internationalists in reaction to Japanese aggression in China and Hitler's "imperial ambitions." Herring accepted that Roosevelt hated war and coveted peace but noted Roosevelt believed "conflict with the dictatorships is inescapable" and the democracies "must call a halt" to the aggression of Japan, Germany, and Italy. Roosevelt had, therefore, begun a campaign to educate the American people to another "crusade." This had "aroused apprehension of his policy in the minds of many Americans." Roosevelt's motives might be "pure" but "the wisdom of his course" was open to question. Herring ended by coming down solidly on the side of the isolationists, arguing the United States should preserve "a zone of sanity, a bulwark for democracy in the midst of madness.[15]

In June, Will Durant pleaded there be "No Hymns of Hatred" among Americans. While the twentieth century was "troublous," "men had always been troublesome" and only "a soul innocent of history" could expect wars to end. Yet, while "all nations have a rendezvous with war," one should see "if anything can be done to halt them for a while." The next war, when it came, would not be over ideologies but over "nationalistic rivalries for material goods." Therefore, an effort should be made at reconciliation through concessions. For example, the *Anschluss* was "natural and forgivable" while even "the cantonization of Czechoslovakia" would "be a small price to pay for the unity of Europe." A prosperous Germany would "probably" be less of "a threat to her neighbors and to her racial and religious minorities." Given a restored unity in Europe, Japan would not be able to long trouble China. Further, the restoration of world trade on an equitable basis would be a potent force for peace. Ultimately, however, no American could assert "the need for going to war every time a distant nation misbehaves." Some "issues should be left for settlement to those nations that have engendered them." Democracy could be best preserved, not by forcing it "upon peoples that show no eagerness or aptitude for it," but by "making it function more successfully than dictatorship."[16]

The Nation insisted it was foolish for America to agree to a united front against Hitler. Russia was "a bloodily self-purging dictatorship" itself. France was "under the thumb" of Great Britain, which had determined on a "course of cowardly compromise, of buying off the dictators, and confirming them in their wrongdoing." To ally with these three would be "a disaster."[17]

On the diplomatic front, *Newsweek* opened 1938 with a report Britain and France had achieved "a harmony" that was "unequaled since the World War" by reaching agreement on "air co-operation so comprehensive as almost to constitute a military alliance." Their foreign offices believed, however, that the Reich was not "yet ready to fight" and "Hitler may still be bought off with a few foreign 'triumphs'."[18]

The Nation insisted Hitler could not "be bought" by Anglo-French retreats and concessions. The policy of these governments, managed by "poor-spirited incapables," was "bankrupt." Their four year pattern of "capitulations and concessions to gangsters and blackmailers" had produced only "disastrous consequences." The only hope for Europe lay in a tripartite alliance of Britain, France, and Russia that would attract the smaller nations of eastern Europe to a policy of collective security. Britain, however, refused to cooperate with Russia and was pulling France away from an understanding with Moscow. In such a situation, Hitler felt encouraged to pursue his ambitions. Already the nations of eastern Europe, with the exception of Czechoslovakia, were moving into the Nazi orbit.[19]

That Britain intended to pursue its appeasement policy was confirmed when Vansittart was elected to the Order of the Bath and promoted to the post of "Chief Advisor to the Foreign Office." This post, combined with his control of the secret service, gave Vansittart "the widest conceivable authority and mobility in conducting British foreign policy." Further, the "pro-German political group in London" secured the appointment of Lord Cadogan to Vansittart's former post of permanent under-secretary to the Foreign Office. Cadogan, *Time* averred, had "an open mind toward Hitler." *The London Times* adopted an increasingly pro-German attitude. It argued Germany was "patently destined" to absorb Austria and dominant eastern Europe and, if there were to be peace, there could "be no exemption from contribution and concession" by Britain, Germany, and even the Czechs. *The Times* insisted its "main purpose" was to further the policy of rapprochement with Germany. *Time* labeled this attitude as straight "pro-German propaganda" better than any designed by Goebbels.[20]

French ability to withstand the British policy of appeasement was weakened when Chautemps' Popular Front government collapsed due to its inability to control the epidemic of communist inspired strikes and the fall of the franc to an eleven-year low. Chautemps reorganized the cabinet as a Radical Socialist ministry but it was so weak it collapsed on March 10. At the very moment, then, that Hitler was expected to increase his demands, French foreign policy was directed by a weak coalition government unable to keep its eastern allies in line. Neither was it able to suggest a viable alternative to British line of appeasement. *Newsweek* concluded French authority in Europe "obviously was in a bad way" with no bright hope for the future.[21]

On February 4, Hitler abruptly dismissed Werner von Blomberg, Minister of War, and Werner von Fritsch, Commander of the Reichswehr. Hitler assumed supreme command of the army with Keitel and Brauschitsch as his immediate subordinates. Goering was elevated to Field Marshal while thirteen generals were retired. At the Wilhelmstrasse, Ribbentrop replaced von Neurath. Our magazines gave a variety of reasons for this "bloodless purge." Von Fritsch, according to *Time* and *Newsweek,* had long sought to oust von Blomberg because of his Nazi sympathies. When von Blomberg married his secretary, von Fritsch insisted on his resignation as the marriage violated the Potsdam Code, which required officers to obtain War Office approval of their marriages. "The army" had long objected to the Nazi attack on the churches, the alliance with Italy, intervention in Spain, and continued, dangerous snubs to Britain. Above all, the officers led by von Fritsch insisted "Germany was not ready for war." Therefore, "the army had actually called a showdown with the Fuehrer." Although Hitler had purged the army command, the army "might" resist again as ultimately the purge was really a long-overdue reorganization of the German military machine.[22]

The Nation, while agreeing the Reichswehr had precipitated the purge by its anti-Nazi stance, believed it meant Hitler had finally attained "absolute and undisputed control and authority" over Germany. The purge, coupled with the appointment of Ribbentrop, meant "we may look forward to a new era of militant aggressiveness" as one more control on Hitler had been removed. *The New Republic* believed, on the contrary, the purge had revealed divisions in the Reich "too deep-seated" to be "exorcised." The army, it was true, had been subordinated directly to Hitler but it was unlikely his control of it would be "more effective than it was before" as the officer corps remained anti-Nazi. Therefore, Hitler's position was "fundamentally insecure, and Nazi Germany is weaker in fact than she appears to the superficial observer."[23] *The New Republic* reiterated this view in a later issue, arguing the German officer corps remained opposed to Hitler's adventurous policies as it "had looked at things as they really are" and realized the Reich was not ready for war. They sensed that, beneath "the calm exterior of the *Volksgemeinshaft,*" there was "division and confusion" in Germany and they wanted peace. *The Nation* came around to this view in its February 19 issue, insisting Hitler had an "unstable hold on his followers" and would have to broaden his base of support before embarking on an adventure.[24]

Speculation about the purge was shelved when, at Mussolini's suggestion, Schuschnigg met Hitler for a "heart to heart talk." *Newsweek* initially speculated, as a result of the "alpine secrecy" thrown over the meeting, that there would be closer economic cooperation between Austria and Germany and the possible inclusion of Nazis in Schuschnigg's cabinet. Such a "meager agreement" would give Hitler a "triumph" he could use in his upcoming speech to the Reichstag. *Time* believed the meeting revealed Hitler had shelved the idea of annexing Austria "to make a deal on lesser but vital issues." Schuschnigg had allegedly agreed to prevent a return of Archduke Otto to the throne while Hitler agreed to curb his Austrian Nazi supporters. The word among Austrian Nazis was "Hitler has betrayed us!" The "Jesuit-trained, rock-pious and astute" Schuschnigg had stood up "persuasively to potent, mystic, unstable Dictator Hitler." *The Nation* wrote the meeting had produced a "reported Austro-German pact" that offered a "permanent settlement of outstanding differences between the two countries" and would result in closer ties between Hitler and Mussolini. It might even lead to a four-power pact between Britain, France, Italy, and Germany "directed against the Soviet Union." *The New Republic* non-committedly commented the agreement, whatever its contents, left grave differences between Austria and Germany.[25]

Schuschnigg's meeting with Hitler was actually overshadowed by, what at the time, seemed to be more important stories. In Rumania, King Carol dismissed Goga and replaced him with Patriarch Cristea of the Orthodox Church. Carol reputedly dismissed Goga for his extreme anti-Semitism that threatened Rumania with potential bankruptcy, for Goga's pro-Nazi alignment, and because of pressure from Britain, France, and Czechoslovakia. Above all, Carol was motivated by the desire to establish a personal dictatorship. Carol had selected Cristea as Goga's replacement because the Patriarch's more moderate anti-Semitism corresponded with Carol's views. *Time* devoted its longest story on Germany to Niemoeller's trial which, though secret, had created a stir within Germany. Niemoeller reputedly conducted a spirited defense of his attacks on Nazi persecution that were "dynamite." It noted he had not shown himself to be "pro-Semitic" but rather, quite to the contrary, had rationalized Nazi anti-Semitism as the result of the Jews having "brought the Christ of God to the Cross." A verdict had not yet been announced by the court.[26]

Newsweek carried a lengthy report on a new anti-Semitic drive in Italy. There, an anti-Semitic weekly had been established, the government had banned all books and plays by Jews unless officially authorized, and Olivetti, a Jew, had been forced to resign as leader of the Fascist corporations of Italy. Mussolini was supposedly motivated by a desire to combat Zionism among Italian Jews.[27]

Major interest, however, centered around Chamberlain's efforts "to push" the idea of a four-power pact that would include Britain, France, Italy, and Germany. Diplomatic relations were in a "state of greater flux than at any time" since Mussolini invaded Ethiopia and Chamberlain was determined to capitalize on the situation according to *Newsweek*. *Time* reported Chamberlain and Eden had "quarreled fundamentally" when Chamberlain suggested to the cabinet Britain loan Italy $125,000,000 and cede colonial territory to Germany to ensure the formation of the pact. Since Eden had not resigned, *Time* believed "Europe was verging upon Business, upon a Big Deal" with Hitler.[28]

When accurate reports of the meeting between Schuschnigg and Hitler finally appeared, they came as a bolt from the blue. *Newsweek* reported Hitler had given Schuschnigg an "ultimatum" after browbeating, threatening, and haranguing him. *Time* was so incredulous of the reports of open threats of violence by Hitler and his generals, that it labeled them "nothing but a cock-and-bull story." Rather than "the Nazis having been such fools" to try and "crack" Schuschnigg "by third degree methods," the agreement was "chiefly remarkable" for the way Schuschnigg had "yielded much" while preserving Austrian integrity and independence. *Time* and *Newsweek* did agree on the details of Schuschnigg's concessions to Hitler. Schuschnigg had agreed to appoint the Austrian Nazi Seyss-Inquart as Minister of Interior and add five pro-Nazi sympathizers to his cabinet. By decree Schuschnigg freed 1,228 Nazis from jail, returned 1,932 ousted Nazis to the civil service rolls, and recommissioned 150 Nazi officers in the Austrian army. The same evening, Vienna's Nazis paraded openly, "rushed opera crowds, and man-handled Jews." Even with this information, *Time* argued "it was clear that Jesuit-trained Kurt von Schuschnigg had not capitulated outright, had driven a bargain with Hitler." Even if Hitler annexed Austria, *Time* believed it would "not be a calamity" unless Hitler made it one.[29]

Newsweek noted "Paris and London" had "offered Vienna no hope" in the crisis. In France the government was paralyzed by a coalition cabinet unable to resolve "the capitalist-labor struggle" while in Britain "a Cabinet crisis of historic proportions" had developed due to Eden's resignation. *Time* reported only that "the British Cabinet itself was 'cracking' with strain" due to the news from Vienna.[30]

In the same issues in which they reported the Austrian crisis, *Time* and *Newsweek* summarized Hitler's long-delayed speech to the Reichstag quite differently. *Newsweek* noted Hitler had "seldom resorted to his frenzy-producing oratorical hysterics" but spoke with a "hard," "new complacency." After the usual attack on communism, Hitler had emphasized his unity with Mussolini, announced he favored a fascist victory in Spain and the Japanese conquest of China, and recognized Manchukua. But, "the crux of the speech" was a Hitler pledge to protect Germans *"outside* the Third Reich." Since he did not mention Austria, *Newsweek* believed the speech "pointed unmistakenly to Prague as his next point of interest." *Time*, however, reported "the big smash of the speech was Hitler's ominous roar" that Germany had "no differences with England—except colonies." *Time* ended its account of the speech with the statement "five hours later" Eden resigned from the British cabinet. *The New Republic* interpreted Hitler's speech to mean he was "worried about internal opposition" and it was "big talk to cover real uneasiness." It noted Eden had been characterized as a "troublemaker" by Hitler.[31]

Eden and Chamberlain had long disagreed over British policy. According to *Newsweek*, their final disagreement came when Chamberlain "flatly refused France's demand for a joint protest" about Austria and intimated Czechoslovakia "must shift for herself." *Time* believed their rupture came when Chamberlain informed Eden he intended to placate Mussolini at any cost. *The New Republic* praised Eden and castigated Chamberlain and Halifax, who had replaced Eden. It asserted the British Tories were "not only anti-socialistic but also anti-democratic" and appeared ready to "sacrifice Czechoslovakia and the Soviet Union" to Hitler. *The Nation* believed Eden's resignation meant Chamberlain had repudiated the League and given the dictators a blank check. On March 12, *The Nation* returned to this theme. It insisted "the pro-German gang" represented by Chamberlain were "not mere craven imbeciles" but "more like traitors," who put the interests of "their class before those of their country."[32]

The resignation of Eden led to a major debate in Commons. There were charges Chamberlain had engineered Eden's resignation at the insistence of Mussolini, that Chamberlain had neglected to inform Eden of major concessions to Italy, and that Chamberlain had given Hitler a free hand in central Europe. Chamberlain, however, won a vote of confidence even though he affirmed his intention to placate Mussolini and Hitler.

Even if Chamberlain were willing to write off Austria and Czechoslovakia, the leadership of those nations expressed a determination to resist Hitler. Schuschnigg, speaking to the Austrian Federal Diet, pledged "what we have we will hold! Austria must remain Austrian!"[33] Krejci, Chief of the Czechoslovakian General Staff, announced Prague was building additional fortifications, moving the Skoda factory to the interior, and would refuse "autonomy" to the Sudetenland Germans. France renewed its pledge to aid the Czechs a few days later. When Goering subsequently threatened to use his air force to protect "German minorities," Premier Hodza of Czechoslovakia asserted Prague would meet force with force.[34] Chamberlain, however, refused to be deterred from his search for a four-power pact that would conciliate Hitler. When Henderson, the British ambassador to Berlin, remarked "to a prominent member of the German government" that he could not understand why Hitler had not already annexed Austria, Chamberlain refused to publicly repudiate the statement.[35]

If Chamberlain expected Hitler to annex Austria, his expectations were amply fulfilled on March 12. Schuschnigg, on March 9, announced a plebiscite on the question of Austrian independence. At Graz, Linz, and Innsbruck Nazis rioted and seized public buildings. On March 11, Hitler gave Schuschnigg an ultimatum demanding his resignation and the postponement of the plebiscite. German troops appeared on the frontier. Schuschnigg reigned and Seyss-Inquart, became chancellor. The following morning, as German troops entered Austria, President Miklas resigned. Seyss-Inquart, on March 12, proclaimed the union of Austria and Germany and, the next morning, Hitler arrived in Vienna.

Frederic Sondern, Jr., who was in Vienna during the *Anschluss*, reported in August Hitler had indeed subjected Schuschnigg to a "terrible two hours" of harangue and browbeating. Schuschnigg had been forced into agreeing to add Nazis to his cabinet. On his return to Vienna, Schuschnigg had rallied his spirit and announced the plebiscite. This made Hitler "livid with rage" and he sent General Muff, the German military attache, to deliver Schuschnigg an ultimatum demanding his resignation and the appointment of Seyss-Inquart as chancellor. Schuschnigg, unwilling to subject Austria to "fraticide" and "bloody" invasion had resigned as the first German army units crossed the border. Seyss-Inquart assumed the chancellorship of an "independent Nazi Austria." Hitler had not made the decision to annex Austria outright until he reached Linz on his way to Vienna. There, telegrams informed him France was without a cabinet, Britain would not march, and that Mussolini had no objections to outright annexation. Hitler immediately ordered the *Anschluss—*

the "end" of Austria "had come." Hitler had bluffed and blustered his way to another success.[36]

On March 13, the day of *Anschluss*, Nazis paraded and cheered at St. Stephen's Cathedral, others "chased Jews about the Leopoldstadt ghetto section, crying: 'Hop the twig, Judah! [hang yourself]'." Police, donning swastika armbands, made no effort to stop the violence. Those Jews who could, "sought places on outgoing trains." In the Jewish section of Vienna, *Time* reported "boys were frogged, the eyes of old men watered as their beards were jerked, Nazis spat in the faces of Jewesses" and everyone, Jew or Aryan, soon appeared wearing a swastika. Decrees promptly prohibited Jewish lawyers and doctors from practice of their profession. When Hitler announced a plebiscite on the *Anschluss* for May 10, Jews were barred from voting.[37] Himmler immediately mobilized the Vienna police and began arresting socialists, communists, union leaders, and Jews.[38]

In France, Chautemp's cabinet had fallen on March 10 in a struggle with the Socialists in the Chamber. At the time of the *Anschluss*, therefore, France had no government and was leaderless. Delbos, however, agreed to join Chamberlain in a protest to Berlin objecting to "coercion backed by force" in Austria. A "minor official" in Berlin dismissed the note as "irrelevant."[39]

Some 20,000 Britons gathered in Trafalgar Square shouting "Chamberlain must go!" and "Ribbentrop get out!". Eight hundred police had to be called out to restrain the crowd. The Trade Union Congress leadership demanded Chamberlain break diplomatic relations with Germany and insist on a Nazi withdrawal from Austria. Chamberlain, addressing Commons, took the line, however, that nothing could now be done to prevent the *Anschluss*. He "hinted" at increased British rearmament and conscription. Chamberlain concluded that Britain would "make fresh reviews" of the situation.[40]

The Nation was roused to a new level of denunciation of Hitler by the *Anschluss*. Hitler, it wrote had disregarded "all legal and humane considerations" in his attack on Austria and was already planning to assault Czechoslovakia and the Soviet Ukraine.[41] Hitler had acted as a "gangster" who used "pure force, untarnished by scruple, pity, hesitation, indecision" and was "contemptuous of the weakness" of his victims. In short, "Austria was murdered" and Hitler would not be stopped by "inaction, compromise, and an anxious hope." His "gun" remained loaded and Czechoslovakia had already been selected as his next victim—to reach it, he would step across "the corpse of Austria." *The New Republic* demanded an immediate "vigorous protest against the conventional Nazi program of brutality and suppression" directed against Austrian Jews. Only such action might cause Hitler "to restrain his young cohorts of sadists."[42] It called Hitler "a psychotic individual who is so obsessed with the realm of his own emotions" that he was unaware he would ultimately bring down on himself "disaster and defeat from united enemies." He was so out of touch with reality that he "slapped the faces of the British statesmen who were just about to succumb to his wooing."[43]

Joseph Barber, responding to the *Anschluss* in the May issue of *The Atlantic Monthly*, insisted that it "was something of a miracle" that Austria had maintained its independence for "as long as she did." Following the "folly enacted at Versailles," Austria had experienced repeated financial crises in 1921, 1922, 1929, and 1931. It had riots and attempted revolution in 1927 and 1934, leading to the dictatorship of Dolfuss and his murder in 1934. Schuschnigg had a chance for a new beginning but chose to continue the dictatorial policies of Dolfuss. The result was the alienation of the laboring classes from the ruling classes. In the absence of any political solidarity, the Nazi party grew geometrically. Austrian Nazis, "predominantly youthful" and "fanatic," were "absolutely fearless" and imbued with what they believed to be a "holy mission." Austrian Nazis could thus be expected to be, if anything, more radical than German Nazis. The Leopoldstadt area of Vienna would assume "more and more the character of the medieval ghetto" under their control of Austria. Certainly, the *Anschluss* would lead to a new flow of political refugees while the "shadow of Hitler over Europe" would grow "ever more ominous."[44]

Secretary of State Hull, usually quite phlegmatic, delineated the administration's attitude in a major speech before the National Press Club. He chastised Japan, Italy, and Germany for acting like "gangsters" who fostered "international anarchy based on brute force." Germany was singled out for its "relapse into barbarism." He stressed "the startling events" in Austria were an example of "the contagious scourge of treaty-breaking and armed violence" rampant in Europe. While emphasizing the United States could no longer pursue a policy of isolationism, he refused to spell out probable American action in each "particular set of circumstances." Hull argued that, in any case, the United States needed to rearm. *Newsweek* commented the speech contributed to "a general drop in isolationist and peace-at-any-price sentiment" which, combined with news of the *Anschluss*, "won increased popular backing for a sterner foreign policy." The dictators, it asserted, could "not be too sure America would not fight." Opposition to the Vinson Big-Navy Bill rapidly dissolved in the House.[45]

American indignation over the *Anschluss* was also increased by reports of the brutal anti-Semitic measures instituted by Nazi officials. The "full brunt of the terror" had fallen on Jews who were "reduced in three days to a state" that had taken three years to achieve in Germany. All Jewish doctors were barred from practice, the Kreditanstalt Bank was expropriated along with the Zwieback department stores and five Jewish newspapers, and Jewish financiers arrested. "Loot hungry Austrian Nazis" cleared out stocks in Jewish stores while "Brown-shirted guerrillas" expropriated Jewish restaurants and reopened them "under Aryan management." In Vienna, Brown-Shirts were "breaking in houses" and forcing their inhabitants to scrub pro-Schuschnigg slogans off walls and streets. When the frontiers were closed to Jewish emigration, "police reported wholesale suicides by Jews." *The Nation* editorialized Austria had "been made over into a hell of hate, prejudice, vicious cruelty, sadism." "All Austria" had become "one horrible prison-house of Jews." The "number of wholesale suicides" could "never be estimated, and they are only beginning." *The New Republic* saw in Vienna the full "sickening spectacle of Nazi barbarity" as many Jews killed themselves rather than become one of "the thousands of Jews" arrested and sent to "concentration camps."[46] *Newsweek* reported Jews had been barred from all schools "pending the establishment of ghetto institutions." Mixed Jewish-Gentile couples were ordered to separate. The Vienna Medical School ordered only "Aryan corpses" could be used in dissection classes when Jewish suicides jumped to eighty-eight a day. Freud's passport and funds were taken from him. Goering declared in Vienna that in "three years" the city would be exclusively Aryan.[47] By April 11, the Jewish suicide rate had climbed to 132 a day and was rising. On April 17, all Jews were expelled from within thirty miles of the Czech frontier and their "houses, money, even spare clothes" were confiscated. The 2,000 "Jews thus made destitute" were "dumped" in Vienna's ghetto. Fifty were taken to a jetty in the Danube and abandoned. Prague shipped them to Hungary which returned them to the jetty. After several days without food or water, a French tug rescued them. Books by Jews in Vienna's public library were burned.[48]

M.W. Fodor described Austria after the *Anschluss* as "The Cemetary of Europe" and stated "Hatred is celebrating its victories in Vienna." The first Nazi act was to commandeer Jewish automobiles and vans which were then used to not only carry away plundered merchandise but "even the counters, desks, and shelves" of Jewish stores. Jewish women in movie houses had their hand-bags taken from them by roving Nazi bands. Jewish males were beaten or taken to prison after being made to scrub the streets in their best clothes. The Rothschild home was despoiled of its art by an entire fleet of vans. Approximately three thousand Jews had committed suicide and the rich cultural contribution of Jews to Austria had ended overnight.[49]

The New Republic argued Nazi anti-Semitism in Austria made it clear "that Nazi racial theory" served "primarily a social purpose as a deadly instrument of destruction of the upper and upper-middle classes." This destruction, rather than being the by-product of invasion, "was one of the major objectives of Germany's conquest" and had "been one of the most thorough, most ruthless and most rapid social revolutions in modern history." Austria had been "handed over to the most radical, openly totalitarian, and anti-bourgeois faction of the Nazi Party" and "600,000 non-Aryans" had seen their livelihood, profession, or property expropriated by these Nazis. The wealth stolen through this expropriation was being used to strengthen the German war machine and to purchase the allegiance of the Austrian workers and peasants. The Jews of Austria had begun their own *via dolorosa.*[50]

Some indication of the changing mood of American public opinion following the *Anschluss* can be gained from a poll taken by *The Nation.* Although its editor, Oswald G. Villard, remained a staunch pacifist, he did mail out a ballot to all *Nation* subscribers and "130,000" other "non-readers" on March 19, 1938. It asked the respondents to vote on whether isolationism or a system of collective security afforded the United States "the better chance of security." The ballot was also printed in *The Nation.* On April 2, he reported that out of the initial 1,328 ballots returned to *The Nation,* 1,144 favored "a policy of cooperation with other nations in defense of peace"—184 voted for a policy of isolationism. In letters accompanying their ballots, Upton Sinclair, Thomas Wolfe, and Paul Douglas expressed support for a system of collective security. William Allen White wrote he believed the foreign policy of America could only be solved by "a transcontinental earthquake plus an oceanic inundation" and that he had no answer to the question.[51] The following week Villard reported "partial returns" were running "five-to-one for collective action." *Nation* subscribers favored collective action by 86.5 percent while "non-readers" favored it by eighty-two percent. Out of 4,457 ballots, 3,372 wanted the United States to join in collective action against Japan and Germany. The week of April 16, Villard reported 83.3 percent of all those polled favored collective security.[52]

In October, 1938, *Harper's* published the results of a series of polls by George Gallup. It stressed the results were correct to one-half of one percent. Although the poll covered both domestic and international issues, only those results pertinent to this study are included here. The date of a particular poll is given in parenthesis. The results are in the order presented:

If you had to choose between Communism and Fascism, which would you choose? (June, 1938) Communism, 50 percent; Fascism, 50 percent.

Are you in favor of permitting Nazis who are American citizens to wear uniforms and parade in this country? (September, 1937) No, 83 percent.

Do you think there will be another World War? (August, 1937) Yes, 73 percent.

Should the United States: Build a larger navy? Yes, 74 percent. Increase the strength of its army? Yes, 69 percent. Enlarge its air force? Yes, 80 percent. (January, 1938)

Do you think a larger navy, as now proposed by President Roosevelt, will be more likely to get us into a war or keep us out of war? (March, 1938) Keep us out, 73 percent; Get us in, 27 percent.

Do you think the cause of world peace will be hurt if the League of Nations is dissolved? (December, 1937) No, 63 percent.

Which nation can be least trusted to keep the treaties it makes? (April, 1938) Germany, 66 percent.

Do you think that the United States will have to fight Germany again in your lifetime? (April, 1938) No, 54 percent.

Which nation do you think is most likely to start the next war? (August, 1937) Germany, 30 percent; Italy, 27 percent; Russia, 11 percent; Others, 13 percent.

Should the colonies taken from Germany after the World War be given back to her? (November, 1937) No, 76 percent.

Which European country do you like best? (April, 1937) England, 55 percent; France, 11 percent; Germany, 8 percent; Finland, 4 percent; Ireland, 4 percent; Others, 8 percent.

Should the United States go to war to help any South American country attacked by any European or Asiatic country? (February, 1938) No, 68 percent.

F.S. Wickware, the author of the article, summarized the results as indications Americans had "a deep determination to stay out of the next general war" and that "half of us think the country can stay out."[53]

The crisis occasioned by the *Anschluss* precipitated a number of other crises in its wake. When Hitler spoke in Berlin following his return from Vienna, banners proclaimed "Fuehrer! Your *Sudetenland* Awaits you also!" Hitler referred to German "racial kinsmen" being "suppressed" in neighboring countries to shouts of acclaim. The following day, Benes announced Germans would be given "a proportionate share" in the Czech civil service. Hitler responded by sending an army of 300,000 into Austria and Silesia.[54] Poland bullied Lithuania into a statement that Vilna was Polish by dispatching 100,000 troops to its border with Lithuania and giving Kaunas an ultimatum.[55] There was a flight of capital from western Europe to the United States with the franc dropping to a twelve year low against the dollar while London transferred $30,000,000 to New York in one week. The foreign funds went into securities as Wall Street dropped to its 1938 low point.[56] The French cabinet dismissed French Foreign Minister Delbos and replaced him with Paul-Boncour, who favored Chamberlain's plans for the four-pact. *The Nation* argued the week would "be recognized as crucial" in years to come even though the threat of war had momentarily passed. Hitler's "Cold War" had claimed its first victim and he had escaped unopposed by the democracies—a move sure to whet his appetite. The fate of Czechoslovakia was now the key to war or peace in Europe.[57]

At the end of March, Chamberlain, under prodding from Labor and even fellow Tories, made a formal, major foreign policy address in Commons to define British policy. He announced "Britain would go to war" to defend the empire, France, Belgium, Portugal, Iraq, and Egypt. Chamberlain pointedly stated Britain would give no "prior guarantee" to defend Czechoslovakia. Indeed, he "hoped" Prague would take "practical steps to meet the reasonable wishes" of *Sudetenland* Germans. Chamberlain added there had been "considerable progress" in the Anglo-Italian negotiations for a "gentlemen's agreement" in the Mediterranean. *The New Republic* believed the speech was tantamount to inviting Hitler to invade Czechoslovakia, the key to eastern Europe.[58] In a by-election following the speech, the Tories lost the formerly "safe" seat of West Fulham London to a Laborite who characterized Chamberlain's policies as a "wobble to war."[59] When Premier Blum asked the Chamber of Deputies for authority to impose a new capital levy, he was shouted down with cries of "Down with the Jews!". The French Senate refused to even discuss the proposal and Blum resigned to be replaced by Daladier on April 10. Daladier announced French policy would correspond to that of Chamberlain in Europe and the Mediterranean.[60] *The Nation* stated French policy would henceforth seek agreements with Mussolini and Hitler "in preference to a policy of resisting aggression." Chamberlain's hand was sure to direct future French foreign policy. *The Saturday Evening Post* later editorialized that French diplomacy had become a "subordinate member of Sterlingaria" and the City would henceforward determine French policy. *The New Republic* believed that Chamberlain, who would unilaterally conduct British and French policy, had "told Hitler to take Czechoslovakia, without war if possible." By this deal, Chamberlain had "condemned the continent to doom." The same day Daladier became premier, Hitler received a 99.75 percent vote of support for his *Anschluss* from Germans. *Collier's* reported at the end of 1938 that Joseph Buerckel, who had "engineered" the Saar plebiscite and was "a specialist in plebiscites," had been sent to Vienna ahead of the German army to lay the groundwork for the vote. He had used both the stick and the carrot and, as always, had delivered the vote Hitler expected.[61]

Buerckel's tactics were illustrated by his treatment of Vienna's Cardinal Innitzer. During the preparations for the plebiscite on the *Anschluss*, Primate Cardinal Innitzer of Vienna urged all Austrian Catholics to support Hitler and had even ended a radio speech with "Heil Hitler!" The Vatican radio thereupon broadcast a statement "denouncing Nazism by implication" which warned Catholics to be wary of "wolves in sheep's clothing." Catholics were told to vote according to their conscience and not to dictates of the Primate. A script of the broadcast was distributed to all foreign correspondents in Rome.[62] Innitzer was subsequently summoned to Rome and forced to withdraw his statement publicly.[63]

Following the *Anschluss*, Innitzer became an anti-Nazi because of Nazi attacks on church schools and Catholic youth organizations. On October 8, after an Innitzer sermon critical of the regime, "Nazi hotheads," stormed the cardinal's palace where they "smashed windows, burned pictures and prayer books, hurled a priest from a second-story window, and cut the prelate's face with flying glass." Buerckel, the Nazi Commissioner for Austria, publicly attacked the cardinal in a speech before 100,000 people and ordered him placed in "protective custody."[64]

Meanwhile, on April 16, Chamberlain finally achieved his long-sought accord with Mussolini resolving their differences in the Mediterranean. He stated he intended to use the agreement as a spring-board to a four-power pact that included Germany.[65] *Newsweek* and *The Nation* predicted Daladier would quickly reach a similar accord with Italy and, to align his policies with Chamberlain's, would seek to evade French commitments to Czechoslovakia and Moscow.[66] The American State Department stated Chamberlain had made a "realistic" contribution to peace and vastly improved the chances for the proposed four-power pact.[67] Chamberlain's hopes for the pact were immediately dealt a body-blow by Hitler, who through his puppet Heinlein, demanded absolute autonomy for *Sudetenland* Germans, the institution of Nazi anti-Semitic laws in Czechoslovakia, and the alignment of Czechoslovakian foreign policy to Berlin's lead. *Time* reported the demands were so "outrageous" that "even the now violently pro-German London *Times*" was shocked by them. In Budapest, Hungarian Nazis "clamored 'Czechoslovakia must be dismembered'!" *The New Republic* interpreted the blast, coming when it did, as symbolic of Hitler's belief "the Chamberlain government will do nothing" to resist his *Drang Nach Osten*. *The Nation* predicted the Nazi demands were so far-reaching that "even Chamberlain" would not be able to reach an accord with Hitler over Czechoslovakia.[68]

Chamberlain immediately sought and attained an unwritten military agreement with France that provided for French direction of their combined armies in the event of war, for British direction of their combined air forces, and coordinated action by their combined fleets. The action was supposedly taken to offset the Rome-Berlin Axis and to drive a wedge between Hitler and Mussolini during Hitler's visit to Rome from May 3 - 9.[69] If the wedge was driven, it was not apparent to *Newsweek* a week later. It argued the meeting produced "no grandiose political results" and the Rome-Berlin axis seemed as solid as ever. *Time* believed the meeting had given a "free hand in Czechoslovakia" to Hitler—a judgment concurred with by *The Nation* and *The New Republic.*[70] On May 23, *Newsweek* reported "time to prevent an explosion" over Czechoslovakia "seemed to be running out." Heinlein, in a visit to London, rejected *a priori* all possibility of compromise with Benes and suggested a German attack on Czechoslovakia might be ignited by upcoming municipal elections in the *Sudetenland.* *Time* believed the visit meant Chamberlain was seeking a way to allow Hitler to achieve his Czechoslovakian "aspirations" without war. *The Nation* insisted the "capitulation of Czechoslovakia to Hitler" had been arranged by "back-stairs negotiations" while *The New Republic* believed "Hitler can be stopped only by force" but that force was now unlikely to be used.[71]

According to M.W. Fodor, the racial and nationality problems of Czechoslovakia were unsolvable. Czechs, Slovaks, and Germans were so intermixed geographically that it would be impossible to demarcate politically autonomous areas for them. Yet, it was impossible for them to live together without resentment and strife. Germans resented the loss of their superior position prior to 1918. The Czech government then compounded the problem by employing "chiefly their own people in the state administration" and by not implementing any of the minority guarantees promised the Germans. Economically, the Czech government awarded most of its contracts to Slavic firms and neglected to provide adequately for its minorities when the depression hit. Whatever the intentions of Prague toward the German minority, its policies met "a good deal of sabotage on the part of subordinates." Now virtually all the Sudeten Germans demanded autonomy. Having gained Vienna, Hitler looked to Czechoslovakia for his next success. His intervention in the *Sudetenland* was dangerous for "war in Czechoslovakia probably means a general conflagration in Europe."[72]

For a moment, the anticipated "Second World War" threatened to become a reality when two *Sudetenland* Germans attempting to cross into Germany were killed by a Czech border guard. *Sudetenland* Germans rioted, German planes overflew the Czech border, and there were reports Hitler had moved his army up to the border. Benes promptly mobilized 400,000 Czech troops and stationed them in his "Little Maginot Line." Daladier reacted by breaking off his negotiations with Mussolini while the British embassy in Berlin was alerted for evacuation. Hitler quickly acted to defuse the situation by "guaranteeing Chamberlain" he had no intention of using military force against Czechoslovakia. Our magazines gave varying reasons for Hitler's action. *Time* stressed Hitler was motivated equally by a warning from Chamberlain and by Benes' show of force. *Newsweek* believed simply that Benes had finally called Hitler's bluff. *The New Republic* believed "an unequivocal declaration" from Daladier had stayed Hitler's hand. *The Nation,* however, argued Chamberlain had informed Hitler that the use of force would cause Britain to mobilize.[73]

Following the deescalation of this crisis, there was momentarily almost an air of diplomatic anti-climax in the magazines. There were limited reports of continued irritation and counter-charges between Berlin and Prague. Heinlein's *Sudetenland* organizations continued to harass Benes but in a much subdued key.[74] Attention, however, quickly shifted to other topics that had been somewhat shunted to the side during the Czech crisis. For example, renewed fighting had erupted in Palestine on Easter Sunday as British units ambushed Arab terrorists and the terrorists attacked Jewish farm settlements. Arabs, for some weeks, "punctured oil lines, spiked railroads, tore down telegraph wires, and sniped off travelers." Arab posters had appeared offering $20 for the murder of a Jew and $800 for the assassination of a governmental official.[75] A Tory, Locker-Lampson, introduced a bill in Commons to confer Palestinian citizenship upon "oppressed European Jews." This would provide them with papers and protection by the British government. By a margin of one vote, it was "admitted to first reading" but was subsequently dropped. The measure was intended primarily to succor Austrian Jews.[76]

Austrian Jews were certainly in dire straits. They, like Jews in Germany, had been made "stateless persons" with no legal rights. On April 26, "the Vienna edition of the *Volkischen Beobachter* warned Jews to abandon all hope" and emigrate as Austria would be *"Juden-frei* by 1942" at the latest. "Hundreds of Jews" had been forced to parade through Vienna doing "a burlesque of the goosestep." Others were made to "scrub floors and wash windows" for Aryans. On April 27, Goering announced that all Jewish property in Austria and Germany had to be registered with the government pending its "Aryanization." Goering announced he thereby expected to "recover" for the Reich some $2,800,000,000. *The New Republic* identified the Austrian Nazis as "gangsters in uniform" who had surpassed all previous records "of brutality and injustice" by "supposedly civilized" nations. It reported Austrian Jews were being "systematically tortured" as "the bestiality" of the SA ran rampant. It noted there had been, within one three day period, "537 authenticated instances of suicide among the Viennese Jews." Nazis hung signs on the doors of suicides that read "go and do likewise." *The Nation* insisted Austria represented the "most harrowing instance of Nazi brutality" against the Jews. Austrian Jews had become the primary target for "the sadism of the swastika." Vienna had become, with Palestine, a "Death Trap for Jews."[77]

William E. Dodd, recently the American ambassador in Berlin, wrote it was "almost impossible to realize the horrors" being visited upon Jews by the Nazis for "never in modern times has a sovereign power bent itself so savagely" to kill its own citizens or to transgress "every tradition of culture and humanity." This anti-Semitism was "not a rational movement" but stemmed from "Hitler himself" and his twisted emotions and political motives. It was both the "lubricant and fuel for his Nazi machine." Hitler confidently predicted "that by 1950 no Jew" would be living within German boundaries for they "will all have been killed or driven into exile." Hitler's anti-Semitism was unique in history and would profoundly alter history.[78]

Nazi persecution in Austria following the *Anschluss* ended all pretense that private organizations and the League commission on refugees could solve the refugee crisis. The Nazi effort to force Jews to emigrate moved into high gear and there was little doubt Hitler was using every possible pressure to speed the exodus. Roosevelt, who had remained aloof from all comment on the refugee crisis to this point, surprised everyone with his call at the end of March for thirty-two nations to meet at Evian to ease the emigration crisis and to establish a new international organization for refugees. He stressed the cost of refugee emigration would have to be provided by private agencies and that no nation would be asked to increase its immigration quotas. Our magazines gave varying reasons for Roosevelt's action. *Newsweek* believed he was motivated by a desire to wean Americans away from isolationism and to "an active opposition to 'international gangsters'." *Time* insisted Roosevelt took the action to express his disapproval of the *Anschluss*. *Time* later argued Dorothy Thompson had convinced Roosevelt to finally move.[79] The conference was set to open on July 6, 1938.

The emigration of Freud demonstrated the difficulties facing even a major world scientist who sought to escape from Austria. His publishing house in Vienna was expropriated as were his home and liquid assets. Penniless and eighty-two years old, it took strong pressure on Whitehall by his admirers to secure him a British visa. Even then, his permit to leave Vienna was not issued until Prince George of Greece agreed to pay the Nazis $50,000 for his release. *The New Republic* drew a contrast "between the gentle doctor in London and the paranoid dictator in Berlin," declaring that "the inmates of the asylum have expelled the physician." Two weeks later, *The New Republic* wrote it had become clear that Hitler was "holding the Jews for ransom." However, his "code is a little lower than that of the American gangsters" who, after robbing their victims, let them go free.[80]

In Germany proper, persecution of Jews was also intensified in May and June, 1938. This was especially true in Berlin where many Jews had fled to escape "even greater persecution in the provinces." *Newsweek* reported "night after night Jews were herded out of homes, cafes, and theatres" by "cursing mobs" and "individual Jews were beaten in the streets." Entire streets were "roped off while Jewish blocks were searched" and "more than 1,000 Jews" were arrested for trivial reasons. A new decree was issued "to suffocate what is left of Jewish economic life": all Jewish shops were ordered to display special signs, even one Jewish member of a corporate board made the corporation Jewish, while one-fourth of the capital of a company made it Jewish. Aryan trade with a Jew was to be considered a "deliberate demonstration" against the government. *Time* concluded "no doubt was left last week that the Nazi aim is complete elimination of Jews from the Third Reich." Both *Time* and *Newsweek* agreed the persecution was intended to demonstrate to Evian Conference representatives that barriers to Jewish immigration into their countries had to be relaxed.[81]

Time reported that, as a result of the intensified persecution, "long lines" of Jews "formed at the U. S. and British consulates for visas." It asserted 126,000 Jews had emigrated from Germany since 1933 and that the Jewish death rate exceeded the "birth rate by an average of 5,000 a year." As the emigrants were "usually young Jews," *Time* predicted that by 1940, sixty-five percent of Germany's Jews would be forty-five or older. According to *Newsweek*, 23,500 Jews emigrated from Germany in 1937, with 8,800 admitted to the United States. At this rate, it would take thirty years for all Jews to emigrate from Germany. A complicating factor was that the *Anschluss* had made an additional 250,000 Jews the target of Nazi persecution.[82] To aid the German authorities and populace in the identification of Jews, the Nazi government announced that, beginning January 1, 1939, all Jewish males had to adopt the name Israel, Jewish females the name Sarah.[83]

The Evian Conference, according to *The New Republic* "opened in an atmosphere of gloom" for doors were "closing against the refugees almost everywhere throughout the world." The problem was no country "wanted a victim of persecution" unless he was so "well financed, and otherwise so desirable," that his future was no problem. It noted Italy had refused to attend because Germany had not been invited and wrote one "could as reasonably refuse to attend a funeral because the murderer had not been asked. *The Nation* believed most countries would limit their aid to Jews to "verbal sympathy" although "the Jewish question" had "become the moral responsibility of the whole non-fascist world." The British delegation especially was "incredible" as it was led by Lord Winterton, a known anti-Semite. He had insisted it was unwise to aid German Jews as it would lead to "similar expulsions from Poland and Rumania." *The Nation* responded this argument meant it was wrong "to save people from a burning house" on the ground it would "encourage arson."[84] *Time* wrote the first week of the conference had produced "many warm words of idealism, few practical suggestions." Two days had been spent electing a president as "no delegate wanted the post." Because Roosevelt had called the conference, "the chief U. S. delegate" Myron Taylor had finally accepted the task. When he insisted on prompt action, *Newsweek* noted "most governments" reacted "by slamming their doors." Most European countries wanted "the burden shifted to the New World." The Australian delegate stated Australia had no racial problems and was "not desirous of importing one." Some Latin Americans agreed to take a limited number of agricultural workers but only Mexico and the Dominican Republic promised havens with no restrictions attached. The only real agreement was to establish an intergovernmental committee, separate from the League, "to bargain with Germany."[85]

Time concluded the conference was a failure as it had produced no tangible results and would, in the future, be reduced to "endless bickering with Germany." *The New Republic* believed the conference revealed "annoyance at the Nazis" was due as much to the fact they had created the problem of Jewish refugees as to the cruelty practiced by the Nazis. The committee set up by the conference selected August 3 for its first meeting in London. Joseph Kennedy, American ambassador to Britain, was to convene the meeting. One significant note about the conference was that Britain had ruled out Palestine as a haven for Europe's Jews.[86]

When the permanent Refugee Organization met in London, Earl Winterton of Britain was elected as its chairman while George Rublee, a Washington lawyer, was selected as its director. It was immediately apparent that "no nation" was "willing to receive penniless Jews." Yet, it was certain Germany would not allow Jews to take cash or even their household possessions out if they emigrated.[87] Dorothy Thompson, at this point, published her book, *Refugees: Anarchy or Organization,* in which she suggested formation of "an international corporation for trading in refugees." Blocked German marks, owed refugees and foreign investors, would be passed to Germany in return for industrial and capital goods for the use of emigrants in their new homes. The arrangement would resemble that made between Germany and the Palestinian Jewish agency *Ha'avara. Ha'avara* had assisted 14,000 Jewish families to reach Palestine.[88] Hitler, however, had just decreed that when a Jew attempted to auction off his goods prior to emigration, no Aryan could bid on them. If not bid on, the goods were immediately forfeited to the state. *Time* remarked it would be simpler for the Nazis "to order Jews to stay or starve or emigrate naked." In the same article, it noted Prague had just "forcibly driven" 400 Austrian Jews back across a secluded section of its border with Germany as it had reached a "refugee saturation point.[89]

Myron Taylor told the new organization's delegates it would take sixteen years, at the rate visas were being issued, to find homes for the 660,900 refugees needing a haven. To earlier refugee estimates, he added a new section for Italian Jews. In July, the Italian government announced all Italians, with the exception of Italian Jews, were "Aryan-Nordic" in their "orientation" and that a "racial under-secretary" would be added to its Ministry of Interior. Italians were warned not to lose their "racial purity" through marriage with Jews. The immediate effect was to warn Jewish refugees Italy was no refuge for them.[90] All Italian schools were subsequently closed to foreign Jews and the Fascist party declared only one Italian Jew out of every 1,000 could participate in the "full life of the state." Ludwig Lore argued Italian Jews had loyally supported the Fascist party and state. They had volunteered for service in Ethiopia, supported the war with donations, and denounced Zionism. Yet, they were now under attack because Mussolini wanted to demonstrate his solidarity with Hitler and to insist on unconditional allegiance from all Italians. This demonstrated, according to Lore, that there was "no place for the Jew in a fascist world."[91] Pope Pius XI promptly denounced the new anti-Semitic laws and was, in turn, denounced by the fascist press.[92]

In September, Mussolini further ordered all Jews who had settled in Italy, Libya, and the Dodecanese Islands after January 1, 1919, to leave Italian soil within six months. A "Jew" was defined as a person who had Jewish parents—grandparents were not mentioned. There were between 10,000 to 20,000 Jews who fell under this definition. A second decree prohibited Jews from attending or teaching in any school or university after October 16. Approximately 10,000 students and 300 professors and teachers were affected by this decree.[93]

The same week of the Italian decree, the Grand Duchy of Luxemburg closed its frontiers to all Jewish refugees while the Swiss government announced it would string barbed wire along its frontiers "to stop the Jewish flood." In Danzig, Nazis destroyed the Jewish synagogue and declared the city's 400 Jews had to sell their property to the government "at Nazi dictated prices." In Kiev, the Red Army had to be used to suppress anti-Jewish riots.[94]

The Nation alleged anti-Semitism was also subtly increasing in the United States. Opponents of Roosevelt and the New Deal had begun "to damn the Jews for Roosevelt's alleged sins." Businessmen could be overheard equally damning Jewish financial and labor leaders as "subversives." When Morris Ernst fought Boss Hague of New Jersey, he was called "a Jew communist." Even conservative Jews now looked upon the Jew who defended "the cause of free speech" as "a person of dubious judgment." It called for a campaign to refute the anti-Semites.[95] Henry Ford, on his seventy-fifth birthday, accepted with great publicity Hitler's award of the Grand Cross of the German Eagle.[96] There seemed to be no limit or end to the Jewish tragedy. No nation wanted them and there was no place for them to hide.

The British partition of Palestine, according to John Gunther, was the "best amelioration in sight" for the persecuted Jews. The partition, however, was certainly going to meet resistance from the Arabs, who were aware of *"their own economic, political and cultural inferiority."* The Arabs had become increasingly not only "anti-Jew, but anti-British" and had launched "a real civil war" in the form of "mass terrorism." The terrorism sought "to disorganize the forces of authority by secret and subterranean means." Only time would tell if the British would be able to repress the terrorists. Jews were initially "bitter" about the Peel Report until they realized "the Arabs opposed it more vehemently than they did." Palestinian Zionists had then become "partitionists" and sought "their own state no matter how small." They insisted only a Jewish state could offer succor and refuge to persecuted Jews.[97]

If Palestine was to provide a haven for European Jews, there was little reason to believe that it would be a safe refuge. Arab terrorism, combined with the partition proposal had led to a violent three-way conflict there. When the British proved unable to suppress the Arab terrorists, Vladimir Jabotinsky organized the Revisionist movement out of "firebrands" of the Zionist party. The Revisionists were sworn to meet Arab terror with counter-terror and to drive the British from Palestine. In early July, the British hung a young Jew, Ben Yosef, for ambushing an Arab bus with gunfire—the "first" Jew executed in Palestine "since the fall of their Temple in 70 A.D." The result was increased Revisionist attacks on both the British and Arabs.[98] *Time* reported the following week that Revisionists, one of whom was a twelve-year old girl, had repeatedly tossed bombs into Moslem crowds. For "the first time in recent history," Jews had resorted to violence to defend themselves. In "ten days of terrorism," forty-five Arabs and twenty-three Jews were killed, 145 Arabs and eighty-one Jews were wounded. The British rushed the *Repulse* to Haifa and ordered 1,600 more British troops to Palestine. *Newsweek* reported the Arab terrorists were being armed in Trans-Jordan and Syria. According to *The Nation*, Palestine had become a "Death Trap for Jews."[99] On August 15, *Time* reported that Arab bands, nicknamed "Oozlebarts" by British Tommies, had virtually become the rulers of Palestine at night—when British troops withdrew into the safety of their forts. Arab "military courts" were punishing any Arab who did business with Jews or the British. The bands were increasingly attacking Jewish collective farms. The following week, the Imans of Iraq issued a *fativa* declaring the terrorism against the Jews and British in Palestine a *"jihad"* or holy war. The Jews and British braced themselves for a new level of fanaticism in the Arab attacks.[100] When the Nazis met at Nurnberg for their 1938 Congress, 100 Arabs were present and received a clamorous welcome each time they made a public appearance.[101] The struggle continued, with varying degrees of intensity, to October—when it escalated once again to an even higher level of violence.

During the first half of 1938, our magazines continued their pattern of reporting the effects of Nazism on German domestic life. In February, *The Reader's Digest* reported German women had been driven from the universities and work-force and reduced to the level of bearing "the children the Fatherland needs for future wars." In the secondary schools, stress was placed on their "physical training," the "glorification of the State and war," "loyalty to Hitler," and the "acceptance of racial superiority." The majority of German girls and women accepted the situation and were "satisfied with household cares and the bearing of children." "Young girls" were "enthusiastic over the promise of husbands." In actuality, "drudgery" was the destiny of the German female.[102]

In April, the *Digest* noted Germany had mounted a "herculean effort to achieve self-sufficiency." As one result, flour and clothing were being made from wood fiber. There was even an *ersatz* margarine made "of fats extracted from wood." Initially intended as machine grease, "after trying it on prison inmates," the government declared it "edible" and made it part of the food ration. As part of this program of self-sufficiency, housewives had to turn into the government even used soup bones. Stage magicians were forbidden "to use eggs, milk, or other eatables" in their acts. The use of barter in foreign trade had produced some "odd transactions." Standard Oil, "in one deal," had accepted "40,000,000 mouth organs" in payment. The Budd Machinery Company of Philadelphia accepted "200,000 canary birds" in lieu of a $43,000 payment. Metro-Goldwyn-Mayer accepted "a live hippopotamus" in payment— which it resold to an American circus. Germany had adopted the economy of a "blockaded country" or a "beleaguered fortress" and Germans had adopted their lives to "synthetic living" with "notable patience."[103]

Hitler's efforts to reduce unemployment in Germany had met great success and by July, 1938, there were only 37,000 Germans, out of 20,500,000 workers, who had no jobs. *Time* called this unemployment reduction "remarkable," noting Hitler "had actually created a labor shortage." Much of German labor was not employed in war production but in the creation of roads, the "production of cheap *Volkswagen* automobiles," and the "rebuilding of Berlin and Munich." To meet the labor shortage, Goering had decreed a draft of all German workers. *Newsweek* was far more critical of the new labor law. It noted even Russia had not openly adopted such severe measures. *Newsweek* attributed the unemployment reduction to public-works projects, the removal of women from the industrial force, and the expansion of the bureaucracy of the Nazi party and the state. It added, however, arms production and army conscription had played a significant role in the labor shortage. Berlin correspondents, it averred, forecast that Jews would be made to work for Hitler "as their forebears once did for the Pharoahs." A week later, *Time* called the German labor "Strength Through Joy" movement "spectacular," pointing out that "in 1936, 6,000,000 workers" had enjoyed inexpensive vacations across Europe.[104]

In May, *Collier's* ran one of its customary biographical sketches on leading Nazis—this time on Heinrich Himmler. Himmler headed the entire police organization in the Third Reich, including the "black-shirt stalwarts" of the SS. He had initially risen in Nazi ranks by making "the Nazi party in Bavaria" the "best gang of hell-raisers in Germany." Now Himmler, rather than the better publicized Goering or Goebbels, was "the most likely heir apparent" to "the Fuehrer." He was the "wily, slight, anemic-looking" man who wielded "the iron fist" for Hitler. A "cunning, crafty" man with a "genius" for organization, he kept a dossier on every important person in Germany—probably even "on himself." Six days a week, he could "liquidate Germans" and then retire, on the seventh day, to "his chicken-farm" convinced the heads had rolled "for the good of the Reich." As long as Hitler lived, Himmler would be "his trusted lieutenant, his man Friday." For Hitler, Himmler had given up God and killed even "his closest comrades." As police chief, he had remade German law into "the law of the jungle."[105]

This "law of the jungle" was described when, in June, *Collier's* published an account of the imprisonment for seven months of an "Aryan" German in Dachau. The victim, who had subsequently emigrated to the United States, had been imprisoned for referring to Hitler as "that actor." Without even the formality of a trial by the Gestapo, he was placed in a prison battalion and subjected to physical and mental abuse that reduced him to a shell of his former self. Prisoners were systematically starved, beaten, and degraded to the point where they were afraid to speak even to their fellow inmates. The slightest offense brought a beating—severe offenses carried the death penalty. Many inmates committed suicide rather than face the prospect of continued imprisonment. The victims were "Communists, Socialists, Jews, priests, ex-officials and back-slid Nazis." The guards were "young, black-uniformed SS troops, 200-per-cent Nazi," usually "18 to 20" years old. Although heavily armed, their "real weapons" were "kicks" and clubs. Jews received the worst labor details and abuse in the camp. The narrator was released from Dachau only because, prior to his imprisonment, he had been granted an American visa.[106]

The military nature of the Third Reich was also emphasized by our magazines. Emil Ludwig wrote that Germany stood "in clattering armor before the world demanding vengeance" for Versailles. German "honor" demanded "victory by arms." Any understanding of the Third Reich had to be based on this tenet. Hitler, the perfect embodiment of the German mind, did not want territory or raw materials, but "war for the sake of victory." Nothing less could erase the "feeling of inferiority" in every German's breast. If

"Americans and the English" realized this "frenzy," they might avert war but it was improbable war could be prevented. The "German Soul" had become "the Sword."[107]

In the view of Stephan H. Roberts, Germany had become "The House That Hitler Built." After spending sixteen months driving 8,000 miles across Germany, Roberts concluded Hitler epitomized a "great upsurge of the unconscious in the German people." With the continual cry of *"Deutschland erwache!,"* he had galvanized the latent military spirit of the German people and endued them with a *Weltanshauung* based on the myth of *"Blood and Soil."* The "only outcome" of this myth "must be a fight" against all "inferior races" on the "ultimate stage" of history. Hitler had thus "resurrected tribal instincts and the mystical sanctions of a savage society." Without thought for the basic laws of economics, he had created "the finest" army and air force in Europe and launched a drive for self-sufficiency. Only conquests in the future would be able to balance the debts he had already incurred. Hitler, to support the drive for conquest, had transformed the youth of Germany into "clean-living zealots" pledged to sacrifice life itself for the Fuehrer.

Roberts, although describing Nazi anti-Semitism as "a campaign of annihilation," revealed his own anti-Semitism when he wrote that "the undoubted facts that a Jewish minority had secured an overlarge measure of professional success," due "in some cases" to "racial influence," had produced Hitler's Jewish policies. Roberts went on to say "50.2 percent of the lawyers" and 48 percent of the doctors" in Berlin were Jews. These Jewish doctors had "systematically seized the principal hospital posts," "two thirds of the school and welfare positions," and half the teaching posts of the medical faculty of the University of Berlin. Further, he alleged, Jews owned the "largest and most important Berlin newspapers" and "had made great inroads on the educational system." Roberts asserted, however, that the "program" had reached the point where it was "utterly incomprehensible." Roberts concluded "Hitler's ideas...of necessity lead to war" and it was inevitable unless Hitler modified his policies or there was a transition "to some other regime." If war came, it seemed most likely it would be ignited by the *Sudetenland* issue.[108]

Diplomatic activity over the *Sudetenland* increased in June. Chamberlain's "policy of recounciliation and peace," which was supposed to lay the foundation for a four-power pact to guarantee peace in Europe, received a number of diplomatic and domestic set-backs in June, 1938. Hitler refused to mute his aggressive designs against Czechoslovakia over the *Sudetenland* and unleashed a massive propaganda campaign charging it was systematically persecuting its German minority and that it was a communist bastion in central Europe.[109] Heinlein, leader of the Czech Nazis, although supposedly negotiating with Premier Hodza about *Sudetenlander* conditions, was privately stating that any concessions by Benes would be rejected outright. Heinlein told Ward Price of the pro-Nazi *London Daily Mail,* owned by Lord Rothermere, that he expected the *"Sudetenland* problem" would "simply" be solved "next fall" by "direct action by the German Government." According to *Newsweek,* the Czech crisis was "apt to grow more serious" as Hitler showed no intention of accepting any settlement that denied him hegenomy in central Europe. *Time* subsequently asserted "the Fuehrer will accept no 'solution' of the Sudeten problem" as he was determined to force Czechoslovakia into Germany's orbit.[110]

The Czechs, for their part, seemed determined to resist Hitler's demands even if it meant war. Hodza and Benes extended Czech compulsory military service from two to three years, issued decrees making every Czech from six to sixty liable for some type of auxiliary service, and promoted the *Sokol* sports organizations as paramilitary forces. They further announced, in response to informal pressure from Chamberlain, that they had no intention of releasing France and Russia from their military alliances with Czechoslovakia. In repeated public speeches, Hodza affirmed "Czechoslovakia would defend itself to the last."[111] *Collier's* asserted the Czechs were "united in their will" and were waiting for Hitler, "not afraid, but surely not glad," and would defend their nation to the bitter end. *The Nation* asserted Chamberlain was also losing his influence with Daladier as French public opinion was swinging around to a decision to defend Czechoslovakia. Daladier and Bonnet were now urging Benes to resist making any concessions to the *Sudeten* Germans. Any attempt by Chamberlain to appease Hitler by sacrificing Prague was therefore likely to run into the shoals of French intransigence.[112]

Chamberlain's pact with Mussolini, intended as a foundation block for the proposed four-power pact, was also revealed to be worthless by events in Spain. Mussolini not only rejected Chamberlain's efforts to end the bombing of civilians in Spain but also ignored his appeals for negotiations between Franco and the republicans. Even more importantly, after twenty-two British ships had been attacked in republican ports by fascist planes, Chamberlain could not secure Mussolini's help to end the attacks. He was reduced to informing the Commons Britain was unable to protect its ships and that they would henceforth enter Spanish waters at their own risk. Chamberlain's Italian policy had therefore lost all its "deceptive plausibility."[113] A vote of censure moved by the Labor party was voted down by 275-to-141. Churchill led ten Conservatives to desert the government.[114]

In addition to these international rebuffs, Chamberlain's policies were also coming under increasing domestic criticism. Maurice Hankey, who held the three posts of Permanent Secretary for Imperial Defense, Clerk of the Privy Council, and Permanent Secretary to the Cabinet, had to be dismissed by Chamberlain for his growing opposition to official policy. Eden, increasingly under Churchill's influence, broke the silence he had maintained since his resignation as Foreign Secretary and moved over to open opposition against Chamberlain. A number of Tories began to look to Eden for leadership.[115] On June 1, Hitler renounced all Austrian foreign debts. This repudiation antagonized the "potent" Association of British Chambers of Commerce which insisted Chamberlain impound German credits in Britain. Chamberlain thus had the choice of alienating the bondholders by accepting the repudiation or of antagonizing Hitler by freezing Nazi credits, a move that "would blight" his "hopes of an Anglo-German appeasement."[116] Hitler, however, defused the issue by reaching a private agreement with Chamberlain to repay the Austrian loan bonds held in Britain. Britain agreed to lower the interest rate on the Austrian debt and threw in lower rates on the Dawes and Young loans. Other creditors were left to fend for themselves.[117]

Chamberlain, who had been searching for a means to bind French policy closer to that of Whitehall, finally discovered a method to achieve his purpose. The last week of July, King George of Britain made a state visit to France to "cement" the alliance between London and Paris. Halifax accompanied the king and met privately with Daladier, who was under pressure from some of his cabinet to defend Czechoslovakia. Immediately before leaving London, Halifax had received Hitler's "suggestions" for a settlement with Prague from Fritz Wiedemann, Hitler's "confidential emmisary."[118] There were rumors Hitler had insisted the "Czechoslovak Question" be resolved by a four-power conference of Britain, France, Italy, and Germany. Prague and Moscow had to be excluded from the conference. Halifax was instructed by Chamberlain to secure French acceptance of this plan. From London, Chamberlain announced Viscount Runciman would visit Prague at the request of Hodza to arbitrate differences between the Czechs and the *Sudeten* Nazis. Benes promptly denied any such invitation but agreed to meet Runciman anyway.[119] Hitler increased the pressure on Chamberlain by moving troops to Germany's border with the *Sudetenland*, demanding a "solution" had to be found by the middle of August, and hinting he would agree to Chamberlain's long-sought four-power pact. *The Nation* asserted that, under these conditions, Runciman was the man selected to throw out "the baby just before the wolves catch up with the sleigh." *Newsweek*, however, asserted Europe pinned "its hope" on Runciman's ability to make peace.[120]

On the weekend of August 8, while Runciman was "studying" the *Sudetenland* problem, Hitler ordered the harvest gatherered as quickly as possible so horses could be released to the German army, requisitioned private trucks in Germany, ordered the Siegfried Line manned, and mobilized all German reserves for "autumn maneuvers." He declined to name a terminal date for the maneuvers. France planned to mobilize its reserves and defend Czechoslovakia although it was in a financial crisis and was totally unprepared for war.[121] However, if Hitler's announcements were designed to panic Chamberlain and, through him, Daladier, they succeeded beautifully. Chamberlain, horrified at the thought of conflict, stated at a luncheon given by Lady Astor that he was "in favor" of a territorial revision awarding the *Sudetenland* to Germany.[122]

Willson Woodside argued in *Harper's* that Germany did not possess the necessary raw materials to fight a major war. If war did come, Germany would have to move quickly to seize materials and transport from "Lapland to the Black Sea." This would place her at war simultaneously with Czechoslovakia, France, Rumania, Russia, Poland, Yugoslavia, "probably Britain," and "perhaps Scandinavia." Only "someone insane" could believe Germany would prevail against these odds. Yet, it must be remembered "saner heads" were "not in control of Germany to-day" and war might well come. Hitler seemed determined to take the *Sudetenland*—by agreement or force.[123]

By the first week of September, there were clear indications the *Sudetenland* situation was reaching the crisis point. Germany was fully mobilized, the Nazi press was hysterically reporting Czech attacks and atrocities against *Sudeten* Germans, and the *Sudeten* Nazis were arming to the teeth. The Hungarian minority in Czechoslovakia declared its support for Heinlein, the Nazi leader. There were rumors Hitler had informed Budapest and Belgrade he might invade the *Sudetenland* to "restore order." Runciman spent increasingly large periods of time conferring with *Sudetenland* Nazi leaders. Goering told diplomats from central European states he had "definite information" the "British will not lift a finger" if Hitler decided to march. Chamberlain, however, ordered the British Home Fleet to its war station at Scapa Flow by September 6. The Foreign Office reiterated Chamberlain's statement of March that Britain would give no "prior guarantee" to Prague.[124] *The New Republic* reported "the war panic has therefore been renewed, worse than before." *The Nation* argued "the next weeks will settle the fate of the world." Even if the British succeeded in securing Czech agreement to a cession of the *Sudetenland*, Hitler would view it only as a "temporary compromise" and would not alter his plans to destroy Czechoslovakia at the first opportunity.[125]

As Europe balanced on the edge of war, American insurance firms doubled their premiums on American property abroad and the pound dropped to a three year low. Lloyd's announced it would no longer issue war-risk insurance policies. The Royal Navy recalled recently pensioned reserves to the fleet, the Royal Air Force moved to its dispersal bases, and the War Office ordered specialists into the army. On September 5, Paris called up "thousands of reserves," cancelled all military leaves, brought the Maginot Line up to strength, and provisioned its battle fleet for sea duty. Tons of sand was trucked into Paris for possible use in sand-bags. The "Third Reich was an armed camp" with 1,500,000 in uniform. All former officers and technicians of the air force were recalled, doctors had to report their whereabouts, and all non-military construction suspended.[126] Rumania agreed to allow Russian troops to cross its territory to aid the Czechs provided Warsaw did not protest. Moscow announced it would stand by its pact with Czechoslovakia.[127] *The New Republic* wondered if there would be "War Now, or Later," while *The Nation* wrote diplomacy had reached a "Dead End in Europe."[128] *The Nation* demanded that, given the likelihood of war, Congress repeal the Neutrality and Johnson Acts because they stood "in the way of help to possible victims of aggression."[129]

While these military preparations were being made, Runciman continued to pressure Hodza and Benes for greater and greater concessions to Hitler. Hitler adamantly held out for even larger concessions each time Runciman presented a new series of concessions—"Plans" one to three were quickly rejected. The final offer of Benes was to cantonize each area of the *Sudetenland*, apportion state jobs according to the percentage of each minority in a canton, establish a separate minority post in each ministry of the common government, and provide $35,000,000 to revitalize the economy of the *Sudetenlanders*. Even this plan was rejected by Heinlein although talks and negotiations were allowed to continue.[130]

At the tenth Nazi Party Congress in Nuremberg, Hitler demanded the *Sudetenlanders* be given "self-determination" immediately. *The London Times* editorially observed Czechoslovakia might best cede the area to Germany and instantly created consternation both in Britain and on the continent. Paris and Prague demanded to know if it was Britain's official position while Berlin papers stated Chamberlain approved of the annexation. Chamberlain had to repudiate the statement and reassure Paris "to nip a cabinet crisis."[131] *Time* believed that, given Chamberlain's statement, Hitler would accept the determination of Chamberlain to protect Czechoslovakia and the crisis had passed.[132]

The treatment of the Munich crisis by *The Atlantic Monthly* of September, 1938, demonstrates an inherent problem faced by our magazines, especially the monthlies, when dealing with a fast-breaking story. In attempting to keep their readers informed, they had to run either "background material" which was so broad as to be of little news value or take the chance of being superceded by events. For example, Carl J. Frederick asserted Benes would be "firm" in the crisis and, though "not ruthless," would resist any cession to Hitler. Slow "to strike," Benes knew when "you cannot compromise on principles" and would maintain his principles "even against overwhelming odds." Everyone, including "the British Conservatives" knew that he could not be bluffed. Czechoslovakia would meet force with force. The only remaining question was whether the democracies would support him in his moment of trial.[133] By the time this issue reached all its readers, Chamberlain was already meeting with Hitler to arrange the Munich pact.

To simply rehearse the events leading from Godesburg to Munich would serve little purpose here. What is important here is to identify the interpretations placed upon the chief characters of the conference and the reaction to their agreement by the magazines studied.

The New Republic and *The Nation* spared few invectives in their criticism of the conduct of Chamberlain and Daladier both during and after the Munich Conference. Following the announcement they would meet with Hitler and Mussolini at Munich to transfer the *Sudetenland* to Germany, *The New Republic* asserted Daladier had been driven by fear to join Chamberlain in a "Great Surrender" to the "psychologically abnormal fanatic" of "Berlin." For his part, Chamberlain, under the influence of the "Clivenden clique," had surrendered out of a desire to block communism in central Europe and "to safeguard the interests of the propertied classes of the Empire." The two, led thus by their fears, had joined to "sacrifice Czechoslovakia to the Nazi Moloch" in an act which was "the ultimate in cowardice and faithlessness." They had, by "their betrayal," not won peace but merely postponed temporarily, the coming "great war." According to *The Nation*, the two leaders had made a "brutal and irresponsible betrayal" of Prague in order to give "Hitler his pound of flesh" in return for his wall against bolshevism in central Europe. Their "Great Betrayal" originated in their undiluted "cowardice" which prevented them from joining with Soviet Russia.[134]

Time believed "there was never any doubt that Chief Chamberlain would *not* quarrel with Chief Hitler" as Chamberlain was determined not to fight "with the Soviet Union" as his ally. He therefore had to obtain the cession peacefully and so prevent France and Czechoslovakia from declaring war and bringing Moscow into central Europe as their ally. *Newsweek* insisted Chamberlain and Daladier had "suddenly discovered that their people would not fight for such a remote issue as Czechoslovakia" and, in addition, were "influenced by strong opinion" in their "respective nations" in "favor of coming to terms with the new Germany.[135] The British and French public had been "terrified" by the prospect of an attack by the German air force. In Britain "the strong opinion" was identified as "the Astor, Rothermere, Beaverbrook, and Camrose press" which collectively controlled "55 of the country's largest newspapers." Lord Londonderry, leader of "the Clivenden group," even wrote a letter to Hitler at the height of the crisis and had flown to Munich to confer with Goering and give him his advice. In France, deputies in the Chamber informed Daladier their electorates were opposed to war.[136]

Chamberlain returned home to be met by overwhelming cheers and acclaim. Chamberlain was nominated for the Nobel Peace Prize for 1938. Although Duff Cooper, First Lord of the Admiralty, resigned in protest over Munich, Chamberlain won a vote of confidence in Commons 366—144. A poll showed fifty-seven percent of the British public approved the Munich Agreement.[137] Chamberlain did reorganize the Territorial Guard or army reserve system, request funds for an enlarged navy and air force, and for the stockpiling of foodstuffs. In early November, the Conservative party gained twenty new seats in the British elections for municipal offices while Chamberlain won another vote of confidence on his foreign policy by a vote of 345—138.[138]

Daladier, like Chamberlain, was met by wild acclamation on his return home. He won an immediate vote of confidence in the Chamber 366—144. Although his Popular Front cabinet was dissolved by the resignation of the communists, Daladier was given power to rule by emergency decree until November 15, when the Chamber was due to reconvene. As France swerved to the right, Daladier announced a major rearmament plan for the army and air force.[139] Daladier, speaking at a Radical Socialist party meeting, urged a French pact with Hitler and Mussolini and bitterly denounced the communists. *Newsweek* predicted he was lining up "his party for friendship with dictators."[140]

Benes and Hodza, who had mobilized the Czech army and prepared to resist Hitler, were overwhelmingly supported by the Czech populace, Russia, and Rumania. However, they had been bluntly told that Britain and France did not intend to fight. This rendered null and void any Russia assistance as Russia was not required, nor could fight, until France and so Rumania, came to the aid of the Czechs.[141] Benes, realizing he could not fight Hitler alone, had accepted the inevitable and resigned. A pro-Nazi ministry had been formed which had surrendered Teschen to the Poles and immediately sent a delegation to "coordinate Czech policy" with that of Germany.[142]

Upon the resignation Benes and Hodza, General Jan Syrovy assumed the premiership of the Czech state and appointed Frantisek Chvalkovsky as foreign minister. Autonomy was immediately granted to Slovakia and Ruthenia. The communist party and the Free Masons voluntarily dissolved their organizations. The government promptly instituted compulsory work camps for all unemployed youth under eighteen. When Syrovy announced all German and Austrian refugees had to leave Czechoslovakia, numbers of these refugees promptly committed suicide.[143] "Hundreds of desperate Jews," "booted" from the *Sudetenland* by the Nazi SA, were refused permission to enter Czechoslovakia by Prague as they "were technically citizens of Germany." The "starving, penniless refugees" took shelter "under hedges" between the German and Czech armies. They were finally saved by the Czech Red Cross at the urging of Wilbur J. Carr, American minister to Prague. In Prague, "university students and young doctors" attacked Jews in cafes and on the streets with shouts of "Down with the Jews!"[144]

There was little agreement in American magazines about Hitler's motives. Even in the same magazine there were often sharply divergent interpretations at times. On September 24, and October 1 for example, *The Nation* insisted Hitler had precipitated the crisis to seize the Skoda works and the Czech armaments industry. On October 1, *The Nation* also asserted Hitler's bombast over the *Sudetenland* had placed him in a position where he had to act because he "couldn't afford to back down." It asserted in the same issue Hitler was motivated by the desire to remove the "last barrier" to his control of Central Europe or again, by his determination "to break the Franco-Soviet pact."[145]

The New Republic believed on September 28 that Hitler acted in order to destroy the Franco-Russian pact and isolate Moscow, but on October 5 that Hitler was driven by the revolution he had created and which he could not stop without his own destruction. On October 12, it asserted Hitler was motivated by an urge to establish Teutonic domination over Slavs. In the same issue, it insisted he wanted the Czech industry and raw materials along with the use of the Czechs as "vassals" for his "master race."[146]

The one consistent theme in *The New Republic* and *The Nation* was that Hitler was *not* motivated by concern for the *Sudetenlanders*.

Hitler, following the cession, toured the *Sudetenland* where he was met with wild acclaim and bouquets of flowers. He vowed the area would be German "forever." Riding on the crest of his triumph, he denied Hungary any share of Czech territory until the pro-Nazi Admiral Horthy assumed the premiership of Hungary. He then unilaterally gave Hungary a cession of Czech provinces. Chamberlain and Daladier were not consulted about the cession. At Hitler's direction, generous trade and barter arrangements were concluded with Bulgaria, Yugoslavia, and Poland. They were assumed to have moved over into the German orbit. In Germany, the army reserves were demobilized but construction of the Siegfried Line was speeded up.[147]

Of our magazines, only *Time* defended the Munich settlement. *Time* argued "the triumph of Germany was enormous, but not without limits." Hitler had demanded 14,200 square miles of Czech territory but had received only 12,000 square miles. Although he had destroyed the Little Entente and the French-Czech pact with Russia, he now faced a British guarantee to Czechoslovakia "even more definite" than Britain's "unwritten entente" with France. Further, the crisis had "proved with finality" that "modern communication and enlightenment of the peoples reduce the chances of an outbreak of war." With less than an accurate reading of history, *Time* insisted "for the first time in history," a major crisis had been "settled by talking instead of shooting first." "Realists" could take "heart from one fact"—the conference had at least "set a precedent, which might flower into a great influence for peace, for aggressors being persuaded to follow legal—diplomatic forms." The following week, responding to charges Chamberlain had traded the *Sudetenland* for peace, it argued "any man could see last week" that "the Munich Agreement was not a trade." Chamberlain had wisely decided to preserve the British empire and its navy so as to preserve the peace. The British navy was the surest guarantee of peace both in Europe and the Pacific."[148] Only *Time* attempted to defend the Munich Pact in this way. It is noteworthy that neither *Time* or our other magazines argued Chamberlain had signed the Munich Pact in order to buy time for rearmament.

It was unanimously agreed by our magazines that, in the words of *Time*, "U. S. opinion had performed a major shift." It noted "pacifists like Thomas Mann" and "realists" like Dorothy Thompson had joined to attack Hitler and Nazism and to defend Czechoslovakia. Episcopal Bishop Manning of New York, formerly a staunch pacifist, reversed his attitude and insisted that, at "some point," force would be needed to stop Hitler. *Newsweek* reported that in "28 cities, citizens jammed into halls and stadiums" to cheer the Czechs while they "booed and hissed every mention of Hitler's name." In Chicago, one such rally attracted 30,000 people. In New York, "a rabidly pro-Czech gathering in Madison Square Garden" cheered "for three hours" its organizer's attacks on Hitler.[149] *The Nation* pointed out the "Hearst press supported the Nazi program in its headlines" and that the New York *Daily News* had defended the partition of Czechoslovakia. However, *The New York Times, The Chicago News,* and *The New York Herald Tribune* had sharply taken Hitler to task and their reports had been those that galvanized the American people—not those of Hearst. *The New Republic* wrote American opinion was "solidly against Hitler" and was "far more bitterly aroused against Germany" than it had been prior to April, 1917. There was "no use in advising 'neutrality of thought' " to Americans any longer. A group of "war veterans," stirred up by the news reports, attacked and beat Bund members at a rally of the organization in Union City, New Jersey.[150]

According to *Newsweek* and *The Nation*, radio had, for the first time, dominated all reporting on an international crisis. *The Nation* was profuse in its praise of H.B. Kaltenborn's erudition and forceful delivery. It also praised "Edward R. Morrow of C.B.S." for "the superb job" he had done in his day to day broadcasts and for his coup in broadcasting Jan Masaryk's speech live and direct from London. Radio had brought news "of the rush of events" to "millions of listeners in rural districts" of America and, again for the first time, provided them with "a generous stream of facts and interpretations." *Newsweek* commented that although "Americans were still isolated emotionally—radio took care of that." It reported "443 news programs and bulletins in three weeks." Of these, "113 originated in Europe." "C.B.S., again with only two men abroad," had devoted 2,847 minutes or "nearly two full broadcasting days" to the crisis and had presented "98 programs from fourteen European news centers."[151]

As a result of these radio broadcasts, "in every American city and crossroads village, men and women thought and talked of little" but the crisis. Villard of *The Nation* reported he had seen "seven men—attendants and customers— with their heads in a car in a Vermont filling station" listening to radio reports from Europe. *Newsweek* correspondents from around the United States telegraphed reports of "citizens crowded around loud-speakers in taverns, cigar stores, and parked automobiles to hear the voices from abroad." From Oklahoma and Texas came reports "even some farmers quit work in the fields to hear Hitler's September 26 speech."[152] Americans had emotionally been pulled into the European cockpit by their ears.

Yet, these American emotions did not translate into a determination to oppose Hitler by sharp diplomatic protest or collective security arrangements with the European democracies. Roosevelt, during the period of the crisis, was under tremendous pressure from the isolationists to do and say nothing. According to *Time*, the State Department "turned its deafest ear, its stoniest silence" to all appeals for American action. Prominent "Congressional leaders" urged caution on both Roosevelt and the American people. Much official action was devoted by the administration to making arrangements to absorb the $500,000,000 in gold rushed from European treasuries, banks, and private investors to the United States.[153] When Roosevelt did act, he was cautious and sent "innocuous" cables to Europe pleading for peace. With his ear close to the ground as always, he realized that, for many Americans, even this was too much. One positive effect was the call, from all quarters, for the increased rearming of America.[154]

Roosevelt promptly called for an increase in the rearmament of the navy and air force. Bernard Baruch was asked to organize the necessary technical and economic infrastructure for the production of dies, tools, and jigs for national defense. When Hitler included the United States with Britain and France in an attack on the rearming of the democracies, Hull replied the defense of the United States was a purely domestic matter.[155] Roosevelt had Hull urge the Lima Conference of Latin American states to "place their houses in order" to resist Nazi infiltration and totalitarianism. *Newsweek* noted even "Post-Munich pacifists did not complain" about these actions of Roosevelt. They believed rearmament would provide a shield behind which the United States could insulate itself from the vexations of Europe.[156]

A number of our magazines, although bitter in their denunciations of Hitler, were solidly in the pacifist camp. Desirous of seeing an end to the Nazi threat, they still wanted the menace to disappear without American military involvement. As one result, their suggestions for keeping the peace, while restraining Hitler, appear surrealistic and utopian. *The Nation* urged Roosevelt to convene an international conference to resolve "the whole problem of European minorities." To support agreements reached by the conference, the United States "could offer favorable trade agreements" accompanied by "credits and loans." *The New Republic* stressed Roosevelt's aims should be "to keep out of war" while refraining from "action which would materially injure the success of those whose cause we favor." He should certainly avoid making promises "the American people are not prepared to fulfill." On October 12, *The New Republic* insisted America help "the West" to "redefine" its "economic and spiritual concepts" in "dynamic terms" as an alternative to Nazi ideology.[157] The following week it urged "a real experiment in the way of a civilization" that would demonstrate the futility and folly of Nazism. Both agreed the United States should avoid pledges to Britain and France for the crisis had revealed they could not be trusted. *Newsweek* advocated placing "strong moral pressure on dictatorial powers" and, if war broke out, "unequivocally placing the blame on Hitler's shoulders." However, America must not resort to force unless attacked.[158]

Demaree Bess, writing in *The Saturday Evening Post* prior to Munich, argued pacifists had divided into two camps, not only domestically but internationally. One group believed in and fought for peace, but was willing to defend the concept of "collective security" against "totalitarian" governments and, if pushed, would fight a "holy crusade" against "aggressor nations." A second group was "logically more consistent" in stressing wars created more problems than they settled and that they were not fought on "any such artificial issue as 'totalitarianism' or 'Fascism' or 'dictatorship'." This latter group knew wars were always fought for "self-interest." The crusaders either deceived themselves or were attempting to "mislead their followers" and genuine pacifists should be wary of them.[159]

After Munich, Demaree Bess continued to insist on strict pacifism as the only intelligent course for Americans. In his view, "Munich was not a duel"— "it was a deal." It revealed the true struggle in Europe was not one of "democracy versus dictatorship" but another example of the "everlasting game of European power politics." Any "moral issue" of aid to "democracies" like Britain and France was "neatly cleared off the board" by the action of Chamberlain and Daladier. There should be no more talk of "quarantining aggressor nations" after Munich. America must look to its own self-interest and, if war came anyhow, defend its self-interest only.[160]

Norman Thomas also attacked the idea that the "present conflicts" in Europe were "a clash of ideologies" or "dictatorships and democracies." Hewing to a pure pacifist line, he asserted American participation was not necessary to crush fascism. Russia alone had an army large enough to defeat both Germany and Japan. If America did enter the coming war, democracy would be lost here at home as modern war called for a totalitarian state. Finally, America had no interests to defend against either Germany or Japan except those of monopoly capitalism. What was ultimately necessary was to stop wars by keeping the peace.[161]

The debate, however, did not run entirely one way. Thomas Mann urged the United States to prepare for war as it was an "illusion that compromise with fascism is possible" or that fascists could be "won over to the idea of peace and collective reconstruction by forbearance, or amicable concessions." In "every concession" fascists would only see "a sign of weakness, of resignation, and of abdication." What was needed was "a humanity strong in will and firm in the determination to preserve itself," for "freedom must learn to walk in armor." Pacifism that would not fight in any circumstances would "surely bring about war."[162]

Yet another view was represented by Charles A. Lindbergh. During the Munich crisis, Lindbergh had declared, at a dinner party given by Lady Astor, that the German air force was stronger than the combined air strength of the rest of Europe. After Munich, at a dinner given by Hugh R. Wilson, American ambassador in Berlin, Lindbergh "glowed with embarrassed pride" when Goering "hung the Service Cross of the Order of the German Eagle around Lindbergh's neck and pinned on his chest the six-pointed star that goes with it."[163]

Even as this American debate was going on, it became apparent Hitler had gained more from the Munich agreement than the *Sudetenland.* Hungary moved into his orbit and demanded its own slice of the Czechoslovakian state. Poland swiftly moved to seize Teschen and identify itself with the aggressor states. Turkey, which had just accepted a British loan designed to pull it closer to London, reversed its course and accepted a large line of credit from Germany. The Franco-Soviet pact was destroyed along with Prague's pact with Moscow. Litvinov, a consistent supporter of Russian cooperation with the West, was recalled to Moscow. The Scandinavian states announced they no longer felt bound to join the League in applying sanctions to an aggressor.[164] Japan adopted a more aggressive posture toward British outposts and interests at Canton and Hong Kong. *The New Republic* twice predicted the way had been prepared for a Nazi-Soviet pact to join their economic resources and to partition Poland.[165] The Munich agreement also directly led to increased persecution and suffering of Jews in both Europe and Palestine.

The Munich conference provided a direct stimulus to the "war in Palestine" according to Abert Vitron. The "anti-Zionist movement" had exploded into "a revolt against Great Britain" as the Arabs believed Chamberlain had lost his nerve. Arabs, armed by attacks on British depots and financed by robberies of British and Jewish banks, agreed upon a unified command and expanded the magnitude of their assaults. The British army had been placed totally on the defensive as entire districts of Galilee and southern Judea were conquered by Arab battalions. While it could kill Arabs, it could no longer protect British courts, land registry offices, or the Mosul pipeline. No British soldier or policeman dared venture out at night. Were it not for the Jewish defense organizations, the whole of Palestine would have "long since been in the hands of the rebels." *Newsweek* reported Britain was rushing 8,000 additional troops to join the 10,000 already in Palestine.[166] Taufik al-Suwadi, Iraq's Foreign Minister, appeared in London to pressure Chamberlain to establish Palestine as an independent state and to prohibit further Jewish emigration into the Mandate. Chamberlain, as one result, had requested the British ambassador in Rome to sound out Mussolini about "diverting further Jewish emigration from Europe to Ethiopia." Mohammed Ali Pasha, an Egyptian parliamentary leader, demanded Chamberlain "give Palestine Arabs what he gave *Sudeten* Germans." Anything less, he warned, would lead to the Jews being "eradicated."[167]

By October 24, *Time* could report Palestine was "host to the largest British military force since Lawrence's time." Some 10,000 British troops were being "rushed direct from transports to the main trouble zones." Mt. Carmel was recaptured, along with Bethlehem, in all-night battles. Yet, "these punitive actions" brought "no end to terrorism." The Old City of Jerusalem was still totally in Arab hands. Taufik Suwadi was predicting that, if Jewish immigration continued, "a Hitler would arise in Palestine." London, according to *Time*, had to fight a full-scale war in Palestine or make "concessions at the expense of the Jewish colony" there. *The New Republic* believed it "problematical" whether Britain could defend its position against "Arabs backed by Germany and Italy."[168]

The following week, *Newsweek* wrote "all Palestine" was "on a war basis." Chamberlain felt he could not make concessions to the Arabs until Palestine had been pacified. However, there were indications he would meet Arab demands to halt Jewish immigration once peace had been restored. The Coldstream Guards had to be pressed into service to reconquer the Old City of Jerusalem against strong Arab resistance. When Cordell Hull, under heavy pressure from American Jews, requested London to make no radical decisions about Palestine without consulting with the United States, Arab leaders in Palestine ordered "a boycott of American goods and institutions." Arabs in Lebanon and Syria rioted and demonstrated against the British. Arabs in Palestine staged a general strike on November 1-3. Ary Abdul Razik, a prominent Palestinian "rebel," addressed a letter "to Franklin Rosefelt (sic)" threatening reprisals if the United States "continued to support the immigration of Jews to Palestine."[169]

The same week that news of a new ferocious Nazi pogrom appeared in our magazines, they reported Britain had abandoned the idea of partition and had suggested "a London round-table conference between Jews and Arabs." Invitations were immediately sent to Jews and Arabs in Palestine—also invited were Arabs from Egypt, Iraq, Saudi Arabia, Trans-Jordan and Yemen. Whitehall further announced that if the conference proved impossible to hold or if it deadlocked, Britain would "make and impose" its own decisions.[170]

The already desperate fate of German and Polish Jews took a turn for the worse on October 6, 1938. On that date, Warsaw commanded all holders of Polish passports residing in foreign countries to obtain special visas by October 29 or forfeit their citizenship. Berlin, alleging fear that thousands of Polish Jews in Germany would be denied the visas, ordered a mass deportation of Polish Jews on October 28. Some 20,000 were "herded" up to the Polish frontier and expelled into the one-mile open strip between the frontiers. Approximately 12,000 were able to slip into Poland, but 8,000 remained in the strip with only the $4 allowed each emigrant. Most ended up in Zbaszyn, "their fate unknown." A small three sentence note in *Newsweek* for November 14 reported Herschel Grynszpan, a "17-year-old German-born Polish Jews" had shot "Secretary Ernst von Rath" at the Germany embassy in Paris. Grynszpan told the police he had "come to avenge his Polish brethren."[171]

The first of our news magazines to report on the November Nazi pogrom was *The Nation* in its issue of November 19, 1938. It asserted Hitler had declared "War Against the Jews." "In every city and town Nazi youths in party cars" toured the streets and "smashed and plundered Jewish shops, burned synagogues, beat and arrested helpless Jews" while police and firemen "looked with smiling approval." It further reported Goering had leveled a fine of $400,000,000 on the Jewish community and had forbidden Jews to conduct any retail, mail-order, commission, or handicraft business after January 1, 1939. Goebbels prohibited, effective immediately, any Jew from attending movies, theaters, or concert halls.[172]

Time reported "the Fuehrer was beside himself" due to the death of von Rath and had unleashed the SA in retaliation. In "every part of Germany mobs smashed, looted, burned Jewish property." Synagogues had everywhere been "fired or dynamited." The "so-called mobs" were actually SA youths in civilian clothes—however, they had forgotten to remove their hob-nail boots. Jews of all ages were "spat upon, cuffed, nose-jerked, kicked, and given black eyes"— the "synthetic mobs" had only "stopped short of rape and firing squads." Jews who managed to reach the Dutch frontier were turned back on instructions from The Hague. *Time* reported in Frankfurt "every male Jew between the ages of 18 and 60 was taken into custody." It alleged the Nazis hoped to force "the international Jewish community" to send German Jews large sums of "good money" to pay for Germany's imports.[173]

The Saturday Evening Post had already insisted on October 1 that Germany was "a nation already at war." By rigid control of "credit inflation," Hitler and Goering had made Germany into a great military power at the expense of the German people. Their economic policies were so "geared and streamlined for war" it had become "a serious question" whether the German economy "might not be undermined by a prolonged period of peace." The *Post* suggested there were rumors the state would have to adopt a policy of "confiscation" to support its economy. Certainly, the German people, already suffering economically, could not easily accept any more sacrifice.[174] On this assumption, Hitler had found his solution in the confiscation of what little wealth belonged to the Jewish community.

Newsweek reported the pogrom had begun all over Germany at exactly "2 a.m. Nov. 10 (sic)." It reported the "marauders" had all worn SA boots and were provided "with gloves." Some squads were evidently detailed to attack stores while others attacked synagogues. Approximately "25,000 or more Jews, nearly all men," were "rounded up"—twenty or more committed suicide. Goebbels summoned foreign correspondents to allege the attacks had been spontaneous and there had been no looting. To the reports of *The Nation* and *Time, Newsweek* added that Goering had ordered Jews to repair their own damage and had confiscated their insurance claims. The fine alone, it insisted, would take "between a third and fourth of realizable German wealth." It believed the purpose of the pogrom was to force Jews abroad to end their criticism of the Third Reich by demonstrating German Jews were hostages.[175]

In its issue of November 9, which went to press prior to the November pogrom, *The New Republic* wrote "one of the commonest observations in public conversations" was that "Hitler is mentally unsound." It noted this judgement was shared by a number of leading American psychiatrists "recently consulted by Science Service." A.A. Brill described Hitler as "a psychopathic paranoid personality" whose "sole need is hatred" for his algolagnia or "pleasure in pain." Oscar Raeder identified Hitler as an "infantile personality" who acted on "childhood fixations" and was "amoral and probably sadistic." Karl A. Menninger believed Hitler mentally saw "other people" as aggressors against whom he had to take action—hence, his "fantastic," "dangerous" attacks on Jews. Ordinarily, "such individuals" were committed to institutions but in a "sufficiently inflammable society" such as Germany, they could become leaders. *The New Republic* believed, given these diagnoses, Hitler was "a far greater menace to the world" than a "sane and rational individual would be."[176]

On November 19, in its initial report on the pogrom, *The Nation* called Hitler a "perverse mentality" who had unleashed a "bestial" act of "vengeance." *Time* quoted with approval a statement by Archbishop Kurley of Baltimore which called Hitler a "madman" assisted by "cripple-minded Goebbels."[177]

News of the pogrom caused a wave of horror and disgust to sweep across the United States. *The New Republic* declared "from one end of the country to the other" there was "a public outburst of angry feeling such as has rarely been seen in our history." Newspapers unanimously "excoriated the Nazis." *The Nation* reported "newspapers in every county" were aghast at "the orgy of terror." *Newsweek* wrote "newspapers, public officials, civic organizations, and religious groups from coast to coast" were united in their protest against the Nazi barbarism. The Federal Council of Churches broadcast a radio program in which Herbert Hoover and Alf Landon joined Harold Ickes in protest against the pogrom. La Guardia organized a "Nazi Guardian Squad" of Jewish New York policemen to protect the German consulate from protesters.[178] A radio program by Dorothy Thompson attacking the pogrom received 3,000 telegrams of support in a few hours time. Pickets were spontaneously set up before German consulates across the country. There were widespread demands for Ford and Lindbergh to return their Nazi decorations.[179] *Newsweek* declared a "state of psychological estrangement" existed between the United States and Germany. *Time* asserted that, when "on any issue Alf Landon joins Al Smith, William Green joins John Lewis, Georgia Baptists and Tennessee Episcopalians join Manhattan rabbis," something momentous had "happened in U.S. public life." It declared Roosevelt "had a mandate from the people" to respond to the pogrom.[180]

Roosevelt, however, either failed to perceive he had a mandate to act decisively or perceiving it, failed to act on it. He did recall the American ambassador from Berlin for "consultations"—a move Hitler countered by recalling his ambassador to Berlin for "talks." He did publicly denounce the pogrom as an act he thought could not happen in the twentieth century—but did not break diplomatic relations with Berlin. Roosevelt did extend the visas of the "12,000 to 15,000 refugees" in the United States for an additional six months—he did not request Congress to change the immigration quotas for refugees or order the State Department to expedite visas to take up the unfilled spaces in current quotas. Even though magazines as diverse as *The New Republic, The Nation,* and *Collier's* believed a change in the immigration laws was both possible and desirable, Roosevelt refused to test the "mandate" directly or indirectly.[181]

Joseph Kennedy, American ambassador to Britain, who had already been rebuked for a speech supporting Chamberlain's policy of appeasement, was again rebuked by Roosevelt for conviving "with the British Prime Minister to impede the efforts of Mr. Rublee and the Intergovernmental Committee" to find a haven for Jews. The form or tone of the rebuke was, however, not made public as was the first rebuke. *The Nation* asserted Kennedy had ignored Rublee, had insisted the plight of German Jews was not "an American problem," and had stated the refugee crisis could not be allowed to affect other important "causes."[182]

Albert Einstein, in an article for *Collier's* written in response to the pogrom, attempted to rationally understand what was basically irrational—the Nazi war against the Jews. Einstein defined "Jewishness," not as a racial term, but "as a community of tradition." This community stressed a "democratic ideal of social justice, coupled with the ideal of mutual aid and tolerance among all men." Supporting this ideal was a "high regard" for "every form of intellectual aspiration and spiritual effort." Where these were the ideals of the nation or society, the Jew was accepted for himself without persecution. Where the society insisted on regimentation and "uncritical acceptance of dogma," the Jews were seen as "nonassimilable element." In Nazi Germany, therefore, anti-Semitism was used to protect "the privileged classes" and to enable "a small, unscrupulous and insolent group to place the German people in a state of complete bondage." The Jew was also regarded as a threat to Nazi authority because of the Jewish "insistence on popular enlightenment of the masses" and on recognition of the common humanity of mankind.[183]

According to our magazines, the November pogrom and the subsequent reports of continuing Nazi anti-Semitic brutality had a greater effect on democratic public opinion and diplomacy than did the *Anschluss* or the Munich Pact.

Reports from Germany stressed there was no easing in the persecution of Jews. In Berlin, 8,000 Jewish apartments were expropriated. In Breslau, all telephone service "to Jews was cut off." In Munich, police "raided rich Jewish homes for art works." Across Germany, rabbis were jailed. Jews were forbidden to sell their securities or to draw more than 100 marks a day from their bank accounts. Jews were no longer given receipts even when they paid their fines or taxes. Sixty-two Jews were made "to run a bloody gantlet (sic)" at Sachsenhausen Concentration Camp—twelve were beaten to death. A total of

"1,500 major anti-Semitic mass meetings" were staged across Germany. A Jewish director and actors were forced to re-open the Jewish Theater of Berlin so Goebbels could insist that "rich Jews laugh and applaud while poor Jews are starving." *Das Schwarze Korps* "descended from appalling generalities to particulars" by writing "we should...face the hard necessity of exterminating the Jewish underworld...by fire and sword."[184]

Although the extortion of the $400,000,000 "fine" from Jews was expected to disrupt the German economy, Goering announced all Jews with more than $2,000 would have to pay twenty percent of their capital in four bi-monthly installments as a down payment on the fine. When the first 200 of a projected 5,000 Jewish children were allowed to leave Germany for Britain, they had "everything of value taken from them" and were allowed to take only forty cents apiece out of the Reich. Jews were banned from downtown Berlin districts and officially advised to move to "the Scheunenviertal region, a squalid slum." Himmler banned Jewish possession of automobiles, motorcycles, and driving licenses.[185]

Nazi anti-Semitism proved to be exportable, at least at points. The rump Czech and Slovak governments announced they intended to introduce "anti-Semitic laws based on Germany's Nuremberg code." In South Africa, Boers in Johannesburg staged "an anti-Jewish demonstration" with shouts of "Down With the Jews!"[186] Father Coughlin, broadcasting from Detroit, praised the pogrom as a German "defense mechanism" against "Jewish-sponsored Communism." He openly borrowed materials from a Nazi pamphlet printed at Erfurt accusing Jews of having masterminded and financed the communist revolution. The Jersey City Council of the Knights of Columbus passed a resolution "approving" his allegations even though Cardinal Mundelein of Chicago publicly repudiated Coughlin—as did Catholic laymen led by Al Smith.[187]

American outrage mounted steadily as reports of the on-going pogrom appeared in newspapers, magazines, and on the radio. Mass protest meetings were held across the United States. The usually pacifistic *Nation*, although acknowledging an official boycott was an act tantamount to war, called for a diplomatic break with Berlin, a freezing of German assets in the United States, and an embargo of German trade. *The New Republic* also endorsed the call for an embargo to support the voluntary boycott increasingly being implemented by growing numbers of Americans. Both called for an immediate relaxation of American visa procedures and quotas.[188] *The Nation* pointed with pride to the cultural contributions of refugees who had reached America. Groups of all types collected relief funds to aid the refugees. Eleanor Roosevelt gave her support to a proposal for a Leon Blum Colony in Palestine. Walter Lippmann called for Africa to be colonized with a million refugees a year.[189] There was no mass demand for the refugees to be admitted into the United States.

The British government took the lead in the effort to find a refuge for German Jews. Chamberlain and Daladier agreed to accept 10,000 refugees apiece in their colonies. Chamberlain flatly refused, however, to increase the 12,000 a year quota for Palestine. The best he offered was to settle Jews in Tanganyika and British Guiana as agricultural workers. Chamberlain did, however, agree to accept immediately 5,000 Jewish children into the British Isles.[190] Australia agreed to accept 15,000 Jews as permanent settlers provided each entered with $1,000 capital. *The New Republic* summarized the problems and obstacles of aid to the refugees. No nation wanted to accept the Jews as anything but "agricultural pioneers" for they were unwilling "to endanger their own jobs and economic opportunities in order to help them." Further, German expropriation of the refugees' capital meant they would enter their hosts' country as paupers. Psychologically, the democracies were "really far more interested in punishing the guilty" than succoring the victims. Finally, the German government seemed more interested in holding the Jews for ransom and as hostages than in aiding their emigration. It concluded with a plea for increased American quotas for the refugees, noting that to accept all of them would only amount to an increase in the American population of "four-tenths of one percent."[191]

Following Munich and the pogrom, Chamberlain attempted to continue his policy of appeasement and accommodation with Hitler. He issued no official statement against the pogrom. As this entailed accepting German domination of south-eastern Europe, he refused to consider loans or arm sales for Rumania and Yugoslavia. Chamberlain also sought to "Dicker with Germany on Colonies" and appointed Oswald Pirow, Defense Minister of South Africa, "to act as go-between" in colonial negotiations with Hitler.[192]

Chamberlain found, however, that public sentiment against further concessions to Hitler had suddenly stiffened because of the Jewish persecution. Polls showed seven out of ten Britons were so appalled by the pogrom that they wanted no further British negotiations with Hitler. Lloyd's of London announced it would not transfer to Germany any insurance payments occasioned by the pogrom. The funds were to be held "in escrow" until they could be paid to their rightful recipients. In by-elections, Chamberlain's Tory party lost three out of five seats where the elections were fought out on the issue of foreign policy. Commons unanimously passed a resolution condemning the pogrom—its mood was so determined Chamberlain was himself forced to vote for the resolution.[193] Even those who had earlier pressed appeasement upon him reversed their position. *The London Times* vehemently attacked Hitler and the pogrom, the Earl of Hardwicke declared "Germany wasn't fit to have colonies," and Lord Mount Temple, "one of the country's foremost pro-Germans," resigned the presidency of the Anglo-German League. Lord Londonderry, Chairman of the Conservative Party and a leader of "the pro-German clique," publicly called upon Chamberlain to pledge he would not "sacrifice an inch of territory or one individual" to Hitler. Chamberlain was forced to recall Pirow from Berlin and announce there would be no colonial concessions to Hitler. He even had to drop the term "appeasement" from his speeches.[194]

When Schacht privately visited London to confer with Montagu Norman, Governor of the Bank of England, and Chamberlain to forestall a trade war and to secure more British trade, he also suggested a "ransom" arrangement for German Jews. He proposed German Jewish emigrants be given "trading certificates" in exchange for their property. These certificates could be used only to buy German goods and so increase German exports. Schacht also met with Rublee of the Intergovernmental Committee on refugees though no report on their discussion was issued. Public sentiment was so set against Germany, however, that not only did Schacht's mission fail, but Commons voted a trade subsidy bill to increase economic pressure on Germany.[195]

Following Munich, Daladier, like Chamberlain, attempted to continue a policy of appeasement and business as usual with Hitler. He secured a pact of non-aggression with Hitler similar to the one concluded by Chamberlain with Hitler at Munich. After the pogrom broke, public indignation was so great he had to publicly renounce any possible cession of French colonial territory to Hitler. When former premier Flandin, who had supported a pro-Nazi attitude, went to place a wreath on the Tomb of the Unknown Soldier, he was publicly assaulted. Dorothy Thompson was able to raise easily large sums of money, both in France and America, "from Gentiles" to hire eight of France's best defense lawyers to defend Grynszpan.[196]

As 1938 ended, the appeasement policy of Chamberlain and Daladier had been shattered. British and French reaction to the November pogrom precluded any possibility of accommodation with Hitler. Mussolini's demand for the cession of Tunisia to Italy ended any immediate possibility of his appeasement by France.[197] Chamberlain and Daladier continued their efforts at rearmament. For his part, Hitler unleashed a propaganda campaign aimed at the Ukraine so intense that Poland and Russia began diplomatic discussions on the subject.[198] Pirow, who had returned from Berlin, warned that Hitler was in a dangerous mood and that "international tension" would "reach a breaking point during the spring of next year."[199] Hitler's war on the Jews had already begun, his war on Europe was about to begin.

Chapter VI

Krieg, 1939

In its January 2, 1939 issue, *Time* nominated Hitler as its "Man of the Year" for 1938. Gone, however, was any description of Hitler as "Handsome Adolf" or any defense of the Munich Conference. The *Kristal Nacht* had profoundly affected its viewpoint. *Time's* cover depicted "Organist Adolf Hitler" playing a "hymn of hate in a desecrated cathedral" while his victims "dangle on a St. Catherine's wheel" as the "Nazi hierarchy looks on." Hitler was now a "moody, brooding, unprepossessing" ascetic, a "sexless, restless, instinctive" dictator who had founded a "demagogic, ignorant, desperate movement." After becoming chancellor, he had conducted "an audacious, defiant, ruthless foreign policy" for five and a half years. Hitler had made France a "second-rate power," had shown that Chamberlain's "peace with honor" policy had brought neither peace nor honor, and had reduced Mussolini to "a decidedly junior partner." In the process, Hitler had become "the greatest threatening force that the democratic, freedom-loving world faces today" and had created the issue "over which men may again, perhaps soon, shed blood"—that of "civilized liberty v. barbaric authoritarianism." He had already launched a religious war against Jews. Because of Hitler, Germany's 700,000 Jews had been "tortured physically, robbed of homes and properties, denied a chance to earn a living, chased off the streets." These wars had occurred within Germany—Europe now faced the prospect of military conflict and it "seemed more than probable that the Man of 1938 may make 1939 a year to be remembered."[1] The pogrom had not only radically affected *Time* but all Americans and their government.

Certainly, relations between the United States and the Third Reich opened in 1939 on a distinctly sour and strident note. It began when Harold L. Ickes, the Secretary of the Interior, speaking to a Zionist Society dinner in Cleveland at the end of 1938, declared Hitler had taken Germany back to "a period when man was unlettered, benighted, and brutal." The November pogrom demonstrated Hitler counted "the day lost when he can commit no crime against humanity." Ickes attacked Ford and Lindbergh for accepting decorations from the "same hand" that was "robbing and torturing thousands of fellow human beings." Ickes, who had just barred the shipment of American helium to Germany, was immediately and bitterly blasted by the German press. Roosevelt was included in the attack because he had accepted the 1938 American Hebrew Medal for improving relations between Jews and Christians. The Nazi press attack was followed by the demand by Hans Thomsen, the German charge, for an official apology. Sumner Welles, who received him at the State Department, "bluntly refused" to apologize, adding Ickes "spoke for all Americans" and represented "the feeling of the overwhelming majority of the people of the United States" following the recent pogrom. Welles' statement, contrary to normal diplomatic procedure, was released to the press. It was also announced that Roosevelt, to show his solidarity with Ickes, would spend the weekend at Ickes' Maryland farm. The same day, Key Pittman, chairman of the Senate Foreign Relations Committee, publicly asserted as "a beneficial statement of fact" that the American people did not "like" the government of Germany and the United States would defend the principles of law and morality "because it had the power" to do so. After two days of silence, Goebbels told foreign correspondents the "incident was closed."[2]

Newsweek asserted America had given Germany "a public scolding unparalleled in recent United States history." The most significant thing about the interchange was that it was "clearly part of a Roosevelt maneuver" to apply "diplomatic and moral pressure on the dictators." It noted British and French papers had headlined Roosevelt's handling of the matter. *Time* agreed Roosevelt had masterminded the American response—which was the diplomatic equivalent of "Nuts to You!" Not since 1917 had "the U.S. given any nation such a come-uppance." The message was "just blunt enough" to make "Hitler understand" and "the result appeared salubrious." While *The New Republic* concurred with the thrust of Welles' remarks, it believed "there is a possibility of overdoing this sort of thing" and there was "a time when dignity demands doing more or saying less." Of Pittman's statement, *The New Republic* wrote it "was uncalled for and *apropos* of nothing in particular." *The Nation*, however, believed Ickes deserved "a Congressional medal" and had spoken "directly for the American people for the first time in many a month." It called for an increased moral and economic attack to check "the dictators here and now" by "short-circuiting their ability to make war."[3]

There was a growing anti-Hitler and anti-Nazi attitude among most Americans with sixty-one percent favoring a boycott against German goods while forty-six percent believed "the United States will have to fight Germany again within their lifetimes."[4] This attitude existed in spite of growing Nazi efforts to propagandize the United States. *The Reader's Digest* insisted the Nazis had "established a network of cells, agencies, organizations, and press bureaus in every population center of the country." Fritz Kuhn, fuehrer of the *Amerikadeutscher Volksbund*, had organized fifty-six units "coast to coast" which printed twenty Nazi newspapers in the United States that sought "to enflame anti-Jewish and pro-German" attitudes. This propaganda was not intended to convert Americans to Nazism but to create "enough dissension and pro-German sentiment in the United States" to prevent American aid to the democracies. *The Reader's Digest* emphasized Americans realized the propaganda was racial, anti-Semitic, and anti-labor and were offended by it. In addition to this German-American Bund propaganda, Goebbels was beaming six hours of daily short-wave programs from Nauen, Germany, to the United

States over station DJD. This signal was so strong it was "clear as a bell" even in San Francisco. Only one-sixth of the content was devoted to news and its interpretation—"German supremacy, the Bolsheviks Are Coming, Jew-baiting, and the rest of Hitler's invidious staples." The remaining content was devoted to German and American music and to lectures on the New Germany. *The New Republic* insisted this radio propaganda was having little effect on Americans but did not dismiss its effectiveness entirely. NBC received 20,000 letters a year from its world-wide listeners.[5]

The November pogrom, coming on the heels of Munich, also had a profound effect in Europe, especially in Britain and France. The entire policy of appeasement was attacked. Although there was a Tory victory in a by-election in December, 1938, Chamberlain came under increasing attack as 1939 opened. Lloyd-George criticized him in Commons for his "lack of courage" at Munich. The Permanent Under-Secretaries for War, Overseas Trade, and Colonial Affairs made an unprecedented and united attack on Chamberlain's rearmament program, asserting it was in a shambles, was inadequate in extent, and unworkable. Chamberlain was forced to renew his pledge to hasten rearmament and to remove ministerial snags associated with the program. Graham Hutton alleged Chamberlain supported rearmament only to silence his critics and was still determined to rearm "neither too rapidly nor too extensively." Chamberlain's great fear was that British rearmament might antagonize Hitler. Forced to drop the term appeasement, Chamberlain still hoped to "conciliate Mussolini" at the cost of France, to negotiate an air pact with Hitler, and to elbow Germany into "a collision with the Russian left-wing regime."[6]

Daladier was also experiencing increasing criticism, not for Munich, but for his measures to increase taxation. He was deserted by many of the Radical Socialists and nearly toppled from office. Mussolini chose this moment to declare the Franco-Italian Pact of 1935 invalid. Mussolini, in addition, demanded Paris cede French Somaliland and the Jibuti-Addis Ababa railway to Italy. It had already been predicted that Chamberlain, stymied in his efforts to appease Hitler, would next seek to appease Mussolini. Chamberlain, responding to Mussolini's demand, announced he would leave for Rome on January 11 to consult with Mussolini.[7]

In the interim, Daladier despatched 10,000 Senegalese troops to Somaliland, sent two warships to Jibuti, and declared France "would cede no territory" to Rome. When Mussolini also demanded the cession of Tunisia to Rome, Daladier announced he would visit Tunisia and Algiers and pointedly and publicly requested Chamberlain not to discuss French affairs while at Rome. On his visit, Daladier was enthusiastically cheered by the populations of Corsica, Tunisia, and Algeria. Daladier made a point of touring the French Mareth line fortifications on the border with Italian Libya.[8]

Prior to his departure for Rome, Chamberlain was a harried man. Even those who had urged the policy of appeasement on him deserted in droves. Lady Astor, whose country estate had provided a synonym for the pro-Hitler "Clividen Set," chose "to whip out a flat denunciation of Adolf Hitler" that criticized him for warping "the lives of Jewish children" and for being a "lunatic." The opposition of other groups also increased. "Several hundred men and women" demonstrated along Whitehall with placards reading "Appease the unemployed—not Mussolini!" In addition, Duncan Sandys, Churchill's son-in-law, and Liddell Hart, military correspondent for *The Times*, announced the formation of a "Hundred Thousand" party that would fight Chamberlain's appeasement policy toward the dictators.[9] When Roosevelt attacked the aggressor nations in his State of the Union speech, most influential British newspapers, apart from *The Times*, scored Mr. Chamberlain for having abdicated the leadership of the democracies to Roosevelt. The Federation of University Conservatives passed a resolution against appeasement "and in particular the policy of renewing friendship with Italy."[10] Chamberlain, however, chose to ignore this rising swell of protest. *The New Republic* surmised Chamberlain had embraced appeasement so tightly that he had no choice but to play the game to its bitter end. To repudiate appeasement would be to repudiate himself, acknowledge his disastrous failure, and to commit political suicide. *The Nation* called Chamberlain "that pilgrim of appeasement" whose trip to Rome might well provide the final spark to ignite the resentment of the "smoldering electorate." Chamberlain seemed a sleep-walker unaware of events around him.[11]

In the event, Chamberlain's visit to Rome "produced no great decisions." Both leaders insisted in public news releases that they had "not given away anything." *Time* wrote of the discussions that "Nothing good went Italy's way and nothing bad went Britain's." To this extent, Chamberlain had come off "with a sort of negative triumph."[12] *The New Republic* stated there were rumors Hitler had told "his ally not to press his demands against France for another year." Chamberlain himself was constrained by Daladier's clear refusal to make any concessions to Mussolini. However, it believed the "way is still open for further 'appeasement' " as it was unlikely Chamberlain would return from Rome repentant of his ways. *The Nation* wrote Chamberlain had "accomplished nothing" at Rome—and for "this the world can be profoundly thankful." Chamberlain had, for once, taken note of British and French public opinion.[13]

While Chamberlain was preparing to negotiate with Mussolini, Roosevelt was not idle. Roosevelt called for a vast new armaments program, particularly for the army air force, and for the necessary air fields and bases to train and support an armada of 13,000 planes. Congressmen were not slow to realize the armament program was supported by the majority of Americans. Even isolationists, on the whole, supported the program. This action, combined with his recall of Wilson from Berlin, Hull's work with the Lima Conference, and Roosevelt's denunciation of the dictators, were interpreted as signs Roosevelt indicated to assume the leadership of "the democratic peoples which Britain and France relinquished at Munich."[14]

In his address to Congress, Roosevelt declared that, although Munich had averted an immediate war, peace was not assured. There were threats of new, perhaps military, aggression and no nation was safe merely because it had a "will to peace." The United States had, therefore to prepare itself morally, economically, and militarily to defend its heritage of freedom. Three institutions, he insisted, were "indispensable" to Americans—freedom of religion, democracy, and international good faith. All three institutions were under attack by aggressor nations and Americans must prepare to command "a decent respect for the opinions of mankind."[15]

Newsweek wrote Roosevelt believed Germany was already attacking the United States by interfering in South America, by upsetting world trade with its "self-sufficiency" policies, by fostering an arms race, by encouraging un-American groups in the United States, and by creating race hatred that had repercussions in America. It endorsed his actions wholeheartedly. *Time* believed Roosevelt had "struck vigorously the keynote of contemporary U.S. feeling" and lauded his action and remarks.[16]

The New Republic stated Roosevelt was "now engaged in a sort of undeclared war of his own against the Fascist triumvirate" that was both "economic and political." He hoped to frighten "the bullies" and to "put a little backbone into the leaders of the so-called democracies of Europe." While approving his rearmament efforts, it urged Americans to consider that undeclared wars often evolved into "shooting wars." *The Nation* declared Roosevelt's actions "rang out like a bugle across the world" and that his address to Congress in both "its manner and matter" placed "it among the great state papers of our history." To Americans, it was "a call to recognize the crucial nature of the fascist challenge and to accept it firmly and coolly."[17] The great neutrality debate of 1939 had begun.

The majority of Americans, including the isolationists, favored naval rearmament as a way to guarantee the defense of the United States. Many also accepted the mechanization and the expansion of the army. What they protested in the rearmament program was Roosevelt's call for 13,000 aircraft and the training of military aviators in American colleges and universities. *The New Republic, Collier's,* and *The Saturday Evening Post,* were typical of this latter group, arguing far fewer planes were needed for "defense," that the planes would rapidly become obsolete, and that Roosevelt actually intended to build the planes for British use.[18] It was also argued additional pilots were not needed if Roosevelt's intention was only to defend the western hemisphere. Additional pilots were needed only if, contrary to the desires of the American people, Roosevelt intended to fight a war in Europe. *Newsweek* reported on January 16 that Americans were disquieted by the possibility of the abandonment of neutrality. *The New York Daily News,* formerly a loyal Roosevelt supporter, "savagely attacked the new foreign policy." On January 23, *Newsweek* stated the military budget for 1939 would be $10.54 per capita but that Senators Borah and Nye were leading a move to tighten rather than relax the neutrality act. Sixty-one percent of Americans favored a boycott of German goods but only forty-six percent thought war with Germany was likely.[19] The same week, *Time* reported Senator Lynn Frazier of North Dakota had proposed a constitutional amendment to ban preparation for, or the use of, war as a national policy. Senator Robert Reynolds of North Carolina asserted France and Britain would not risk war so there was no need for America to prepare for war. The isolationist threat led Roosevelt to call Ambassador Bullitt home from Paris and Ambassador Kennedy from London to report to a joint meeting of the House and Senate Military Affairs Committees. Moreover, Roosevelt felt it necessary to declare the United States had no thought of taking part in a European war.[20] The debate reached out of Washington committee rooms into our magazines.

Henry Wolfe argued in *Harper's* that Hitler posed little immediate threat to the New World and the concern about defense of the western hemisphere was misdirected. Hitler thought in continental terms as *Mein Kampf* amply demonstrated. The Nazi demand for colonies merely screened "the Reich's major objective, her drive to the East." The Anglo-Naval pact of 1935 indicated Hitler was not concerned with an overseas colonial empire and the Siegfried Line was only a shield behind which Hitler could pursue his real goal— *Lebensraum* in the east. Munich was actually "the beginning, not the end, of Germany's *Drang nach Osten*." To complete that drive Hitler first had to solve "the perennial Polish problem" which itself could only be done by defeating Russia or winning it as an ally. No one should assume German relations with Moscow were static and "a second Rapallo" was not inconceivable. Even so, a serious Nazi military threat "must await the accomplishment of Hitler's long-range plans in Europe." Americans needed to decide whether to cooperate with the western democracies to stop Hitler before, at some future date, with the combined resources of Europe under his control, he threatened their peace and security.[21]

In the April issue of *Harper's*, Nathaniel Peffer insisted the United States should "proceed with armament on a grand scale." While Americans could possibly stay out of a European war, they would not want to remain aloof once it started. They felt a cultural affinity with Britain and France and disliked Nazism. Rather than see "the present German and Italian governments become dominate in Europe," Americans would be psychologically impelled to "put a stop to the excesses of organized terrorism, the institutionalized barbarism, and psychotic dictatorships." Regrettably, it was obvious the last war had been fought in vain. Regrettedly, "the ruling principle of international security" was now force. Since it was, however, Americans would be unable to accept becoming "a democratic island surrounded by fascist states." The menace of fascism was "immediate" and would become more so with each fascist success. It therefore followed American "armament," both speedy and massive, was "advisable and necessary."[22]

David L. Cohn argued the United States should cooperate with Britain and France to defeat Hitler if he began a war in Europe. While three-fourths of Americans wanted to avoid war, eighty-two percent favored overt economic aid to the allies should war erupt. In the event of war between Germany and Russia, eighty-three percent wanted Russia to win. Although these statistics could be read several ways, Cohn insisted it was clear Americans "do not want Germany victorious in a world war" and they "do not want Britain and France to be crushed by Germany." In their minds and hearts, Americans knew they could not ultimately avoid war for they knew "fascist conquests" would "not stop with Europe and Africa." If Hitler were to win Europe, he would dominate South America, first economically and then politically. A Hitler difficult to defeat in Europe would be almost impossible to defeat if he had the combined resources of Europe behind him. Therefore, of all the alternatives open to the American people, neutrality was the least attractive and least acceptable policy.[23]

Drew Pearson insisted it was as impossible to legislate isolation as it was to legislate morality. The Spanish Civil War and subsequent events had demonstrated the president could ignore the neutrality laws and, in turn could be ignored by bureaucrats. While Congress, the president, and the American people denounced dictators, the diplomat could make "neutrality become the tool of the dictators." Americans should simply look to their own interests, openly oppose the dictators, and forget about neutrality.[24]

Eddie V. Rickenbacker urged the immediate production of, not 13,000, but 50,000 airplanes. The United States needed an aircraft industry in being if war broke out for it would not have the grace period it enjoyed between 1914—1917. Only that volume of aircraft could support the industry, ensure the training of the requisite number of pilots, and ensure American domination of the air in any conflict. The planes need not be military planes, which regularly became obsolete, but civilian planes that, in the meantime, could fly the mail, provide transportation, and stimulate public flying. Complacency and isolationism were not adequate defenses in the current state of the world.[25]

The Saturday Evening Post was the most staunchly isolationist of our magazines. S. Paul Johnston argued Hitler undoubtedly held "the balance of power in the air today" and was not bluffing when he asserted the German air force could destroy entire cities. His first-line air force was not only formidable but was backed up by well-equipped and bomb-proof factories that could replace any losses incurred in combat. However, it would be years before his bombers could reach the United States and Americans had time to consider rationally the potential threat he posed to our security. What was necessary at the moment was to reject "political pressure" from high offices.[26]

The *Post* left little doubt about what office it was talking about in its pages—the Oval Office occupied by Roosevelt. Europeans, Demaree Ross asserted, were "more apprehensive about the foreign policy of the United States than they are about that of Hitler." They desired peace and had secured it at Munich. Roosevelt, who did not understand the game of power politics like European statesmen did after centuries of practice, wanted to scrap the traditional American foreign policy of isolation and meddle where he was not wanted. Europeans had done "the decent thing" at the time of the pogrom in Germany by providing funds and seeking a home for the refugees. In the United States, there was "an emotional orgy" that bore the marks of being "artificially whipped up" by "interested groups and individuals for purposes of their own." Americans needed to avoid such emotional outbursts as they had "enough to do at home."[27]

Demaree Ross returned to this latter theme two weeks later when he argued Americans should be rational and not allow Hitler's anti-Semitism to affect their foreign policy. They needed to understand the Jews were "Pawns in Power Politics." Anti-Semitism was "a deliberate, systematic policy, aimed at definite objectives" the Axis powers sought to achieve. Mussolini used it to stir up the Arabs against the British empire, the Japanese used it as an anti-Soviet slogan in the Orient, and Hitler used it as a political weapon in Central Europe and the Balkans. In Austria, "brown bolshevists" like Goebbels had used anti-Semitism to attack established wealth and religion—goals the communists would have approved. In the Balkans, which were over-crowded and anti-Semitic to the core as a result, Hitler used it as a political weapon. Ross insisted Americans needed to avoid allowing their emotions to affect their foreign policy.[28]

On April 8, the *Post* returned to its attack on Roosevelt. It believed it "strange that Americans were inviting themselves to a war before it even begins." Roosevelt, however, seemed determined to defend Canada and Latin America before there was any threat to them. Indeed, his "Quarantine Speech" indicated he wanted to defend everyone against everything. In the same issue, Demaree Ross insisted Roosevelt had been so shocked by Munich he had decided European statesmen were incompetent and he needed to conduct the game of power politics even though he did not understand the rules since he was only a novice. Americans should mobilize to "tell him to stay out" of Europe.[29] If Americans were now ready to abandon traditional isolationism, it was because, for "one and a half years," Roosevelt had conditioned them into the "cultivated obsession" of intervention in Europe.[30] The *Post* was for peace at any price except a direct attack on the United States.

Alfred North Whitehead came down solidly on the side of peace at almost any price. Only "excited intellectuals" in Britain refused to see Britain was not a European, but an imperial power. To maintain and exercise the benefits of the empire for its people, it was necessary for Britain to remain at peace through isolation from the internecine quarrels of Europe. Furthermore, the problems of nationalism in central Europe could not be solved through war. Certainly, to "have a world war" to oppose the "Pan-German movement would be madness," particularly since the allies themselves had promoted nationalism in the Treaty of Versailles. Resistance to German nationalism would only result in a war from which "Europe would emerge exhausted, with its emotions barbarized, its ideals brutalized"—and the problem of nationalism would remain unresolved. The "only certainty would be a ghastly slaughter leading to an unknown future." One problem that did need resolution was the tragedy of the Jews. Germany was the "main seat of the vicious explosion" of anti-Semitism in Europe and German Jews needed to be saved. The answer, however, did not lie in the establishment of a Jewish homeland in Palestine. Such a Palestinian Jewish homeland could only be maintained, and then only temporary, by British bayonets. Jews, moreover, had no "large experience" in political management and because Jewish thought always dealt on "specific ideals, conceived in the abstract, devoid of compromise and of the requisites for survival," it was unlikely they could maintain a homeland on their own. The answer lay in another direction—the resettlement of German Jews in "the large stretch down the East Coast of Africa" and in dispersal among the Arab states. For this resettlement to succeed, however, the Jews would have to learn to compromise and cooperate. In the final analysis, peace was also required for this plan to work. War against Hitler would, indeed, "probably lead to the massacre of hundreds of thousands of Jews." For all these reasons, war should be the last resort of Britain and avoided entirely if possible.[31]

Oswald G. Villard, former editor of *The Nation* and still a regular columnist for it, was opposed not only to cooperation with Britain and France but also to American rearmament. There was no national defense plan, no joint service defense plan, and no limit to the funds requested by the army and navy. Invasion of the United States was both improbable and impossible. The real danger was that "the rising tide of military and naval preparedness" would "in itself drive us well along the road to fascism." Why arm "to the utmost limit" if "thereby we lose our democratic soul"—"that soul we are supposed to preserve" by producing armaments without end.[32]

To C. Hartly Grattan, "the proper policy" was "clear: No American shall ever again be sent to fight and die on the continent of Europe." Democracy was truly endangered, not by fascism in Europe, but "by war." Americans should therefore "oppose war" unless it was "forced upon us by the absolute necessity of defending this continent." The United States had entered the last war because Americans had "lost our heads, failed in our job—which was to maintain neutrality." The same slogans were again being brought forward and republished with their content only slightly altered. All hands were being asked to make the world "safe for democracy" but there was no agreement on how that was to be accomplished. The issues in 1939 were even "more confused than ever before." To fight for "an unanalyzed negative objective—stopping fascism—would be the quintessence of folly" for it was impossible to assume the defeat of fascism would "release forces of a variety pleasing to American democrats." Certainly, the "difference between the opposed powers of Europe are not sufficiently clear-cut to justify sending Americans to fight and die for one side or the other." To go to war in Europe would only be a fight to preserve the reactionary *status quo* of Britain and France and impose that reactionary *status quo* on Italy and Germany. Neutrality was the only "sensible policy for the United States" for if Americans did "rush into a European war, early or late, democracy in this country is finished."[33]

J. B. Priestly attempted to convince *Harpers'* readers the "reactionary" government of England, led by Chamberlain, Simon, Hoare, and Halifax, did not represent the real Britain. They had gained power because of the inadequacies and deficiencies of the electoral system which, for example, made one Tory vote in Cheltenham worth more than four votes in industrial boroughs. Moreover, the Tories controlled "about four-fifths of the Press." As the government was only required to hold a general election every seven years, the Tories were not required to pay attention to British public opinion in the interim. The "Inner Cabinet," the very essence of Torism, had "a deep-seated fear of 'the Reds' " and based their foreign policy on the hope "Hitler would move eastward, become embroiled with Russia, and then dog would eat dog." Actual British public opinion understood the Axis powers were "thinking in terms of world domination" and knew "that at the heart of the Nazi and Fascist movements" there was "an evil principle, something that will have to be destroyed." In deciding upon their foreign policy, Americans needed to beware of confusing the aiding of Chamberlain and assistance to the cause of democracy in defeating Hitler.[34]

These same basic arguments were to be interminably repeated by each side during the debate over the neutrality laws during the late spring and summer of 1939.

The crash of a new Douglas bombing plane in Los Angeles led to a new row in Washington over American foreign policy in early February. The crash would have passed largely unnoticed except for the injury of Paul Chemidlin, a French arms purchaser. The crash thus led to a flurry in Congress as War Department regulations forbade the sale of new aircraft designs to a foreign power. The Senate Military Affairs Committee discovered Roosevelt had approved the sale of the planes to both France and Britain. Roosevelt thereupon defended his actions by saying the democracies needed the planes for their defense, that the sale would relieve unemployment, and that payment would be made by "cash on the barrelhead" and so not violate the neutrality laws. Angry isolationists turned out in force. Senator Nye charged Roosevelt had allied the United States militarily to France. Clark of Missouri alleged Roosevelt was preparing for war. There were repeated calls in the Senate for a clear statement of American foreign policy. Senator Pittman, on the other hand, received 35,000 telegrams in one week demanding a change in the neutrality laws which would allow sales to democratic nations.[35] *Newsweek* noted "the stay out of it at any cost camp" was steadily growing in Congress even though fifty-seven percent of Americans believed the United States would be at war with Germany within a year. *Newsweek* concluded the defense program would pass but the neutrality laws would remain in place. *The New Republic* asserted "Americans everywhere were resolutely opposed to war and to anything that might savor of war." However, business leaders supported rearmament for defense as "an avenue of recovery" from the depression.[36]

Time reported American public opinion had undergone a profound change. Americans, it asserted "had developed a sudden and violent dislike for Japan and Germany." Germans, who were disliked by "only 17.3% of the people in 1935, were disliked by 30% in 1938." Fifty-seven percent believed the United States would become engaged in a general European war in 1939 "to scotch the dictators." Yet, Americans did not want to go to war—sixty-nine percent still wanted to remain neutral. There was near unanimous agreement, however, that all Americans wanted a strong defensive capability. The isolationists, led by Hiram Johnson, Herbert Hoover, "Cotton Ed" Smith of South Carolina, and Bob Reynolds of North Carolina, agreed Europe "had best be left to take care of itself" but, nevertheless, insisted "they wanted a big stick just in case." A second camp, which included "liberals," "practically all U.S. Jews and militant Christians," Dorothy Thompson, and communists, wanted action against the dictators ranging from boycotts and embargoes to alliance with Britain and France. Roosevelt was firmly in this latter camp but was handicapped by the isolationists.[37]

The Nation argued the "simon-pure isolationists" were "no more than a small minority in Congress." They were undoubtedly "a sincere, vocal, and influential group" quite capable of supporting Senator Nye's threat of a summer-long filibuster to prevent the repeal or drastic revision of the Neutrality Act. Such tactics would likely succeed as those who sought overt American aid to the European democracies were also a minority. The debate centered on the "cash and carry" clause which was due to expire on May 1. Unless reenacted, all commodities except weapons of war could be sold and exported to belligerents in American ships. The "interventionists" believed its lapse would aid Britain and France. The isolationists, on the other hand, did not want American ships traveling to war zones but equally did not want to open up the issue lest the Neutrality Act be emasculated. They were therefore limited to conducting "untiring opposition to any serious change in the act." Most Americans wanted to supply Britain and France with food if war began, a bare majority would sell them war material, but almost all were overwhelmingly opposed to military support for the democracies.[38]

By April, there were five alternative neutrality plans before Congress. One would allow trade with any nation on a cash-and-carry basis. A second provided Roosevelt could decide who would be allowed to buy American arms. A third repealed existing laws and relied on international law to determine American trade. A fourth forbade trade with any belligerent. A final plan was simply to allow the cash-and-carry provision to lapse on May 1. A *Newsweek* poll indicated twenty-two senators opposed broadening Roosevelt's powers, ten favored broadening his authority, with the remaining senators equivocating or undecided. House Minority Leader Joseph Martin insisted there was absolutely no common meeting ground in the House. Most Congressmen believed Chamberlain could not be trusted and acted on this belief.[39]

While this debate had been taking place in the United States, Hitler had begun his campaign for "an independent, but Berlin-dominated Ukraine" to be established with territory taken from Russia, Poland, Czecho-Slovakia, and Rumania. Beck, Foreign Minister of Poland, attempted to gain French support against the concept of an independent Ukraine but met with no success. He subsequently visited Hitler for the same purpose. There were rumors Beck had agreed to the Nazi annexation of Danzig and to a "special status" for the Germans in Memel. On January 23, *Time* reported Hitler had sent Nazi "organizers" into the Carpatho-Ukraine, despatched a military mission to the Ruthenians, and was forming a Ukrainian "Free Corps." Daily radio broadcasts from Berlin called for a "free Ukraine." The Soviet government had responded by purging unreliable persons in the Ukraine.[40]

Domestic reports from Germany stated the German economy had been tilted toward preparation for an immediate war, the Skoda works had been placed on a war footing, and that the increased military production had caused a labor shortage which could only be met by the importation of Czech workers.[41] *The New Republic* insisted this regimentation and speed-up of the German economy had created unrest among both employers and labor. The most significant news item, however, was that Schacht had been replaced by Walter

Funk, a former newspaper man. The German need for capital had reached such a crisis point it could be met only by forced inflation. When Schacht refused to create "printing press money," Hitler had sacked him and turned on the presses. *The New Republic* interpreted Schacht's dismissal as one more preparation for war. *The Nation* saw it as presaging "another running jump into foreign adventure."[42]

As 1939 began, there were some apparent glimmers of hope for the plight of refugees. Goering not only invited Rublee, Chairman of the Intergovernmental Committee on Refugees, to Berlin but also announced he had approved a four-point program with American Quakers to ameliorate the condition of German Jews. Under the program, Jews would be allowed to emigrate to transient camps outside Germany where they would be housed until they received an immigration visa. 150,000 Jews could emigrate immediately to establish colonies outside of Europe. This group would be allowed to raise money to aid the emigration of Jews still within Germany. Finally, the Quakers were allowed to establish Jewish relief stations in Germany itself. To support these efforts, Roosevelt cabled Mussolini to request Ethiopia be used as a haven for the emigrants and that Mussolini use his influence with Hitler to persuade him to allow emigrants to take enough capital with them to begin life anew. Roosevelt appeared ready to assume leadership of the refugee crisis.[43] Montague Norman, President of the Bank of England, went to Berlin to discuss an international loan for Germany on condition Jews were allowed to emigrate with some capital. Former Prime Minister Baldwin organized a Jewish refugee fund that quickly raised $1,500,000 to aid their resettlement. The new Czecho-Slovakian government not only arranged with London the immediate emigration of 5,000 German, Austrian, and *Sudeten* Jews, but agreed to finance the emigration with part of a loan from Britain.[44]

Rublee, meeting in Berlin with first Schacht and then Funk, achieved what seemed a fresh and even conciliatory arrangement to provide succor for Germany's Jews. Jews would be allowed to return to work in Jewish enterprises until they could emigrate, there would be no new anti-Semitic legislation, and part of Jewish wealth would be placed in a fund from which emigrants could draw money for passage, equipment, and machinery. As in the Quaker program, 150,000 youthful Jews would be allowed to leave at once provided they agreed to arrange later for the emigration of their parents. After reaching this agreement, Rublee resigned and was replaced by Sir Herbert Emerson, League High Commissioner for Refugees.[45]

Time and *The Nation* asserted Hitler's agreement to these plans did not represent a change of heart or method on his part. The German economy had been badly jolted by the November pogrom and subsequent Jewish sales of securities and real-estate to meet the fine imposed by Goering. Furthermore, foreign reaction to the pogrom had caused German exports to drop "12 1/2 percent, forcing an even greater fall in vital imports." Diplomatically, the pogrom had caused the democracies to reassess their appeasement efforts and attendant economic policies.[46]

The assessment of Hitler's motives and reliability made by *Time* and *The Nation* was amply verified when *Time* reported on March 6 that "Adolf Hitler's two-weeks-old promise" to Rublee had already been "knocked into a cocked hat." The Berlin police issued new orders requiring the Jewish community to provide the police with the names of 100 Jews who would leave Germany within two weeks. After they had paid their taxes, their share of the "von Rath fine," their capital flight tax, their "contribution" to the fund for aged Jews, and sold their jewels "to the State at the State's own price," they would be given a passport stamped with "a large 'J' (for Jew)." The emigrants then had two weeks to leave or face "dire penalties."[47]

Quentin Reynolds argued the anti-Semitic "plague of hate that has swept over Germany like a pestilence continues without abatement, growing in intensity each day." Nazi persecution was much worse than the heavily censored reports from Germany were allowed to reveal and "how long" Jews "will remain alive was a moot question" for "the pogrom, the complete pogrom, is coming." The Jew "must think even the Supreme Being he has worshipped has deserted him." One should make no mistake—the intention of Hitler was to "liquidate" the Jews. Reynolds, in a second article for *Collier's,* demonstrated how the unrelenting Nazi persecution had finally driven the shy, introverted Grynszpan to shoot von Rath. Nazi hounding and brutality, moral, psychological, and physical, had produced the desperation which led to the shooting. No decent human being could fail to sympathize with the young man.[48]

There were other disheartening reports on the Jewish refugee crisis. Although Czecho-Slovakia had agreed to assist 5,000 refugees emigrate, there were 12,000 "utterly destitute" Jews housed in camps near Prague, where they received "a maximum of 28 cents a day for food." In point of fact, moreover, only about 1500 visas had been made available to them. As a result, they were "living in a sort of purgatory, between salvation in a free country and damnation in what they regard as a German hell." Czecho-Slovakia also gave all Jewish teachers "vacations for an indefinite period." Danzig ordered all of its 6,000 Jews out of the city by April 1 with only twenty dollars apiece. After April 1, they would be "dumped on outgoing ships."[49] Between the German-Polish border, ten Jews froze to death. Mussolini rejected outright the idea of an Ethiopian haven and there was no sign he had intervened with Hitler. In Hungary, Premier Imredy presented a parliamentary bill "admittedly aimed at forcing the emigration of Hungary's 500,000 Jews." Ironically, he was shortly forced to resign when it was discovered his great-grandfather had been a Jew. He was, however, replaced by Paul Teleki, who reaffirmed Hungary's intention to proceed with the anti-Semitic legislation.[50]

The basic problem for refugees fleeing from Nazi persecution continued to be the lack of emigration visas. Nazi permission for Jews to emigrate was meaningless without them. A new twist in the refugee crisis appeared when 300 Jewish emigrants were stranded in Montevideo, Uraguay, when Paraguay canceled their immigration visas as they were awaiting further transportation. Ten Austrian Jews, immigrating to the Dominican Republic, were likewise stranded in New York when the Dominican government imposed a new $500 head tax on immigrants although they had been allowed to leave Germany with only twelve dollars apiece.[51]

These were, furthermore according to *Time*, signs of growing anti-Semitism in the United States. New York employment ads increasingly specified "Christian," "Gentile," or "Anglo-Saxons only," job opportunities. Many Jewish women had begun "wearing crosses" to obtain work. The New York Telephone Company, questioned about its discrimination against Jewish telephone operators, responded it did not employ Jewish women "because their arms are too short" to operate a switchboard. A major restaurant owner refused to employ Jews because they "did not like to serve non-kosher food."[52]

There was an anomalous article in *The Atlantic Monthly* in January that smacked of a subtle anti-Semitism. Purportedly written by an "anonymous" Gentile wife married to a Jew, it managed to repeat many of the more common anti-Semitic libels. Identifying herself as an "American-born girl" whose parents were " 'Aryan' Germans," she wrote she "frequently" found herself "trying to see things from the Nazis' point of view" following "a happy thirteen-month sojourn in the *Vaterland* a few years ago." The author's mother was quoted as saying "The Jews are essentially an Oriental race" that are "sensual, aggressive, ostentatious, cunning"—"a heritage they can never overcome." Or again, Jews are successful in business "because they are shrewder than Christians and never hesitate to seize an unfair advantage." In science, they develop "windy theories like those of Einstein and Freud," while "Jewish painters like Picasso (sic) and Modigliani are clever but never great." The "Jews' god" was always "money." The author argued, however, that it "must not be inferred that Mother, because of her German background, was particularly anti-Semitic" for "the same things" were said by "one-hundred-percent Americans." The mother was "happy to say" her son-in-law was "not all Jewish in his make-up" and did not "look Jewish" and one would not "think he was a Jew at all."

The wife stated that "in our discussions," she had to "choose the more tactful way" because "Ben" still had "the Jewish hypersensitivity toward all criticism of his race." When attending the synagogue with him, she "found strange, and a little comical, the presence of men in black derbies at the altar, the squeaky notes of the Shofar," and "the absence of the reverent hush that makes the Catholic or Episcopal service inspiring." Ben, however, was "not at all sure there is a God." His lips clamped "shut" when she ventured to "suggest" Judaism was dogmatic and played "politics quite as much as Rome." Ben agreed "you can baptize a Jew and turn him into an outward Christian" but you could not "take away his feeling for his people, his racial appearance, or his tastes."

Jewish publications "openly vaunt the superiority of their race" and never "mince words when it comes to criticizing the Goy on whose land they live," yet she had never met a Jew "who is willing to admit that some repairs might also be made in the House of Israel." Rarely was a Jew ready to place his "country" above his own interests for he "instinctively desires first the welfare and advancement of his own people." The Jew had always been alien because of "his alien culture, his alien tradition, his fierce pride" in what he believes is "a superior race."

The wife stated she had tried to tell Ben "Hitler is merely writing another page" in the history of Jewish persecution and "that it is no use trying to tell him that a hundred years hence the world will no more call Hitler a swine" for expelling the Jews than it did Edward I of England.

The article ended with a one sentence statement that Ben was the best husband in the world. To anyone familiar with anti-Semitic canards, it is readily apparent that this article, in disguise, includes many of them. It had been paraphrased at length here because it was so strange and so atypical of *The Atlantic Monthly* and yet, reflected current American anti-Semitic attitudes.[53]

The Nation described the German-American Bund meeting in Madison Square Garden on February 20 as "the worst exhibition of Jew-baiting ever seen in the United States." Huge banners read "Stop Jewish Domination of Christian America!," and "Wake Up, America! Smash Jewish Communism!" Bundists strong-armed dissenters and led applause for Coughlin and Hitler. Dorothy Thompson was ejected for repeated laughter at the speeches. Jews were stabbed before and after the meeting on the New York subways.[54]

Ominously, the Bund had begun to proselytize among Hungarians, Syrians, and Arabs. A similar group, the Irish-led Christian Front, "Coughlin's storm troopers," repeatedly attempted to disrupt meetings where Jews were scheduled to speak. Jews were habitually jeered as "kikes, the Christ-killers, the mockies." Anti-Semitics picketed station WMCA in New York each Sunday because it edited out Coughlin's remarks against Jews. Italian Fascists were using the weekly *Il Grido della Stirpe* to attack Jews. This open anti-Semitism was a recent phenomenon but had "ceased to be whispered" and had "an open instrument of demagoguery, a vast outlet" for poison.[55]

The New Republic believed there were 800 organizations in the United States that could be called pro-fascist or pro-Nazi. Individually, they were not large but collectively, they were influential. Only a few carried the Nazi banner openly, most talked of "constitutional democracy," but all were anti-Semitic. All of them claimed they were Christian or that they supported Christianity. Their technique was to pin the label "Jewish" or "Communist" on anyone opposed to them while, at the same time, claiming for their cause every great American hero. The respected Institute for Propaganda analysis estimated one out of every three Americans was subjected to the message of these groups but it did "not know how many ears are dear" to the anti-Semitic message.[56]

The Saturday Evening Post insisted there were actually only approximately 100-150 pro-fascist organizations in the United States. Their numbers only seemed larger because they were so militant and vocal. Although they owed their immediate origin to Hitler, they recruited from the ranks of former klan members. These groups might give some Americans "ideological indigestion," but they were no danger to American freedoms.[57]

In April, *The New Republic* reported a *Fortune* survey revealed "urban white-collar workers in the industrialized Northeast" thought anti-Semitism was on the increase. *Fortune,* according to *The New Republic,* believed between

"18.7 and 33.4 percent of the total population" carried "the symptoms of latent anti-Semitism."[58]

Retired Major-General George Van Horn Moseley, who had been "roaring around the country," made national news when he spoke to the Women's National Defense Committee in Philadelphia in April. He denounced Jews, declaring the next war would be fought for their benefit, and "rasped" at Roosevelt for appointing Frankfurter to the Supreme Court. He predicted the army would "demur" if given "un-American orders." Moseley concluded "Fascism and Nazism" would be "good 'anti-toxins' " against Jews and communists in the United States.[59] Representative Martin Dies, chairman of the Un-American Activities Committee, insisted there was an organized anti-Semitic campaign hiding under the cloak of "a patriotic program to stamp out subversive isms." The campaign, he averred, was directed by George Deatherage of the Fascist Knights of the White Camellias, James E. Campbell, and George Moseley. It was largely financed by Dudley P. Gilbert, a wealthy New Yorker. Moseley was attempting to organize a private army with headquarters in Atlanta. The campaign was exposed by James F. Cook, American Legion Commander of the Department of Tennessee, who sent Dies literature circulated by the group.[60]

In April, hearings were held on the Wagner-Rogers Bill that provided for the admission, outside quota limits, of 20,000 German-born children into the United States in 1939 and 1940. All the children were under fourteen and represented all races and creeds. Witnesses supporting the admission insisted funds had already been collected to provide for their transportation and care and pointed out the children would not take jobs away from Americans. Helen Hayes made an especially dramatic appeal for the bill. However, the American Legion and "an assortment of patriotic societies" opposed the bill, insisting American children were ill-fed, ill-clad, and ill-sheltered and they needed assistance before "alien children" were admitted to the United States. *The Nation* predicted the bill would not pass as there was a rising tide of public opinion against the admission of any immigrants. The bill did pass the committee, but with the proviso that the number of the children admitted had to be deducted from current quotas.[61] Senator Wagner, realizing the result might be the death warrant for an equal number of adults, withdrew the bill from consideration.

Jewish hopes for a Palestinian homeland met continued frustration. The British plan for a round-table conference between Jews and Arabs seemed increasingly unpromising. George Antonius, an Arab Christian visiting New York prior to going to the conference, verbalized vehemently the Arab viewpoint. He insisted Arab terrorism in Palestine was merely "the corollary of the moral violence" done to the Arab by the Briton and the Jew. A Jewish Palestinian homeland would be resisted by unlimited force because the Palestinian Arab preferred death to the loss of his land and could depend for support upon the entire Arab world. The persecution of Jews in Germany was irrelevant because no "code of morals" could "justify the persecution of one people in an attempt to relieve the persecution of another." The conference, he concluded, was useless and doomed to failure.[62]

When the conference convened on February 7, tension between the Arab and Jewish delegations was so intense they would not sit at a common table and Chamberlain had to address each group separately.[63] When Chaim Weizmann made "a two-hour plea" for a Jewish homeland, Jamal Husseini, the cousin of the Grand Mufti, took "only twenty minutes" to denounce the British rule in Palestine and to reject any partition plan. Each session ended with total deadlock. The Arabs demanded the abrogation by Britain of its League mandate, the creation of a sovereign Arab state, an immediate end to all Jewish immigration and sales of land to Jews, and the abandonment of all discussion of a Palestinian Jewish homeland. The Jewish delegation demanded the continuance of the mandate, effective protection of the Jewish minority there, large-scale Jewish immigration, and the eventual development of a sovereign Jewish state.[64]

Chamberlain's objective all along had been to secure Britain's life-line to India and the Orient. More desirous, therefore, of placating the Arabs than providing Jews with a haven, he tentatively proposed to end the League mandate in 1942-1944 by the establishment of an independent Palestinian state bound by treaty to Britain. The treaty would provide for British bases in Palestine, common access for all faiths to the various holy sites, and guarantees for the protection of Jewish minority rights. The Jewish delegation rejected the proposal but requested continued negotiations on a different basis. For the Arabs, "the British proposal was a big victory." In Palestine, Arab crowds celebrated "the reconquest of Palestine from the British." The same week bloody fighting among Arabs, Jews, and the British left thirty dead and scores wounded. *The New Republic* believed Britain would "cook up her own plan, sugar it heavily with sweet phrases and cram it down the throats of Jews and Arabs alike." *The Nation* insisted the British proposal was "as great a betrayal as the Munich pact."[65]

In April, following the failure of the London conference, Chaim Weizmann flew to Cairo to appeal for King Farouk's aid in arranging a temporary truce in Palestine due to the critical European situation. While Weizmann's appeal failed, the Arab terror campaign received a serious setback when the British army killed one major Arab leader and French troops in Syria captured and imprisoned another. The level of violence thereupon declined for the first time in months.[66]

On May 17, a British White Paper revealed Chamberlain's proposal for Palestine. Over a five year period, 75,000 more Jews would be admitted until the Jewish population was frozen at 500,000 or one-third the number of Arabs. At the end of an additional ten years, Britain would grant Palestine its independence and a state established tied to Britain by a firm alliance. The new state would be governed by Jews and Arabs in proportion to their population. Jews of all factions immediately united to oppose "this bitter blow." In Tel Aviv, angry Jews tore down the Union Jack over Government House and hoisted a blue and white Zionist flag with a six-pointed star. Revisionists staged riots in which a British soldier was killed and 200 people were injured. This was followed by a twenty-four hour general strike and a refusal by landowners to pay British taxes. It took two days for the British army to stop the agitation. The Arabs remained quiet but rejected the plan as it admitted more Jews to Palestine and as they desired immediate independence.[67]

The Nation and *The New Republic* attacked the plan as another "Munich." The British had, in cold blood, made a bid for Moslem support in the next war at Jewish expense. It knew the Jews could not, in any case, support the Axis. No more than Munich would it bring peace to Palestine for the Arab was implacable in his hatred and opposition to Jews. Jews, for their part, were increasingly motivated by the realization they faced annihilation in Europe and could not peaceably accept the British proposal. Villard, a thorough-going pacifist, suggested the Jews should find themselves a Gandhi and conduct a campaign of non-violent passive resistance.[68]

In Commons, the British proposal was heavily assaulted by Lloyd-George and Churchill. When put to a vote, the plan received approval by a vote of 268 to 179, although the normal government strength was 413. Colonel Josiah C. Wedgewood stated the cabinet's betrayal of its pledge to the Jews meant only one thing—Jews in Palestine should begin blowing up bridges and pipelines. The Revisionist organization responded by setting off bombs in Haifa that killed eighteen Arabs and wounded twenty-four more in a market. Ben Gurion promptly denounced the Revisionist organization for the attacks.[69]

Meanwhile, other events had long been distracting Europeans and Americans. When Barcelona fell on January 26 to Franco, Mussolini mobilized 60,000 troops and aviators and renewed his demands for Corsica and Tunisia. Daladier replied, on the same day, France would "not yield a single acre or concede a single right" without war. The French General Staff announced plans to double the speed of French mobilization if needed. Minister of Finance Reynaud announced French plans to buy "5,000 planes abroad."[70] Chamberlain went on the radio to announce a plan for "voluntary registration" of 1,800,000 Britons to "make us ready for war." Home Secretary Hoare followed to declare Britain was prepared to win if war were forced on it while First Lord Stanhope stated Britain was launching a warship each week. Air Minister Wood concluded for the government with the assertion British air production would treble in 1939. This government statement was followed by a program in which eighteen British notables such as the Earl of Derby, Norman Montagu, and John Masefield appealed for the "leaders and people of the great German Reich" to join in an effort "to lay the specter of war." British housewives were officially advised to start storing food for emergencies.[71]

For his part, Hitler held a conference with "several hundred admirals and generals," canceled all military leaves after February 15, and moved two divisions to the Italian border where they could quickly aid Mussolini. In his address to the Reichstag, celebrating his sixth anniversary as chancellor, Hitler again demanded the return of Germany's former colonies and further, declared he would stand by Mussolini in any Mediterranean crisis that developed. He accused the United States of "interfering" in German affairs and forbade "Americans to interfere in our affairs." The Reichstag repeatedly interrupted his speech with shouts of approval and extended his dictatorial power until 1943.[72]

Subsequent close examination of his speech revealed "it was actually one of the most sensational and threatening talks ever made by the head of a State." Hitler had averred "Europe cannot settle down until the Jewish question is cleared up." The most ominous statement, however, followed:[73]

> If the international financiers in and outside Europe should succeed in plunging the nations once more into a world war, then the result will not be the bolshevization of the earth, and thus the victory of Jewry, but the annihilation of the Jewish race in Europe.

The new crisis caused a 9.74 drop in stocks on the New York exchange to a close of 136.42, down from a January 4 close of 154.85. British securities in London slumped and had to be supported by the Bank of England. Speculators transferred an "immense volume" of gold to the United States. The pound sterling dropped in value and could be stabilized only by inflation. Rearmament and "appeasement by loans" were bankrupting Britain. Prior to Munich, approximately $50,000,000 a month was sent to New York from London. By October, 1938, the amount jumped to $443,403,000 a month.[74]

As the crisis deepened, Roosevelt allegedly told the Senate Military Affairs Committee that "America's frontier was on the Rhine." When the remark was reported in the press, the French Chamber of Deputies "echoed with cries of 'Long Live Roosevelt'!" The British and French praised the president for his courage. Although Roosevelt publicly labeled the rumor a "lie," most senators and foreign diplomats believed he had made the statement.[75] *Newsweek* wrote "Mussolini thought so and wavered in his intention" to attack France. Germany "thought so and a note of concern crept into the usually arrogant Nazi press." Senators "fumed in the straitjacket of secrecy the President had imposed on them." The American press generally praised the supposed remarks of Roosevelt. Neye, Borah, and Hiram Johnson insisted again on "mandatory neutrality to keep America out of war" as they believed Roosevelt was intent on war to aid the democracies.[76]

Following Roosevelt's supposed statement, the French Deputies, in a rare show of solidarity, unanimously passed a resolution declaring the French empire indivisible and that it could not be "transmitted, delegated, or shared." Chamberlain asserted in Commons Britain would tolerate no "threat to vital interests of France, from whatever quarter it came." Chamberlain also insisted before there could be any further appeasement of the dictators, they had to demonstrate "some concrete evidence of willingness" to work for peace that went beyond words. He continued to push preparations for war. The cabinet announced plans to de-centralize the government, to provide 1,200,000 gas masks for children, to mobilize British medical services, and that it would compensate British citizens for loss of life or property in case of war. The defense budget was dramatically increased. Both Britain and France began cautious approaches to Franco, seeking his friendship and neutrality if war broke out.[77]

At the end of February, although Italy and France were continuing to reinforce their African garrisons, *Newsweek* believed the crisis had largely passed and saw signs Mussolini was retreating before the prospect of war with France. He made no protest when French troops moved up to the borders of Italian East Africa and Libya and he also placed a freight contract with the French railways in Somaliland. Britain had publicly stood by France, Franco seemed anxious to reach an understanding with them following their recognition of his regime, and Roosevelt apparently had joined the democracies—events which were noted in Rome.[78]

Time, however, saw no reduction in the North African crisis and thought only a "Mediterranean Munich" would prevent war. Furthermore, *Time* stressed there were numerous and consistent reports in the British and French press that Hitler was about to unveil a new "Hitler surprise" on March 6. The German army was fully mobilized and on a wartime footing. The British, French, and Dutch governments were busily transferring large amounts of gold to New York to buy food and meet the "cash and carry" requirements of American neutrality laws. *The New Republic* also believed in the immediate possibility of war. Both Italy and Germany were mobilized and prepared for war and if they encountered firm resistance from Britain and France might well unleash their legions—Germany to the east and Italy in the Mediterranean. They could not sit idle as their economies were too unstable.[79]

Both the fascist and democratic states continued to arm at an ever increasing pace. *The Reader's Digest* reported Germany had between sixteen and eighteen thousand planes and was producing a thousand more each month. London planned to "handle a million casualties the first week of war" due to the awesome power of this German air force. France was spending $65,000,000 in the United States to purchase 1,000 planes. Britain planned to spend $2,900,000,000 for defense in 1939, almost double the amount budgeted in 1938. Italy, whose economy was so much smaller, had budgeted $500,000,000 for arms in 1939.[80]

The opposing camps also began a desperate search for allies. Ciano attempted to form a Balkan alliance with Yugoslavia, Rumania, and Hungary that almost materialized. Ciano visited Warsaw in an attempt to seduce Poland by the offer of Madagascar as a place to ship Poland's 3,200,000 Jews. He sought and concluded a trade agreement for Russian oil and rare ores. Ribbentrop induced Hungary to sign the Anti-Comintern Pact.[81] Both camps bid for Franco's support or, barring such support, his benevolent neutrality. Chamberlain proposed a large loan to Poland, attended a reception at the Russian embassy for the first time and despatched a trade mission to Moscow. Vice Admiral C.V. Usborne was sent on a good-will mission to Rumania while Lady Stanley, wife of the President of the Board of Trade, was hurried off on a visit to Latvia, Estonia, Poland, and Greece.[82]

Chamberlain, seemingly of two minds during the crisis, again doubled the British budget for arms, again asserted Britain would stand by France, and prepared a British Expeditionary Force of eighteen divisions for quick despatch to France in the event of war.[83] The British civilian population was prepared for aerial and gas attack. Yet, at the same time, Chamberlain despatched his Secretaries for Overseas Trade and the Board of Trade to Berlin to discuss a trade agreement and the possibility of a worldwide market agreement. Chamberlain also put out feelers for a conference to discuss arms limitations and a "general settlement" for Europe. As the arms build-up was quickly and surely bankrupting both camps in Europe, Chamberlain believed the solution of that problem would resolve the second problem.[84]

The Reader's Digest for March predicted Hitler might plunge into a foreign adventure due to the impending collapse of the German economy. Wages had been cut and prices inflated with the result the average German was reduced "to a bare level of subsistence." Even with the *ersatz* program, there were shortages of all types. One result was a growing political discontent which Goebbels could not counteract. Much of the economic collapse was due to the effects of the November pogrom which had disrupted the German economy by the slump in securities and real estate values. A new foreign adventure to recoup the German economy was therefore likely.[85]

On March 1, *The New Republic* asserted German economic reserves were exhausted, with both exports and imports rapidly dropping, and that discontent was "prevalent." Any further hardships would need to be off-set by a "new psychological compensation" and Hitler believed, in addition, "another political victory will provide the resources necessary for still further advance." War was, therefore, likely in the spring. *The Nation* also reported Germany was in desperate financial straits. Hitler had been reduced to paying government contractors with "non-interest-bearing I.O.U.'s without definite redemption dates." These were used as collateral for bank loans which meant an increase in note issue and inflation. Brinkmann of the Reichsbank had been driven to a "nervous breakdown" by the phony money. With the Ides of March, "Hitler's open season for treaty-breaking," was at hand and war might well result as Hitler's answer to his economic situation. Czecho-Slovakia lay at hand for the taking.[86]

Following the Munich Conference, Czecho-Slovakia had been divided into the three autonomous areas of Bohemia-Moravia, Slovakia, and the Carpatho-Ukraine. The latter two immediately became the scene of Nazi-supported separatist movements. On March 6, President Hacha had to forestall a separatist coup in Carpatho-Ukraine. On March 9, Hacha had to place the Slovakian premier, Joseph Tilso, under house arrest to prevent a planned separatist coup in Bratislava. When Bratislava was placed under martial law and garrisoned with Czech troops, there were numerous clashes with the fascist, anti-Semitic Hlinka Guards. Slovaks paraded with shouts of "Slava (Heil) Hitler" and joined Slovakian-Germans in singing the Horst Wessel Lied. Tiso smuggled out a telegram asking for Hitler's aid in the establishment of an independent Slovakia. Released due to Nazi pressure, Tiso hurried to Berlin and conferred with Hitler. Hitler then sent Hacha an ultimatum demanding he announce the independence of Slovakia and the Carpatho-Ukraine. Simultaneously, the Nazi press and radio unleashed an "anti-Czech tirade." London and Paris announced that internal rearrangements of Czecho-Slovakia was not their concern.[87]

Hitler summoned Hacha and Foreign Minister Chvalkovsky to Berlin on March 14, brow-beat them by threatening to bomb Prague "out of existence," and so obtained their "request" that German troops occupy Bohemia-Moravia and the provinces he placed under German "protection." On March 15, German troops moved in with Hitler in their train and occupied Prague. Ribbentrop announced Hacha would remain as president but would be subordinate to a Nazi protector who would have an absolute veto power over laws and the courts. The protectorate would have "local autonomy" but would have to act in total harmony with the Third Reich. Czechs were to become "subjects" of the Reich with only "racial Germans" enjoying Reich citizenship. The following day, Tiso requested Hitler to place Slovakia under his "protection." The Gestapo immediately began the round-up of anti-Nazis and ordered Jews fired from their jobs. A wave of suicides followed. With Hitler's permission, Hungary immediately marched in and seized the Carpatho-Ukraine. By this move, Hitler satisfied both Hungary and Mussolini, who had pressed Hungary's claims to the province.[88]

Time wrote the seizure of Czechoslovakia "was Adolf Hitler's most sudden, shocking surprise," There had been only three days of preparatory propaganda accusing the Czechs of attacking Germans, harboring communists, and favoring Jews. It believed Hitler was motivated by a desire to seize Czecho-Slovakia wealth to bolster the sagging German economic situation.[89] *Time* asserted the British and French secret services had predicted the aggression but that Chamberlain and Daladier, believing they could do nothing about it and that their peoples were "bored" with central Europe, had pretended they were unaware of the invasion. When they realized their peoples were angry and indignant, Chamberlain and Daladier suddenly assumed a mantle of indignation and anger. *Time* ended by contrasting selections from Hitler's speeches about his desires for peace, a purely German Reich, and an end to Nazi demands for territory after Munich with his actions from 1935 to his attack on Prague.[90]

Newsweek believed Nazi tanks in Prague "crushed the final illusion that Nazi imperialism had been appeased by concessions." Recognition of this Nazi imperialism "must lead Britain to fight the Reich at every step." Britain would henceforth regard Germany "not as a potential friend but as a certain enemy." Where London led, Paris was sure to follow.[91]

The New Republic accused Hitler of violating "his own code of morals" in invading "the land of a non-German people in order to steal their weapons, their money and, before he is through with them, their gold wedding rings and silver spoons." The invasion was "a marauding expedition" and other such expeditions were to be expected for "Hitler needed hard cash" and much of the Czech gold reserve had been moved to London.[92]

With the death of the rump Czecho-Slovakia, *The Nation* dropped its isolationism: It asserted Hitler was determined upon the domination of Europe and possibly the world. If he succeeded, it would mean "even the semblance of human freedom" would be obliterated "in a large part of the world" and ultimately, Americans would be forced, "in order to survive, to fit into the framework of a Nazi world." His attack meant there should be a "change in the Neutrality Law to permit sales of supplies to the non-fascist powers in case of war" and a "willingness to consult on other possible measures of resistance." Villard continued to insist on isolationism in his column "Issues and Men," but *Nation* editor Kirchwey was henceforth for all aid to the democracies.[93]

Roosevelt was the first democratic leader to react to Hitler's aggression. He had Sumner Welles formally condemn the coup as an act of "wanton lawlessness" that would only temporarily extinguish Czech freedom. Welles also despatched a note to Germany asserting the United States refused to recognize the conquest. The Treasury Department, on a ruling by Attorney General Murphy that German exports were subsidized, slapped a net tax of twenty-five percent on all German goods, including Czecho-Slovakia in the ruling. The American minister at Prague was ordered home immediately. The Post Office Department ordered all mail to Czecho-Slovakia held in New York and Paris until senders could retrieve letters and funds they did not want to fall in Nazi hands. Senator Key Pittman, Roosevelt's spokesman on neutrality, called for an amendment to the neutrality bill permitting a "cash and carry" plan that would aid France and England. *The New Republic* stated it had "no doubt" Americans would support all of Roosevelt's actions except for the relaxation of the neutrality laws. Czecho-Slovakian Americans, approximately 2,500,000 in all, instantly rallied to Roosevelt and began to hold "Stop Hitler" rallies.[94]

Chamberlain "officially and formally" buried his appeasement policy and announced events in central Europe was "decidedly Britain's business." Czech funds in London worth $60,000,000 were blocked. He had Halifax state Britain would not allow Poland or the Balkans to fall into Nazi hands. The British ambassador to Berlin was recalled. Chamberlain declared he would seek a statement against further German aggression signed by Britain, France, and Russia to which Poland, Rumania, Turkey, Greece, and Yugoslavia would be invited to adhere.[95]

Daladier, taking his lead from Chamberlain and Roosevelt, blocked all Czech funds in Paris, denounced Hitler's action, and recalled his ambassador from Berlin. In addition, he requested and received dictatorial powers from the French Parliament. He announced he would call more men to the colors, speed up rearmament, and virtually place France on a wartime footing.[96]

Any expectation Hitler would pause and reevaluate his aggressive conduct due to the action of the democracies was quickly disappointed. Hitler summoned Lithuanian Foreign Minister Urbays to Berlin on March 21 and demanded the immediate cession of Memel and the subordination of Lithuanian policy to that of Germany. Hitler once again visited a conquered city in the wake of his troops while "panic-stricken Jews fled" for their safety. Hitler also simultaneously demanded and received an agreement making Rumania an economic vassel of Berlin. A diplomatic note to Poland offered to settle Hitler's differences with Warsaw provided Poland agreed to the Nazi annexation of Danzig. If anything, Hitler had accelerated his pressure and aggression.[97]

The reaction of Britain and France was tepid at best. Sir Samuel Hoare said Britain would not protest the seizure of Memel and evaded questions in Commons about Rumania. Chamberlain later insisted Rumania had not signed away its economic freedom. Foreign Under-Secretary Richard Butler insisted Britain was not contemplating a boycott or economic sanctions against Germany. The "Stop Hitler" movement had been derailed by Russia and Poland and Chamberlain was again taking counsel of his fears.[98]

When approached by Chamberlain for a "declaration" against Hitler, Russia countered with the suggestion of an "anti-Hitler conference" of Britain, France, Poland, Rumania, Turkey, and Russia. Chamberlain replied the idea of a conference was "premature." Warsaw, however, thoroughly frightened Chamberlain. It mobilized another class of its reserves, withdrew its rolling-stock from the Corridor, and moved 10,000 troops to the city of Gdynia. Warsaw further informed Chamberlain it would not join a merely rhetorical gesture that would only antagonize Hitler and asked for absolute guarantees of military assistance from Britain, France, and Russia. *The New Republic* stressed Russia and Poland dared not trust Daladier and Chamberlain. They duped public opinion but dared not put teeth in their "Stop Hitler" campaign. *The Nation* insisted there was "an uneasy feeling" Chamberlain simply could not be trusted.[99]

The "Stop Hitler" movement by Roosevelt, however, continued to gain momentum even if it was only moral and economic. The State Department announced a plan to force countries selling gold to the United States to cooperate in an anti-Nazi boycott. The State, War, and Navy requested Congress to pass the Pittman resolution to allow Latin American nations to rearm. Under presidential urging, Congress passed a bill to provide the army with 6,000 planes and considered bills to increase naval air power. Roosevelt, it was openly rumored, was leading a move to "starve" Germany economically. Further, Roosevelt extended recognition to Franco's regime to cooperate with British and French efforts to keep him out of the Axis orbit.[100]

The British press split almost evenly "over the way to cope with Hitler." Rothermere's *Daily Mail* stated there had been "no logic or justice about Czecho-Slovakia" and that "Europe should rejoice that more frontiers had been changed without resort to a big conflict." Beaverbrook's *Daily* Express also adopted the same line. *The Daily Mirror* and *The New Chronicle* which had long opposed appeasement, demanded the immediate resignation of Chamberlain. What was more significant was that the Tory dailies, *The Daily Telegraph* and *The London Times*, called for all measures needed to stop any further Nazi aggression. The Rothermere and Beaverbrook chains had a combined circulation of 5,000,000 while the opposition had a combined circulation of 4,000,000. British public opinion, however, had "welded" into a "white heat of public indignation" against Hitler.[101]

Swift on the heels of these reactions, Hitler mobilized another class of army reserves and moved large contingents of troops toward the Polish Corridor and Danzig. East Prussia was transformed into an armed camp. Hitler then presented Warsaw with a list of demands that included the cession of Danzig to Germany, a German road across the Corridor, and the adherence of Poland to the anti-Comintern Pact. Chamberlain, faced with a revolt in his cabinet and tremendous pressure from all elements of the British public, finally rose in Commons to announce he and Daladier intended to negotiate a system of outright military alliances to resist further Nazi aggression. He denounced Hitler as a man whose word could not be trusted. To the unanimous cheers of Commons, Chamberlain declared any action which "clearly threatened" Poland would be met by British and French force. On the following day, when *The London Times* interpreted this to mean only the independence, not the integrity of Poland, was guaranteed, Whitehall issued a statement declaring Britain was pledged to the defense of Polish integrity. Major Vernon Barlett applauded the action and stated in Commons that Britons "shall not be able to enjoy" themselves "until Franco's widow tells Stalin on his deathbed that Hitler has been assassinated at Mussolini's funeral."[102]

Poland, meanwhile, called up additional reserves and announced a national defense loan of $228,000,000. Colonel Beck, however, was reluctant to publicly accept the British guarantee for fear of antagonizing Hitler and because he was not sure Chamberlain and Daladier could be trusted. Chamberlain had to appeal directly to Marshall Smigly-Rydz and President Moscicki before the guarantee was accepted.[103]

Newsweek interpreted the Anglo-French guarantee to Poland to mean "the British Empire and Greater Germany had recognized each other as the ultimate enemies in a struggle for world power" and "as in 1914, the threat of German domination evoked the determination to fight it out to a finish" among all Britons. *Time* wrote Britain, "step by step, like a long-harried elephant finally facing an enemy," had finally "turned in her tracks." Chamberlain's pledge was "an impressive and world-shaking spectacle." If war came, it noted, "Germany will again have to fight both on eastern and western fronts." *The Nation* believed "the initiative in Europe" had finally "passed to the Western democracies." *The New Republic*, however, insisted "we are not justified in hoping for too much from the latest turn of events." People everywhere believed Chamberlain simply could not be trusted and might yet make a deal with Hitler. Chamberlain would have difficulty, therefore, in creating a Stop-Hitler system of alliances.[104] To a lesser degree, *Time*, *Newsweek*, and *The Nation* shared this suspicion of Chamberlain.

Hitler responded to Chamberlain in speech from Wilhelmshaven delivered from behind bullet-proof glass. Delivered extemporaneously, the broadcast was cut off by Goebbels after Hitler's first sentence. While the official explanation was there had been broadcast difficulties, *Time* asserted it was because Hitler was in "a state of high emotion and intense anger" and had looked "much tenser than usual." His entourage simply could not trust what he might say "in a moment of oratorical ecstasy." Those who heard the speech in person asserted "Hitler had rarely delivered a worse speech" and that it had been "weak, unconvincing, rambling, discussive, formless." Never had "Hitler seemed less sure of himself." The speech was an anti-British diatribe of the *"Gott strafe England"* genre. He accused Chamberlain of plotting an encirclement policy and threatened to denounce the Anglo-Naval Treaty. *Time* noted "one noticeable feature of the world's reaction to this latest Hitler oratory. Nobody paid much attention to it."[105]

If Hitler was nonplussed by Chamberlain's unexpected *voltra-face*, Mussolini was not taken aback by it. For some time, there had been hopes Mussolini might yet be separated from Hitler. Following Munich, Mussolini had pointedly not pressed seriously his earlier demands against France. He had studiously avoided public comment on Hitler's assassination of the rump Czech-Slovakian state. On April 7 then, there was a tremendous shock when, "in accordance" with the Axis' "newly adopted schedule of a country a week," Mussolini attacked and overran Albania without warning. Once again, *The Nation* asserted, the aggressors had the initiative.[106] King Zog, after his troops put up a futile one day resistance, fled to Greece. From there, he issued a statement declaring there were "in Europe two madmen who are destroying the world—Hitler and Mussolini." There were also "in Europe two damn fools who sleep—Chamberlain and Daladier."[107]

The seizure of Albania struck "again the already overworked alarm bells all the way from the Thames to the Dardanelles." Hitler, who had been continually in touch with Mussolini, concentrated troops along the Dutch and Yugoslavian borders, despatched Goebbels to the Italian island of Rhodes and Goering to Libya, and announced he would neither "understand or approve" if "the democratic Western powers" interfered with "the legally irreproachable position and behavior" of Mussolini. Chamberlain, who was fishing in Scotland, rushed back to London, called an emergency cabinet meeting, and reconvened Parliament. Chamberlain, without waiting for Parliament to assemble, extended an unconditional British guarantee to Greece and Turkey. The British fleet was mobilized and its Mediterranean units were ordered to defend Corfu. Franco announced Spain would sign the anti-Comintern Pact.[108] Across Europe, "precautionary measures" were taken by all armies. In Holland, all army leaves were canceled. Carol of Rumania inspected his army and its border defenses. British and French air staffs opened planning conferences. Gas masks were issued at the Vatican and special air-raid shelters built for the Pope and the cardinals. Daladier ordered the French fleet to sea and met with the French Council of National Defense. Dictator Metaxas of Greece "hinted he would not oppose the British occupation of Corfu" to assure the integrity and independence of Greece.[109]

Roosevelt issued an official statement which declared "the inevitable effect of this incident" directly affected "our own welfare." *Newsweek* wrote that, in America, "war hysteria" was "not very far under the surface these days." Major General William Haskell, commander of the New York National Guard, asked the Guard be brought up to wartime strength. Radio networks carried "staccato appeals for recruits." Assistant Secretary of War Louis A. Johnson officially reported American industry was "substantially" mobilized for war production. Pulpits across the country "reverberated with Easter imprecations on the dictators." The percentage of Americans willing to sell arms to Britain and France during wartime jumped to sixty-six percent "as compared with

55 percent a month ago." The New York Stock Exchange dropped to a new low for 1939.[110] Herbert Hoover, who *Time* asserted was the leading American isolationist, urged Congress to take action to prevent Roosevelt from taking the United States into war against the wishes of the American people.[111]

During April, tensions daily increased across Europe as alarms poured in from every sector. Lithuania reported Hitler was demanding a further cession of territory. Hungary and Bulgaria mobilized their forces and took action against native Nazi groups. Portugal reported Franco was moving Spanish and Italian units to its border. In ever greater volume, gold was sent abroad, primarily to the United States. Berlin announced forty units of the German fleet would "maneuver" off the Spanish coast. Paris countered by mobilizing its fleet and despatched a naval force to protect the International Zone of Tangier while London strengthened its forces at Gibralter. There were reports Franco, not Hitler, would attack Gibralter. German troops were reported to be moving into Italy to assist an Italian "adventure."[112] The Dutch strengthened their border battalions, mined their roads and harbors, and prepared to blow their dikes if attacked. Belgium mobilized its forces as did the Swiss. The Nazi press demanded the return of Danzig and launched a propaganda campaign which alleged Poles were beating Polish-Germans with "clubs and wire whips." Berlin and Warsaw moved new divisions to their common border. Both mobilized new classes of troops.[113] *Newsweek* reported 8,000,000 men were under arms in Europe, with the number increasing each day. This was roughly the number mobilized in 1914. *Time* believed these tensions had produced a war hysteria in all parts of Europe. The French "regarded the beginning of war as the end of civilization" but were "ready to die game." In Britain there was an evident "desire to go ahead and get it over with." The Italians and Germans were unenthusiastically reconciled to the inevitability of war.[114]

Chamberlain insisted he was attempting to enlist Russia in his Grand Alliance with Poland and France. There were few signs he was succeeding. The central European nations hesitated "to call in the Red horde as a defense weapon." Poland in particular was opposed to the enlistment of Russia. For his part, Stalin was hesitant to trust Chamberlain and demanded an outright military alliance with Paris and London. A German delegation was invited to Moscow to discuss a new trade agreement. Chamberlain suggested Russia agree to supply Poland and Rumania with war material and part of the Red air force—but withhold its army if war broke out. The Russians rejected the proposal outright. Chamberlain did extend an Anglo-French guarantee to Rumania which King Carol accepted, insisting, however, he had not requested it. Yugoslavia, fearful of provoking the dictators, asked *a priori* that no guarantee be extended to it.[115]

Responding to the growing tensions in Europe, Roosevelt moved on several fronts to stiffen the resolve of the democracies and to galvanize the American people into action. In the week beginning on April 9, he "made so many headlines" that "the typesetters could hardly keep up" with his remarks. On April 9, he left Warm Springs saying he would return in the fall "if we don't have a war." On April 11, Roosevelt pointedly endorsed a *Washington Post* editorial that insisted the United States had to take the lead in stopping Hitler "by threat and, if that failed, by war." On April 14, he told Latin American representatives the United States was determined "to defend American peace, matching force with force." On April 15, Roosevelt ordered the American battle fleet back to the Pacific where it could counterbalance any Japanese threat to British, French, and Dutch possessions in the Orient and so free up their naval units for service in Europe. He also despatched identical telegrams to Hitler and Mussolini offering to convene a world peace conference if they would pledge not to attack thirty-one specified countries for ten to twenty-five years.[116]

Newsweek believed "the Roosevelt gesture was foredoomed to failure" as Hitler and Mussolini had "gone too far to turn back." The dictators might try either of "two diametrically opposite" courses—fight before the democracies tightened a ring around them or try to talk their way out of the ring. *Time* wrote Roosevelt's actions had "clarified once and for all the fact" he "positively expected war abroad unless some one's will-to-peace" was "stronger than the Dictators' will-to-war." Whatever the reaction of Hitler and Mussolini, it "could only be a prelude to even greater deeds by Franklin Roosevelt." *The Nation* identified Roosevelt "as the world's leading peace-monger" and called his appeal to the dictators "bold and generous and honest." He had "voiced the passionate desire for peace of every sane man and woman in the world." If the appeal was rejected, the rejection itself would "stiffen the spines of wavering elements" in the democracies against the dictators. The American people were solidly behind Roosevelt's efforts to prevent war and would be aroused if Hitler forced war upon the world.[117] *The New Republic* believed Roosevelt had made the appeal to the dictators, "not primarily to bring peace, but to be rejected." If they accepted the appeals, they could no longer blackmail Europe. If they rejected the appeal, they would only facilitate the mobilization of a "Grand Alliance against them." It agreed with Roosevelt on the necessity to prepare to resist evil, but also called upon him to state what the Grand Alliance would "be fighting *for*" in the event of war.[118]

Newsweek reported Roosevelt's action had produced "a rising tide of hope and a consequent stiffening of attitude in Britain, France, and most of the small powers" of Europe. In the Senate, it produced bitter attacks on the president by Reynolds, Borah, and Walter George. The upcoming end of the cash-and-carry clause on May 1 lent an air of urgency to Roosevelt's actions as well as those of the isolationists. *Time* reported the most recent Gallup poll revealed sixty-five percent of Americans favored a boycott of Germany, fifty-seven percent wanted the Neutrality Act revised to allow war material sales to Britain and France, fifty-one percent expected a European war in 1939, and fifty-eight percent believed the United States would be drawn into any European war that broke out. *Time* asserted "preoccupation with the war question was general" across the United States. Americans were opposed to war but sided with the allies if there was a war. If war did erupt, they had "a fatalistic, unhappy, shoulder-shrugging belief" the United States would be drawn into it. While Alvin York of World War fame believed "Hitler and Mussolini jes' need a good whippin' and it looks like Uncle Sam's gonna have to do it," the American Legion remained opposed to foreign wars. A *Time* poll of its reporters in the United States revealed the Far West generally approved of armament for defense but opposed involvement in a European war. The Middle West was mixed in its attitude with some measure of pro-Nazi sentiment among Detroit tycoons. Detroit editors believed, however, that war was inescapable and "U.S. participation was obligatory." The South "appeared solidly disgusted with Hitler and Mussolini" but believed they were a European problem. There was "annoyance at Jews for having helped precipitate so much fuss and bother." The North East was the "most agitated by the war atmosphere" but unable to see a way to avoid war. Sympathy for "Hitler's Jewish victims was a chief sinew of militant sentiment." Most people showed "the strain of prolonged suspense" and wanted a European war to "get this damn thing settled."[119]

Two interesting and exceptional in-depth background stories appeared in American magazines on the weekend of April 24-26. They interrupt our narrative at this point because they indicated a growing awareness the democracies were dealing with a pathological political system dominated by a pathological dictator.

Time devoted its cover story of April 24 to Heinrich Himmler. It provided an accurate and detailed biography of his life which attributed his power to his utter devotion and "undying love for his Fuehrer." More significant was its description of his personality, his organizations, and his brutality. For the first time in these magazines, American readers were provided with a detailed picture of the organization of the Nazi police state and the man who administered it.

Himmler, according to *Time*, was a "weak, fleshy-chinned, owlish" individual who was "inordinately ambitious, a weaver of grandiose political dreams" and a "cold, selfish, remorseless fanatic." "No orator," he was "scarcely a figure calculated to arouse much personal enthusiasm." Himmler, of all the Nazis, was "the most uncompromising, the least likely to show mercy or kindness." He was not so much seen or heard in Germany as he was felt as "the shadow behind the swastika." As Police Commissioner and "supreme director of law and order in all Germany," Himmler had "purged, sacked, centralized, reorganized" the German police system to make it a Nazi "cult." His role in the Third Reich was to accuse, abuse, and kill anyone even suggested to him by Hitler. Not even the most loyal Nazi felt safe or believed he could speak freely over his telephone.

Himmler held two important titles. As "Inspector" of the "dread, notorious" Gestapo, he imposed a total dictatorship upon the life of every "German, every dissenter, and every Jew." As Reichsfuehrer of the *Shutzstaffel* or SS, he had organized it into three branches. The General SS included those who did no more than attend Nazi meetings, police demonstrations, sports events, and auxiliary police functions. The Service Troops were the military arm of the SS. Organized into four motorized military units, they served in peace-time as honor and body guards of the Nazi leadership. In wartime, they would be an elite striking force for the German army. The Death's Head Brigade guarded the concentration camps. These camps were, under Himmler's orders, made permanent prisons where "Communist agitators, homosexuals, disgraced Nazis, Jewish university professors, Protestant conscientious objectors" were "thrown together in common cells." "Few steps were taken" to prevent "Jewish adolescents from being attacked or molested." "Sadism and brutality" were the prime marks of the prisoner's daily life—the "whipping-post is used freely; men are forced to run while carrying heavy loads are prodded with bayonets if they fall out of step." Jewish boys were frequently thrown into latrines and their heads pushed under the mire by rifle butts. Out of these SS groups, Himmler intended to breed a "great race of supermen." In the event of war, Himmler could be expected to build "a personal political machine," blindly obedient to Hitler, but otherwise able to dominate German economic and political life for Himmler's benefit. Hitler's outlook and obsessions were reflected faithfully by Himmler.[120]

The New Republic ran a series of three articles condensed from Reinhold Hainish's memoir of his association with Hitler in Vienna. Hainish depicted Hitler as a lonely, moody, introverted individual who would, at unexpected moments, break into loud, extended monologues on political questions of the day. He alleged Hitler, at this period, was not anti-Semitic and, indeed, often survived by selling his watercolors to Jews. Hainish described Hitler as a man obsessed with hatred of the Austro-Hungarian empire and its minorities and as one who was unable to forgive any imagined or real slights given to him. Hainish, according to *The New Republic* had died or been killed while in the custody of the Gestapo.[121]

These articles provided much of the material for a psychiatric portrait of Hitler in the April 26 issue of *The New Republic*. The article tentatively diagnosed Hitler as a "schizophrenic" who had been profoundly disappointed by his mother and, therefore, was unable to relate to others. Hitler reacted to that disappointment by turning a hostile and aggressive face to the world. The psychiatrist asserted such "aggressive neurotics" knew no limits to their hatred. These neurotics, on reaching the "height of their powers," however, "automatically" collapsed mentally. Hitler was already showing symptoms of increasing confusion, indecision, and fear. Medically, a "purely pathological outcome" for Hitler was "not at all excluded." Democratic statesmen needed to realize they were not dealing with a rational man who could be approached on a rational basis but, rather, a man driven by compulsions he could not control and who hated without limit.[122]

Time, on May 8, reported Freud's disciple, Carl Jung, placed Hitler in "the category of the truly mystic medicine men" who believe they are "acting under the command of a higher power" within them. Such men could not be simply told to disobey this higher power as they would not respond to such treatment. Jung could only induce such a patient "to behave in a way less harmful to himself and society." Western leaders should not, therefore, touch "Germany in her present mood" as "she is much too dangerous." Jung's prescription was to tell Hitler to go "to Russia" as that was "the logical cure" for Hitler's mania.[123]

In short, both psychiatrists believed Hitler was irrational and sociopathic. As such, he was not less, but more, dangerous to the world.

At the end of April, the magazines in this study reported Chamberlain, with the assistance of French Foreign Minister Bonnet, was determined to make yet another effort at appeasing Hitler. Both returned their ambassadors to Berlin. The British ambassador, Henderson, was specifically instructed to tell Hitler that Britain and France were not aiming at the encirclement of Germany. This statement was also made by Lord Halifax in the House of Lords. Hitler was urged to be moderate in his reply to Roosevelt which he had scheduled for a Reichstag speech on April 26. If Chamberlain had truly intended to extend guarantees to selected nations and to seek alliances with others to deter Hitler by the threat of war, this was now undone by his overtures to Hitler. *The Nation* observed he had displayed once again "his usual exquisite sense of bad timing" for his actions were "almost an invitation" to Hitler "for added truculence."[124] The Nazi press proclaimed the British move demonstrated London was displaying weakness and indecision and there was no reason to fear war. Russia, already cautious about trusting Chamberlain, grew even more cautious. To central European nations already having qualms about accepting "a British guaranty," there seemed even more reason than ever to attempt their own accommodation with Hitler.[125]

In France, the extreme right promptly seized the opportunity to attack both Britain and Russia. They argued Britain could not be trusted but, if war did break out, Frenchmen could be expected to do the dying while the British took cover behind their navy and air force. They also disparaged Russian intentions and the strength of the Russian army. Stalin reacted with a demand for an outright Anglo-French-Soviet military alliance designed to protect the three from both German and Japanese aggression.[126] *Time* believed Chamberlain had so squandered the respect and authority of Britain by his latest action that Stalin might very well decide to ally himself with Hitler. *The Nation* believed Chamberlain's behavior was "a queer way of backing up" Roosevelt's telegram to the dictators and would produce an adverse reaction to the British cause in the United States and in Russia. It could not understand why Chamberlain had not immediately initialed an accord with Moscow. It was dangerous to allow the matter to drift.[127]

The "Secret Nightmare" of Europe, according to Henry C. Wolfe, was the "specter of a German-Russian coalition." To many Americans, this fear might seem "fantastic" but to the *Zwischenland* states of central Europe it was a real possibility. They were aware there was no affinity between "the taciturn, mysterious Stalin and the hysterical, flamboyant Hitler." They were also aware both Hitler and Stalin were masters of *Real-politik* and neither "would permit his personal feeling toward the other to wreck a long-range foreign policy." The *Zwischenland* remembered Rapallo and the cooperation between the Reichswehr and Moscow. These states realized that, for all Hitler's bombast and rhetoric against *"Bolshevismus,"* he had never broken German commercial relations with Russia. Further, they knew Stalin resented Russian exclusion from the Munich conference and the Anglo-French desire to see Hitler move east for his *Lebensraum*. For his part, Hitler knew that, in Russia, bolshevism had been replaced by Stalinism. Rather than face *Einkreisung*, Hitler might deal with Stalin. Italy would be urged toward the Mediterranean, Japan toward the Dutch East Indies, and Hitler would be free to move into the Balkans and the Middle East. Stalin, free of the fear of a Japanese attack, would be free to move toward the Persian Gulf. To initiate this program, "the Nazis would undoubtedly suggest to the Soviets a fourth partition of Poland." Litvinov, the opponent of Hitler, was "the man to watch." If he was purged, the *Zwischenland* would "be certain that Hitler and Stalin have reached an agreement." Chamberlain seemed oblivious to the danger.[128]

When the general reaction to his latest appeasement effort finally registered in his mind, Chamberlain again veered and attempted to repair the damage he had done. He announced the formation of a Ministry of Supply to mobilize British production behind its military services and, under extreme pressure from Daladier, announced British would institute its first peace-time conscription since the time of Charles II. Significantly, however, when Hitler celebrated his fiftieth birthday with a military parade, delegates from all the Balkan states were present to offer him their felicitations. *Time* began, with the issue reporting these events, to run a series of articles under the title "Background for War" which reviewed the political and economic history of Europe from 1914—1939.[129]

Meanwhile, the reply of Mussolini and Hitler to Roosevelt was eagerly and anxiously awaited. Mussolini finally responded with a rather mild statement Italy could not trust grand international conferences after its experience at Versailles. Moreover, in his typical turgid verbiage, he asserted "the proposal of reciprocal guarantees lasting ten years" did not "take into account the pyramidal errors of geography." For his part, Hitler prepared for his reply by circulating a note to each of the thirty-one powers mentioned by Roosevelt with the notable exceptions of Britain, France, and Russia. Each was asked if felt "menaced by Germany" or if it had requested or known of Roosevelt's telegram. All replied negatively with the exception of Switzerland and Rumania, which gave qualified negative responses.[130]

In his speech to the Reichstag on April 26, Hitler justified his conquest of Czecho-Slovakia as necessary and in the best interest of Europe. More ominous was his tirade against Poland. He asserted he had asked Poland to return Danzig to Germany and allow him the right to a fifteen mile wide extraterritorial highway across the Corridor. In return, he had offered the Poles a guarantee of their economic rights in Danzig and a twenty-five year guarantee of their borders. In addition, he had offered to have Germany, Poland, and Hungary guarantee Germany would not absorb Slovakia and so further extend its frontiers around Poland. This "one and only offer" had been rejected by Poland. Since Britain and Poland had entered into an alliance, he declared void the Anglo-German naval treaty and the Polish-German non-aggression pact. In his reply to Roosevelt, Hitler used a mixture of bitter humor and plain bitterness. The response was divided into "twenty-one questions and answers" that allowed Hitler to unleash his gift for invictive and sarcasm. With material provided by the Germany embassy in Washington, he was able to employ most of the isolationist arguments that had already been directed against Roosevelt.[131]

Newsweek reported "Millions of Americans crawled out of bed at a quarter to 6" to hear Hitler's speech. Editors attending the American Newspaper Publishers Association meeting in New York believed Hitler had scored soundly on Roosevelt. *Newsweek* asserted the speech had "strengthened isolationist sentiment over the country" and had not reduced the possibility of war. In actuality, Hitler's denunciation of the pacts with Britain and Poland had only served to further divide Europe into hostile camps. *Time* also believed Hitler had adroitly embarrassed Roosevelt and strengthened isolationist sentiment in the United States—clearly it was "Hitler's Inning." However, it insisted world opinion now knew Hitler could not be stopped with words. *The New Republic* described Hitler's tone as insulting to Roosevelt and as "an example of magnificent virtuosity." Nothing, however, could disguise the fact Hitler's actions spoke louder than his words and that he was still bent on the conquest and domination of Europe by threats if possible and by war if necessary. *The Nation* believed Hitler had "managed to sound like a mélange of American isolationist senators." Like them, he had also ignored the question of what could be done to save civilization without the price of German domination. Therefore, Hitler's reply was meaningless in the face of his determination to have a war.[132]

If Europe was not technically at war in the week following Hitler's speech, it was certainly far from being at peace. Chamberlain's elusive hope of separating Mussolini from Hitler was revealed for the foolishness it had been all along. Ribbentrop and Ciano initialed a firm political and military alliance which would be formally signed on May 22. Under its terms, Hitler could demand Italian military support at his whim. In Warsaw, Beck diplomatically called Hitler a liar by denying Hitler had suggested negotiations over Danzig and the Corridor and asserted Poland would not surrender Danzig without a fight. Chamberlain, who never profited from the lessons of his errors, nevertheless again raised the spectre of appeasement by offering to "mediate" the Danzig issue between Poland and Germany and asserted in the Commons Britain would welcome an amicable settlement of the issue.[133] In the French Chamber, there were isolated demands for Danzig to be given to Germany. Pius XII, the new pope, seized the moment to also offer to mediate the Polish-German dispute. *Time* believed the pattern of events leading to Munich seemed "to be duplicating itself."[134]

Stalin, given to distrust even in the best of times, retired Litvinov at this point. Litvinov had long been associated with anti-Nazi efforts. He was replaced by the more unknown and compliant Molotov. The move was interpreted to mean Stalin was no longer willing to trust Chamberlain and join the Stop-Hitler movement. Chamberlain was bitterly attacked by Lloyd-George and others for having failed to reach an agreement with Russia. *The New Republic* surmised the groundwork had been laid for the "acceptance by Moscow of Hitler's immediate program" due to Stalin's distrust of Chamberlain.[135]

The reaction among isolationists in the United States was profound. Alf Landon insisted America should stay out of European affairs because "we cannot be sure what nation we can rely on in Europe." A Gallup poll showed the overwhelming majority of Americans opposed any involvement in Europe. Roosevelt felt it necessary to say he would not reply to Hitler's Reichstag speech. *Newsweek* conducted its own poll of Democratic and Republican state chairmen, "more than a score of Congressional leaders, key businessmen, and editors from every part of the country." The party chairmen broke party lines but, nevertheless, split "exactly" fifty percent to fifty percent on aid to Britain and France. Of the Congressional leaders, "only two were unqualifiedly in favor of helping Britain and France." There was near unanimous agreement the United States should develop an adequate defense for itself and the western hemisphere.[136]

By the middle of May, tensions had begun to ebb across Europe. War insurance rates were cut across the board. Belgium discharged one-third of the technical experts it had mobilized a month earlier. Franco demobilized 200,000 men. Mussolini allowed his daughter, Edda Ciano, to sail on a vacation to Brazil and, speaking in Turin, made a speech that was universally interpreted as conciliatory. The King and Queen of England began their trip to visit Canada and the United States.[137] The American public heaved a collective sigh of relief and congratulated itself that it had maintained its policy of isolationism during the crisis. More than ever, that policy seemed confirmed by events.

The democracies and the Axis continued to posture but in a subdued key. Hitler toured the Siegfried Line but made no threatening gestures. Lord Halifax and Daladier insisted their nations could outlast Germany and Italy economically, militarily, and psychologically in any war of nerves. Although the Scandinavian states reaffirmed their neutrality, Chamberlain did succeed in getting the British guarantee to Turkey accepted by the Istanbul parliament. With immediate tensions reduced, Chamberlain reverted to hints of possible appeasement over Danzig and continued negotiations with Russia, but more slowly and warily.[138]

As always when there was a lull or deescalation in international affairs, the news magazines turned to reporting on domestic events in the European nations. From England, there was a report Lady Astor had decided to crusade to have flogging removed from the British naval and criminal codes. In Hungary, Count von Bethlen announced his retirement from politics. While Mussolini pleaded with Italians to replace coffee drinking with the tippling of good Italian wines, Hitler had Goebbels launch a campaign to reduce alcohol consumption in Germany.[139]

On the weekend of May 28, despatches from London predicted Britain, France, and Russia were on the brink of signing a firm tripartite agreement designed to hold Hitler in check. The only point that supposedly remained unsettled was whether the guarantee between the three states should be extended to include smaller border states such as Estonia and Latvia. The British government reportedly believed the treaty "was in the bag." In Germany, however, *Time* reported there were "hints" Hitler would soon reach an agreement with Russian partitioning Poland.[140]

Molotov rejected the British proposal on May 31. He declared it was inadequate as it did not include guarantees for the smaller states bordering on Russia and made no coordinated provision for the amount of aid to be given to these smaller states. Molotov openly voiced doubts whether Chamberlain could be trusted and hinted Chamberlain still wanted to appease Hitler. He ominously declared Russia would continue to observe its trade agreements with Germany and hinted Moscow would seek a 200,000,000-mark German line of credit for industrial goods. Latvia, Estonia, and Finland declared their neutrality and asked it be respected. Denmark signed a non-aggression pact with Germany.[141]

Chamberlain promptly resorted to his policy of appeasement. Halifax suggested Britain would ensure an "economic *Lebensraum*" for Germany if Hitler agreed not to attack neighboring states. The following day Chamberlain declared he still hoped to achieve an understanding with Hitler. When Pius XII suggested a new four-power conference from which Russia was excluded, there were rumors it was closely connected with Chamberlain. Chamberlain and Simon, to show the sincerity of their latest appeasement policy, released to Berlin the $30,000,000 of Czech gold held by the Bank of England.[142]

Reaction to Chamberlain's suggestion of appeasement was swift. Laval called for a policy of reconciliation with Mussolini while Flandin suggested "a policy of mediation" with Germany. In Britain, *The Times* demanded no further concessions be made to the Axis while "some" British newspapers called upon Chamberlain to resign. The Labor Party bitterly attacked Chamberlain in the Commons. In Italy and Germany, the press "welcomed the change of temperature in London." Chamberlain moved to counter the storm of protest in Britain by the announcement William Strang would leave immediately for Moscow to resume negotiations with Stalin.[143]

Hitler refused to reply to Chamberlain's hints of appeasement. He entertained Regent Prince Paul of Yugoslavia for four days, repeatedly pledging undying friendship between their two nations. On June 7, he simultaneously signed non-aggression pacts with Estonia and Latvia. There were reports he had supplied Stalin with intercepts of cables from Chamberlain to Daladier that suggested Hitler be given a free hand in eastern Europe. Strang's reception in Moscow was decidedly cold. To escape the summer heat in Berlin, Hitler went to the Berghof.[144]

Throughout June, there were disparate events in the United States that provided both comfort and tragic misfortune to Jews. On one hand, American anti-Semitic groups received a series of sharp blows. New York District Attorney Thomas Dewey indicted and arrested Fritz Kuhn, German-American Bund leader, on a charge of grand larceny and forgery. The Dies Committee released evidence that the American anti-Semite Moseley, supported by the wealth of D.P. Gilbert of New York, had been in touch with an "international fascist headquarters in Rome." Moseley had recently been gaining national attention with his allegations "the war now proposed is for the purpose of establishing

Jewish hegemony throughout the world" and that the Russian revolution had been financed with Jewish money. Called before the Dies Committee, Moseley alleged the Jews were a "schizophrenic cult" supporting capitalism on Tuesdays and communism on Fridays. Jews should therefore be spied on by Army Intelligence, brought before martial courts, and driven into the Atlantic and Pacific. Kuhn was an American patriot on alert against the Jewish peril which included Jewish plans to poison the water systems of large cities. He further told the committee "I approve of Mr. Hitler insofar as he had handled the international Jews." The entire testimony was so ludicrous that the Dies Committee unanimously struck his two-day statement from its record.[145] In addition to the deflation of these two anti-Semitics, American Jews were heartened by the organization of two groups to fight anti-Semitism. A Committee of Catholics to Fight Anti-Semitism was begun with the full blessing of the American Catholic hierarchy. The Grand Lodge of the Sons of Italy, which had 200 local chapters in the United States, formed a Bureau for Good Will between Italians and Jews in America. Both organizations were praised by Jews and were promised the support of American Jewish groups.[146]

If this news heartened Jews, the pain was all the more terrible when the news broke of the voyage of the Hamburg liner *St. Louis*. Prior to the voyage, all of its 937 Jewish passengers had received temporary immigration visas from the Cuban government of Fedrigo Bru. These visas would allow them to remain in Cuba until American visas became available. On board were 152 children, 106 of them under ten years of age. On May 5, nine days before the *St. Louis* left Germany, Bru announced the temporary visas had to have the approval of the Cuban Departments of State, Labor, and Treasury. The ship sailed under the belief Bru would relent once the refugees were under way. When the ship reached Havana on a Monday, however, only twenty-nine Jews were allowed ashore. The remainder were refused admission. One passenger committed suicide while another attempted it. On Thursday, Bru ordered the *St. Louis* out of Havana with a twenty-six boat escort to see that no passengers committed suicide by leaping overboard. Bru then offered to land the group on the Isle of Pines provided Jewish relief agencies posted a bond of $453,500 and guaranteed the cost of their care. When Lawrence Berenson, representative of American Jewish relief agencies, attempted to negotiate the amount, Bru withdrew his offer. Although Berenson thereupon accepted the original offer, Bru refused to discuss the subject and ordered the *St. Louis* out of Cuban waters. The American government refused to intervene or offer immediate visas to the refugees from the unfilled German quota. Leaving Cuba, the refugees could see the lights of Miami as they sailed slowly up the coast of the United States. They finally found refuge in Britain, France, Belgium, and Holland. *The New Republic* ended its report of the incident by writing "Bureaucratic cruelty was at the top of its form" in Washington as "Pilate Washed His Hands" of the event.[147]

Off the coast of South America, 200 Jews with Paraguayan visas, sailing on the ships *Caporte*, *Monte Olivia*, and *Mendoza*, were refused admission to Uruguay when Paraguay voided their visas. They were returned to Germany. At Veracruz, 106 German Jews were refused permission to land from the freighter

Flandre—327 Spanish loyalist refugees on board were given permission to debark.[148]

At the end of June, fear of war flared again in Europe. The crisis centered on Hitler's demand for the cession of Danzig to the Reich. *Time* asserted there was "no doubt Adolf Hitler is determined to have Danzig this summer." Hitler mobilized 2,000,000 men and declared Germany had taken its destiny into its own hands. The mobilization depleted the German labor force to the point where compulsory labor drafts were instituted in Czecho-Slovakia and Jews were recalled to their former jobs.[149] Mussolini mobilized the Italian army and announced it would hold maneuvers on the border of France. Daladier immediately declared France was ready for war and would fight if Hitler annexed Danzig or attacked Poland. Chamberlain was initially conciliatory toward Germany. Churchill, however, denounced Hitler, demanded increased mobilization, and a declaration Britain would fight to defend Poland and Danzig.[150] A survey revealed fifty-six percent of the British electorate wanted Churchill in the cabinet as they approved of his consistent anti-Nazi stance and his oft-repeated optimism Hitler could and would be defeated if war erupted. Every major British newspaper except *The London Times* demanded Churchill be made First Sea Lord as signal to Hitler that Britain would honor its commitment to Poland.[151] Chamberlain was finally forced to pledge publicly Britain would fight and to advance the date for annual fall naval and army maneuvers.[152]

As pressure on him increased, Chamberlain mobilized British naval reserves, despatched the Royal Air Force on long-distance flights to show it could reach German targets, called up the Territorial Army reserves, and announced Britain was spending $10,000,000 daily for military preparedness. A loan of $23,400,000 was given to Warsaw for the purchase of war material and Ironside, the Inspector General of the British army, was sent to Warsaw for staff talks.[153]

The most sensational story from Paris was the expulsion of Nazi Otto Abetz and the arrest of 150 French reporters. The *Deuxieme Bureau* revealed Abetz had spent 350,000,000 francs in bribes to the French press between May and November, 1938. Julien Poirier, advertising manager of the reactionary *Le Figaro*, had accepted 3,500,000 francs from Abetz. Aubin, news editor of *Le Temps*, received 1,000,000 in return for military information. Police were reportedly searching for Pierre Gaxotte, editor of the right-wing *Je Suis Partout* and Ferdinand de Brinon, editor of the financial paper, *l'Information*. Daladier, using his emergency powers, announced that henceforth the French press would be censored.[154]

It was the report of another of Chamberlain's interminable attempts at appeasement, however, that shook all the capitals of Europe. It came when Helmut Wohltat, German Export Minister, visited London to attend a whaling conference. Robert Hudson, the Secretary for British Overseas Trade, asked Wohltat to meet with him privately and secretly. Hudson thereupon proposed Britain grant Germany a loan of "perhaps $5,000,000,000" and guarantee Hitler access to world markets and raw materials. In return, Britain wanted German disarmament and a pledge by Hitler to keep the peace. Hudson hinted the proposal came from Horace Wilson, Chamberlain's personal adviser. Foreign correspondents in Berlin were told by Goebbels that Hitler was "100 percent for peace" and there need be no war over Danzig. The Poles only needed to be told "Danzig is not worth a world war." When word of the proposal was leaked to the press by Wohltat, however, Liberals, Laborites, and anti-appeasement Tories blasted Chamberlain. Chamberlain did not deny the discussion had occurred but insisted it was "private and unofficial" and that Hudson had exceeded his authority improperly. Hudson informed the press he would not become a scape-goat for Chamberlain and, if forced to resign, would "tell all before the House of Commons." Confidence in Chamberlain dropped still lower across Europe and in Washington.[155]

Beginning in July and extending into August, there were several news reports that demonstrated the increasing desperation of Jews. In the middle of July, Wilhelm Frick announced all Jews and Jewish organizations in Germany henceforth had to join a single Reich's Union of Jews. He announced the union would arrange for the emigration of Jews and would assume financial responsibility for destitute Jews and all Jewish orphanages and hospitals. War pensions to Jewish war veterans were discontinued and their support assumed by the new organization. *Newsweek* asserted this new decree, combined with payment of the *Kristal Nacht* fine, meant the final annihilation of Jewish financial resources in Germany.[156]

As if Nazi persecution were not enough, Britain added its bit to the Jewish tragedy. Thousands of Jews, including refugees from Germany, Poland, the *Sudetenland*, and Rumania, had been smuggled into Palestine by various Jewish organizations that chartered every tramp steamer available for the trip. The depth of Jewish desperation could be measured by this continuing effort despite the horrors attendant upon it. Jews making the journey faced starvation, the plague, extortion, and death—only to chance interception by the British navy off the coast of Palestine and be forced out to sea again. The S.S. *Parita*, after steaming without a captain for eleven weeks, tried to beach itself near Tel Aviv. Its 875 passengers were rounded up by the British army and interned—most were near starvation. Colonial Secretary MacDonald announced in July that Britain would halt all legal Jewish emigration into Palestine for six months beginning on October 1. If the smuggling were not stopped, the ban might be continued indefinitely.[157]

In New York, the *Irgun Zevai Leumi* denounced the British declaration, asserted it had alone smuggled 15,000 Jews into Palestine, and vowed it would fight Britain with a force organized along the lines of the Irish Republican army. *The New Republic* described the *Irgun* as a well-organized "Jewish National Army" with well-defined aims and a disciplined, dedicated body of volunteers. Its symbol was a clenched fist holding a rifle superimposed on a map of Palestine. Its aims were to save as many Jews as possible from Europe, organize a Jewish army and navy, and compel the establishment of a Jewish Palestinian Homeland. With the cooperation of anti-Semitic governments in Europe, including Germany, it had established escape routes down the Danube and through Athens. In Palestine, it had an army of 5,000 which was daily growing as young Jewish refugees reached Palestine. Around the world, it numbered 100,000 persons. Many Jews in America and Britain, though opposed to the *Irgun* in public, secretly supported it financially and prayed for its success.[158]

When the World Zionist Congress met in Geneva in August, the *Irgun*, which had not been invited, "flooded" the delegates with broadsides that proclaims "The *Irgun* is beginning a struggle for the Jewish State!" The Congress, undership of Chaim Weizmann, however, decided to "support British Democracy in the present darkest hours." Any objections delegates might have had toward British policy "were silenced by the spectre of other powers" controlling Palestine. They were aware the only alternative for the moment was for Hitler or the Moslems to control Palestine—a prospect even less acceptable to the delegates. Freda Kirchwey insisted that, given the course of events, she was convinced "that only the end of Hitler can end the torture of the Jews."[159]

The last month of peace, August, 1939, had a strange air about it in the magazines. On the one hand, it resembled a Greek tragedy with its inexorable march toward doom. On the other, it resembled a surrealistic play improvised from moment to moment by its characters. There were a number of reasons for this type of coverage. Radio reports, which had become the prime source of news during the Munich Conference, played an even larger role in August, 1939, as events reached the ignition point in Europe. American magazines could not hope to compete with the immediacy of radio and tended to stress the "significance" of events already known to their readers.[160] For example, the first of the magazines utilized in this study to report the beginning of the war was *The Nation* on September 9—when the war had already been blazing for a week and a half. When *Time* did finally announce the attack on Poland in its issue of September 11, it took pains to stress it could not cover the daily course of the war but would only "interpret" events after the fact.[161]

A second factor in the change in coverage was occasioned by the sheer volume of reports from Europe as events reached their climax. The European pot was boiling over with reports of diplomatic and military posturing and maneuvering all during August. Much of this voluminous reporting was speculative and difficult to interpret in a proper context. Were the Anglo-French negotiations with Moscow stalemated or moving to a successful conclusion? When Ciano met with Ribbentrop, was it to synchronize their aggressive designs or was it an Italian attempt to moderate Hitler's demand for war?[162] It was impossible to know due to the volume of disparate rumors reaching the wire services. Speculation and rumor perforce became the stock-in-trade of correspondents as censorship was increasingly imposed in each capital of Europe.

August opened with another Chamberlain attempt at appeasement of the Axis, this time with Japan. By this "Oriental Munich," made without consultation with France or the United States, Chamberlain recognized "the special requirements" of the Japanese army in China and undertook not to impair those requirements. Chamberlain put the best face on the agreement by claiming he had denied Japan recognition as a belligerent and that aid to China was still possible.[163]

Reaction in the United States, where fifty-one percent of the voters favored an embargo on war material sales to Japan, was swift. Roosevelt, with the support of Republican Senator Vandenberg, denounced the American 1911 treaty of commerce with Japan and hinted that when the treaty expired in six months, America might embargo all sales to Japan. The action received almost universal approval from all quarters.[164]

Earlier in the year, Hull had finally spelled out the administration proposals for a new neutrality bill. It asked for the repeal of the automatic arms embargo, that American ships be prohibited from entering combat zones, the travel of American citizens in war zones be restricted, the title of export goods to belligerents be transferred before shipment, loans and credits to combatants be restricted, and the licensing of arms import and export continued. Sol Bloom, Chairman of the House Foreign Affairs Committee promptly introduced the proposals in Congress. Nye, Clark, and Borah just as promptly threatened a filibuster if the bill reached the Senate.[165] By the middle of June, Nye had twenty-one senators pledged to support his projected filibuster. Senate Minority Leader McNary of Oregon counted thirty-six senators pledged to vote against any change in the neutrality laws. In July, as tensions increased daily in Europe, the deadlock continued between the White House and Congress. Even though Roosevelt made a last-ditch appeal to leaders of both parties to save the Bloom Bill as a deterrent to the Axis, the Senate Foreign Relations Committee voted to defer action on it by a vote of twelve to eleven. On August 5, Congress adjourned without any alterations in the neutrality laws.[166]

The failure of Congress to modify American neutrality laws, however, had little apparent effect in Europe where events marched at their own pace. *Time* and *Newsweek* reported the Anglo-French pact with Russia was "ready for signing" with only a "minor" disagreement over the definition of "indirect aggression" against the Baltic states still needing resolution. Negotiations had reached the point where Britain and France had despatched a military mission to Moscow to coordinate defensive measures in the event of war. It was anticipated signature of the pact would cause Hitler to pause and the peace of Europe would be ensured. *The New Republic*, however, insisted the negotiations had "reached a stalemate." Moscow felt Chamberlain was untrustworthy, was merely using the talks for propaganda purposes, and was still seeking an arrangement with Hitler. It was most likely Hitler believed the pact to be still-born and that he had a free hand to attack Poland. On August 9, *The New Republic* predicted war might begin during "the third week of August or September 1 as the pact remained a moot question."[167]

Chamberlain, who still asserted the pact with Russia was near signature and peace assured, recessed Parliament until October 3. There were rumors he thereby hoped to secure a free hand to reach an agreement with Hitler.[168] His action was bitterly but unsuccessfully resisted by Laborites and Conservatives who read daily reports the German army was concentrating on the Polish border and within and around Danzig, that the German army was constructing a pontoon bridge on the Vistula that was due for completion on August 29, and that there were border clashes between Nazis and Polish customs officials. Smigly-Rydz and Beck were almost daily asserting Poland would meet force with force.[169] Over the next two weeks, there were increasing reports of troop movements and maneuvers, air-raid drills, and of a growing German press propaganda blitz against Poland.[170] There were confusing and often contradictory reports Mussolini was mobilizing for war or that he was negotiating a peace settlement through the Vatican. Rumors Hitler had determined to seize Danzig by force were contradicted by rumors Chamberlain would negotiate the return of Danzig to Hitler to preserve the peace.[171] *Collier's,* however, insisted the crisis had passed and that the democracies had finally won their "White War" against Hitler. It was now only necessary to give the totalitarian states "a sporting chance to work out their salvation in their own way, and to gain their fair share of this world's goods and trade by peaceable means."[172]

On August 23, these rumors and speculations were suddenly put to rest when Hitler and Stalin blew "to pieces" all "international calculations" by their alliance between the "Red Star and Swastika." *The Nation* declared Chamberlain, "the double-crosser," had been "double-crossed by Stalin." Chamberlain, now more than ever, would seek to negotiate the return of Danzig and the Corridor to Hitler. Poland, however, would remain firm, resist negotiation, and fight if attacked. The following week, *The Nation* wrote there could be no thought of making peace with Hitler. Another "deal with Hitler" would mean "the end of the hopes of civilized people." Jews, "over vast areas of the earth," would be "persecuted—perhaps largely exterminated" if Hitler were not stopped. All Americans needed to rally behind Roosevelt, arm their nation, and be prepared, if necessary, to aid in the defeat of Hitler.[173]

Newsweek asserted the Berlin-Moscow pact had left Europe "Thunderstruck" and had undoubtedly "shifted the foundations of the world balance of power." The immediate effect was to increase the probability of war. Germany and Poland were rushing troops to their borders and, within a week, Hitler would likely "launch an overwhelming attack on the Poles." Chamberlain was described as "astounded" by the pact even as Beaverbrook's papers insisted there would be no war. However, Britons of all political persuasions were determined not to permit a new Chamberlain effort at appeasement. The following week *Newsweek* believed that, although war was now certain, the Hitler-Stalin pact had solidified the opposition to Hitler "more firmly than ever."[174]

Time declared the pact had created "bewilderment and consternation" all over the world. The whispered "nightmare" of the democracies had finally happened and Hitler had achieved his "greatest victory." Hitler, only hours after the signing of the pact had begun to move the bulk of the German army to the Polish border and war was likely. The smaller states of Europe were declaring their neutrality or seeking to reach an arrangement with one side or the other. Some of these states, due to the threat of war, were now truly united as a nation for the first time in their existence.[175]

The New Republic believed Stalin had finally decided Chamberlain was untrustworthy and so had negotiated his own "Munich." Nothing now stood between Hitler and the "complete domination of all Central Europe." Not only was war with Poland likely, but, at the proper moment, Hitler would probably attack Russia. Stalin had bought neither honor or peace.[176]

In their issues of September 4, which had gone to press prior to the beginning of war on September 1, *Time* and *Newsweek* reviewed the events of the last week of peace and predicted war was inevitable. The German press campaign had reached a crescendo, German trains stopped at the frontiers, the bridges to France were blocked, and the Danish border closed. Civilian train service and *Lufthansa* flights were suspended. Ration cards were distributed and German diplomats in London, Paris, and Warsaw were recalled.[177]

Daladier mobilized the French army and navy, recalled vacationing factory workers, ordered the harvest gathered, and manned the Maginot Line. All bridges over the Rhine were blocked and mined. Art treasures were moved to safety or sandbagged and Paris darkened. Daladier went on the radio to encourage the French populace and announce France would fight if Poland were attacked.[178]

Chamberlain recalled Parliament to request war powers and received them with only four dissenting votes. Plans for evacuating London were posted, zoo animals were gassed or moved to rural areas, and the first contingent of British troops unloaded at Dieppe.[179] Winston Churchill, recalled to the cabinet as First Sea Lord, mobilized the British naval and merchant fleets. The British empire nations were requested to pledge their support and did so promptly.[180] A most revealing comment from Britain, according to *Time*, was this exchange between a reporter and a militiaman:[180]

> Are you going to fight for King and Country?
> To hell with King and Country!
> Well, are you fighting for Democracy?
> I don't give a damn for Democracy!
> What are you fighting for?
> To beat that bloody Hitler!

Domestic reports the last week of peace centered on the reaction of Americans to the Hitler-Stalin pact and their attitude toward neutrality in the event of war.

Time reported Roosevelt had been "caught off-base with the rest of the world" by "the Hitler-Stalin deal." In the "absence of any sharp new angle" that would keep the peace, Roosevelt wired King Victor Emmanuel of Italy, President Ignace Moscicki of Poland, and Hitler to suggest direct negotiations, arbitration by "an impartial umpire," or conciliation through the good offices of a neutral. He then moved to cushion the anticipated shock of war to the American economy and money markets.[181]

For "millions of suspicious isolationists," the pact had "merely confirmed" their "worst opinion of the Reds." Isolationism was simplified for many of them as it placed "the dictatorships in one neat pile." The American Legion and Veterans of Foreign Wars cheered isolationist speakers at their respective conventions. The great mass of Americans were first bewildered and then angered by the pact.[182]

American communists were "befuddled, appalled, embarrassed" by the signing of the pact. The party first went "into a silence, then into a great writhing." Browder asserted the pact had not affected party membership, that Russia had not compromised with Nazism but had contributed to world peace, and Stalin would disavow the treaty "if Germany turned aggressor." Heywood Broun, however, asserted Russia had "here and now contributed to the might and menace of Hitler...the masquerade is over." In Boston, Trotskyites fought in a hotel ballroom with Stalinists who tried to defend the pact. In San Antonio, 5,000 Texans angered by the pact stormed the municipal auditorium to break up a communist rally. In spite of police attempts to stop the attackers, forty communists were badly injured.[183]

Newsweek reported a Gallup poll revealed seventy-six percent of all Americans favored selling all war materials except munitions to the democracies; eighty-two percent insisted on cash payment; fifty-seven percent, on a separate question, favored lifting the arms embargo entirely; seventeen percent wanted to go to war against Hitler at once if war erupted.[184]

The same week *Newsweek* conducted its own poll of "the policy-making executives of 50 representative newspapers in 37 states." Thirty-two out of the fifty unqualifiedly wanted the arms embargo lifted. Fourteen of the fifty wanted to exploit any possible "war boom" on a cash-and-carry basis; twenty-four were opposed, twenty-two had no comment. Four favored a war referendum bill; twenty-four opposed such a bill, twenty-two had no comment. Thirty-seven opposed early American participation in the coming war designed to shorten the conflict; eight reserved judgement, four declined comment.[185]

The New Republic cited a *Fortune* poll which showed eighty-three percent of Americans wanted the United States to work for peace without saying what its policy should be if war did break out. However, 65.5 percent believed no American troops should be sent to Europe even if the democracies were losing. The same number felt the United States should develop its own industries so it would not need to buy anything abroad. Some 61.5 percent wanted to stop trading with aggressor nations if they declared war.[186]

At 5:45 A.M., on Friday, September 1, 1939, Hitler attacked Poland. At noon on September 3, Chamberlain and Daladier finally mustered up their courage, honored their treaty with Poland, and declared war on Hitler. Hitler's war against Jews had expanded into a war against Europe.

Chapter VII

Conclusions

Americans were well served by the coverage given to Adolf Hitler, the Nazi party, and the Third Reich in their magazines.

As early as 1923, concurrently with the earliest mention of Hitler in major German newspapers, American magazines initiated their own reports on Hitler and the Nazi party. They accurately delineated his origins, his political intentions, the composition and characteristics of his followers, and his rabid anti-Semitism. They found it difficult to believe that Hitler, with his absurd racial theories, his hysterical oratory, and his Chaplainesque mustache, could become the leader of a modern, industrialized, and civilized nation. The magazines therefore pictured him as a reactionary demagogue hired by German capitalists as a tool against communism. After 1929, as Germany dropped into the depression and unemployment rose, they perceived that Germans were, in their desperation, turning to the Nazi party. Even so, they believed Bruening, von Papen or von Schleicher would block Hitler's path to the chancellorship.

This attitude is understandable for the magazines were confronted with a phenomenon that was *sui generis*. They found it difficult, for example, to draw the proper inferences from their own reports of Nazi attacks upon Jews. Their experience of anti-Semitism was limited to instances where it had been used as a means to an end. Initially, therefore, they interpreted Hitler's assaults on the Jews as an ideological and political ploy intended to attract the German masses. At other times, the magazines attributed it to excesses committed by Nazi rowdies who had gotten out of hand. What was inconceivable to sensible people was that Hitler's anti-Semitism was an end in itself devoted to the destruction of European Jewry. By the late fall of 1932, when Hitler was increasingly seen as the only alternative to communism in Germany, they still asserted that, if and when he became chancellor, Hitler would moderate his attitude and rein in his followers.

When Hitler did become chancellor in January, 1933, American magazines were quick to recognize and report Germany had fallen into the hands of a criminal who ruled by lynch law and the brutal suppression of all dissent. They perceived Hitler had replaced German law and democracy with mass hysteria and a reign of terror, that he had subdued civilized political discourse with a club, and had enlisted the professional German bureaucracy under the leadership of a gang of thugs. Yet, even then, they speculated the German

214

officer corps, the monopoly capitalists, or the state of the German economy would topple Hitler or, at least, cause him to moderate his policies.

As a result of the voluminous reports out of Germany that appeared in their newspapers and periodicals, Americans were organizing boycotts and staging demonstrations against Hitler and his regime as early as April and May, 1933. Most Americans, Jews and Gentiles alike, already disliked Hitler, many hated him. This repugnance grew deeper and became more fixed over the years. It is worth noting this repugnance developed, not out of a perceived Nazi threat to peace, but out of an awareness of Hitler's domestic brutality and anti-Semitism. Tragically, this attitude was accompanied by the belief that a boycott of German goods, or an embargo of commerce with Germany, or protests by the State Department, constituted an acceptable response to events within Germany. Even though Americans disliked Hitler, he was defined as a Jewish and German problem. Americans were unwilling to abandon their isolationism.

Isolationism was a long-standing tradition of the American people. Washington's final address was enshrined as a Delphic injunction to avoid involvement in the affairs of Europe. Only for a brief period in World War I had the American people embraced a vision of international cooperation. The Versailles settlement, however, killed that vision and renewed their commitment to isolationism. In the decade of the twenties, revisionist historians reinforced American isolationism with their studied conclusion that the United States had been duped into war in 1917 and then betrayed by traditional European power struggles. This attitude was strengthened in 1933 and 1934 by Congressional investigations of the role financiers and munition-makers played in leading Americans into World War I. Most Americans resolved that such a pattern must not be allowed to repeat itself and became even further entrenched in their isolationism. One result was the neutrality legislation of 1935.

There was another potent factor that increasingly became intertwined with isolationism during the period surveyed by this study—anti-alien nativism. Like isolationism, this type of nativism had a long history in the United States. Earlier its purported intention had been to preserve American resources and culture for Americans. To this, the depression developed the added element of preserving American jobs for Americans. The desperation of Jews to find a haven intensified this attitude, especially after the pogrom of November 10, 1938. Anti-alien nativism took on a distinctly anti-Semitic cast. Willing to express moral outrage and indignation, Americans were unwilling to provide succor for the Jewish victims of Hitler's murderous intentions. Americans tended to blame the helpless victim as well as Hitler for creating the problem. In 1939, this anti-alien nativism reached a new height of influence within Congress and upon the administration. The development of this attitude occurred against a background of other events that diverted the attention of the American people.

When Hitler assumed the chancellorship of Germany, the United States was in the throes of the greatest depression in its history. The American banking system had collapsed, millions of Americans were unemployed, and every sector of its economy was in a shambles. New Deal attempts to conquer, or at least ameliorate, the crisis dominated American political discourse and the life of every American. While Hitler was "coordinating" Germany, instituting the Nuremburg Laws, and demolishing the Versailles settlement, the New Deal was moving from one pragmatic experiment to another in its effort to revive the American economy. In 1937, when it was obvious Hitler posed a threat to the peace of Europe, Roosevelt was caught up in his futile effort to alter the Supreme Court in a bid to clear the judicial path for his New Deal legislation. By the time of the *Anschluss* and Hitler's assault on Czechoslavakia in 1938, the American economy had slipped into another trough. Roosevelt, seemingly bereft of any new ideas to combat the depression, attempted a purge of his own party in an effort to overcome the growing inertia of the New Deal. Throughout this period, Americans were drawn in upon themselves due to their economic concerns.

There were also a series of international incidents and crises, apart from those involving the Third Reich, that directly or indirectly claimed the attention of the American people. In 1933, Japan withdrew from the League due to the Lytton Report. Following the failure of the Disarmament that same year, Japan denounced the naval accords of 1922 and 1930 in early 1934. Japan seemed to pose a distinct challenge to American interests and power in the Pacific. In 1935, Mussolini attacked Ethiopia and raised specific questions about the neutrality legislation of the United States. 1936 saw the beginning of the Spanish Civil War which divided Americans along religious and ideological lines. Once again, a foreign conflict caused extended discussion of American neutrality. In 1937, Japan attacked China, long a special interest of Americans. Throughout this period, Latin America was racked by coup attempts and revolutions that threatened American economic interests in the area. In short, there were other international events that were, at times, regarded as more immediate challenges to American interests.

After the Munich Conference, most Americans accepted that Hitler was intent on the domination of Europe and had ceased to be only a Jewish or German problem. However, they insisted the problem he presented needed to be resolved by Europeans themselves. This attitude was reinforced, as each crisis arose, by the obvious determination of Chamberlain to appease Hitler. Secure behind two oceans, Americans were content to rearm and allow the perfidious statesmen of Europe to quarrel among themselves.

It is to the credit of American periodicals that, throughout this tumultuous period, they perceived the threat posed by Hitler and his Third Reich. It is true some were more perceptive than others and that they varied in their attitudes and interpretations. *The Saturday Evening Post*, although it published several excellent articles on Hitler's rise to power on the crest of the depression, did not maintain this early excellence. It became consumed with its attack on the domestic policies of the New Deal, never abandoned its isolationism, and never repented its nativistic nationalism. Its response to the rearmament of Britain and France was to ask why, if they had the money to rearm, they did not repay their earlier war debts. Its reaction to the refugee crisis was continued opposition to any increase in immigration quotas. In the face of growing Axis aggression, it protested against American rearmament.

Collier's and *The Reader's Digest* tended to feature biographical and anecdotal material about the personalities and events in the Third Reich. *The Reader's Digest* displayed the shock and horror of civilized people confronted by monstrous evil. Its articles, while heavily emotive, did alert a certain type of general reader to the nature of the Third Reich. *Collier's*, in 1938 and 1939, had altered its approach. It ended by supporting all measures short of war in its opposition to Hitler and sought to open the gates of the United States to refugees. In time, it developed into a mirror of the best in the conscience of the American people.

The Atlantic Monthly and *Harpers* provided space to a number of acute interpreters of the European scene and the situation of Jews in Hitler's Germany. Henry C. Wolfe quite early discerned that Hitler's foreign policy was directed at the conquest of Europe, his anti-Semitism at the annihilation of European Jews, and that Stalin, given the policies of Chamberlain, would likely come to his own accommodation with Hitler. M.W. Fodor astutely interpreted the Nazi assault on Austrian Jews following the *Anschluss* as a qualitative escalation in Hitler's war against the Jews. Elmer Davis eloquently asserted the United States had a distinct interest in the European crisis and could not rest content behind its oceans. The Neutrality debate was especially handled in a fair-handed manner by both magazines.

The Literary Digest, Time, and *Newsweek,* the primary news magazines utilized in this study, performed a yeoman task in keeping the American people apprised, week by week, of events. *The Literary Digest,* until it ceased publication in early 1937, admirably reported events and provided excellent synopses of both foreign and domestic newspaper attitudes and editorials. *Newsweek* was the solid, essentially neutral and objective news work-horse of the three. Its reports were concise and voluminous, covering every aspect of Third Reich and its foreign policy. *Time* was the brash interpreter of events, given to perjorative titles and slangy slogans, yet comprehensive in its coverage. Although it largely accepted and defended the policy of appeasement through the Munich Conference, the November pogrom radically altered its attitude toward Hitler and Germany. It immediately became a staunch opponent of all that Nazism represented.

Some might be tempted to criticize these news magazines for relying essentially upon wire-service reports and newspapers for their material. It is true that none of them maintained a regular staff of correspondents in Europe and the Third Reich. Closer consideration, however, suggests this practice may well have been a strength. Of necessity, they had to utilize reports filed by a broad spectrum of correspondents supplemented by the use of domestic and foreign newspapers. This wide range of sources allowed them to interpret events from a broader perspective. Further, they had the relatively greater leisure, as they appeared only weekly, to place specific events in a larger time frame and to assess their significance more accurately than most newspapers. It was not until Munich that their value as a source of news was reduced by radio reports.

Even then they maintained their ability to place events in a larger context and assess their significance more acutely than radio was able to do.

The New Republic and *The Nation*, the most liberal of our magazines, brought to their reports a moral indignation that was refreshing. From the first, they provided their readers with penetrating insights into the political nature of Nazism, its economic policies and, above all, its anti-Semitism. Alone among the magazines in this study, they quite early called for immediate and practical aid to the victims, Jewish and Gentile, of Nazi spleen and hatred. Theirs was a continual crusade for the relaxation of the immigration barriers. Their ideological bias was a definite handicap, however, when it came to suggestions of how Nazism should be confronted. *The New Republic* remained pacifistic and isolationist to the bitter end. *The Nation*, following the *Kristal Nacht* pogrom and the rape of the rump Czech state, did finally abandon its pacifism and isolationism and support American rearmament and aid to the democracies.

It is also to the credit of these magazines that they never embraced appeasement at any price, never allowed themselves to be subverted by Nazi ideology and propaganda, and never supported Hitler as an almost indispensable barrier to communism. The same cannot be said of the British and French press. American magazines were also quick to denounce and expose fascist and racist factions in the United States. To a greater or lesser degree, they expressed indignation at all that Hitler represented and practiced. By 1939, the majority of them realized Hitler had ceased to be a Jewish problem, a German problem, or even a European problem but, rather, had become a problem for civilized people everywhere. If Americans failed to respond to the threat to civilization posed by Adolf Hitler and his Nazi minions, it was not because they were ill-informed by their periodicals.

As this work has demonstrated, it is possible to write a survey history of the rise of Hitler and the subsequent course of the Third Reich from a limited selection of American magazines. It has also demonstrated it is possible to place that survey in a developmental sequence that enables the student of history to understand how events were interpreted at the time they occurred. To approach the period through the study of its magazines is to enter metaphorically into a type of time warp. The magazines are redundant with color, anecdotal material, comment, and interpretation not usually found in standard historical studies. Much more work, however, is needed in the study of the Jewish magazines, Catholic periodicals, and general circulation magazines. This work is only a brief *prolegomenon* to that task.

If American magazines failed to galvanize the American people to oppose Nazism, it is well to remember that even Roosevelt, the quintessential interpreter of the public pulse, was unable to do any more. He perhaps would have pursued a different policy if he had received even the passive consent of the American people, but he knew he did not have it. Certainly he understood the threat posed by the probable consequences to the United States. Dedicated to the defeat of the depression, highly sensitive to Congressional pressure, and aware of the mood of the American people, he was more the captive of their insularity than its transformer.

Notes

Chapter 1

[1]Ludwell Denny, "France and the German Counter-Revolution," *The Literary Digest*, 14 March 1923, p. 295.

[2]"Misfire of the German Mussolini," *The Literary Digest*, 17 March 1923, p. 23.

[3]"Is Poincare to Blame for the German Smash?," *The Literary Digest*, 3 November 1923, pp. 5-7.

[4]Paul Gierasch, "The Bavarian Menace to German Unity," *Current History*, November 1923, pp. 222-229.

[5]"Germany," *The Independent*, 1 March 1924, p. 123.

[6]"Invisible Government in Germany," *The American Monthly Review of Reviews*, 19 July 1924, pp. 94-95.

[7]F. Goetz, "How Hitler Failed," *The Living Age*, 22 March 1924, p. 595.

[8]"National Socialist," *Time*, 25 August 1930, p. 27.

[9]"Handsome Adolf," *Time*, 6 October 1930, p. 23. *Time* used the sarcastic phrase "Handsome Adolf" until readers' letters objected to the practice: "Letters," *Time*, 17 April 1933, p. 6.

[10]"Hitler—Germany's Would-Be Mussolini," *The Literary Digest*, 19 December 1930, p. 40.

[11]"Handsome Adolf, The Man Without a Country," *The Literary Digest*, 18 October 1930, p. 34.

[12]H. L. Binsee, "Adolf Hitler, German Hypnotist," *The Reader's Digest*, December 1930, pp. 711-713.

[13]"Hitler—Germany's Would-Be Mussolini," *The Literary Digest*, 11 October 1930, p. 36.

[14]"Handsome Adolf, The Man Without a Country," *The Literary Digest*, 18 October 1930, p. 36.

[15]"Three Against Hitler," *Time*, 21 December 1931, p. 18. A photograph of Hitler in an oratorical pose was *Time*'s cover for this week with the sub-title "Right goes hand in hand with Might."

[16]"National Socialists," *Time*, 25 August 1930, p. 27.

[17]"Handsome Adolf, The Man Without a Country," *The Literary Digest*, 18 October 1930, p. 34.

[18]*The Nation*, 24 September 1930, p. 309.

[19]"Handsome Adolf," *Time*, 6 October 1930, p. 23.

[20]"Dictator or Parliament," *The Nation*, 8 October 1930, p. 365.

[21]*The Nation*, 20 October 1930, p. 459.

[22]"Dangerous Days in Europe," *The Literary Digest*, 25 October 1930, p. 14.

[23]Isaac F. Marcosson, "Germany Goes to Extremes," *The Saturday Evening Post*, 1 November 1930, p. 120.

[24]"Handsome Adolf, The Man Without a Country," *The Literary Digest*, 18 October 1930, p. 36.

[25]"Handsome Adolf," *Time*, 6 October 1930, p. 23.

[26]Marcosson, "Germany Goes To Extremes," *The Saturday Evening Post*, 1 November 1930, p. 120.

[27]"Germany's Inflamed Youth," *The Literary Digest*, 1 November 1930, p. 16.

[28]*The Nation*, 24 September 1930, p. 309.

[29]Binsee, "Adolf Hitler," *The Reader's Digest*, December 1930, p. 713.

[30]"Red and Brown Winnings," *Time*, 22 September 1930, p. 22.

[31]"Germany's Inflamed Youth," *The Literary Digest*, 1 November 1930, p. 16.

[32]"Handsome Adolf," *Time*, 6 October 1930, p. 23 *The Nation*, 1 October 1930, p. 336.

[33]"Dictator or Parliament," *The Nation*, 8 October 1930, p. 365.

[34]"Brunning Uber Alles," *Time*, 27 October, 1930, p. 21.

[35]*The Nation*, 29 October 1930, p. 459.

[36]Binsee, "Adolf Hitler," *The Reader's Digest*, December 1930, p. 713.

[37]"National Socialists," *Time*, 25 August 1930, p. 27; "Handsome Adolf," *Time* 6 October 1930, p. 23.

[38]*The Nation*, 29 October 1930, p. 459.

[39]*The Nation*, 17 December 1930, p. 664.

[40]Oswald G. Villard, "Germany Nears the Crisis," *The Nation*, 3 December 1930, p. 603.

[41]"National Socialists," *Time*, 25 August 1930, p. 27; "Strap Helmets Tighter," *Time*, 29 September 1930, p. 25; "Plate Glass Riots," *Time*, 27 October 1930, p. 22.

[42]"Dangerous Days in Europe," *The Literary Digest*, 25 October 1930, p. 14.

[43]Binsee, "Adolf Hitler," *The Reader's Digest* December 1930, p. 712.

[44]"Strap Helmets Tighter," *Time*, 29 September 1930, p. 25.

[45]*The Nation*, 1 October 1930, p. 336.

[46]"Schacht Shocks," *Time*, 13 October 1930, p. 22.

[47]*The Nation*, 17 December 1930, p. 664.

[48]"Power of Jews, Of Press," *Time*, 12 January 1931, p. 17.

[49]"Germany the Key of the New Europe," *The Literary Digest*, 17 January 1931, p. 13.

[50]William Martin, "Europe: A Continent in Travail," *The Atlantic Monthly*, February 1931, p. 243.

[51]"Hitler's Great Walkout," *The Literary Digest*, 28 February 1931, p. 14.

[52]Isaac F. Marcosson, "The New German Leadership," *The Saturday Evening Post*, 16 June 1931, p. 4.

[53]"Traitor Hitler!," *Time*, 13 April 1931, p. 21.

[54]*The Nation*, 15 April 1931, p. 39.

[55]"Traitor Hitler!," *Time*, 13 April 1931, p. 21; *The Nation*, 15 April 1931, p. 39.

[56]Marcosson, "New German Leadership," *The Saturday Evening Post*, 16 June 1931, p. 5.

[57]"Power of Jews, Of Press," *Time*, 22 January 1931, p. 17.

[58]"Ballyhooer's Return," *Time*, 22 January 1931, p. 23.

[59]Oswald G. Villard, "Can Germany Pay?," *The Nation*, 28 January 1931, p. 91; Martin, "Europe," *The Atlantic Monthly*, February 1931, p. 244; "Gratified," *Time*, 4 January 1932, p. 7.

[60]"Washington Moves at Last," *The Nation*, 24 June 1931, p. 568.

[61]Dorothy Thompson, "Something Must Happen—German Youth Demands a Different World," *The Saturday Evening Post*, 23 May 1931, pp. 18-19.

[62]"German Fears of a Revolution," *The Literary Digest*, 11 July 1931, p. 15.

[63]"Beggar No Chooser," *Time*, 20 July 1931, p. 20; "Pan-Chaos," *Time*, 3 August 1931, p. 16.

[64]"Quickly Done," *Time*, August 1931, p. 16.

[65]"Unmitigated Gloom," *Time*, 10 August 1931, p. 16; "Severe Flutter," *Time*. 17 August 1931, p. 12; "Wiggin for President," *Time*, 17 August 1931, p. 12.

[66]"Pan-Chaos," *Time*, 3 August 1931, p. 16; "Bull-by-the-Tail," *Time*, 10 August 1931, p. 16.

[67]*The Nation*, 16 September 1931, p. 269.

[68]George P. Auld, "That International Millstone," *The Atlantic Monthly*, September 1931, pp. 375-376; *The Nation*, 21 October 1931, p. 417.

[69]"Eliza Bruning," *Time*, 26 October 1931, p. 17; *The Nation*, 21 October 1931, p. 417.

[70]*The Literary Digest*, 31 October 1931, p. 14.

[71]*The Nation*, 11 November 1931, p. 555.

[72]*The Nation*, 11 November 1931, p. 555; "Pax Gallica," *The New Republic*, 18 November 1931, p. 4; "Germany in Fear," *The New Republic*, 18 November 1931, pp. 7-8.

[73]"Adolf Hitler States His Case," *The Literary Digest*, 21 November 1931, pp. 14-15; "Why Germans Hold We Must Pay," *The Literary Digest*, 21 November 1931, p. 15.

[74]"The Wildfire Spread of German Fascism," *The Literary Digest*, 28 November 1931, p. 13; "Hitler's Astounding Outburst," *The Literary Digest*, 19 December 1931, p. 10.

[75]"Repudiators," *Time*, 7 December 1931, p. 13; "Three Against Hitler," *Time*, 21 December 1931, p. 17.

[76]"Deadlock in Berlin," *The New Republic*, 16 December 1931, p. 124; "Bruning's Last Stand," *The Nation*, 23 December 1931, pp. 685-686; "We Are Not Carthage," *Time*, 14 December 1931, p. 20.

[77]John Elliott, "Germany in the World Crisis," *The Nation*, 16 December 1931, pp. 662-663.

[78]"Debts and Darkness," *Time*, 21 December 1931, p. 17; "We Are Not Carthage," *Time*, 14 December 1931, p. 20.

[79]*The Nation*, 16 December 1931, p. 654.

[80]"The Transformation of Adolf Hitler," *The Literary Digest*, 9 January 1932, pp. 13-14.

[81]T.R. Ybarra, "Best Since Bismarck," *Collier's* 6 February 1932, pp. 12 ff.

[82]"May Anticipated," *Time*, 18 January 1932, p. 14; "Hep! Hep! Oberst Epp!," *Time*, 25 January 1932, p. 16.

[83]*The New Republic*, 3 February 1932, p. 306.

[84]Gerhard Friters, "Who Are the German Fascists?," *The Reader's Digest*, March 1932, pp. 63-65; Nicholas Fairweather, "Hitler and Hitlerism: A Man of Destiny," *The Atlantic Monthly*, March 1932, pp. 380-387; Nicholas Fairweather, "Hitler and Hitlerism: Germany Under the Nazis," *The Atlantic Monthly*, April 1932, pp. 509-516.

[85]William H. Hale, "Ten Years of Hitler; One Hundred of Goethe," *The Nation*, 16 March 1932, pp. 307-308.

[86]"Nominations" *Time*, 29 February 1932, p. 20; *The New Republic*, 2 March 1932, p. 56; John Elliott, "Germany Seeks a President," *The Nation*, 2 March 1932, pp. 255-256.

[87]"The Hindenburg Victory," *The New Republic*, 23 March 1932, p. 140; "Hindenburg Making Germany Safe for Everybody," *The Literary Digest*, 26 March 1932, p. 15.

[88]"Hitler Stopped?," *Time*, 18 April 1932, p. 15; "Hitler Versus Prussia," *The Nation*, 20 April 1932, p. 455; "Munich Night, 1932," *Harper's*, April 1932, pp. 546-550; "Hitler Versus Prussia," *The Nation*, 20 April 1932, p. 455.

[89]"Braun v. Brownshirts," *Time*, 2 May 1932, p. 19; "Shifting Politics in Germany," *The New Republic*, 4 May 1932, pp. 314-315; "Hitler's Star Still in Ascendancy," *The Literary Digest*, 7 May 1932, p. 12.

[90]"Bruning Out," *Time*, 6 June 1932, p. 17; "Cabinet of Monocles," *Time*, 13 June 1932, p. 16; "The German Republic Totters," *The Nation*, 22 June 1932, p. 695.

[91]"Bruning Out," *Time*, 6 June 1932, p. 17; "Undressing and Upholding," *Time*, 27 June 1932, p. 19; "Radical Reactionaries," *Time*, 4 July 1932, p. 16.

[92]"Rough Riots," *Time*, 11 July 1932, p. 16; "Fair or Foul," *Time*, 11 July 1932, p. 17; "Bloody Sunday," *Time*, 25 July 1932, p. 16.

[93]"Bloodshed in Germany's Political Campaign," *The Literary Digest*, 16 July 1932, p. 12; *The Nation*, 17 August 1932, p. 1.

[94]"Germany's Supreme Effort to End the Terror," *The Literary Digest*, 20 August 1932, p. 10.

[95]*The Nation*, 27 July 1932, p. 66; William C. White, "Germany's Lost Generation," *The Atlantic Monthly*, July 1932, pp. 118-124; "Radical Reactionaries," *Time*, 4 July 1932, p. 16; "Lausanne Peace on Earth," *Time*, 18 July 1932, p. 13.

[96]"The End of Hitler?," *The Nation*, 10 August 1932, p. 115; "Useful Adolf," *Time*, 15 August 1932, p. 13.

[97]"Velvet Glove," *Time*, 22 August 1932, p. 14; *The Nation*, 24 August 1932, p. 1; "The Hitler-Von Papen Duel that Rocks Germany," *The Literary Digest*, 10 September 1932, p. 11.

[98]Frank H. Simonds, "If Hitler Comes to Power," *The Reader's Digest*, August 1932, pp. 61-63.

[99]"Brown Trout and Bitterness," *Time*, 5 September 1932, p. 14; cf. "Clemency for Nazi Murderers," *The Literary Digest*, 17 September 1932, p. 12.

[100]"Uber Alles!" *Time*, 12 September 1932, p. 15; cf. *The Nation*, 28 September 1932, p. 1; "Germany's Demand to Arm as a First-Class Power," *The Literary Digest*, 17 September 1932, p. 10.

[101]"Partitioning Prussia," *Time*, 12 September 1932, p. 16.

[102]"Reichstag in Revolt," *Time*, 19 September 1932, pp. 14-15.

[103]"Fine People," *Time*, 26 September 1932, pp. 14-15; "Vorwarts mit Gott," *Time*, 17 October 1932, p. 20.

[104]"Hitler Tamed," *Time*, 14 November 1932, pp. 17-18; "Hitler's Shattered Dream of Dictatorship," *The Literary Digest*, 19 November 1932, p. 13; *The Nation*, 16 November 1932, p. 2.

[105]Karl F. Geiser, "Hitler's Hold on Germany," *The Nation*, 16 November 1932, pp. 474-475.

[106]" 'Ware' Hohenzollerns!," *Time*, 21 November 1932, pp. 14-15; "Hitler Gets Warm," *Time*, 18 November 1932, pp. 18-19; *The Nation*, 30 November 1932, p. 1

[107]"Only One Man...." *Time*, 5 December 1932, pp. 15-16; *The Nation*, 7 December 1932, p. 1.

[108]"Europe's Fears of Germany's Military Chancellor," *The Literary Digest*, 17 December 1932, pp. 9-10.

[109]"Something More Important," *Time*, 19 December 1932, pp. 15-16.

[110]"Something More Important," *Time*, 19 December 1932, p. 16; "Gregor Strasser, Big Hitlerite Rebel," *The Literary Digest*, 28 January 1933, p. 13.

[111]"Miraculous Deeds," *Time*, 26 December 1932, p. 12; "Germany's New 'War Spirit,' " *The Literary Digest*, 7 January 1933, p. 13; *The New Republic*, 21 December 1932, p. 145; *The Nation*, 4 January 1933, p. 3; "Happy New Year?," *Time*, 2 January 1933, pp. 14-15.

[112]*The Nation*, 4 January 1933, p. 3; "Brasses and Plots," *Time*, 16 January 1933, p. 16.

[113]"Germany's New 'War Spirit,' " *The Literary Digest*, 4 February 1933, p. 12; "How They Put a Nazi on the Spot," *The Literary Digest*, 4 February 1933, p. 13.

[114]"Hitler in Power," *The Nation*, 8 February 1933, pp. 137-138; "Hitler Wins," *The New Republic*, 8 February 1933, pp. 336-337.

Chapter II

[1]*The Nation*, 15 February 1933, p. 163.

[2]"Scared to Death," *Time*, 27 February 1933, p. 16; "Hitler and Secret Treaty Reports Stir Europe," *Newsweek*, 25 February 1933, p. 17. *Newsweek* first began publication on 17 February 1933. Like other American news magazines, it relied on newspapers and not correspondents for its material.

[3]"Whizzing Bullets Herald Hot Election Tactics," *Newsweek*, 4 March 1933, p. 13; "Flaming Reichstag," *Time*, 6 March 1933, p. 20; "Scared to Death," *Time*, 27 February 1933, p. 15.

[4]"National Revolution," *Time*, 13 March 1933, p. 16.

[5]"Hitler Wins," *The Nation*, 15 March 1933, p. 277; the same week *Newsweek* reported Albert H. Wiggin succeeded in having the private creditors of Germany extend their loans for another year: "Private Creditors Extend German Short-Term Loans," *Newsweek*, 25 February 1933, p. 13; "Third Standstill," *Time* 27 February 1933, p. 16.

[6]"Hitler's Role," *The Nation*, 15 February 1933, p. 164.

[7]Frederick Kub, "The Most Talked of Army in Europe,"*The Reader's Digest*, March 1933, pp. 60-64; "Rift Widens in Arms Conference," *Newsweek*, 18 March 1933, pp. 15-16; "March on Berlin," *The New Republic*, 15 February 1933, p. 4; "Sparks Hissing Around Europe's Powder Magazine," *The Literary Digest*, 25 March 1933, p. 12.

[8]"National Revolution," *Time*, 13 March 1933, p. 18; "Hitler Wins," *The Nation*, 22 February 1933, p. 197.

[9]"Hitler Wins," *The Nation*, 22 February 1933, p. 197; "One People—Two Flags," *Time*, 20 March 1933, p. 15; "Hitler's Bright Sun Shines on Bloody Acts,: *Newsweek*, 18 March 1933, pp. 16-17; "American Outcry at German Jew-baiting," *The Literary Digest*, 1 April 1933, p. 4; "Terrorism Rules Germany," *The Nation*, 29 March 1933, p. 332; "A Week's Vignettes of Nazi-Land," *Newsweek*, 25 March 1933, pp. 13-14; "Terrorism Rules Germany," *The Nation*, 29 March 1933, p. 332.

[10]"Prayers and Atrocities," *Time*, 3 April 1933, p. 16; "All Fool's Day," *Time*, 10 April 1933, p. 24; "A Week's Vignettes of Nazi-Land," *Newsweek*, 25 March 1933, p. 13.

[11]"Hitler's Bright Sun Shines on Bloody Acts," *Newsweek*, 18 March 1933, p. 16; "Prayers and Atrocities," *Time*, 3 April 1933, p. 17; "Nazi Anti-Semitic Atrocities Denounced Here," *Newsweek*, 1 April 1933, p. 17.

[12]"Nazi Anti-Semitic Atrocities Denounced Here," *Newsweek*, 1 April 1933, p. 17; "The Week," *The New Republic*, 5 April 1933, p. 198; "The Two-Edged Sword of Nazi Boycotts," *The Literary Digest*, 8 April 1933, p. 3.

[13]"All Fools' Day," *Time*, 10 April 1933, p. 23; "Nazis Heed an Indignant World," *Newsweek*, 8 April 1933, p. 17; "Co-ordination," *Time*, 17 April 1933, p. 17; *The Nation*, 19 April 1933, p. 430.

[14]"All Fools' Day," *Time*, 10 April 1933, p. 23; "The Jews in Fascist Germany," *The New Republic*, 12 April 1933, p. 236; "Back to Barbarism" *The Nation*, 12 April 1933, p. 338; Ludwig Lore, "Nazi Revolution at Work," *The Nation*, 19 April 1933, p. 440; "Co-ordination," *Time*, 17 April 1933, p. 17; "Steel Helmets Now Part of Hitlerism's Forces," *Newsweek*, 6 May 1933, p. 15.

[15]"Nazis Against the World," *The Nation*, 5 April 1933, p. 36; "Escaping the German Hell," *The Nation*, 26 April 1933, p. 470; "Co-ordination," *Time*, 17 April 1933, p. 17.

16"Shaping Germany to the Nazi Model," *Newsweek*, 15 April 1933, p. 12; "Co-ordination," *Time*, 17 April 1933, p. 17; "Germany," *Newsweek*, 22 April 1933, p. 12; it was with this book-burning that the term "Holocaust" initially occurred in the magazines under study: "Students Exult as 'Un-German' Books Burn," *Newsweek*, 20 May 1933, pp. 14-15.

17"Students Exult as 'Un-German' Books Burn," *Newsweek*, 20 May 1933, pp. 14-15; "Chancellor Hitler's Anti-Semitic Laws Explosive Item on League Council Agenda," *Newsweek*, 27 May 1933, p. 16.

18"Student's Exult as 'Un-German' Books Burn," *Newsweek*, 20 May 1933, pp. 14-15; "Hitler Goes to Sea; Reviews Reich's Fleet," *Newsweek*, 3 June 1933, p. 12; "Nazis Against the World," *The Nation*, 5 April 1933, p. 360; "Polish-German Clashes that Perturb Europe," *The Literary Digest*, 22 April 1933, p. 10; "England Critical; Italy Friendly; Poland Angry," *Newsweek*, 22 April 1933, pp. 11-12.

19"Jews, Non-Nazis Still Feel the Lash of Hitler," *Newsweek*, 29 July 1933, pp. 12-13; *The New Republic*, 2 August 1933, pp. 299-300; "Six Months of Hitlerism," *The Nation*, 2 August 1933, pp. 122-124.

20"Nazis Make Jews Act Communist Mob for Movie," *Newsweek*, 16 September 1933, p. 13; "Aryans on Horseback," *Time*, 16 October 1933, p. 16; "Nobles Arrayed," *Time*, 4 December 1933, p. 18.

21"Blindfolded," *Time*, 7 August 1933, p. 19; *The Nation*, 9 August 1933, p. 142; *The New Republic*, 20 September 1933, p. 139.

22"Hitlerism Is Cracking," *The Nation*, 11 October 1933, p. 397; "Nazi Bishop Elected to Head United German Protestants," *Newsweek*, 7 October 1933, p. 12; *The Nation*, 18 October 1933, p. 423; "The Suppressed Advertisement Concerning R.H. Macy," *The Nation*, 25 October 1933, pp. 478-480; *The New Republic*, 1 November 1933, p. 320.

23"Nazis Against the World," *The Nation*, 5 April 1933, p. 360.

24"Getting the Jews Out of Germany," *The New Republic*, 19 July 1933, p. 255; "Arabs Riot Against Palestine Jew Influx," *Newsweek*, 21 October 1933; "Peace of Holy Land Shattered as Arabs Continue Anti-Semitic Immigration Riots," *Newsweek*, 4 November 1933, p. 11; "Jews Not Wanted," *Time*, 6 November 1933, p. 22.

25Waldo Frank, "Why Should the Jews Survive," *The New Republic*, 13 December 1933, p. 121; Edward S. Martin, "The Nazis and the Jews," *Harper's*, June 1933, pp. 125-128.

26"A Week's Vignettes of Nazi-Land," *Newsweek*, 25 March 1933, pp. 13-14; "Hitler Enabled," *Time*, 3 April 1933, pp. 15-16; "Germany Throws Her Republic Overboard," *Newsweek*, 1 April 1933, pp. 3-5.

27"Shaping Germany to Nazi Model," *Newsweek*, 15 April 1933, p. 12; "Co-ordination," *Time*, 17 April 1933, p. 17; Dorothy Thompson, "Room to Breathe In," *Saturday Evening Post*, 24 June 1933, pp. 4-5; "Steel Helmets Now Part of Hitler's Forces," *Newsweek*, 6 May 1933, pp. 15-16.

28"Swastika or the Cross," *Time*, 17 April 1933, pp. 18-19; *The New Republic*, 5 April 1933, p. 198; "Co-ordination," *Time*, 17 April 1933, p. 18; "Nazis Adopt Compulsory Labor Measure. Reorganize Industry, Curb Nationalists," *Newsweek*, 13 May 1933, p. 12; "Hitler Crushes the Labor Unions," *The New Republic*, 17 May 1933, pp. 4-5; "Naziland Hails Hitler, Continues Hitlerizing," *Newsweek*, 29 April 1933, pp. 13-14.

29"Totalitarians Rampant," *Time*, 3 July 1933, p. 20; "We Demand," *Time*, 10 July 1933, p. 16; "Hitler Turns on Catholics, Protestant Politicians," *Newsweek*, 8 July 1933, p. 14; Dorothy Thompson, "Room to Breathe In," *Saturday Evening Post*, 24 June 1933, pp. 4-5; F. Britten Austin, "Old-Time Germany Looks at Hitler," *Saturday Evening Post*, 5 August 1933, pp. 10-11.

[30]"Feast of Labor," *Time*, 8 May 1933, p. 18; "Nazis Adopt Compulsory Labor Measure, Reorganize Industry, Curb Nationalists," *Newsweek*, 13 May 1933, p. 12; "Hitler Crushes the Labor Unions," *The New Republic*, 17 June 1933, p. 4.

[31]"Scared to Death," *Time*, 27 March 1933, pp. 15-17; "Terrorism Rules Germany," *The Nation*, 29 March 1933, p. 332; *The New Republic*, 29 March 1933, p. 170; "Back to Barbarism," *The Nation*, 12 April 1933, p. 383.

[32]T.R. Ybarra, "The Hitler Jitters," *Collier's*, 24 June 1933, pp. 10-11, 36-37; "Feast of Labor," *Time*, 8 May 1933, p. 18; *The Nation*, 19 April 1933, p. 443.

[33]"Co-ordination," *Time*, 17 April 1933, p. 17; T.R. Ybarra, "You Can't Get to Heaven That Way," *Collier's*, 29 July 1933, pp. 19-20; "Making a German Christ for Germany," *The Literary Digest*, 22 April 1933, p. 16; "Naziland Hails Hitler Continues Hitlerizing," *Newsweek*, 29 April 1933, pp. 13-14.

[34]"Nazis Speed Toward a 'Totalitarian' State," *Newsweek*, 1 July 1933, p. 13; "The Cross Still Standing Triumphant Above the Swastika," *The Literary Digest*, 1 July 1933, p. 17.

[35]"Miracle," *Time*, 31 July 1933, p. 16; *The New Republic*, 2 August 1933, p. 300; "Sub-Dictator," *Time*, 21 August 1933, p. 12; "Church Militant," *Time*, 9 October 1933, p. 20.

[36]"Nazi Church Adviser Rebukes Anti-Jewish Radicals," *Newsweek*, 25 November 1933, pp. 14, 16; "New Heathenism," *Time*, 27 November 1933, p. 16; *The Nation*, 29 November 1933, p. 607.

[37]"Reichsbishop Mueller Struggles for Church Unity," *Newsweek*, 16 December 1933, p. 13; "Christian Conglomeration," *Time*, 11 December 1933, p. 26; *The Nation*, 13 December 1933, p. 664.

[38]*The New Republic*, 19 April 1933, p. 264; *The Nation*, 19 April 1933, p. 443; "England Critical; Italy Friendly; Poland Angry," *Newsweek*, 22 April 1933, pp. 11-13.

[39]"Religious Clashes; Nazis Rout Catholics; Prevent Mass," *Newsweek*, 17 June 1933, p. 14; "Will-to-Arms," *Time*, 19 June 1933, p. 19; "The Cross Still Standing Triumphant Above the Swastika," *The Literary Digest*, 1 July 1933, p. 16; "Hitler's Steam Roller Moves at Top Speed," *The Literary Digest*, 8 July 1933, p. 13; "Hitler Turns on Catholics, Protestant Politicians," *Newsweek*, 8 July 1933, p. 14; *The Nation*, 12 July 1933, p. 33.

[40]"Hitler Achieves Third Aim, A One-Party State," *Newsweek*, 15 July 1933, pp. 12, 14; "Concordat," *Time*, 17 July 1933, p. 19; "Peace Guaranteed Between Germany and the Vatican," *The Literary Digest*, 22 July 1933, p. 11.

[41]Only approximately 100 books were burned in Munich: "Bibliocaust," *Time*, 22 May 1933, p. 21; "Germany—The Twilight of Reason," *The New Republic*, 4 June 1933, p. 117; "Compulsory Labor in Germany," *The New Republic*, 7 June 1933, p. 89; "Job Control," *Time*, 12 June 1933, p. 23.

[42]Quentin Reynolds, "Woman's Place," *Collier's*, 25 November 1933, pp. 21-22; *The Nation*, 5 July 1933, p. 2; "Hitlerite Marriages as Unemployment Relief," *The Literary Digest*, 15 July 1933, p. 13; " 'Painted Dolls' Out, Nazi Women Are Warned," *Newsweek*, 19 August 1933, p. 13; "Nazi Babies," *Newsweek*, 5 August 1933, p. 12; "Nazi Unification," *The Nation*, 12 July 1933, p. 33; "Nearly Half Million 'Unfit' Will Be Sterilized," *Newsweek*, 30 December 1933, p. 11; C. Thomalla, "Sterilization in Germany," *The Reader's Digest*, October 1934, pp. 103-104, summarizes implementation of the edict.

[43]"Rift Widens in Arms Conference," *Newsweek*, 18 March 1933, pp. 15-16; "Germany's Stand For Semi-Military Force Deadlocks Conference," *Newsweek*, 20 May 1933, pp. 12-13.

[44]*The New Republic*, 24 May 1933, p. 29; "Germany Will, the U.S. Too," *Time*, 29 May 1933, p. 12; "Conference Adjourns as Davis Clarifies America's Stand on War Commitments," *Newsweek*, 10 June 1933, p. 10 "Hitler Proclaims Peace By Equality,"

The Literary Digest, 27 May 1933, pp. 10-11; "How Pacific Is Hitler?," *The Nation*, 31 May 1933, p. 602.

45"Must," *Time*, 3 July 1933, p. 21; "We Demand," *Time*, 10 July 1933, p. 16; "Totalitarians Rampant," *Time*, 3 July 1933, pp. 20-21; Clifford Sharp, "How Strong Is Hitler?," *The Reader's Digest*, September 1933, p. 44.

46"Germany Will, the U.S. Too," *Time*, 29 May 1933, pp. 12-13; "The Four-Power Pact: Il Duce Declares It Has Been Initialed and War Chapter Is Closed," *Newsweek*, 17 June 1933, p. 12.

47"Germany Will, the U.S. Too," *Time*, 29 May 1933, pp. 12-13; "Spouters and Specifiers," *Time*, 26 June 1933, pp. 16-17; "Henderson Takes to 'the Road' for Peace," 24 June 1933, *Newsweek*, p. 10; "The Wrong Road to Peace," *The New Republic*, 28 June 1933, p. 171; "Hitler's Anti-Russian Plot," *The New Republic*, 21 June 1933, p. 140.

48"Austria's Struggle Against Hitlerism," *The Literary Digest*, 3 June 1933, p. 10; "Austria Keeps Up Its War on the Nazis," *The Literary Digest*, 24 June 1933, p. 10; "Border War," *Time*, 21 August 1933, p. 13; "Two Men in a Boat," *Time*, 28 August 1933, p. 13; "Europe's Bewildered Angel of Peace," *The Literary Digest*, 9 September 1933, p. 13; "Germany's Drive on Austria," *The Literary Digest*, 30 September 1933, p. 14.

49*The Nation*, 13 September 1933, p. 281; "Austrian's Sad Plight," *The Nation*, 13 September 1933, p. 383; "Nazi Agitation and Propaganda Tempt Nation to Adopt Fascism as a Solution," *Newsweek*, 16 September 1933, p. 13; "What a Conflict," *Time*, 18 September 1933, p. 14.

50Emil Lengyel, "Austrian's Fight Against Hitlerism," *The Literary Digest*, 16 December 1933, pp. 17, 44.

51Sidney Hugh, "Hitler and the New Germany," *The Literary Digest*, 7 October 1933, pp. 5, 43; "Diplomats at Dinner Consider German Rearmament," *Newsweek*, 7 October 1933, p. 11; "Hitler Is Cracking," *The Nation*, 11 October 1933, p. 397.

52"Nazi Pilot Hitler Casts Off From the League; His Nation Drifts into Isolation, Watched By an Anxious World," *Newsweek*, 21 October 1933, pp. 3-4; "High Time," *Time*, 23 October 1933, p. 16; "Quintuple Dynamite," *Time*, 23 October 1933, pp. 15-16.

53"Quintuple Dynamite," *Time*, 23 October 1933, pp. 15-16; "Nazi Pilot Hitler Casts Off From the League; His Nation Drifts into Isolation, Watched By an Anxious World," *Newsweek*, 21 October 1933, pp. 3-4; "America, the Allies and Hitler," *The Nation*, 1 November 1933, p. 499; Sidney Hugh, "Hitler and the Peace of Europe," *The Literary Digest*, 4 November 1933, pp. 28-29.

54"Effective Political Machine and One-Party Ballot Bring Expected Nazi Landslide," *Newsweek*, 18 November 1933, p. 13; "Kämpfen Mit Uns," *Time*, 20 November 1933, p. 19; "The Third Reich Votes," *The New Republic*, 22 November 1933, p. 38; "Chancellor Hitler's Expected Election Triumph," *The Literary Digest*, 25 November 1933, p. 11; "Effective Political Machine and One-Party Ballot Bring Expected Nazi Landslide," *Newsweek*, 18 November 1933, p. 13; "Totalitarian State Finally Achieved By Hitler," *Newsweek*, 9 December 1933, p. 14.

55"Germany's All-Nazi Womanless Parliament," *The Literary Digest*, 30 December 1933, p. 15; "Deputies in Brown Shirts Quickly Approve Hitler's Policies," *Newsweek*, 23 December 1933, p. 12.

56"How Pacific Is Hitler?," *The Nation*, 31 June 1933, p. 602; *The Nation*, 5 July 1933, p. 2; *The New Republic*, 2 August 1933, p. 299; *The New Republic*, 25 October 1933, p. 292.

57"Formenter Ousted," *Time*, 6 November 1933, p. 24.

58"How Shall We Meet Nazi Propaganda?," *The Nation*, 8 November 1933, p. 526.

[59]Ludwig Lore, "Nazi Politics in America," *The Nation*, 29 November 1933, pp. 615-617.

[60]Lore, pp. 615-617; Johan J. Smertenko, "Hitlerism Comes to America," *Harper's*, November 1933, pp. 660-670.

[61]Harold Loeb and Selden Rodman, "American Fascism in Embryo," *The New Republic*, 27 December 1933, pp. 185-187.

[62]*The New Republic*, 25 July 1934, p. 274; *The Nation*, 25 July 1934, p. 85; *The New Republic*, 25 July 1934, p. 275.

[63]*The New Republic*, 25 July 1934, p. 275.

[64]"Hitler's Year: An Audit of Twelve Months Which Shook Germany, Alarmed Neighbors, and Amazed the World," *Newsweek*, 27 January 1934, pp. 7-8.

[65]"Adolf and Ignatz," *Time*, 1 January 1934, p. 13; "Bless Me, Natzi!," *Time*, 8 January 1934, p. 21; "Gentle Adolf," *Time*, 8 January 1934, p. 21; "Hitler Tickets," *Time*, 29 January 1934, p. 20.

[66]"Peace," *Time*, 9 April 1934, p. 21; "Hitler Uses Gentle Hand in Religious Troubles," *Newsweek*, 14 April 1934, p. 18.

[67]"Bishops Blasted," *Time*, 15 January 1934, p. 27; T.R. Ybarra, "Hard-Boiled Hermann," *The Reader's Digest*, February 1934, pp. 13-16; "Ernst Roehm—The Mailed Fist of Hitler," *The Literary Digest*, 20 January 1934, p. 12.

[68]Stephard Stone, "Hypnotist of Millions," *The Reader's Digest*, February 1934, pp. 10-12; T.R. Ybarra, "Hard-Boiled Hermann," *The Reader's Digest*, February 1934, pp. 13-16.

[69]"Goering Out?," *Time*, 15 April 1934, p. 28.

[70]"Monarchists Fools?," *Time*, 29 January 1934, p. 20; "Obedient Deputies Give States' Rights to Reich," *Newsweek*, 10 February 1934, pp. 16-17.

[71]*The New Republic*, 7 February 1934, p. 348; "Wilhelm at 75," *Time*, 5 February 1934, p. 21; "Author, Hunter, Policeman," *Time*, 5 February 1934, p. 21.

[72]"Death of the States," *Time*, 12 February 1934, p. 17.

[73]"Organic Upbuilding," *Newsweek*, 26 March 1934, p. 16; "Hitler's Chickens Come Home to Roost," *The New Republic*, 4 April 1934, p. 202.

[74]*The New Republic*, 3 January 1934, pp. 207-208; "Hitler Prepares for the Olympics," *The Literary Digest*, 6 January 1934, p. 27.

[75]"Kosher and Kulter!," *Time*, 8 January 1934, p. 20.

[76]" 'Self-Help' of Mob Stops Film Starring Jewess," *Newsweek*, 17 March 1934, pp. 15-16; "Hitler Has Had No Insubordination From Cabinet," *Newsweek*, 7 April 1934, p. 14; "Death of Auntie Voss," *Time*, 9 April 1934, p. 22.

[77]"Boycott Front Line," *Time*, 26 March 1934, p. 16. See earlier, p. 109.

[78]" 'Putzy' and 1909," *Time*, 9 April 1934, p. 22' " 'Putzy' and '09," *Time*, 16 April 1934, p. 21; Ernst F.S. Hanfstaengl, "My Leader," *Collier's*, 4 August 1934, pp. 7-9. This is a laudatory article of Hitler—one of the few of its kind in American magazines.

[79]"Bishops Blaster," *Time*, 15 January 1934, p. 27; "Clergy in Rebellion Against Reich Bishop," *Newsweek*, 13 January 1934, p. 16; *The New Republic*, 24 January 1934, p. 293.

[80]"Hindenburg Alive to Issues, Rebukes Nazi Bishop," *Newsweek*, 20 January 1934, p. 16; "Rosenberg Prefers Heroes' 'Fiery Spirit' to Crucifixion," *Newsweek*, 10 February 1934, p. 17.

[81]"Peace," *Time*, 9 April 1934, p. 21; "Hitler Uses Gentle Hand in Religious Troubles," *Newsweek*, 14 April 1934, p. 18; "Bishop, Pressed By Hitler, Seeks Church Peace," *Newsweek*, 21 April 1934, p. 20.

[82]"Church Leaders Defy Nazis' Control of Religion," *Newsweek*, 9 June 1934, p. 14; "Pagans and Gags," *Time*, 23 July 1934, p. 18.

[83]"My Leader," *Time*, 20 August 1934, p. 16; "Against Protestant Revolt, Catholic Rebuff, Primate Mueller Forces His United Church," *Newsweek*, 29 September 1934, p. 13; "Shame and Sorrow," *Time*, 1 October 1934, p. 17; "A Lutheran Primate for Nazi Germany," *The Literary Digest*, 6 October 1934, p. 18.

[84]"Protestants Parade By Nazi Headquarters, Chanting Protest," *Newsweek*, 22 September 1934, p. 16; *The Nation*, 3 October 1934, p. 366.

[85]"Some Sabers Flash in Protestant-Nazi Conflict," *Newsweek*, 29 October 1934, p. 14; "Meisser v. Muller," *Time*, 22 October 1934, pp. 20-21; "Militant German Protestants Block 'Hitlerizing,' " *The Literary Digest*, 27 October 1934, p. 20; *The Nation*, 24 October 1934, p. 463; *The New Republic*, 24 October 1934, p. 295.

[86]"Reichsbishop v. Toothache," *Time*, 5 November 1934, p. 18; "Protestants Cheered as Hitler Snubs Reich Bishop," *Newsweek*, 3 November 1934, p. 14; *The New Republic*, 7 November 1934, p. 352.

[87]"Bishops Blasted," *Newsweek*, 15 January 1934, p. 28; *The New Republic*, 24 January 1934, p. 293; "Immune Cardinal Wars on 'Paganism' of Nazis," *Newsweek*, 10 March 1934, p. 14.

[88]"Hitler Uses Gentle Hand in Religious Troubles," *Newsweek*, 14 April 1934, p. 18; "Conflict Between Germany and Vatican," *The Literary Digest*, 21 April 1934, p. 16; "Against Protestant Revolt, Catholic Rebuff, Primate Mueller Forces His United Church," *Newsweek*, 29 September 1934, p. 13.

[89]"Beneath the Censor's Lid Boils Hitler's First Crisis, a Bitter Feud Between Brown Shirt and Junker," *Newsweek*, 30 June 1934, pp. 3-4; "Second Revolution," *Time*, 2 July 1934, p. 16; "Beneath the Censor's Lid Boils Hitler's First Crisis, a Bitter Feud Between Brown Shirt and Junker," *Newsweek*, 30 June 1934, pp. 3-4.

[90]"Von Papen Shows His Hand," *The New Republic*, 4 July 1934, pp. 196-197; "Beneath the Censor's Lid Boils Hitler's First Crisis, a Bitter Feud Between Brown Shirt and Junker," *Newsweek*, 30 June 1934, pp. 3-4.

[91]"Beneath the Censor's Lid Boils Hitler's First Crisis, a Bitter Feud Between Brown Shirts and Junker," *Newsweek*, 30 June 1934, pp. 3-4; "Second Revolution," *Time*, 2 July 1934, p. 16; "Revolt Within Germany," *The Nation*, 4 July 1934, p. 5; "Von Papen Shows His Hand," *The New Republic*, 4 July 1934, pp. 196-197; "Crux of Crisis," *Time*, 16 July 1934, pp. 15-18.

[92]"The Threats to Hitler's Rule," *The New Republic*, 9 May 1934, pp. 356-357.

[93]"German Upheaval Follows Nazi Split," *The Literary Digest*, 7 July 1934, p. 13.

[94]"Blood Purge," *Time*, 9 July 1934, p. 17; "Nazi Against Nazi, Hitler 'Liquidates' Some of His Former Comrades in a Desperate Gamble with the Future," *Newsweek*, 7 July 1934, pp. 3-4; "Revolt in Germany," *The New Republic*, 11 July 1934, pp. 222-223; "Hitler Moves Right," *The Nation*, 18 July 1934, pp. 61-62; cf. Dorothy Thompson, "The Germany Revolution—Continued Story," *The Saturday Evening Post*, 8 September 1934, p. 63; "Nazi Germany's Second Revolution," *The Literary Digest*, 14 July 1934, p. 1.

[95]"German Upheaval Follows Nazi Split," *The Literary Digest*, 7 July 1934, p. 13; "Blood Purge," *Time*, 9 July 1934, p. 17; "Revolt in Germany," *The New Republic*, 11 July 1934, p. 223; "Hitler Turns to the Right," *The New Republic*, 18 July 1934, p. 251.

[96]"The New Fascism in Germany," *The New Republic*, 25 July 1934, p. 279; Dorothy Thompson, "The German Revolution—Continued Story," *The Saturday Evening Post*, 8 September 1934, p. 64; Frank H. Simonds, "The Turn of the Tide in Europe," *The Atlantic Monthly*, October 1934, p. 486; "The Nazi Blood Bath," *The Nation*, 11 July 1934, p. 32; "Nazi Against Nazi, Hitler 'Liquidates' Some of His Former Comrades in a Desperate Gamble with the Future," *Newsweek*, 7 July 1934, p. 4; "Black Shirts Gain to Brown Shirts' Distress," *Newsweek*, 4 August 1934, p. 13.

[97]"Deadline," *Time*, 5 February 1934, p. 22; "Chancellor Takes His Nazi Troubles to the League," *Newsweek*, 10 February 1934, p. 18.

[98]"Crescendo," *Time*, 12 February 1934, pp. 18-20; cf. "Europe Marches," *The New Republic*, 21 February 1934, pp. 32-33.

[99]"Dolfuss on the Danube," *Time*, 19 February 1934, p. 18; "Socialists, Soldiers, Police and Heimwehr Shot It Out in Vienna and Other Cities," *Newsweek*, 17 February 1934, p. 15; "Dogged by the Past and in Fear of the Future, Austria Licks Her Self-Inflicted Wounds," *Newsweek*, 24 February 1934, pp. 5-6; "Interlude," *Time*, 26 February 1934, pp. 15-17; "Heimwehr Move Stirs Cafe Table Talk of Monarchy, Civil War, or Perhaps a Fascist Coup," *Newsweek*, 3 March 1934, p. 13; "Rumors of the Week," *Time*, 5 March 1934, p. 15; "Habsburg Hopes," *Time*, 19 March 1934, pp. 17-18.

[100]"The Meaning of Austria," *The New Republic*, 28 February 1934, p. 60; *The New Republic*, 7 March 1934, p. 86; John Gunther, "The Struggle for Power in Austria," *The Nation*, 16 June 1934, pp. 557-599.

[101]*The New Republic*, 27 June 1934, pp. 165-166; John Gunther, "After the Dolfuss Murder," *The Nation*, 22 August 1934, pp. 204-105; "Mussolini, Dolfuss, and Goemboes Sign 'Coordination' Pact; France a Watchful Observer," *Newsweek*, 24 March 1934, p. 16; "Family to Safety," *Time*, 23 July 1934, p. 20.

[102]"Dolfuss Killed, Nazi Crushed, Germany Isolated; Italy Sends Troops to the Border, and an Anxious World Watches," *Newsweek*, 4 August 1934, pp. 3-5; "Death For Freedom," *Time*, 6 August 1934, pp. 17-19; "Austria and After," *The New Republic*, 8 August 1934, pp. 331-332; "Europe v. 'Dillinger,' " *Time*, 6 August 1934, p. 14.

[103]"Austria and After," *The New Republic*, 8 August 1934, pp. 331-332; "Nazism's Defeat in Austria," *The Nation*, 8 August 1934, pp. 144-145; John Gunther, "After the Murder of Dolfuss," *The Nation*, 22 August 1934, pp. 204-205.

[104]Frank H. Simonds, "The Turn of the Tide in Europe," *The Atlantic Monthly*, October 1934, pp. 484-491.

[105]*The New Republic*, 23 May 1934, p. 30.

[106]"The Chancellor-Reichsfuehrer Watching His Step," *The Literary Digest*, 18 August 1934, p. 12.

[107]"End of Three Lives," *Time*, 13 August 1934, pp. 15-18; "Hitler, From His Mountain Retreat, Keeps Watchful Eye on a Vexed and Troubled Nation," *Newsweek*, 18 August 1934, p. 11; "What Next in Germany?," *The New Republic*, 15 August 1934, pp. 5-7; "Hitler Coordinates," *The Nation*, 15 August 1934, pp. 172-173; "What Next Germany?," *The New Republic*, 15 August 1934, pp. 5-7; "Hitler, Master of Germany, Faces Supreme Test," *The Literary Digest*, 11 August 1934, p. 12.

[108]"Ja Ja Ja Ja Ja Ja Ja Ja Ja: Nein,"*Time*, 27 August 1934, pp. 16-17.

[109]*The New Republic*, 29 August 1934, p. 57; Robert Dell, "The Future of Hitler," *The Nation*, 19 September 1934, pp. 320-322; " 'Goose Step' To Polls Gives Reich 'One Leader,' With 'One Will,' For 'One People,' " *Newsweek*, 25 August 1934, p. 14.

[110] *The New Republic*, 26 September 1934, p. 171; "Holy Roman Adolf," *Time*, 17 September 1934, pp. 18-19; "Girl, 27, Tells Der Fuehrer How and When to Smile," *Newsweek*, 15 September 1934, p. 16. *Newsweek* used Riefenstahl's picture for its cover on 15 September 1934. The film received the English title "Triumph of the Will"; "Hitler Predicts Grey Old Age for the Brown Shirts," *Newsweek*, 15 September 1934, p. 15.

[111]"Hitler' Chickens Come Home to Roost," *The New Republic*, 4 April 1934, p. 202.

[112]"Exit Versailles," *The New Republic*, 2 May 1934, pp. 324-325.

[113]"The Drift in Germany," *The Nation*, 23 May 1934, p. 579; "Air and Sun," *Time*, 11 June 1934, pp. 22-23; "Germany Strikes Back Against Trade Boycott," *The Literary Digest*, 16 June 1934, p. 15.

114"Ware Marks!," *Time*, 18 June 1934, pp. 17-18; "Nazi Germany's Grave Economic Crisis," *The Literary Digest*, 30 June 1934, p. 15; *The New Republic*, 20 June 1934, p. 3.

115"Six-Month Debt Moratorium, Result of Reparations, Depression, Adverse Trade Balance," *Newsweek*, 23 June 1934, pp. 10-11; "Moratorium," *Time*, 25 June 1934, pp. 18-20; for one view of the effects of the boycott, see T.R. Ybarra, "Germany Takes the Rap," *Collier's*, 24 November 1934, pp. 21, 28; "Germany Decides Not to Pay," *The Nation*, 27 June 1934, pp. 718-719.

116*The Nation*, 1 August 1934, p. 115; *The New Republic*, 1 August 1934, pp. 302-303; "Hand to Mouth," *Time*, 6 August 1934, pp. 15-16.

117"Hand to Mouth," *Time*, 6 August 1934, pp. 15-16.

118*The New Republic*, 12 September 1934, p. 114; *The New Republic*, 10 October 1934, p. 226; *The New Republic*, 24 October 1934, p. 12.

119"The Race Begins," *Time*, 30 April 1934, p. 15.

120Ludwig Lore, "How Germany Arms," *Harper's* April 1934, pp. 505-517; condensed and reprinted in *The Reader's Digest*, June 1934, pp. 8-12.

121*The Nation*, 9 May 1934, p. 1; "America, Britain, and Even France Help Goering in Building up Reich's Air Force," *Newsweek*, 19 May 1934, pp. 10-11.

122"Arm's Week," *Time*, 21 May 1934, p. 17; "Soft Words Inaugurate Parley; Hard Words Bring Temporary Adjournment," *Newsweek*, 9 June 1934, p. 10; "Gravity of the Grave," *Time*, 11 June 1934, p. 19; "War Clouds over Geneva," *The Nation*, 13 June 1934, p. 662; "Parley Fails in Europe, League in Chaco, While Russia Welds Her Security," *Newsweek*, 16 June 1934, p. 10; "No Disarmament Again," *The New Republic*, 20 June 1934, p. 142.

123E. Howlitt, Jr., "Making Germany Gas-Proof," *The Reader's Digest*, October 1934, p. 58; "Germany Arming Alarms British Parliament," *The Literary Digest*, 8 December 1934, p. 13.

Chapter III

1"Time Approaches to Decide Fate of Powder Magazine in Franco-German Relations," *Newsweek*, 2 June 1934, p. 12; "Germany's Advance Work on the Saar Plebiscite," *The Literary Digest*, 19 June 1934, p. 17.

2"Hitler Fires a Big Gun in Saar Plebiscite Drive," *Newsweek*, 1 September 1934, p. 11.

3"Peace But Equality," *Time*, 3 September 1934, p. 20.

4"Deutsch Ist Die Saar!," *Time*, 7 January 1934, pp. 18-19.

5"Troops Armed, Tempers Taut as Fatal Day Arrives," *Newsweek*, 12 January 1935, p. 15; Jack Fischer, "Election in the Saar," *The Nation*, 23 January 1935, p. 97.

6"Hitler and the Saar," *The Nation*, 9 January 1935, pp. 33-34; Dorothy Thompson, "Knox of the Saar," *The Reader's Digest*, January 1935, pp. 73-76.

7"Troops Armed, Tempers Taut as Fatal Day Arrives," *Newsweek*, 12 January 1935, p. 15; Jack Fischer, "Election in the Saar," *The Nation*, 23 January 1935, p. 97.

8*The New Republic*, 23 January 1935, p. 287; "Saar: Fifteen Years of Tension Reaches Climax in Quiet Vote; Blood Tells; Geneva Diplomats Have the Final Say," *Newsweek*, 19 January 1935, pp. 5-6.

9"Saar: Fifteen Years of Tension Reaches Climax in Quiet Vote; Blood Tells; Geneva Diplomats Have the Final Say," *Newsweek*, 19 January 1935, pp. 5-6; *The Nation*, 23 January 1935, p. 85; *The New Republic*, 23 January 1935, p. 287; "German Is the Saar!," *Time*, 21 January 1935, p. 27; "The League Awards Saar to Germany," *The Literary Digest*, 26 January 1935, p. 15.

10"Hitler, Elated Over Saar Victory, Looks Coyly at the League, Covetously at Memel," *Newsweek*, 26 January 1935, p. 11.

[11]"On to Rearmament," *Time*, 28 January 1935, p. 26; "Jews Out of Germany," *The New Republic*, 13 February 1935, p. 5; James K. Pollock, "The Saar Problem After the Plebiscite," *The Literary Digest*, 16 February 1935, p. 35.

[12]"Hitler, Elated Over Saar Victory, Looks Coyly at the League, Covetously at Memel," *Newsweek*, 26 January 1935, p. 11; Oswald G. Villard, "Hitler After the Saar," *The Nation*, 13 February 1935, p. 175; *The New Republic*, 27 February 1935, p. 56; "On to Rearmament," *Time*, 28 January 1935, p. 26.

[13]"Toasted Entente," *Time*, 14 January 1935, pp. 18-19; *The New Republic*, 16 January 1935, p. 260.

[14]"Downing Street Pact: Britain and France Offer to Treat Germans as an Equal If She Signs New 'Locarno' Plan," *Newsweek*, 9 February 1935, p. 5.

[15]"Gentleman's Peace," *Time*, 11 February 1935, p. 17; *The Nation*, 13 February 1935, p. 170; "Hitler Retires to Do Heavy Thinking on Peace Pact," *Newsweek* 16 February 1935, pp. 12-13.

[16]"Germany and the Anglo-French Bid," *The Literary Digest*, 16 February 1935, p. 14; "Pact Making," *Time*, 18 February 1935, p. 21.

[17]"Premier Mussolini Mobilized Reserves as a 'precaution' Against Attacks by Abyssinian Tribes," *Newsweek*, 16 February 1935, p. 12; "Negroes v. Blackshirts," *Time*, 25 February 1935, pp. 18-19; "Il Duce Demands Bare Heads; The Lion of Judah Demands Bayonetless Diplomacy," *Newsweek*, 23 February 1935, pp. 12-13.

[18]"Hitler Finds Pact Unpalatable, Blames 'Cooks,' " *Newsweek*, 23 February 1935, pp. 13-14; "Hitler to the Powers," *Time* 25 February 1935, p. 19; *The New Republic*, 27 February 1935, p. 57; cf. "Germany and the Anglo-French Bid," *The Literary Digest*, 16 February 1935, p. 14; "Germany for Safeguarding Peace," *The Literary Digest*, 23 February 1935, p. 16; *The Nation* 27 February 1935, p. 233.

[19]"Conversation Threat Improves Herr Hitler's 'Cold' " *Newsweek*, 16 March 1935, p. 15; "Blow for Blow," *Time*, 18 March 1935, p. 18; "Hitler's Famous Cold and Its Cure," *The Literary Digest*, 16 March 1935, p. 7; *The New Republic*, 20 March 1935, p. 143; *The Nation*, 6 March 1935, p. 262; *The Nation*, 20 March 1935, p. 318.

[20]"The Reich Returns to Conscript Army in Open Defiance of Versailles Treaty, But 'Exclusively for Defense,' " *Newsweek*, 23 March 1935, pp. 5-7; T.R. Ybarra, "Hitler Changes His Clothes," *Collier's*, 27 April 1935, pp. 12, 46-47.

[21]"Chains Broken!," *Time*, 25 March 1935, pp. 20-21.

[22]*The New Republic*, 27 March 1935, p. 169; "Europe's Tragedy: Act II," *The New Republic*, 27 March 1935, pp. 173-174.

[23]"Hitler Liquidates Versailles," *The Nation*, 27 March 1935, p. 348; "Adolf Hitler's Stroke at Versailles Stirs All Europe," *Newsweek*, 23 March 1935, p. 9.

[24]"Germany Scraps Warnings; War Fever Spreads; Britain Steps In; France Boosts Budget," *Newsweek*, 30 March 1935, pp. 12-14; *The Literary Digest*, 30 March 1935, pp. 9-10.

[25]"Berlin Mission," *Time*, 1 April 1935, pp. 18-19; "London Envoys Meet Frankness and Gloom in Berlin, 'Clarity' and Optimism in Moscow; Peace Dove Flutters," *Newsweek*, 4 April 1935, pp. 5-6.

[26]"Berlin Mission," *Time*, 1 April 1935, pp. 18-19; "London Envoys Meet Frankness and Gloom in Berlin, 'Clarity' and Optimism in Moscow; Peace Dove Flutters," *Newsweek*, 4 April 1935, pp. 5-6.

[27]*The New Republic*, 3 April 1935, p. 197; "Europe Must Choose," *The Nation*, 3 April 1935, p. 376; *The Literary Digest*, 6 April 1935, p. 9.

[28]"Slap in Germany's Face Threatens Peace; Pros and Antis Demonstrate on Frontiers," *Newsweek*, 6 April 1935, pp. 12-13; "Bleeding Frontiers," *Time*, 6 April 1935, pp. 19-21; "Memel: Europe's Most Acute Trouble Spot," *The Literary Digest*, 13 April 1935, p. 16.

29"Mr. Eden Makes Few Sales on Trip; Britain and France Fearful; Hitler Extends Offer," *Newsweek*, 13 April 1935, pp. 12-13; *The Literary Digest*, 13 April 1935, p. 11.

30"Danzig: Nazis Get Rude 59.9 Percent Majority Surprize," *Newsweek*, 13 April 1935, p. 15; "Danzig Is Danzig!," *Time*, 15 April 1935, pp. 20-21; *The Nation*, 17 April 1935, p. 430.

31"Castles of Illusion," *Time*, 15 April 1935, pp. 19-20.

32*The Nation*, 17 April 1935, p. 429; *The New Republic*, 17 April 1935, p. 267.

33"Mussolini Splurges as Host at Stresa; Britain, France, and Italians Chat Hopefully of Non-Aggression Pacts," *Newsweek*, 20 April 1935, pp. 5-6.

34*The Nation*, 17 April 1935, p. 429.

35"Island Diplomacy," *Time*, 22 April 1935, p. 19; *The Literary Digest*, 20 April 1935, p. 11; "Mussolini Splurges as Host at Stresa; Britain, France, and Italians Chat Hopefully of Non-Aggression Pacts," *Newsweek*, 20 April 1935, pp. 5-6.

36*The New Republic*, 24 April 1935, p. 295; "Good News From Stresa," *The Nation*, 24 April 1935, p. 468.

37"Superman!," *Time*, 29 April 1935, p. 15; "Three-Power Resolution Receives Nearly Unanimous Approval; Germany Refuses to Be Judged," *Newsweek*, 27 April 1935, pp. 12-13.

38"Superman!," *Time*, 29 April 1935, p. 15; "Three-Power Resolution Receives Nearly Unanimous Approval; Germany Refuses to Be Judged," *Newsweek*, 27 April 1935, pp. 12-13; *The New Republic*, 1 May 1935, p. 323.

39"Bear and Cock," *Time*, 13 May 1935, p. 15; "Important Fact," *Time*, 20 May 1935, p. 20; *The New Republic*, 29 May 1935, p. 55.

40Edward P. Bell, " 'Nobody in Germany Wants War'—Hitler," *The Literary Digest*, 11 May 1935, p. 11.

41"Rhetorical Retreat," *Time*, 3 June 1935, p. 21; "Hitler's Peace Bid Conciliatory Toward Everyone But Lithuania and the Bolshevists," *Newsweek*, 1 June 1935, pp. 12-13.

42"Hitler's Peace Bid Conciliatory Toward Everyone But Lithuania and the Bolshevists," *Newsweek*, 1 June 1935, pp. 12-13; "Rhetorical Retreat," *Time*, 3 June 1935, p. 21; "Current Opinion," *The Literary Digest*, 1 June 1935, p. 35; "Can Hitler Be Trusted?," *The Nation*, 5 June 1935, p. 645; *The New Republic*, 5 June 1935, p. 85.

43*The New Republic*, 8 May 1935, p. 351.

44"North Sea Nexus," *Time*, 24 June 1935, pp. 14-15.

45"Submarine Concessions to Reich Anger France and Italy; Eden Ladles Out Soothing Syrup," *Newsweek*, 29 June 1935, pp. 12-13; *The New Republic*, 3 July 1935, p. 205; cf. "One Way to Avoid War," *Time*, 1 July 1935, p. 15; "Anglo-German Naval Pact Stirs Acid and Oil Abroad," *The Literary Digest*, 26 June 1935, p. 12; "England Drops Europe," *Time*, 3 July 1935, p. 5.

46"North Sea Nexus," *Time*, 24 June 1935, pp. 14-15; "One Way to Avoid War," *Time*, 1 July 1935, p. 15.

47"July Off," *Time*, 1 July 1935, p. 18; "Where Is Hitler?," *Time*, 29 July 1935, p. 18; "Tokyo Reaches For Another Helping, Taking Key Province in North While Nanking Fears Either to Yield or to Fight," *Newsweek*, 22 June 1935, p. 5; "Odyssey and Hell-Hole," *Time*, 8 July 1935, p. 15; "Duce Prepares for an Abyssinian Harvest; France Still Bitter Over German Submarines," *Newsweek*, 6 July 1935, p. 11.

48Oswald G. Villard, "Hitler After the Saar," *The Nation*, 13 February 1935, p. 175.

49"Boycott: Berlin Commissar Admits Effectiveness of 'Useless' Movement," *Newsweek*, 9 March 1935, pp. 14-15; "New German Plea," *The Literary Digest*, 9 March 1935, p. 14; "Jews vs. Jews," *Time*, 11 March 1935, pp. 22-23.

50"World Pest," Time, 11 March 1935, p. 23.

[51]William Zukerman, "Anti-Semitism Revives in Germany," *The Nation*, 27 March 1935, p. 357.

[52]"War Odds," *Time*, 1 April 1935, p. 18.

[53]"Berlin Enjoys a Riotous 'Holiday'; Nazi Purges Take Minds Off Mounting Food Prices," *Newsweek*, 27 July 1935, p. 12 *The Nation*, 31 July 1935, p. 114.

[54]*The Literary Digest*, 27 July 1935, p. 11. *The Literary Digest* also attributed the attack to rising food prices; "Berlin Enjoys a Riotous 'Holiday'; Nazi Purges Takes Minds Off Mounting Food Prices," *Newsweek*, 27 July 1935, p. 12.

[55]"Nazi Reign of Terror Spreads to Socialists and Catholics; But Hitler Wavers After Strong American Reaction," *Newsweek*, 3 August 1935, pp. 3-4; T.R. Ybarra, "Jew-Baiter Number One," *Collier's*, 9 November 1935, pp. 9, 46-47, had the most extensive biography of Streicher in any American magazine.

[56]"Occult Forces," *Time*, 5 August 1935, pp. 14-15; "It All Happened in a Nazi Week," *The Literary Digest*, 3 August 1935, p. 12; "Bay State Rebukes Nazi Policy," *The Literary Digest*, 24 August 1935, p. 12.

[57]*Newsweek* identified the crowd only as "people"; *Time*, *The Nation*, and *The Literary Digest* identified them as "communists": "Nazi Reign of Terror Spreads to Socialists and Catholics; But Hitler Wavers After Strong American Reaction," *Newsweek*, 3 August 1935, p. 4; "Occult Forces," *Time*, 5 August 1935, p. 15; *The Nation*, 7 August 1935, pp. 145-156; "It All Happened in a Nazi Week," *The Literary Digest*, 3 August 1935, p. 12.

[58]"New York Magistrate Wages Private War on Reich," *Newsweek*, 14 September 1935, pp. 19-20.

[59]"Germany's Heavy Burden," *The Nation*, 7 August 1935, p. 145.

[60]"Schacht's Cautions: No Deviation From Task of Rearming, Even to Indulge Racial Prejudice," *Newsweek*, 10 August 1935, p. 15; cf. T.R. Ybarra, "Hitler's Paymaster," *Collier's*, 7 December 1935, pp. 23, 42; "Damned Dangerous," *Time*, 26 August 1935, p. 23; "Schact's Warning to Nazis," *The Literary Digest*, 31 August 1935, p. 13; *The Nation*, 4 September 1935, p. 253.

[61]"Schacht Cautions: No Deviation From Task of Rearming, Even to Indulge Racial Prejudice," *Newsweek*, 10 August 1935, p. 15; "Tar; Hair Dye," *Time*, 12 August 1935, p. 19; *The New Republic*, 14 August 1935, p. 1; "50,000 for Streicher," *Time*, 26 August 1935, p. 22; *The Nation*, 28 August 1935, p. 226, placed the number at 100,000.

[62]"Hitler Decrees Swastika Reich Flag; Bars Intermarriages; Relegates Jews to Dark Ages," *Newsweek*, 21 September 1935, pp. 12-13.

[63]"Little Man, Big Doings," *Time*, 23 September 1935, pp. 22-23; *The Nation*, 25 September 1935, pp. 337-338.

[64]"Hitler Decrees Swastika Reich Flag; Bars Intermarriages; Relegates Jews to Dark Ages," *Newsweek*, 21 September 1935, pp. 12-13.

[65]"Jews Begin to Feel a Soft Spot in the Iron Heel," *Newsweek*, 28 September 1935, p. 17.

[66]"Paradise for Blackmailers," *Time*, 28 November 1935, p. 28; "Army Wins Skirmish With Politicians Over Veterans," *Newsweek*, 28 December 1935, pp. 16-17; *The Nation*, 27 November 1935, p. 607.

[67]"Boycott the Olympics!," *The Nation*, 21 August 1935, p. 201.

[68]*The Nation*, 30 October 1935, p. 493; *The Nation*, 6 November 1935, p. 521.

[69]"America and the Olympics," *The New Republic*, 6 November 1935, pp. 357-358; *The New Republic*, 18 December 1935, p. 456.

[70]Oswald G. Villard, "Russia Aids the Jews," *The Nation*, 28 August 1935, p. 231.

[71]"Bishops and Dolls," *Time*, 2 December 1935, p. 20.

[72]"Bishops and Dolls," *Time*, 2 December 1935, p. 20.

[73]*The Nation*, 11 December 1935, p. 662.

[74]"Fearless Foe of Nazi Church Union," *The Literary Digest*, 23 March 1935, p. 18; "Chains Broken!," *Time*, 23 March 1935, pp. 20-21; "Christ Cleared," *Time*, 8 April 1935, p. 24; "No Alien Gods!," *Time*, 29 April 1935, p. 18.

[75]"Unchecked Pagan Put Hitler's Loyal Lutherans in Quandry; Bishop Rushes to rescue," *Newsweek*, 4 May 1935, p. 12; *The New Republic*, 8 May 1935, pp. 351-352.

[76]"Last Warnings!" *Time*, 8 April 1935, p. 24; "Nun Gets Five-Year Term for Paying Foreign Debts," *Newsweek*, 25 May 1935, p. 14; "Holy Smugglers," *Time*, 3 June 1935, p. 20.

[77]"Berlin Enjoys a Riotous 'Holiday,' Nazi Purges Takes Minds Off Mounting Food Prices," *Newsweek*, 27 July 1935, p. 12; "Where Is Hitler?," *Time*, 29 July 1935, p. 18; "Nazi Reign of Terror Spreads to Socialists and Catholics; But Hitler Wavers After Strong American Reaction," *Newsweek*, 3 August 1935, pp. 3-4.

[78]"Midsummer Ferment in Germany," *The Literary Digest*, 17 August 1935, p. 10; *The New Republic*, 14 August 1935, p. 1.

[79]Emil Lengyel, "The Catholic War on Hitler," *The Nation*, 6 November 1935, pp. 532-534.

[80]"Paganism Doesn't Pay as Well as Old-Time Religion," *Newsweek*, 9 November 1935, p. 16; "Twilight for Nazi Neopagans," *The Literary Digest*, 9 November 1935, p. 12.

[81]"Storm Over German Protestantism," *The Literary Digest*, 5 October 1935, p. 14; "Holy Ghost's Man," *Time*, 7 October 1935, p. 21.

[82]"Nazis Set Up Board of Lords Spiritual Drawn From Lukewarm Foes," *Newsweek*, 26 October 1935, pp. 16-17; "Loud Threats, Little Action, in Nazi Lutheran Fight," *Newsweek*, 14 December 1935, p. 18.

[83]"New In; Old Out," *Time*, 7 January 1935, p. 22; "Native and Foreigner," *Time*, 14 January 1935, p. 20; "New Justice," *Time*, 11 February 1935, pp. 18-19; "Holy Stupidity," *Time*, 22 April 1935, p. 24.

[84]Barbara S. Morgan, "Swastika," *The Atlantic Monthly*, February 1935, pp. 143-150.

[85]Bertrand Russell, "The Revolt Against Reason," *The Atlantic Monthly*, February 1935, pp. 221-232.

[86]Anne O'Hara McCormick, "Nationalism Wins Out," *The Saturday Evening Post*, 18 April 1935, pp. 27, 111-117.

[87]Frank H. Simonds, "From Crisis to Conversation," *Harper's* May 1935, pp. 680-688.

[88]Alfred Vagts, "The Reichswehr Over Europe," *Harper's*, September 1935, pp. 397-404.

[89]T.R. Ybarra, "Six Million Little Brownshirts," *Collier's*, 31 August 1935, pp. 18, 32.

[90]"Memel, Danger-Spot to Peace," *The Literary Digest*, 28 September 1935, p. 16; "Memel, and Nazi 'Push to East,' " *The Literary Digest*, 5 October 1935, p. 13; "Memel Vote Gives Germans an 80 Percent Victory," *Newsweek*, 19 October 1935, p. 16.

[91]"Great General Staff," *Time*, 28 October 1935, p. 19; "Happy Warriors," *Time*, 11 November 1935, p. 19.

[92]"Dares and Scares," *Time*, 20 January 1935, p. 19; war seemed to likely that the Hartford Insurance ran an advertisement headed "When War Comes," *Newsweek*, 25 January 1936, p. 26; "Britain's Rearmament Parliament," *The Literary Digest*, 15 February 1936, pp. 9-11.

[93]John Gunther, "Hitler," *Harper's*, January 1936, pp. 148-159.

[94]"Holy Land Becomes British Empire's Powder Keg as Jews Object to Arabs' 2-to-1 Control," *Newsweek*, 4 January 1936, p. 16.

[95]"Friendly But Firm," *Time*, 6 January 1936, p. 18; *The New Republic*, 8 January 1936, p. 239; *The New Republic*, 15 January 1936, p. 266.

[96]Ludwig Lewisohn, "Jews in Trouble," *The Atlantic Monthly*, January 1936, pp. 53-60; this article was condensed as "German Jewry's Poignant Plight," *The Literary Digest*, 11 January 1936, p. 18.

[97]Kurt Rosenfeld, "What Germany Does to the Jews," *The New Republic*, 15 January 1936, p. 276.

[98]"Maids, Hymns and Salesman," *Time*, 13 January 1936, p. 21; William Zukermann, "Where the German Ghetto Leads," *The Nation*, 5 February 1936, pp. 154-156.

[99]*The Nation*, 5 February 1936, p. 143; "Foreign Jews Invited to Finance Exile of Reich Jews," *Time* 11 January 1936, p. 21.

[100]"New Jewish Exodus Proposed," *The Literary Digest*, 18 January 1936, p. 17; "Foreign Jews Invited to Finance Exile of Reich Jews," 11 January 1936, p. 21; *The New Republic*, 12 February 1936, p. 2; *The New Republic*, 4 March 1936, p. 94.

[101]Raymond G. Carroll, "The Alien on Relief," *The Saturday Evening Post*, 1 January 1936, pp. 16-17, 100-103; Raymond G. Carroll, "Alien Workers in America," *The Saturday Evening Post*, 25 January 1936, pp. 23, 82-86, 89; Raymond G. Carroll, "Aliens in Subversive Activities," *The Saturday Evening Post*, 22 February 1936, pp. 10-11, 84-85, 88-90; Raymond G. Carroll, "American or Aliens First?," *The Saturday Evening Post*, 11 April 1935, pp. 8-9, 115-118, 120.

[102]"Again an Assassin's Pistol Makes Europe Shiver; the Nations Prepare for Next War; Morgan Acquits Himself of Last," *Newsweek*, 15 February 1936, pp. 7-9.

[103]"Holy Land Becomes British Empire's Powder Keg as Jews Object to Arab's 2-to-1 Control," *Newsweek*, 4 January 1936, p. 16; *The Nation*, 5 February 1936, p. 143; *The New Republic*, 12 February 1936, p. 2 and 4 March 1936, p. 94.

[104]"Again an Assassin's Pistol Makes Europe Shiver; the Nations Prepare for Next War; Morgan Acquits Himself of Last," *Newsweek*, 15 February 1936, pp. 7-9; "Jew Kills Nazi," *Time*, 17 February 1936, p. 15.

[105]"New Martyr," *Time*, 24 February 1936, p. 21.

[106]"Brown International," *The New Republic*, 21 August 1935, pp. 44-45; "Spread of Hitlerism," *The Nation*, 5 February 1936, pp. 156-157.

[107]"Swiss-German Crisis Intensified," *The Literary Digest*, 29 February 1936, p. 13.

[108]"Secret," *Time*, 6 January 1936, p. 9; "Bombs Better Than Butter to Help a Nation Grow," *Newsweek*, 25 January 1936, p. 27.

[109]"Rewards of Victory," *Time*, 17 February 1936, p. 15; "Germany's Drive to Regain Colonies," *The Literary Digest*, 22 February 1936, p. 13.

[110]Louis Fischer, "Austria Dams the Nazi Flood," *The Nation*, 26 February 1936, pp. 246-248; "Hitler Prepares," *The Nation*, 26 February 1936, p. 237; Louis Fischer, "Germany Prepares for War," *The Nation*, 11 March 1936, p. 311.

[111]"Tourists May Have to Help the Bankers Collect Their German Debts," *Newsweek*, 29 February 1936, p. 19.

[112]"New Moves on Europe's Chess Board," *The Literary Digest*, 8 February 1936, p. 12; "Frantic Diplomats Draft Rules for Changed Game," *Newsweek*, 14 March 1936, pp. 9-10; "Abominable Triumph," *Time*, 9 March 1936, pp. 19-21.

[113]"Hitler's Final Thrust at Versailles," *The Literary Digest*, 14 March 1936, pp. 12-13; "Bludgeons and Cookies," *Time*, 16 March 1936, pp. 25-26; "Hitler Marches an Army into the Rhineland, Tears Up Treaties, and Then Offers a New Pact of Non-Aggression," *Newsweek*, 14 March 1936, pp. 7-9.

[114]"Glorious Garrisons," *Time*, 16 March 1936, pp. 24-25; T.R. Ybarra, "Dusseldorf-Coblenz," *Collier's*, 23 May 1936, pp. 11, 63-64, was the only one to argue Rhinelanders were "torn between patriotism and dread"; "Frantic Diplomats Draft Rules for Changed Game," *Newsweek*, 14 March 1936, pp. 9-10.

[115]"Rupture," *Time*, 16 March 1936, pp. 22-23; "Seeking Solution of Rhineland Riddle," *The Literary Digest*, 21 March 1936, pp. 11-12; *The New Republic*, 1 April 1936, p. 205; "Germans Preferred," *Time*, 23 March 1936, pp. 25-26, asserted British

movie patrons cheered newsreels of German troops entering the Rhineland; "Fuehrer Wants Equality for Berlin; Paris Wants an Emasculated Reich; London Wants Peace— and a Lot of Arms," *Newsweek*, 21 March 1936, pp. 7-10.

[116]"Parliament Whiles Away the Silly Season with Whiskers and Wine," *Newsweek*, 14 March 1936, p. 19.

[117]"Seeking Solution of Rhineland Problem," *The Literary Digest*, 21 March 1936, pp. 11-12; "Rupture," *Time*, 21 March 1936, pp. 22-23; "Fuehrer Wants Equality for Berlin; Paris Wants an Emasculated Reich; London Wants Peace—and a Lot of Arms," *Newsweek*, 21 March 1936, pp. 7-10, attributed it to Eden's desire to accommodate Flandin.

[118]"A New Watch on the Rhineland," *The Nation*, 18 March 1936, pp. 335-336; "Will Europe Call Hitler's Bluff?," *The Nation*, 25 March 1936, pp. 368-369; "Has Hitler Won Out?," *The Nation*, 1 April 1936, p. 401; John Gunther, "The Rhineland Crisis," *The Nation*, 1 April 1936. pp. 407-408.

[119]"Does Hitler Mean Peace?," *The New Republic*, 18 March 1936, p. 152.

[120]Nathaniel Peffer, "Too Late for World Peace?," *Harper's*, June 1936, pp. 23-28.

[121]"Jury of Nations Finds the Reich Guilty, Outlines 'Suitable Measures,' Then Disperses," *Newsweek*, 28 March 1936, pp. 15-16.

[122]"Germans Preferred," *Time*, 23 March 1936, pp. 25-27; "Hitler Mends His Political Fences—An Admittedly Superfluous Job," *Newsweek*, 28 March 1936, p. 16.

[123]"Ja!," *Time*, 30 March 1936, pp. 24-25; "Hitler Speaks for 67,000,000," *The Literary Digest*, 4 April 1936, p. 12; cf. *The Nation* 8 April 1936, p. 333.

[124]"Best Mouths," *Time*, 30 March 1936, p. 28; "Hitler Speaks for 67,000,000," *The Literary Digest*, 4 April 1936, p. 12; "The Shape of Things," *The Nation* 8 April 1936, p. 333; *The New Republic*, 8 April 1936, p. 233.

[125]*The New Republic*, 8 April 1936, p. 234; "May God Help Us," *Time*, 6 April 1936, p. 25; *Time*, 13 April 1936, pp. 24-26, ran Hitler on its cover with the caption "Adolf Hitler, 99%."

[126]"Jews and Arabs Die, But Germans Spared 'for Hitler's Sake,' " *Newsweek*, 25 April 1936, pp. 14-15.

[127]"Bad for Business," *Time* 4 May 1936, p. 21; "Riotous Palestine," *The Literary Digest*, 2 May 1936, p. 13; "Arab Vengeance in Palestine; Politics in Egypt," *Newsweek*, 2 May 1936, p. 17; "King Fuad's Death Leaves Britain a Heritage of Woe Like One Left by Lawrence of Arabia," *Newsweek*, 9 May 1936, pp. 15-16.

[128]*The Nation*, 3 June 1936, p. 694.

[129]"Young Men With New Rifles Give Religious Uprising the Aspect of Revolution," *Newsweek*, 6 June 1936, pp. 13-14.

[130]"Near East Riots Spread, Vex Britain," *The Literary Digest*, 6 June 1936, pp. 12-13; "Arab vs. Jew," *The Literary Digest*, 20 June 1936, p. 16; "Arabian Knights Press Britain in New Crusade," *Newsweek*, 4 July 1936, p. 19; "Algerian Flare-up," *The Literary Digest*, 11 July 1936, p. 14.

[131]"Algerian Flare-Up," *The Literary Digest*, p. 14.

[132]"Britain's Curfew Brings Jews Ghetto Memories," *Newsweek*, 29 August 1936, p. 11.

[133]"Hammer Blows," *Time*, 14 September 1936, p. 19; "Again, Shopping Days," *Time*, 26 October 1936, p. 24.

[134]"King Opens the Mother of Parliaments With Words of Wisdom and Warnings; Arabs Rise Again," *Newsweek*, 14 November 1936, pp. 23-26.

[135]*The Nation*, 3 June 1936, m.p. 694; *The New Republic*, 3 June 1936, p. 85; "Young Men With New Rifles Give Religious Uprising the Aspect of Revolution," *Newsweek*, 6 June 1936, pp. 13-14; "Near East Riots Spread, Vex Britain," *The Literary Digest*, 6 June 1936, p. 12; "British Ask Who Foots Bills for Arab Unrest," *Newsweek*, 13 June 1936, pp. 16-17.

[136]Albert Viton, "Why Arabs Kill Jews," *The Nation*, 3 June 1936, pp. 708-710.

[137]Benjamin Stolberg, "The Jew and the World," *The Nation*, 17 June 1936, pp. 766-768.

[138]H.N. Brailford, *The New Republic*, "Storm Over Palestine," 1 July 1936, pp. 230-233.

[139]*The Nation*, 29 April 1936, p. 535; "Poland and Hungary Disturbed by Nazi Terrorist Groups," *The Literary Digest*, 13 June 1936, p. 13.

[140]Herbert J. Seligmann, "Anti-Semitism in Europe," *The New Republic*, 30 December 1936, pp. 265-268.

[141]Albert Viton, "Why Arabs Kill Jews," *The Nation*, 3 June 1936, pp. 708-710; Albert Viton, "A Solution for Palestine," *The Nation*, 26 December 1936, pp. 756-758.

[142]"Olympic Trials," *The Nation*, 18 July 1936, p. 62; "Nations Eye Each Other on Eve of 1936 Games," *Newsweek*, 1 August 1936, p. 20.

[143]Louis Gittler, "Death Takes a Holiday," *The Nation*, 1 August 1936, pp. 124-126; cf. "For Kissers, Death," *Time*, 31 August 1936, p. 18; *The Nation*, 8 August 1936, p. 142; Oswald G. Villard, "Issues and Men," *The Nation*, 15 August 1936, p. 185.

[144]*The New Republic*, 19 August 1936, pp. 30-31; "For Kissers, Death," *Time*, 31 August 1936, p. 18.

[145]"Old Heidelberg," *The Literary Digest*, 4 July 1936, pp. 11-12.

[146]*The Nation*, 11 July 1936, p. 30; *The New Republic*, 15 July 1936, p. 281; *The New Republic*, 28 October 1936, p. 237.

[147]"Kicked While Down," *Time*, 13 July 1936, pp. 17-18; "The Death Rattle of an Orphan and an Empire Provoke Racist Hootings, and Nazi Insults," *Newsweek*, 11 July 1936, pp. 15-16; "Thumber Home," *Time*, 20 July 1936, pp. 30-31; "Defiant Danziger," *The Literary Digest*, 18 July 1936, pp. 12-13; "Gone Fishing,"*Time*, 3 August 1936, p. 20.

[148]Henry C. Wolfe, "Danzig Under the Terror," *The Nation*, 17 October 1936, pp. 447-448.

[149]"Scrap of Paper," *The Literary Digest*, 25 July 1936, pp. 11-12; *Newsweek*, 8 August 1936, carried a cover showing Nazi warships at sea with the caption "Hitler's Ships-Waiting."

[150]"Berlin, Vienna Become Friends; Britain Snubbed Anew," *Newsweek*, 18 July 1936, pp. 22-23; "Might, Right and *de Facto*," *Time*, 3 August 1936, p. 15.

[151]"Business of Empire," *Time*, 20 July 1936, pp. 25-27; "Peace or War in Berlin-Vienna Pact?," *The Literary Digest*, 18 July 1936, p. 10.

[152]"Austria-Dictator's Pawn," *The New Republic*, 22 July 1936, pp. 309-310; "Farmers and Workers Rise Against Military Coup; Fascists Lose Ground in Nationwide Slaughter; Americans Flee," *Newsweek*, 1 August 1936, pp. 7-8; "Fascist and Red March in Spain," *The Literary Digest*, 1 August 1936, pp. 11-12.

[153]"High Wind Over Morocco Blows Battle Fumes Across Continent on 22nd Anniversary of War," *Newsweek*, 8 August 1936, pp. 17-18; "Battleships Steam into Civil War Spotlight; Powers Warn Both Sides After Shells Kill Foreigners," *Newsweek*, 15 August 1936, pp. 10-11.

[154]"Third Major War Scare in 12 Months Finds Powers Playing for Time, Testing Arms; British Guns Police Straits," *Newsweek*, 29 August 1936, pp. 7-9; "Battleships Steam into Civil War Spotlight; Powers Warn Both Sides After Shells Kill Foreigners," *Newsweek*, 15 August 1936, pp. 10-11.

[155]"Drunken Dictators," *The Nation*, 8 August 1936, pp. 144-145; H.N. Brailford, "The Trick of Neutrality," *The New Republic*, 23 September 1936, pp. 174-176.

[156]H.N. Brailford, "The Trick of Neutrality," *The New Republic*, 23 September 1936, pp. 174-176; *The Nation*, 3 October 1936, pp. 377-378.

157"Moscow Uses Civil War as Level to Raise Prestige in Western Europe, Causing Scare; Madrid Evacuates Children," *Newsweek*, 17 October 1936, pp. 7-9; *The New Republic*, 11 November 1936, p. 30.

158"26 Nations Rebuke Moscow on Spain, Absolving Italy; Baldwin Deplores Soviet 'Fanatics,' " *Newsweek*, 7 November 1936, pp. 17-18; "Mussolini, Hitler Form Anti-Red Front; Portugal Breaks with Spain; Franco Wins 'Key City,' " *Newsweek*, 31 October 1936, pp. 14-15.

159"Dictator's 'Five Points,' " *Time*, 2 November 1936, pp. 15-16; "One More Versailles Restriction Goes Down River," *Newsweek*, 21 November 1936, p. 18; *The New Republic*, 25 November 1936, p. 93.

160"Nov. 18: Day of Ignominy, Recognition, Prayer; Eden Loses His Temper But Sticks by Determination to Avert War," *Newsweek*, 28 November 1936, pp. 7-9; "Communists Challenged," *Time*, 30 November 1936, p. 17.

161*The New Republic*, 2 December 1936, p. 127.

162"Fuehrer's Crusade," *Time*, 7 December 1936, pp. 18-19.

163"New 'Holy Alliance' Rouses Communist Fury; Statesmen Talk of War, Count Guns and Planes, Ask for More," *Newsweek*, 5 December 1936, pp. 7-8.

164"Fuehrer's Crusade," *Time*, 7 December 1936, pp. 18-19.

165"Fate of a Monarch, Course of an Empire, Destiny of One-Half Billion Souls Depend on Mrs. Simpson of Baltimore," *Newsweek*, 12 December 1936, pp. 7-8; "Edvardus Rex," *Time*, 14 December 1936, pp. 16-18.

166"The Fascist Front," *The Nation*, 5 December 1936, p. 649; "The Fascist Alliance," *The New Republic*, 9 December 1936, pp. 159-160.

167"Nazi Morale Begins to Crack," *The New Republic*, 30 December 1936, pp. 257-259.

168"Controversy Rages Over Colonies," *The Literary Digest*, 24 October 1936, pp. 13-14; "Number 2 Nazi Eats Less Butter Demands Colonies," *Newsweek*, 7 November 1936, p. 19; "Snooks Cocked," *Time*, 23 November 1936, pp. 22-23; "Nazis Blame Lack of Colonies for Fat Shortage," *Newsweek*, 26 December 1936, pp. 10-11.

169"Fuehrer's Crusade," *Time*, 7 December 1936, pp. 18- 19.

170"Rattling Sabers," *The Literary Digest*, 19 September 1936, pp. 14-15; "Hitler Looks East," *The New Republic*, 23 September 1936, pp. 171-172.

Chapter IV

1"Man on Mountain Makes World Hold Its Breath; Hitler Balances Franco's Salvation and the Peace of Europe," *Newsweek*, 2 January 1937, p. 7; "Hitler's Decision," *The New Republic*, 6 January 1937, pp. 287-288; "Europe Prepares for Another Fuehrer Week End," *Newsweek*, 30 January 1937, p. 17; this had been announced earlier but had not been mentioned due to the press of news coverage of other events. "Saturday Surprise," *Time*, 2 February 1937, pp. 21-22.

2"Hitler's Tangled Web," *The Nation*, 2 January 1937, pp. 4-5.

3"Santa Brings Naziland Food Shortage and Synthetic Goods, Housewives Must Hoard Crusts," *Newsweek*, 2 January 1937, p. 8; "Hitler's Tangled Web," *The Nation*, 2 January 1937, pp. 4-5; "Man on Mountain Makes World Hold Its Breath; Hitler Balances Franco's Salvation and the Peace of Europe," *Newsweek*, 2 January 1937, p. 7.

4Wilson Woodside, "Germany's Hidden Crisis," *Harper's Monthly*, February 1937, pp. 315-325; "Hitler's Decision," *The New Republic*, 6 January 1937, pp. 287-288.

5"Hitler's Tangled Web," 2 January 1937, pp. 4-5.

6"Man on Mountain Makes World Hold Its Breath; Hitler Balances Franco's Salvation and the Peace of Europe," *Newsweek*, 2 January 1937, p. 7.

7"Fascist Eagle and British Lion," *Time*, 12 January 1937, pp. 20-21.

8*The New Republic*, 13 January 1937, p. 311.

[9]"Fascist Eagle and British Lion," *Time*, 11 January 1937, pp. 20-21.

[10]Sir Arthur Willert, "England's Duty," *The Atlantic Monthly*, January 1937, pp. 96-104.

[11]John Gunther, "Britain Returns to Arms," *The Saturday Evening Post*, 30 January 1937, pp. 8-9, 77-78, 80-81, 84.

[12]"Hitler's Tangled Web," *The Nation*, 2 January 1937, pp. 4-5.

[13]"War Cloud From Moroccan Hills Overshadows Battle of the 'Volunteers' in Spain," *Newsweek*, 16 January 1937, pp. 13-14.

[14]"Little World War," *Time*, 18 January 1937, pp. 20-21; "Bumping Off Parties," *Time*, 18 January 1937, pp. 22-23; "The Moroccan Crisis," *The New Republic*, 20 January 1937, pp. 341-342; "Moroccan Front," *The Nation*, 16 January 1937, p. 60.

[15]"Fuehrer Settles 'Crises' in Two Minutes While Assistant Argues With Duce for Days," *Newsweek*, 23 January 1937, pp. 14-15; "Hitler Reassures France in Crisis," *The Literary Digest*, 23 January 1937, p. 10; "Little World War," *Time*, 18 January 1937, pp. 20-21.

[16]"Fuehrer Settles 'Crisis' in Two Minutes While Assistant Argues With Duce for Days," *Newsweek*, 23 January 1937, pp. 14-15; "Butter v. Might," *Time*, 25 January 1937, p. 15.

[17]"War Cloud From Moroccan Hills Overshadows Battle of the 'Volunteers' in Spain," *Newsweek*, 16 January 1937, pp. 13-14; "Butter v. Might," *Time*, 25 January 1937, p. 15.

[18]"Fuehrer Settles 'Crisis' in Two Minutes While Assistant Argues With Duce for Days," *Newsweek*, 23 January 1937, pp. 14-15.

[19]"Saturday Surprise," *Time*, 8 February 1937, pp. 21-22.

[20]"Reich Chief Summarizes Nazi Progress, Upholds Honor, Is Conciliatory," *The Literary Digest*, 6 February 1937, p. 14; "Saturday Surprise," *Time*, 8 February 1937, pp. 21-22.

[21]"Hitler Reviews 4 Year's Struggle, Offers to Cooperate With All Nations Save Russia," *Newsweek*, 6 February 1937, pp. 13-14.

[22]*The New Republic*, 10 February 1937, pp. 1-2; *The Nation*, 6 February 1937, p. 141.

[23]Henry C. Wolfe, "Hitler Looks Eastward," *The Atlantic Monthly*, February 1937, pp. 239-246; Henry C. Wolfe, "Fascism Charts Its Course," *The Nation*, 2 January 1937, pp. 16-17.

[24]"Butter v. Might," *Time*, 25 January 1937, p. 15.

[25]"Ambassador No. 1," *Time*, 15 February 1937, pp. 23-24.

[26]"Duce's Forces Overshadow Hitler's in Spain; Britain Gives Ribbentrop a $2,000,000,000 Rearmament Shock," *Newsweek*, 20 February 1937, pp. 7-8.

[27]"Powers Confine War to Spain as Britain Matches Reich's Billions for Next Battle," *Newsweek*, 27 February 1937, pp. 13-14.

[28]"The Powers Finally Agree to Put Ring Around War-Torn Spain," *The Literary Digest* 6 March 1937, p. 13.

[29]"Powers Confine War to Spain as Britain Matches Reich's Billions for Next Battled," *Newsweek*, 27 February 1937, pp. 13-14; "Peace-Loving Powers Put the War in a Steel Cage; 'Mussolini's Moors' Arrive in Time to Improve the Big Show," *Newsweek*, 20 March 1937, pp. 7-9.

[30]"Stars and Stripes and Bourbon," *Time*, 28 February 1937, pp. 18-19; cf. *The New Republic*, 23 June 1937, pp. 173-174; "Powers Confine the War to Spain as Britain Matches Reich's Billions for Next Battled," *Newsweek*, 27 February 1937, pp. 13-14.

[31]"No. 1," *Time*, 1 March 1937, p. 18; "Cash and No. 2," *Time*, 1 March 1937, p. 18; "No. 3's No. 4," *Time*, 1 March 1937, pp. 18-19; "God and No. 7," *Time*, 1 March 1937, p. 19; "Just Folks," *Time*, 1 March 1937, p. 19.

[32]"La Guardia Suggests Putting Hitler in Horror Chamber; Reich Wants Madhouse for Mayor," *Newsweek*, 13 March 1937, pp. 16-17.

[33]"May La Guardia's Gibe at Hitler Stirs German Vituperation," *The Literary Digest*, 13 March 1937, p. 13; "Nazi Epithets at U.S. Set New High," *The Literary Digest*, 20 March 1937, pp. 3-4.

[34]"Jingles and Jangles Enliven Nazi Week," *Newsweek*, 20 March 1937, pp. 10-11.

[35]"Nazi Epithets at U.S. Set New High," *The Literary Digest*, 20 March 1937, pp. 3-4.

[36]"Envoy Misses Train for Persons in Low Standing," *Newsweek*, 27 March 1937, p. 16.

[37]"Envoy Misses Train for Persons in Low Standing," *Newsweek*, 27 March 1937, p. 16; "New Under-Secretary Receives Heritage of Trouble," *Newsweek*, 3 April 1937, pp. 16-17.

[38]E. B. Ashton, "The New Ambassador," *The Nation*, 5 June 1937, pp. 642-643.

[39]"Hard Future Looms for Fuehrer on 48th Birthday," *Newsweek*, 24 April 1937, pp. 16-17.

[40]"Jingles and Jangles Enliven Nazi Week; Benjamin Franklin Turns Tables on Fascist Forgers," *Newsweek*, 20 March 1937, pp. 10-11; "Nazi Epithets at U.S. Set New High," *The Literary Digest*, 20 March 1937, pp. 3-4; *The New Republic*, 24 March 1937, p. 193.

[41]"Career of Nazi Court Jester Comes to Sad End With Joke on Him," *Newsweek*, 20 March 1937, pp. 10-11; "A Man of Breeding Avoids Meeting His 'Friends,' " *Newsweek*, 21 August 1937, p. 19; cf. "Every Word," *Time*, 12 September 1937, p. 14.

[42]"Undoing of Leni," *Time*, 21 June 1937, p. 23; "Hitler and Mussolini," *Newsweek*, 4 October 1937, pp. 11-14.

[43]"Gospel According to Saint Hitler," *Time*, 25 January 1937, p. 20.

[44]"Hero to Jailbird," *Time*, 28 February 1937, p. 18; "Bernstein Tried," *Time*, 29 November 1937, pp. 20-21.

[45]"Hitler vs. Everybody," *Time*, 3 May 1937, p. 21.

[46]Ralph Thurston, "Hitler Mobilizes 'Mother Goose,' " *The Nation*, 20 March 1937, pp. 317-318; this article was reprinted in *The Reader's Digest*, June 1937, pp. 47-48.

[47]"Aryanisms," *Time*, 30 August 1937, p. 17.

[48]Philip S. Bernstein, "The Fate of German Jews," 23 October 1937, pp. 423-425.

[49]"World's Refugee's Costly to France," *The Literary Digest*, 6 February 1937, pp. 10-11.

[50]"Polish Jews Face Dismal Future," *The Literary Digest*, 20 February 1937, p. 11.

[51]*The Nation*, 22 May 1937, p. 578.

[52]"Fascist Eagle and British Lion," *Time*, 11 January 1937, pp. 20-21; "Loyal Groups Wonder at Mussolini's Attitude, Following Nazi Accord," *The Literary Digest*, 6 February 1937, pp. 11-12.

[53]"Antisemitism? It Could Happen Here," *The Literary Digest*, 5 June 1937, pp. 13-14.

[54]"American Scholars and Gottingen," *The New Republic*, 28 April 1937, p. 346; "Vacant Chairs at Gottingen," *The Literary Digest*, 26 June 1937, pp. 10-11; *The Nation*, 15 May 1937, p. 551; Thomas Mann, "I Accuse the Hitler Regime," *The Nation*, 6 March 1937, pp. 259-261; reprinted in *The Reader's Digest*, July 1937, pp. 84-86.

[55]"No Brown-Shirt Armies!," *The Nation*, 20 March 1937, p. 312; Ludwig Lore, "What Are the American Nazis Doing?," *The Nation*, 5 June 1937, pp. 636-637.

[56]Photo caption, "Germany in America," *Newsweek*, 31 July 1937, p. 8; photo caption, "German-American Day," *Newsweek*, 13 September 1937, p. 11.

[57]"Italy and Germany in America," *The New Republic*, 22 September 1937, pp. 173-174; "Nazi Challenge to American Labor," *The Nation*, 22 September 1937, p. 310.

[58]Joseph F. Dinneen, "Those Nazi Americans," *The Reader's Digest*, October 1937, pp. 10-13.

[59]"Hitler Indicted: The Vatican Charges Nazi With Failure to Keep Concordat," *The Literary Digest*, 3 April 1937, pp. 13-14.

[60]"New Under-Secretary Receives Heritage of Trouble," *Newsweek*, 3 April 1937, pp. 16-17; cf. *The New Republic*, 31 March 1937, p. 221; *The New Republic*, 7 April 1937, p. 249; *The Nation*, 27 March 1937, p. 338.

[61]"Hard Future Looms for Fuehrer on 48th Birthday," *Newsweek*, 24 April 1937, pp. 16-17.

[62]"Hitler Indicted: The Vatican Charges Nazi With Failure to Keep Concordat," *The Literary Digest*, 3 April 1937, pp. 13-14.

[63]"Heathen; and Hitler," *Time*, 12 April 1937, p. 23.

[64]"Holy War," *Time*, 31 May 1937, p. 23; cf. *The Nation*, 29 May 1937, pp. 606-607.

[65]"Hitler Threatens Catholic Church, Which Bismarck Failed to Vanquish," *The Literary Digest*, 19 June 1937, p. 12.

[66]"Caesar Battles Peter as in the Iron Chancellor's Days," *Newsweek*, 19 June 1937, pp. 15-16.

[67]*The New Republic*, 30 June 1937, p. 203.

[68]" 'Happy' Nazis Sadden Pontiff and a Submarine Pastor," *Newsweek*, 3 July 1937, p. 7.

[69]*The Nation*, 14 August 1937, pp. 162-163.

[70]Paul Hutchinson, "The Strange Case of Pastor Niemoeller," *The Atlantic Monthly*, October 1937, pp. 514-520.

[71]"Bombs 'Fall' in Britain, Explode on Nazi Pocket Warship," *Newsweek*, 5 June 1937, pp. 16-18.

[72]"Eden Casts Bread on Germany's Waters; Dirges Accompany Little World War's Worst Crisis," *Newsweek*, 12 June 1937, pp. 5-6; "The New Crisis in Spain," *The Nation*, 5 June 1937, p. 637.

[73]"Diplomacy to the Rescue," *Newsweek*, 12 June 1937, pp. 7-8; "Son of Chamberlain Makes Good; Dame Lucy Still Sniffs at Her Grace, Wallis," *Newsweek*, 5 June 1937, pp. 15-16.

[74]"Diplomacy to the Rescue," *Newsweek*, 12 June 1937, pp. 7-8; "Pro-Fascist Neutrality," *The Nation*, 9 January 1937, pp. 33-34.

[75]"Tantrums into Triumphs?," *Time*, 5 July 1937, pp. 14-15.

[76]" 'Avalanche' Threatens Europe on 18th Anniversary of Versailles Treaty," *Newsweek*, 3 July 1937, pp. 13-15; "Tantrums into Triumphs?," *Time*, 5 July 1937, pp. 14-15; "Europe Nears Zero Hours," *The New Republic*, 7 July 1937, pp. 237-238.

[77]"Tantrums into Triumphs?," *Time*, 5 July 1937, pp. 14-15.

[78]"King Opens the Mother of Parliaments With Words of Wisdom and Warning; Arabs Rise Again," *Newsweek*, 14 November 1936, pp. 23-26.

[79]"Concessions Made to Near East Christians, Jews by Muslim Overlords," *The Literary Digest*, 20 February 1937, pp. 12-13.

[80]"Britain Revives Old Policy of Divide and Rule," *Newsweek*, 10 July 1937, pp. 18-19; "Into Three Parts?," *Time*, 12 July 1937, p. 23; "The Partition of Palestine," *The New Republic*, 21 July 1937, p. 292.

[81]"Might Again Makes Right-Jews, Arabs Divided and Told to Like it," *Newsweek*, 17 July 1937, pp. 12-13; "Mandate Unscrambled," *Time*, 19 July 1937, pp. 16-17; "The Partition of Palestine," *The New Republic*, 21 July 1937, p. 292.

[82]"Into Three Parts?," *Time*, 12 July 1937, p. 23; "Mandate Unscrambled," *Time*, 19 July 1937, pp. 16-17.

[83]Philip S. Bernstein, "Promise of Zionism," *The Nation*, 2 January 1937, p. 12-15.

[84]"Stubborn Facts in Palestine," *The Nation*, 2 January 1937, p. 6.

[85]"Palestine Is Divided," *The Nation*, 17 July 1937, pp. 61-62; "Mandate Unscrambled," *Time*, 19 July 1937, pp. 16-17.

[86]Herbert Solow, "Zionism in Extremis," 31 July 1937, pp. 125-126.

[87]"Near East: Palestine," *Newsweek*, 21 August 1937, p. 18; "300 Alphs," *Time*, 23 August 1937, p. 17.

[88]Pierre Crabites, "Storm Rising in Palestine," *The Atlantic Monthly*, July 1937, pp. 101-107.

[89]H. N. Brailsford, "Should Palestine Be Divided?," *The New Republic*, 1 September 1937, pp. 97-99.

[90]"Arab Terrorists Finally Draw British Wrath," *Newsweek*, 11 October 1937, p. 22.

[91]*The Nation*, 23 October 1937, p. 419; "Holy Land," *Newsweek*, 25 October 1937, pp. 17-18.

[92]"Who Are the Terrorists Who Are Now Paralyzing Palestine?," *Newsweek*, 1 November 1937, pp. 15-16; photo caption, "Palestine," *Newsweek*, 22 November 1937, p. 23.

[93]"Acre Justice," *Time*, 6 December 1937, pp. 22-23; Philip S. Bernstein, "Pogroms or Partition," *The Nation*, 4 December 1937, pp. 607-609.

[94]Bruce Bliven, "Thank You, Hitler," *The New Republic*, 10 November 1937, pp. 11-12.

[95]Herbert J. Seligmann, "Jewish Faith—Christian Civilization," *The New Republic*, 8 December 1937, pp. 123-126.

[96]Ernest K. Lindley, "Can Eight Billion Dollars Stay Neutral?," *The Saturday Evening Post*, 13 February 1937, pp. 8-9.

[97]Henry Cabot Lodge, Jr., "Cutting the Cables," *The Saturday Evening Post*, 1 May 1937, pp. 23, 64, 66-67.

[98]"America Condemns Japan as an Aggressor State—President Roosevelt Finds Civilization in Danger," *Newsweek*, 18 October 1937, pp. 9-11; *Time*, 25 October 1937, p. 18, for initial box.

[99]T.R. Ybarra, "Next to Hitler," *Collier's*, 2 January 1937, pp. 15, 42-43; T. R. Ybarra, "Ace With Nine Lives," *Collier's*, 13 February 1937, pp. 22, 52-53; T.R. Ybarra, "Hitler on High," *Collier's*, 4 September 1937, pp. 21-22.

[100]"Mussolini Provides Experts With a Chess Puzzle," *Newsweek*, 1 May 1937, pp. 16-17.

[101]"Hand-Shakes," *The Literary Digest*, 15 July 1937, pp. 9-10.

[102]"Big Egg?," *Time*, 10 May 1937, p. 19.

[103]Henry C. Wolfe, "Czechoslovakia: Another Spain?," *The New Republic*, 14 April 1937, pp. 283-284; "Mussolini Provides Experts With Chess Puzzle," *Newsweek*, 1 May 1937, pp. 16-17.

[104]George Slocombe, "Europe's Next Battleground," *The Saturday Evening Post*, 24 July 1937, pp. 8-9, 57-58, 60.

[105]Robert Dell, "The Struggle for Czechoslovakia," *The Nation*, 29 May 1937, pp. 611-613.

[106]Elmer Davis, "Czechoslovakia: Bridge or Barricade," *Harper's*, June 1937, pp. 84-93.

[107]Willson Woodside, "The Odds Against Germany," *Harper's*, July 1937, pp. 207-214.

[108]"Genius of British Foreign Office Solves Puzzles—But the War Goes On," *Newsweek*, 31 July 1937, pp. 11-12.

[109]"Robert Vansittart, Europe's Arbiter," *The Nation*, 24 July 1937, pp. 93-95.

[110]"Ebbut, Langen, Putzi," *Time*, 23 August 1937, p. 16.

[111]"Thunderer Regrets Lack of 'Civilized Courtesies,' " *Newsweek*, 21 August 1937, pp. 19-20; "Every Word," *Time*, 12 September 1937, p. 14.

[112]"Submerged Pirates," *Time*, 12 September 1937, pp. 14-15.

[113]Sir Arthur Willett, "The Distempers of Europe," *The Atlantic Monthly*, September 1937, pp. 374-381.

[114]"Imperial Grandeur Crowns Career of Former Socialist in Visit to Brother Ruler," *Newsweek*, 27 September 1937, pp. 7-10; "Strong Peace," *Time*, 4 October 1937, pp. 20-21.

[115]"The Dictator's Meet," *The Nation*, 2 October 1937, pp. 336-377; "Hitler and Mussolini Put Their Heads Together," *Newsweek*, 4 October 1937, pp. 11-14.

[116]"Fuehrer and Duce Stage a Much Ado About—What?," *Newsweek*, 11 October 1937, pp. 21-22; $1,000,000 Bid," *Time*, 11 October 1937, pp. 23-24.

[117]"Chancelleries," *Newsweek*, 22 November 1937, pp. 27-28; "The Dictator's Meet," *The New Republic*, 6 October 1937, p. 225.

[118]"Mussolini Offers a New Axis," *The New Republic*, 6 October 1937, p. 225.

[119]"Contrasting Portraits of the Two Dictators," *The Reader's Digest*, December 1937, pp. 49-51.

[120]"The Windsors," *Newsweek*, 11 October 1937, pp. 22-23; "Windsors in Naziland," *Time*, 25 October 1937, pp. 20-21; "The Windsors" *Newsweek*, 1 November 1937, pp. 19-20.

[121]"Fuehrer and Duce Stage a Much Ado About—What?," *Newsweek*, 11 October 1937, pp. 21-22; "Duce Continues Spanish War on the Front and in London But Fuehrer Offers Pledge to Belgium, Peace for Spain," *Newsweek*, 25 October 1937, pp. 16-17.

[122]Bruce Bliven, "The Second World War Is Here," *The New Republic*, 6 October 1937, pp. 231-233; H.N. Brailsford, "Europe's Power Politics," *The New Republic*, 20 October 1937, pp. 290-292

[123]"Dictators," *Newsweek*, 1 November 1937, pp. 17-18; Henry C. Wolfe, "Nazi Eyes Turn East," *The Nation*, 6 November 1937, pp. 502-504.

[124]"Chancelleries," *Newsweek*, 22 November 1937, pp. 27-28; Robert Dell, "Hitler and Halifax," *The Nation*, 18 December 1937, pp. 685-687; "Hitler Touches Wood," *Time*, 29 November 1937, pp. 18-19.

[125]"Head Hunters," *Newsweek*, 29 November 1937, pp. 21-22; "Hitler Touches Wood," *Time*, 29 November 1937, pp. 18-19.

[126]"Nobel and Nazis," *Time*, 29 November 1937, p. 19.

[127]H.N. Brailsford, "Britain Approaches the Fuehrer," *The New Republic*, 22 December 1937, pp. 190-192; "Bribing Germany To Be Good," *The New Republic*, 8 December 1937, p. 113.

[128]*The Nation*, 4 December 1937, p. 601; "Bounty for Aggressors," *The Nation*, 11 December 1937, pp. 633-634.

[129]Girard Shaput, "What's Wrong With France?," *The Saturday Evening Post*, 18 September 1937, pp. 16-17; 104-105.

[130]John C. DeWilde, "Dr. Schacht and Germany's Future," *The Nation*, 16 October 1937, pp. 202-204.

[131]"Italy at Last Quits League; Democracies Speed Defense," *Newsweek*, 20 December 1937, pp. 18-19; "Traveling Diplomat," *Time*, 20 December 1937, p. 16.

Chapter V

[1]"Palestine," *Newsweek*, 3 January 1938, p. 21; "Wahib the Crooner," *Newsweek*, 17 January 1938, p. 21.

[2]"Nice for Nazis," *Newsweek*, 3 January 1938, pp. 17-18; "God, King and Nation," *Time*, 10 January 1938, pp. 19-20.

[3]"Fascism Comes to Rumania," *The New Republic*, 12 January 1938, pp. 265-266; "Not Rabid," *Time*, 17 January 1938, pp. 26-27.

[4]"Impudent," *Time*, 24 January 1938, p. 16; *The Nation*, 29 January 1938, p. 115; "Rumania's Fascist Pattern," *The New Republic*, 2 February 1938, pp. 350-351; "Rumania and Jews," *Newsweek*, 31 January 1938, pp. 20-21.

[5]"Bloodsucker of the Villages," *Time*, 31 January 1938, p. 17.

[6]*The Nation*, 22 January 1938, p. 87.

[7]"Hebrew Farms," *Time*, 31 January 1938, pp. 17-18; "Hebrew Fur," *Time*, 31 January 1938, p. 17.

[8]"Rumania and Jews," *Newsweek*, 31 January 1938, pp. 20-21; "Bernstein Lines," *Newsweek*, 17 January 1938, p. 22; "Egotistical Bernstein," *Time*, 17 January 1938, pp. 25-26; "Strike for Streicher," *Newsweek*, 7 February 1938, p. 19.

[9]"Pius XI vs. Nazis," *Newsweek*, 3 January 1938, p. 21; "Pagan Night," *Newsweek*, 27 December 1937, p. 23.

[10]"Congress Toil," *Newsweek*, 17 January 1938, p. 12; "Big Navy," *Newsweek*, 10 January 1938, pp. 11-12.

[11]Thomas A. Beck, "Billions for Defense," *Collier's*, 19 February 1938, p. 66; Thomas A. Beck, "Two Oceans to the Good," *Collier's*, 23 April 1938, p. 78; Thomas A. Beck, "Blueprint of a Dictator," *Collier's*, 30 April 1938, p. 78.

[12]George F. Elliot, "We Love a Crusade," *The Saturday Evening Post*, 5 February 1938, pp. 23, 59, 61-62, 64; Stanley High, "Peace, Inc.," *The Saturday Evening Post*, 5 February 1938, pp. 9-10, 89-90.

[13]Wesley W. Stout, "The Case for Isolation," *The Saturday Evening Post*, 23 April 1938, p. 22.

[14]Elmer Davis, "We Lose the Next War," *Harper's*, March 1938, pp. 337-348.

[15]H. Herring, "Where Are You Going, Mr. President?," *Harper's*, May 1938, pp. 562-564.

[16]Will Durant, "No Hymns of Hatred," *The Saturday Evening Post*, 4 June 1938, pp. 23, 48-49, 51-52.

[17]Oswald G. Villard, "Issues and Men," *The Nation*, 9 July 1938, p. 18.

[18]"London-Paris Axle: Harmony Counterbalances Fascist 'Axis,' " *Newsweek*, 3 January 1938, p. 20.

[19]Robert Dell, "Can Hitler Be Bought?," *The Nation*, 8 January 1938, pp. 35-37.

[20]"Vansittart and Honors," *Time*, 10 January 1938, pp. 18-19; "Statesmen vs. Thunderer," *Time*, 24 January 1938, pp. 15-16.

[21]"The Fall of France's Popular Front," *The Nation*, 22 January 1938, p. 88; "France" Strikes, Money Chaos Undermine the Popular Front," *Newsweek*, 24 January 1938, pp. 18-19; "French Compromise," *Newsweek*, 31 January 1938, pp. 19-20.

[22]"Hitler Baffles the World Anew: Bloodless Purge Scares Europe," *Newsweek*, 14 February 1938, pp. 9-10; "Purge No. 2," *Time*, 14 February 1938, pp. 18-19.

[23]"Purge in the Reich," *The Nation*, 12 February 1938, p. 172; "Behind the Nazi Purge," *The New Republic*, 16 February 1938, p. 33.

[24]Leonard Carlton, "Silencing Germany's Generals," *The New Republic*, 23 February 1938, pp. 66-68; *The Nation*, 19 February 1938, pp. 197-198.

[25]"More German Slight of Hand: Army, Church, and Diplomacy," *Newsweek*, 21 February 1938, pp. 16-17; "Adam's Apples," *Time*, 21 February 1938, p. 27; "European Jig-Saw," *The Nation*, 19 February 1938, pp. 199-200; "New Alignments in Europe," *The New Republic*, 23 February 1938, p. 57.

[26]"European Jig-Saw," *The Nation*, 19 February 1938, pp. 199-200; "Rumania," *Newsweek*, 21 February 1938, pp. 17-18; "Dynamite," *Time*, 21 February 1938, pp. 25-27; cf. "More German Slight of Hand: Church, Army, and Diplomacy," *Newsweek*, 21 February 1938, pp. 16-17.

[27]"Italy," *Newsweek*, 21 February 1938, p. 18.

[28]"Britain," *Newsweek*, 21 February 1938, p. 18; "Big Deal," *Time*, 21 February 1938, p. 25; cf. "New Alignments in Europe," *The New Republic*, 23 February 1938, p. 57.

[29]"Hitler Poses as Europe's Master, Foreshadows a Greater Reich," *Newsweek*, 28 February 1938, pp. 9-10; "Windows Opened," *Time* 28 February 1938, p. 19; "Hitler Poses as Europe's Master, Foreshadows a Greater Reich," *Newsweek*, 28 February 1938, pp. 9-10.

[30]"Windows Opened," *Time*, 28 February 1938, p. 19; "Czechoslovakia," *Newsweek*, 28 February 1938, p. 10.

[31]"Give Us Colonies!!," *Time*, 28 February 1938, p. 21; "England Shows Her Colors," *The New Republic*, 2 March 1938, pp. 87-88.

[32]"British Crisis," *Newsweek*, 28 February 1938, pp. 10-11; "Expulsion of Eden," *Time*, 28 February 1938, pp. 22-23; "England Shows Her Colors," *The New Republic*, 2 March 1938, pp. 87-88; "Europe and America," *The Nation*, 5 March 1938, pp. 259-262; Robert Dell, "Chamberlain's Treason," *The Nation*, 12 March 1938, pp. 292-294.

[33]" 'Until Death,' " *Newsweek*, 7 March 1938, pp. 8-9; "Civil War?," *Time*, 7 March 1938, pp. 21-22.

[34]"Soup Temperature," *Time*, 7 March 1938, p. 21; "Necessary, Fight!," *Time*, 7 March 1938, p. 20; "Goering Threatens," *Newsweek*, 14 March 1938, p. 18.

[35]"A Chamberlain Peace?," *Time*, 14 March 1938, p. 17; Robert Dell, "Chamberlain's Treason," *The Nation*, 12 March 1938, pp. 292-294.

[36]Frederic Sondern, Fr., "Schuschnigg's 'Terrible Two Hours,' " *The Saturday Evening Post*, 13 August 1938, pp. 23, 70, 72-74; condensed in *The Reader's Digest*, October 1938, pp. 1-8.

[37]"Austria: Hitler Comes Home, Bismarck's Dream Comes True," *Newsweek*, 21 March 1938, pp. 14-15; "Hitler Comes Home," *Time*, 21 March 1938, pp. 18-19.

[38]" 'Austria Is Finished,' " *Time*, 21 March 1938, pp. 19-21.

[39]" 'Far From Ruined,' " *Time*, 21 March 1938, p. 22; "French Crisis," *Newsweek*, 21 March 1938, pp. 17-18.

[40]"Britain in Crisis," *Time*, 21 March 1938, pp. 21-22; "Great Britain," *Newsweek*, 21 March 1938, p. 17.

[41]" 'Mein Kampf' Unfolds," *The Nation*, 19 March 1938, pp. 315-316.

[42]Freda Kirchwey, "Gangster Triumphant," *The Nation*, 19 March 1938, pp. 321-322; "One Thing to Watch," *The New Republic*, 23 March 1938, p. 177.

[43]"Hitler's Worst Blunder," *The New Republic*, 23 March 1938, pp. 180-181.

[44]Joseph Barber, "Farewell to Austria," *The Atlantic Monthly*, May 1938, pp. 618-623.

[45]"Hull Voices U.S. Anxiety Over 'Gangster' Nations," *Newsweek*, 28 March 1938, pp. 9-10.

[46]"The Ostmark," *Newsweek*, 28 March 1938, pp. 16-18; cf. "Hitler's Cold War," *The Nation*, 26 March 1938, pp. 345-346; Oswald Villard, "Issues and Men," *The Nation*, 26 March 1938, p. 356; "Hitler vs. Freud," *The New Republic*, 30 March 1938, p. 205.

[47]"The Blue Danube," *Newsweek*, 4 April 1938, pp. 17-19; " 'Our Herman,' " *Time*, 4 April 1938, p. 19.

[48]"Distress on the Danube," *Newsweek*, 2 May 1938, p. 18.

[49]M. W. Fodor, "The Cemetery of Europe," *The Atlantic Monthly*, August 1938, pp. 185-190.

[50]Peter F. Drucker, "Social Revolution in Austria," *The New Republic*, 6 July 1938, pp. 239-241.

[51]*The Nation*, 26 March 1938, p. 356; *The Nation*, 19 March 1938, pp. 326-327; "First Peace Poll Returns," *The Nation*, 2 April 1938, pp. 376-378.

[52]"A Foreign Policy for America," *The Nation*, 9 April 1938, p. 403; A Foreign Policy for America," *The Nation*, 16 April 1938, pp. 435-436.

[53]F.S. Wickware, "What the American People Want," *Harper's*, October 1938, pp. 547-552.

[54]"Quick Peace?," *Time*, 28 March 1938, p. 13; "The Ostmark," *Newsweek*, 28 March 1938, pp. 16-18.

[55]"Baltic Blast," *Newsweek*, 28 March 1938, p. 18; "Baltic Peace," *Time* 28 March 1938, p. 12.

[56]"Finance and the War Scare," *Newsweek*, 28 March 1938, p. 33.

[57]"Hitler's Cold War," *The Nation*, 26 March 1938, pp. 345-346; Henry B. Kranz, "Czechoslovakia Holds the Key," *The Nation*, 26 March 1938, pp. 350-351.

[58]"Britain Growls," *Newsweek*, 4 April 1938, pp. 16-17; "Keel Down" *Time*, 4 April 1938, pp. 17-18; George F. Eliot, "Czechoslovakia, Bastion of Europe," *The New Republic*, 6 April 1938, pp. 269-271.

[59]"Britain: A Slap," *Newsweek*, 18 April 1938, p. 21; "Chamberlain's Hat," *Time*, 18 April 1938, pp. 22-24.

[60]"Time for Reflection," *Time*, 18 April 1938, pp. 24-25; "Leftist France Turns to Right," *Newsweek*, 18 April 1938, pp. 19-20.

[61] *The Nation*, 16 April 1938, p. 425; "Britain's Franc," *The Saturday Evening Post*, 18 June 1938, p. 24; Frederick C. Schumann, "The Perfidy of Albion," *The New Republic*, 20 April 1938, pp. 321-323; "Ja!," *Newsweek*, 18 April 1938, pp. 20-21; "Proudest," *Time*, 18 April 1938, pp. 23-24; Paul Schubert, "Hitler's Ward-Heeler," *Collier's*, 31 December 1938, pp. 31-32.

[62]"Pagans and Plebiscites," *Newsweek*, 11 April 1938, pp. 15-16; "Public Enlightenment," *Time*, 11 April 1938, p. 19.

[63]"Ja!," *Newsweek*, 18 April 1938, pp. 20-21.

[64]"The Church in Austria," *Newsweek*, 24 October 1938, p. 20.

[65]"Anglo-Italian Agreement Heartens Shaky Europe," *Newsweek*, 25 April 1938, pp. 17-18; "Peace in Rome," *Time*, 25 April 1938, p. 16; "Mussolini Wins," *The New Republic*, 27 April 1938, pp. 346-347.

[66]"Paris Bows to London," *The Nation* 23 April 1938, pp. 456-458; "Energy in France," *Newsweek*, 25 April 1938, p. 19.

[67]Oswald G. Villard, "Problem in Ethics," *The Nation*, 30 April 1938, p. 505.

[68]". . .Or Else!," *Time*, 2 May 1938, p. 17; "Next," *The New Republic*, 4 May 1938, p. 379; "Hitler Goes to Rome," *The Nation*, 7 May 1938, pp. 520-521.

[69]"Unwritten Alliance," *Time*, 9 May 1938, p. 15; "Chamberlain Puts a Brake on the Rome-Berlin Axis," *Newsweek*, 9 May 1938, pp. 15-16.

[70]"Adolf Hitler's Roman Holiday Dazzles Eye, But Sheds No Light," *Newsweek*, 16 May 1938, pp. 15-16; "$20,000,000," *Time*, 16 May 1938, pp. 22-23; *The Nation*, 14 May 1938, p. 545; "The Dictator's Meet," *The New Republic*, 18 May 1938, p. 29.

[71]"The Czech Problem," *Newsweek*, 23 May 1938, pp. 14-15; "Freiwilliger Schutzdienst," *Time*, 23 May 1938, pp. 14-15; *The Nation*, 21 May 1938, p. 574; George F. Eliot, "Hitler's Balance Sheet," *The New Republic*, 25 May 1938.

[72]M. W. Fodor, "Czech and German," *The Atlantic Monthly*, May 1938, pp. 623-629.

[73]"Second Sarajevo?," *Time*, 30 May 1938, pp. 14-15; "Hitler Meets First Challenge in Czechoslovakia's Show of Strength," *Newsweek*, 30 May 1938, pp. 13-14; "Hitler's Bluff Called," *The New Republic*, 1 June 1938, pp. 88-89; *The Nation*, 4 June 1938, p. 629.

[74]"Germans and Czechs Retire to Business of Making Faces," *Newsweek*, 6 June 1938, pp. 15-16.

[75]"The Holy Land," *Newsweek*, 25 April 1938, pp. 19-20.

[76]"Too Correct Adolf," *Time*, 25 April 1938, pp. 15-16.

[77]"Vienna Jews in Noose," 9 May 1938, p. 19; " 'Land of Justice,' " *Time*, 9 May 1938, pp. 16-17; "Gangsters in Uniform," *The New Republic*, 1 June 1938, p. 89; "Death Trap for Jews," *The Nation*, 16 July 1938, p. 61.

[78]William E. Dodd, "Germany Shocked Me," *The Nation*, 2 August 1938, pp. 176-178; reprinted in *The Reader's Digest*, September 1938, pp. 102-105.

[79]"Foreign Policy," *Newsweek*, 4 April 1938, pp. 10-11; "Refugee Committee," *Time*, 4 April 1938, pp. 11-12; Refugees, Inc.," *Time*, 8 August 1938, pp. 14-15.

[80]"The Austrian Debt," *Newsweek*, 20 June 1938, p. 15; "Holding Jews for Ransom," *The New Republic*, 29 June 1938, pp. 198-199; "The Asylum Expels the Doctor," *The New Republic*, 15 June 1938, p. 141.

[81]"The Nazi Inquisition," *Newsweek*, 27 June 1938, pp. 16-17; " 'Our Sorrow,' " *Time*, 27 June 1938, p. 20.

[82]" 'Our Sorrow,' " *Time*, 27 June 1938, p. 20; "The Nazi Inquisition," *Newsweek*, 27 June 1938, pp. 16-17.

[83]" 'War Is Over!,' " *Time*, 31 October 1938, pp. 18-19.

[84]"Doors Close Against the Refugees," *The New Republic*, 13 July 1938, p. 263; "Death Trap for Jews," *The Nation*, 17 July 1938, p. 61.

[85]"Refugees," *Time*, 18 July 1938, p. 16; "The Refugee Problem," *Newsweek*, 18 July 1938, pp. 13-14.

[86]" 'Happy Augury,' " *Time*, 27 July 1938, pp. 15-16; "Who Wants Refugees?," *The New Republic*, 20 July 1938, pp. 15-16.

[87]"Refugees," *The New Republic*, 17 August 1938, p. 30.

[88]"Refugees, Inc.," *Time*, 8 August 1938, pp. 14-15; Dorothy Thompson, *Refugees: Anarchy or Organization* (New York: Random House, 1938).

[89]"Five-Year-Hope," *Time*, 15 August 1938, pp. 14-15.

[90]"The Duce as Nordic," *Newsweek*, 25 July 1938, p. 17.

[91]Ludwig Lore, "Can a Jew Be A Fascist?," *The Nation*, 13 August 1938, pp. 148-151.

[92]*The Nation*, 6 August 1938, p. 118.

[93]"Italy and the Jews," *Newsweek*, 12 September 1938, pp. 17-18; "Troubles of Jews," *Time*, 12 September 1938, p. 30.

[94]"Troubles of Jews," *Time*, 12 September 1938, p. 30.

[95]"Anti-Semitism Is Here," *The Nation*, 20 August 1938, pp. 167-168.

[96]"Oozlebarts and Cantor," *Time*, 15 August 1938, p. 15.

[97]John Gunter, "Partition in Palestine," *Harper's*, June 1938, pp. 95-103.

[98]"Martyr in Palestine," *Time*, 11 July 1938, pp. 19-20.

[99]"Two to One," *Time*, 18 July 1938, pp. 18-19; "Arab Disunity, Jewish Feuds Complicate Palestine Issue," *Newsweek*, 18 July 1938, pp. 12-13; "Death Trap for Jews," *The Nation*, 16 July 1938, p. 61.

[100]"Oozlebarts and Cantor," *Time*, 15 August 1938, p. 15; "Holy War," *Time*, 22 August 1938, p. 29; "Fatal Fatwa," *Time*, 29 August 1938, p. 18.

[101]*The Nation*, 10 September 1938, p. 233; " 'Centre of the World,' " *Time*, 12 September 1938, pp. 32-33.

[102]Frieda Wunderlich, "It's a Man's World in Germany," *The Reader's Digest*, February 1938, pp. 92-93; condensed from *The American Scholar*, Winter 1937.

[103]Vernon McKenzie, "Synthetic Living in Germany," *The Reader's Digest*, April 1938, pp. 41-44; condensed from Vernon McKenzie, *Through Turbulent Years* (New York: Robert M. McBride and Co., 1938).

[104]" 'Vital Interests,' " *Time*, 4 July 1938, p. 16; "Forced Labor in Reich: German Jews Now Fear Slavery as Under Pharaohs," *Newsweek*, 4 July 1938, pp. 16-17; "Joy Meet," *Time*, 11 July 1938, p. 15.

[105]Ernst von Hartz, "Hitler's Headsman," *Collier's*, 14 May 1938, p. 43.

106Anonymous, As Told to Samuel T. Williamson, "The Nazis Got Me," *Collier's*, 18 June 1938, pp. 12-13, 62-64.

107Emil Ludwig, "The German Soul: The Sword," *The Atlantic Monthly*, February 1938, pp.   ; condensed in *The Reader's Digest*, March 1938, pp. 95-96.

108Stephen H. Roberts, "The House That Hitler Built," *The Reader's Digest* May 1938, pp. 110-128; condensed from Stephen H. Roberts, *The House That Hitler Built* (New York: Harper and Bros., 1937).

109"Central Europe," *Newsweek*, 20 June 1938, p. 14.

110"Inflamed Appendix," *Time*, 6 June 1938, pp. 14-15; "Central Europe," *Newsweek*, 20 June 1938, p. 14; "Optimist," *Time*, 27 June 1938, pp. 16-19.

111"Prague: Preparedness," *Newsweek*, 13 June 1938, pp. 18-19; "Optimist," *Time*, 27 June 1938, pp. 16-19; "Czechoslovakia," *Newsweek*, 27 June 1938, p. 16; "Optimist," *Time*, 27 June 1938, pp. 16-19; "Central Europe," *Newsweek*, 20 June 1938, p. 14.

112Martha Gellhorn, "Come Ahead, Adolf!," *Collier's*, 6 August 1938, pp. 12-13, 43-45; Alexander Werth, "Can Prague Rely on Paris?," *The Nation*, 25 June 1938, pp. 718-720.

113"Spanish Events Put Chamberlain More and More on Spot," *Newsweek*, 20 June 1938, pp. 12-13; "Cautious Britain," *Newsweek*, 27 June 1938, pp. 14-15; "Accelerated Surrender," *The Nation*, 25 June 1938, pp. 713-714.

114"Parliament's Week," *Time*, 4 July 1938, pp. 14-15.

115"Chamberlain's Purge," *Newsweek*, 13 June 1938, p. 18; "Cautious Britain," *Newsweek*, 27 June 1938, pp. 14-15.

116"The Austrian Debt," *Newsweek*, 20 June 1938, p. 15; "Default," *Time*, 20 June 1938, p. 21.

117"Austrian Debts," *Newsweek*, 11 July 1938, p. 21; "Settlement," *Time*, 11 June 1938, p. 16.

118"King on Stage in Paris; Diplomas Maneuver in Wings," *Newsweek*, 1 August 1938, pp. 13-14; "Warning to Dictators," *Time*, 1 August 1938, pp. 14-16.

119"One Staff! One Flag!," *Time*, 1 August 1938, p. 16; "High Stakes on the European Table," *The New Republic*, 3 August 1938, p. 345; "Britain-on-the-Double," *Time*, 8 August 1938, pp. 15-16.

120*The Nation*, 6 August 1938, p. 117; "Czechoslovakia," *Newsweek*, 8 August 1938, pp. 15-16.

121*The Nation*, 20 August 1938, p. 165; "Europe on Edge," *Newsweek*, 22 August 1938, pp. 17-18; "Hitler's Paladin," *Time*, 22 August 1938, pp. 30-31; George Slocombe, "The Paradox of France," *The Atlantic Monthly*, August 1938, pp. 191-195.

122"La Patrie," *Newsweek*, 20 August 1938, p. 18; Robert Dell, "Czech Suicide—London's Solution," *The Nation*, 20 August 1938, pp. 174-176.

123Wilson Woodside, "What Would Germany Fight With?," *Harper's*, September 1938, pp. 426-437.

124"Hint to Hitler," *Time*, 5 September 1938, pp. 14-15; "Europe Mobilizes," *The Nation*, 3 September 1938, pp. 215-216; "Antiwar Pact's Anniversary Finds Britain Ready to Fight," *Newsweek*, 5 September 1938, pp. 13-14.

125"The Chances for Peace," *The New Republic*, 7 September 1938, p. 116; M.W. Fodor, "Hitler Will Decide," *The Nation*, 10 September 1938, pp. 239-241.

126"Plan No. 3," *Time*, 12 September 1938, pp. 29-30; "Britain Moves on Two Fronts to Protect Czechoslovakia," *Newsweek*, 12 September 1938, pp. 15-17; "Ready," *Time*, 19 September 1938, p. 17.

127"'Will' and 'Way,'" *Time*, 19 September 1938, p. 18; "Palace of Peace," *Newsweek*, 19 September 1938, p. 16; "Russo-Czech Communications," *The New Republic*, 21 September 1938, p. 169.

128"War Now, or Later?," *The New Republic*, 14 September 1938, pp. 144-145; "Dead End in Europe," *The Nation*, 17 September 1938, pp. 255-256.

[129]"America's Role in the World Crisis," *The Nation*, 17 September 1938, pp. 256-257.

[130]"Maximum Concessions," *Time*, 19 September 1938, pp. 18-19; " 'Unshakable Faith,' " 19 September 1938, p. 14.

[131]"Nuremberg," *Time*, 19 September 1938, pp. 19-20; "Strategy Underlies Defiance in Hitler's Address to World," *Newsweek*, 19 September 1938, pp. 14-15; "Echoes of Thunder," *Newsweek*, 19 September 1938, pp. 15-16.

[132]"Sawed-Off Sudetens?," *Time*, 19 September 1938, pp. 17-18.

[133]Carl J. Frederich, "Edward Benes," *The Atlantic Monthly*, September 1938, pp. 357-365.

[134]"The Great Surrender," *The New Republic*, 28 September 1938, pp. 200-201; cf. "Deathbed Repentance," *The New Republic*, 5 October 1938, pp. 225-226; "The Great Betrayal," *The Nation*, 24 September 1938, pp. 284-285; cf. Martha Gellhorn, "Guns Against France," *Collier's*, 8 October 1938, pp. 14, 31-32.

[135]"Four Chiefs," *Time*, 26 September 1938, pp. 15-16; Harper's supported this interpretation: Willson Woodside, "The Road to Munich," *Harper's*, December 1938, pp. 28-39; "Talk and Action," *Newsweek*, 3 October 1938, p. 14; "Hangover," *Newsweek*, 10 October 1938, pp. 18-19.

[136]"Reaction," *Newsweek*, 3 October 1938, pp. 18-19; cf. Frank C. Honichen, "Why France Sold the Pass," *The New Republic*, 26 October 1938, p. 323; "Why England Capitulated," *The New Republic*, 26 October 1938, p. 322; Elsuryth Thane, "When London Held Its Breath," *The Reader's Digest*, December 1938, pp. 5-11; "Nordic Dream," *Newsweek*, 10 October 1938, pp. 16-17; "Four Chiefs," *Time*, 26 September 1938, pp. 15-16; "Things arrange Themselves," *Newsweek*, 26 September 1938, pp. 15-16.

[137]"Echoes and Flashes," *Newsweek*, 10 October 1938, pp. 19-20; "Hangover," *Newsweek*, 10 October 1938, pp 19-20; "What Price Peace?," *Time*, 17 October 1938, pp. 19-21; " 'State-of-the-World," *Time*, 31 October 1938, p. 16.

[138]"Territorial Organization," *Time*, 24 October 1938, p. 20; "Britain's Woes," *Newsweek*, 24 October 1938, pp. 14-15; "Business of Government," *Time*, 14 November 1938, p. 20.

[139]"France," *Newsweek*, 17 October 1938, p. 18; "Kiss the Reds Goodbye," *Time*, 17 October 1938, pp. 22-23; "Wrangling in France," *Newsweek*, 24 October 1938, p. 16; " 'State-of-the-World,' " *Time*, 31 October 1938, p. 16.

[140]"France's Swing," *Newsweek*, 7 November 1938, p. 18.

[141]Henry C. Wolfe, "Czechoslovakia at the Zero Hour," *The New Republic*, 28 September 1938, pp. 206-207; "Benes: 'We Are Alone,' " *Newsweek*, 3 October 1938, pp. 16-17; "Crisis and the League," *Time*, 3 October 1938, pp. 18-19; Louis Fischer, "Let the Czechs Stand Firm," *The Nation*, 1 October 1938, pp. 317-318.

[142]" 'Tragedy of Teschen,' " *Time*, 10 October 1938, p. 18; "2,000,000 Sons of Death," *Time*, 3 October 1938, pp. 16-17.

[143]"Hitler's Might," *Newsweek* 24 October 1938, pp. 17-19; "After Munich," *The New Republic*, 26 October 1938, p. 317; "New Constitution," *Time*, 17 October 1938, pp. 19-20.

[144]" 'Jews Under Hedges,' " *Time*, 31 October 1938, p. 19; "Action After Munich," 19 October 1938, p. 292; *The Nation*, 26 October 1938, p. 393.

[145]Vladimir Pozner, "Hitler Wants Skoda," *The Nation*, 24 September 1938, pp. 287-288; Oswald G. Villard, "More Parallel Action," 1 October 1938, p. 352; *The Nation*, 1 October 1938, p. 309; "If Hitler Has His Way," *The Nation*, 1 October 1938, pp. 312-313; John Gunther, "Interim Notes on the Crisis," *The Nation*, 1 October 1938, pp. 316-317.

[146]"The Great Surrender," *The New Republic*, 28 September 1938, pp. 200-201; "The World Waits," *The New Republic*, 5 October 1938, p. 225; "Teuton and Slav," *The*

New Republic, 12 October 1938, pp. 253-254; Vera M. Dean, "Pan-German Redivivus," *The New Republic,* 12 October 1938, pp. 259-260.

147"The Slow Agony of a State: Czechoslovakia Goes into Coma," *Newsweek,* 17 October 1938, pp. 15-16; "Hungary," *Newsweek,* 24 October 1938, p. 18; "Hungary's Bite," *Newsweek,* 14 November 1938, pp. 18-19; "War Is Over!," *Time,* 31 October 1938, pp. 18-19.

148"Four Chiefs, One Peace," *Time,* 10 October 1938, pp. 15-17; "What Price Peace?," *Time,* 17 October 1938, pp. 19-22.

149"Reason v. Force," *Time,* 3 October 1938, p. 9; "Echoes at Home," *Newsweek,* 3 October 1938, pp. 9-10.

150*The Nation,* 1 October 1938, pp. 309-310; "America's Part," *The New Republic,* 5 October 1938, pp. 228-230; *The Nation,* 15 October 1938, p. 366.

151*The Nation,* 8 October 1938, p. 339; "Fruits of the Munich Accord Viewed Skeptically by U.S.," *Newsweek* 10 October 1938, pp. 7-8.

152*The Nation,* 8 October 1938, p. 339; "Fruits of the Munich Accord Viewed Skeptically by U.S.," *Newsweek* 10 October 1938, pp. 7-8.

153"If and When," *Time,* 26 September 1938, pp. 9-10; *The Nation,* 1 October 1938, p. 310.

154"U.S. Policy Still Isolation Despite Gesture of Roosevelt," *Newsweek,* 3 October 1938, pp. 9-10; "Mr. Roosevelt's Appeal," *The New Republic,* 5 October 1938, p. 226; "Mr. Roosevelt and the Crisis," *The New Republic,* p. 253; "Natural Defense," *Newsweek* 24 October 1938, pp. 10-11.

155"Stepped Up U.S. Rearmament a Weapon for Lima Conference," *Newsweek,* 14 November 1938, p. 9; Bruce Blevin, "Picking Up the Pieces," *The New Republic,* 19 October 1938, pp. 294-296; "National Defense," *Newsweek,* 24 October 1938, pp. 10-11; "Nazis vs. U.S.," *Newsweek,* 14 November 1938, pp. 17-18.

156Carleton Beals, "Swastika Over the Andes," *The Reader's Digest,* July 1938, pp. 175-186; "Stepped Up U.S. Rearmament a Weapon for Lima Conference," *Newsweek,* 14 November 1938, p. 9; "Pan American and Guns," *The New Republic,* 16 November 1938, p. 29.

157"A Challenge to America," *The Nation,* 24 September 1938, pp. 285-286; "America's Past," *The New Republic,* 5 October 1938, pp. 228-230; "Mr. Roosevelt's Appeal," *The New Republic,* 5 October 1938, p. 226; Vera M. Dean, "Pan-German Redivivus," *The New Republic,* 12 October 1938, pp. 259-260.

158Bruce Bliven, "Picking Up the Pieces," *The New Republic,* October 1938, pp. 294-296; "The Great Surrender," *The New Republic,* 28 September 1938, pp. 200-201; Oswald G. Villard, "More Parallel Action?," *The Nation,* 1 October 1938, p. 325; "Innocents Abroad," *Newsweek,* 10 October 1938, p. 8.

159Damaree Bess, "Peaceful Wars Aren't Possible," *The Saturday Evening Post,* 27 August 1938, pp. 23, 44, 47-48.

160Damaree Bess, "European Shakedown," *The Saturday Evening Post,* 5 December 1938, pp. 5-7, 77-79.

161Norman Thomas, "We Needn't Go to War," *Harper's,* November 1938, pp. 657-664.

162Thomas Mann, "The Coming Victory of Democracy," *The Reader's Digest,* October 1938, pp. 71-74; condensed from Thomas Mann, *The Coming Victory of Democracy* (New York: Alfred A. Knopf, 1938).

163"Lindbergh on the Spot," *Newsweek,* 17 October 1938, pp. 17-18; "Lindy's Nazi Eagle," *Newsweek,* 31 October 1938, p. 19.

164"A Long Shadow Forward," *The New Republic,* 28 September 1938, p. 197; "If Hitler Has His Way," *The Nation,* 1 October 1938, pp. 312-313; "New Deal," *Time,* 17 October 1938, pp. 24-25; "150,000,000 Bid," *Time,* 17 October 1938, p. 23; "Crisis and the League," *Time,* 3 October 1938, pp. 18-19.

[165]"Japan," *Newsweek*, 10 October 1938, p. 20; "Tangled Threads in the Orient," *The New Republic*, 12 October 1938, p. 254; "Slump in Britain's Prestige Spurs New Japanese Attack," *Newsweek*, 24 October 1938, p. 14; "Nemesis Postpones," *The New Republic*, 12 October 1938, pp. 555-557; "Picking Up the Pieces," *The New Republic*, 19 October 1938, pp. 294-295.

[166]Albert Viton, "It's War in Palestine," *The Nation*, 1 October 1938, pp. 221-223; "Palestine," *Time*, 3 October 1938, pp. 19-20; "Flashes and Echoes," *Newsweek*, 3 October 1938, pp. 20-21.

[167]"Palestine," *Time*, 17 October 1938, p. 22; *The Nation*, 15 October 1938, pp. 366-367; "Islam," *Newsweek*, 17 October 1938, pp. 19-20.

[168]"Britain's War," *Time*, 24 October 1938, pp. 15-16; "After Munich," *The New Republic*, 26 October 1938, p. 317.

[169]"Bullets in Palestine," *Newsweek*, 31 October 1938, p. 17; "Surprise in Gaza," *Newsweek*, 7 November 1938, p. 18; "Palestine Birthday," *Newsweek*, 14 November 1938, p. 21.

[170]"Palestine," *Time*, 21 November 1938, p. 21; "Palestine," *The Nation*, 21 November 1938, pp. 18-19; *The Nation*, 10 November 1938, p. 522.

[171]*The Nation*, 5 November 1938, p. 7; "Misunderstanding," *Time*, 7 November 1938, pp. 19-20; "The Minorities," *Newsweek*, 7 November 1938, pp. 19-20; "The French Cabinet," *Newsweek*, 14 November 1938, p. 21.

[172]"War Against the Jews," *The Nation*, 19 November 1938, pp. 524-525.

[173]" 'These Individuals,' " *Time*, 21 November 1938, pp. 18-19.

[174]Stanley High, "Germany Processes War," *The Saturday Evening Post*, 1 October 1938, pp. 23, 65-67.

[175]"Pogroms Give Reich a Weapon for Spread of Anti-Semitism," *Newsweek*, 21 November 1938, pp. 17-18.

[176]"Is Hitler Crazy?," *The New Republic*, 9 November 1938, pp. 2-3.

[177]"War Against the Jews," *The Nation*, 19 November 1938, pp. 524-525; " 'Madman Hitler,' " *Time*, 21 November 1938, pp. 19-20.

[178]"Let the Jews Come In!," *The New Republic*, 30 November 1938, p. 60; "War Against the Jews," *The Nation*, 19 November 1938, pp. 524-525; "Democracies Uniting to Solve the Problem of Fleeing Jews," *Newsweek*, 28 November 1938, pp. 13-14.

[179]*The Nation*, 26 November 1938, p. 550; " 'Those Individuals,' " *Time*, 21 November 1938, pp. 18-19.

[180]"Democracies Uniting to Solve the Problem of Fleeing Jews," *Newsweek*, 28 November 1938, pp. 13-14; "Singular Attitude," *Time*, 28 November 1938, pp. 10-11.

[181]"Let the Jews Come In!," *The New Republic*, 23 November 1938, p. 60; "The American Way," *Collier's*, 31 December 1938, p. 50; *The Nation*, 26 November 1938, pp. 550-551.

[182]"Kennedy's Speech," *Newsweek*, 31 October 1938, p. 10; "Kennedy on Antagonisms," *Time*, 31 October 1938, p. 17; "More Recklessness in Foreign Affairs," *The New Republic*, 12 November 1938, p. 346; "Singular Attitude," *Time*, 28 November 1938, pp. 10-11; *The Nation*, 26 November 1938, p. 549; "A Special Correspondent, "Kennedy and the Jews," *The Nation*, 26 November 1938, p. 555.

[183]Albert Einstein, trans. Ruth Norden, "Why Do They Hate the Jews?," *Collier's*, 26 November 1938, pp. 9-10, 36, 38.

[184]" 'Woe to the Jews!,' " *Time* 28 November 1938, p. 17; "Democracies Uniting to Solve the Problem of Fleeing Jews," *Newsweek*, 28 November 1938, pp. 13-14; "Ad Nauseum!," *Time*, 5 December 1938, pp. 19-20.

[185]"700,000 Jews," *Newsweek*, 5 December 1938, pp. 17-18; "$.40 Refugees," *Time*, 12 December 1938, p. 22; "Jews," *Newsweek*, 12 December 1938, pp. 16-17.

[186]"Czech Twilight," *Newsweek*, 5 December 1938, p. 17, " 'We Are Wanderers,' " *Time*, 5 December 1938, pp. 17-18.

187"700,000 Jews," *Newsweek*, 5 December 1938, pp. 17-18; *The Nation*, 17 December 1938, p. 650; William C. Kernan, "Coughlin, the Jews, and Communism," *The Nation*, 17 December 1938, pp. 655-658; "Cardinal and Coughlin," *The New Republic*, 21 December 1938, p. 186.

188Oswald G. Villard, "Issues and Men," *The Nation*, 26 November 1938, p. 567; "Refugees and Economics," *The Nation*, 10 December 1938, pp. 609-610; "An Embargo on German Goods," *The New Republic*, 30 November 1938, pp. 83-84.

189"Cultures in Exile," *The Nation*, 17 December 1938, pp. 652-653; "For the Refugees," *The New Republic*, 21 December 1938, p. 189; " 'We Are Wanderers,' " *Time*, 5 December 1938, pp. 17-19.

190"Democracies Uniting to Solve the Problem of Fleeing Jews," *Newsweek*, 28 November 1938, pp. 13-14; "After Munich," *Time*, 28 November 1938, pp. 17-18; "$.40 Refugees," *Time*, 12 December 1938, p. 22; "Jews," *Newsweek*, 12 December 1938, pp. 16-17.

191"The Refugee Puzzle," *The New Republic*, 30 November 1938, p. 87.

192"Empty-Handed Return," *Time*, 28 November 1938, p. 17; "Rebuff," *Newsweek*, 28 November 1938, p. 16; "Yugoslavia," *Time*, 12 December 1938, pp. 20-22; "Britain Prepares to Dicker with Germany on Colonies," *Time*, 7 November 1938, pp. 16-17; "Big Four," *Time*, 14 November 1938, pp. 16-17; "European Whirl," *Newsweek*, 28 November 1938, pp. 15-16.

193" 'We Are Wanderers,' " *Time*, 5 December 1938, pp. 17-18; *The Nation*, 26 November 1938, p. 550; "700,000 Jews," *Newsweek*, 5 December 1938, pp. 17-18.

194"Democracies Uniting to Solve the Problem of Fleeing Jews," *Newsweek*, 28 November 1938, pp. 13-14; "Apparatus Oiled," *Time*, 19 December 1938, pp. 18-19; "Less a Friend," *Time* 26 December 1938, p. 15; "How Stupid!," *Time*, 26 December 1938, pp. 14-15.

195"Private Visit," *Time*, 26 December 1938, p. 14; "Nazi Feeler," *Newsweek*, 26 December 1938, pp. 15-16.

196"Hitler Gesture," *Newsweek* 5 December 1938, pp. 15-16; "Hatchet Buried," *Time*, 19 December 1938, pp. 16-17; "Love!," *Time*, 28 November 1938, pp. 16-17; "Saved?," *Time*, 5 December 1938, p. 22.

197" 'Kill the Duce!,' " *Time*, 12 December 1938, p. 19; "Italy," *Newsweek*, 12 December 1938, p. 17; "Algiers to Asace," *Time*, 19 December 1938, pp. 16-17.

198"Ukrainian Danger Threatens to Rival the Czech Crisis," *Newsweek*, 26 December 1938, pp. 13-14; " 'What Will Mr. Stalin Say?,' " *Time*, 26 December 1938, p. 13; "The Polish-Russian Understanding," *The New Republic*, 7 December 1938, p. 111; "Poland," *Newsweek*, 12 December 1938, p. 18.

199"Apparatus Oiled," *Time*, 19 December 1938, pp. 18-19; "Colonial Caldron," *Newsweek*, 19 December 1938, p. 18.

Chapter VI

1"Handsome Adolf," *Time*, 6 October 1930, p. 23; "Man of the Year," *Time*, 2 January 1939, pp. 11-14.

2"Hairy Man," *Time*, 2 January 1939, pp. 5-7; "U.S. Rebuff to Nazis Is Cue for Stiffer Democracy Stand," *Newsweek*, 2 January 1939, pp. 9-10.

3"U.S. Rebuff to Nazis Is Cue for Stiffer Democracy Stand," *Newsweek* 2 January 1939, pp. 9-10; "Hairy Man," *Time*, 2 January 1939, pp. 9-10; "Ickes, Welles, and Pittman," *The New Republic*, 4 January 1939, p. 241; *The Nation*, 31 December 1938, p. 1.

4"U.S. Arms Bill for New Year Is Put at $10.54 Per Capita," *Newsweek*, 23 January 1939, pp. 9-10.

[5]S. K. Padover, "Unser Amerika," *The Reader's Digest,* January 1939, pp. 3-9; condensed from *The Forum,* January 1939; Damill Lang, "Berlin Sends Radio Greetings," *The New Republic,* 11 January 1939, pp. 279-281.

[6]"Red Kitty," *Time,* 2 January 1939, pp. 14-15; "Munich Shadows: Britain," *Newsweek,* 2 January 1939, p. 16; Graham Hutton, "Where Now Is Britain?," *The Atlantic Monthly,* January 1939, pp. 1-12.

[7]"France and 'Appeasement,' " *The Nation,* 4 January 1939, p. 242; " 'How Stupid!,' " *Time* 26 December 1938, pp. 14-15; "France," *Newsweek,* 2 January 1939, pp. 17-19.

[8]"More Munich?," *Time,* 9 January 1939, pp. 21-22; "Duce's Designs on Somaliland Are Based on Two-Ply Menace," *Newsweek,* 9 January 1939, pp. 7-8; "Triumph in Tunisia," *Newsweek,* 9 January 1939, pp. 7-8; " 'They Are French,' " *Time,* 16 January 1939, p. 21.

[9]" 'I Loathe Dictators,' " *Time,* 9 January 1939, pp. 20-21; "Chamberlain's Troubles," *Newsweek,* 16 January 1939, p. 18; "Second Hundred Thousand," *Time,* 16 January 1939, pp. 19-20.

[10]"Dictator's Challenged," *Time,* 16 January 1939, pp. 11-12; "Mr. Roosevelt Reports on the State of the Nation," *Newsweek,* 16 January 1939, pp. 11-12; "Second Hundred Thousand," *Time,* 16 January 1939, pp. 19-20.

[11]"Chamberlain Goes to Rome," *The New Republic,* 11 January 1939, pp. 273-274; *The Nation,* 14 January 1939, p. 50.

[12]*The Nation,* 21 January 1939, p. 81; "Chamberlain Smooths the Way for French-Italian Harmony," *Newsweek,* 23 January 1939, pp. 15-16; "Umbrella," *Time,* 23 January 1939, p. 19.

[13]"Appeasement at Rome," *The New Republic,* 25 January 1939, p. 328; "Mussolini Stands Pat," *The Nation,* 21 January 1939, p. 81.

[14]"Budget Time," *Time,* 9 January 1939, p. 18; "Reaction," *Newsweek,* 9 January 1939, pp. 13-14; "Swift Rearming Gives U.S. Leadership of Democracies," *Newsweek,* 9 January 1939, pp. 11-12.

[15]"Dictators Challenged," *Time,* 16 January 1939, pp. 11-13; "Mr. Roosevelt Reports on the State of the Nation," *Newsweek,* 16 January 1939, pp. 11-13.

[16]"Reaction," *Newsweek,* 9 January 1939, pp. 12-13; "Dictators Challenged," *Time,* 16 January 1939, pp. 11-12.

[17]Bruce Bliven, "Mr. Roosevelt's Undeclared War," *The New Republic,* 11 January 1939, pp. 281-282; "The President's Message," *The Nation,* 14 January 1939, pp. 51-52.

[18]"13,000 Airplanes," *The New Republic,* 14 January 1939, p. 242; "Ask the Men Who Know," *Collier's,* 28 January 1939, p. 66; "Let's Keep National Defense National," *The Saturday Evening Post,* 11 February 1939, p. 22.

[19]"Mr. Roosevelt's Air Armada," *The New Republic,* 11 January 1939, pp. 270-271; "Mr. Roosevelt Reports on the State of the Nation," *Newsweek,* 16 January 1939, pp. 11-13; "U.S. Arms Bill Is Put at $10.54 Per Capita," *Newsweek,* 23 January 1939, pp. 9-10.

[20]"Arms and the Congress," *Time,* 23 January 1939, pp. 7-8.

[21]Henry C. Wolfe, "Before Hitler Crosses the Atlantic," *Harper's,* February 1939, pp. 253-259.

[22]Nathaniel Peffer, "In an Era of Unreason," *Harper's,* March 1939, pp. 338-343.

[23]David L. Cohn, "Neutrality or Bust," *The Atlantic Monthly,* June 1939, pp. 832-838.

[24]Drew Pearson, "Who Chooses Our Wars?," *Collier's,* 4 March 1939, pp. 12-13, 48-50.

[25]Eddie V. Rickenbacker, "50,000 Planes Can't Be Wrong," *Collier's,* 29 April 1939, pp. 9-10, 60-61.

26S. Paul Jackson, "Hitler Wasn't Bluffing," *The Saturday Evening Post*, 18 February 1939, pp. 5-6, 85.

27Demaree Ross, "Uncle Sam Scares Europe," *The Saturday Evening Post*, 25 February 1939, pp. 23, 37-38, 40.

28Demaree Ross, "Jewish Pawns in Power Politics," *The Saturday Evening Post*, 18 March 1939, pp. 8-9, 33, 34, 38.

29"Who Cultivate War," *The Saturday Evening Post*, 8 April 1939, pp. 24, 109; Demaree Ross, "Gambling With Peace," *The Saturday Evening Post*, 8 April 1939, pp. 25, 118, 120, 122.

30"Cultivated Obsession," *The Saturday Evening Post*, 20 May 1939, pp. 22, 102.

31A. N. Whitehead, "An Appeal To Sanity," *The Atlantic Monthly*, March 1939, pp. 309-320.

32Oswald G. Villard, "Wanted: A Sane Defense Policy," *Harper's*, April 1939, pp. 449-456.

33C. Hartley Grattan, "No More Excursions!," *Harper's*, April 1939, pp. 457-465.

34J.B. Priestly, "Where England Stands," *Harper's*, May 1939, pp. 581-587.

35"French Plane Deal Touches Off New U.S. Foreign Policy Row," *Newsweek*, 6 February 1939, pp. 13-14; "American Planes for France," *The New Republic*, 8 February 1939, p. 2; "Embargoes," *Newsweek*, 6 February 1939, p. 14.

36"Neighbors," *Newsweek*, 6 February 1939, p. 14; "Facts," *Newsweek*, 13 February 1939, p. 16; John T. Flynn, "The Armament Bandwagon," *The New Republic*, 8 March 1939, pp. 121-123.

37"Who's for War," *Time*, 27 February 1939, p. 20.

38*The Nation*, 18 March 1939, pp. 307-308.

39"Bewildered Congress Groping for Sound Neutrality Policy," *Newsweek*, 17 April 1939, pp. 13-14.

40"Ukrainian Snags," *Newsweek*, 2 January 1939, p. 18; "Border Clashes," *Newsweek*, 16 January 1939, pp. 18-19; "According to Hitler," *Time*, 16 January 1939, p. 24; "Liberation," *Time*, 23 January 1939, pp. 15-16.

41"Germany," *Newsweek*, 2 January 1939, pp. 16-17; "Skoda Sale," *Time*, 9 January 1939, p. 22; "Guns for the Reich," *Newsweek*, 19 January 1939, p. 19; "Two Birds; One Stone," *Time*, 30 January 1939, p. 20.

42Gunther Reimann, "Trouble in Hitler's Paradise," *The New Republic*, 25 January 1939, pp. 337-338; "Exit Schacht," *Time*, 30 January 1939, pp,. 18-19; "The Juggenaut Rolls On," *The New Republic*, 1 February 1939, p. 353; Fritz Reiner, "Hitler Takes a New Pilot," *The New Republic*, 8 February 1939, pp. 12-13; "The Reich Tightens," *The Nation*, 28 January 1939, p. 108.

43"Woes of the Jews," *Newsweek*, 2 January 1939, pp. 18-19; "Aid to the Refugees," *Newsweek*, 16 January 1939, pp. 19-20; "Rescue," *Newsweek*, 16 January 1939, p. 9.

44 *The Nation*, 14 January 1939, p. 51; "Rescue," *Time*, 16 January 1939, p. 9; "Aid to the Refugees," *Newsweek*, 16 January 1939, pp. 19-20.

45"Truce," *Time*, 27 February 1939, p. 22; "Escape From the Reich," *Newsweek*, 27 February 1939, pp. 19-20.

46"Pogrom Economics," *The Nation*, 25 February 1939, pp. 219-220; "Truce," *Time*, 27 February 1939, p. 22.

47"Broken Promise," *Time*, 6 March 1939, p. 22.

48Quentin Reynolds, "Unwanted," *Collier's*, 11 February 1939, pp. 12-13, 28-29; Quentin Reynolds, "Portrait of a Murderer," *Collier's*, 25 February 1939, pp. 9-10; 64-65.

49"Refugees in Purgatory," *The New Republic*, 1 February 1939, pp. 355-356; "Woes of the Jews," *Newsweek*, 2 January 1939, pp. 18-19.

50"Christmas Present," *Time*, 2 January 1939, p. 10; "Woes of the Jews," *Newsweek*, 2 January 1939, pp. 18-19; "Ancestor Crisis," *Newsweek*, 27 February 1939, p. 19; "Embarrassing Discovery," *Time*, 27 February 1939, pp. 22-23.

51"The Jewish Problem," *Newsweek*, 23 January 1939, pp. 18-19.

52" 'Christian' Per Inch," *Time*, 19 January 1939, p. 16.

53Anonymous, "I Married a Jew," *The Atlantic Monthly*, January 1939, pp. 38-46.

54George Britt, "Poison in the Melting Pot," *The Nation*, 1 April 1939, pp. 374-376; "America's 'Isms,' " *Newsweek*, 6 March 1939, pp. 14-15; George Britt, "Poison in the Melting Pot," *The Nation*, 1 April 1939, pp. 374-376.

55George Britt, "Poison in the Melting Pot," *The Nation*, 1 April 1939, pp. 374-376.

56"The American Fascists," *The New Republic*, 8 March 1939, pp. 117-188.

57Stanley High, "Star-Spangled Fascists," *The Saturday Evening Post*, 27 May 1939, pp. 5-7, 70-73.

58"Test Vote on Anti-Semitism," *The New Republic*, 19 April 1939, pp. 293-294.

59"Moseley Roars," *Time*, 10 April 1939, p. 18; *The Nation*, 22 April 1939, p. 456.

60"Ism Bombshell," *Newsweek*, 29 May 1939, p. 15.

61*The New Republic*, 26 April 1939, p. 319; "Littler Refugees," *Time*, 26 April 1939, p. 319; *The Nation*, 29 April 1939, p. 481; *The Nation*, 8 July 1939, p. 29.

62"Arab Cause," *Time*, 30 January 1939, p. 17.

63*The Nation*, 11 January 1939, pp. 162-163; "Arab and Jew," *Newsweek*, 13 February 1939, pp. 23-24.

64"Palestine Parley," *Newsweek*, 20 February 1939, p. 21; "Palestinian Deadlock," *Newsweek* 6 March 1939, pp. 25-26.

65"Last Supper?," *Time*, 6 March 1939, pp. 21-22; "Plot Over Palestine," *The New Republic*, 15 March 1939, p. 151; *The Nation*, 4 March 1939, p. 251.

66"Palestine Terror," *Newsweek*, 24 April 1939, p. 24.

67"Palestine Politics," *Newsweek*, 29 May 1939, pp. 18-19; "His Majesty's Policy," *Time*, 29 May 1939, pp. 25-26.

68"Up Arab, Down Jew," *The New Republic*, 24 May 1939, p. 59; "Betrayal in Palestine," *The New Republic*, 31 May 1939, pp. 85-86; "No Peace for Palestine," *The Nation*, 27 May 1939, p. 604; Oswald G. Villard, "Palestine Needs a Gandhi," *The Nation*, 3 June 1939, p. 647.

69"Expediency," *Time*, 5 June 1939, p. 23; "Semitic Friends," *Time*, 3 July 1939, pp. 14-15.

70"Dictator's Bill: Italy," *Newsweek*, 6 February 1939, pp. 20-21; "Europe's New Crisis," *The New Republic*, 8 February 1939, p. 5; "Dictator's Bill: France," *Newsweek*, 6 February 1939, p. 21.

71"Cream-Puff Pleas," *Time*, 6 February 1939, p. 17; "Dictator's Bill: Britain," *Newsweek*, 6 February 1939, p. 21; *The New Republic*, 1 February 1939, p. 356.

72"One Thing or Other," *Time*, 6 February 1939, pp. 17-18; "Dictator's Bill: Germany," *Newsweek*, 6 February 1939, pp. 21-22; "Diagnosing Hitler," *The New Republic*, 8 February 1939, p. 1.

73"Reactions to Hitler," *Time*, 13 February 1939, p. 21.

74"Europe's Crisis and the Market," *The New Republic*, 6 February 1939, p. 43; "Appeasement for the Pound Sterling," *The New Republic*, 8 February 1939, pp. 2-3; "Will Britain Go Broke?," *The New Republic*, 1 March 1939, p. 89.

75" 'Enemy of Peace,' " *Time*, 13 February 1939, p. 17.

76"Where Are U.S. Frontiers? Congress Faces Tough Choice," *Newsweek*, 13 February 1939, pp. 15-16.

[77]"Tough Talk," *Time*, 13 February 1939, p. 17; "Appeasement Next Phase," *The New Republic*, 15 February 1939, p. 29; " 'Deeds, Not Words,' " *Time*, 13 February 1939, pp. 19-20; "New Neighbor," *Time*, 13 February 1939, p. 21; "France and Britain Woo Franco as a Mediterranean Safeguard," *Newsweek*, 20 February 1939, pp. 19-20.

[78]"Spanish War Turns to Tussle of Powers for Franco's Favor," *Newsweek*, 27 February 1939, pp. 17-18; "Colonial Crisis," *Newsweek*, 27 February 1939, p. 18.

[79]"Ides of March," *Time*, 27 February 1939, pp. 19-20; "War This Spring?," *The New Republic*, 1 March 1939, pp. 87-88.

[80]Marc A. Rose, "Hitler's Aerial Force," *The Reader's Digest*, March 1939, pp. 9-10; condensed from *The Forum*, March 1939; "The Armament Bandwagon," *The New Republic*, 8 March 1939, pp. 121-122; "Guns for Peace?: Britain," *Newsweek*, 13 March 1939, pp. 21-22.

[81]"Guardian," *Time*, 6 March 1939, pp. 17-20; "Italy's Salesman," *Newsweek*, 6 March 1939, pp. 24-25; "Pocketbook Friends," *Time*, 20 February 1939, p. 21; "Russia and the Old School Tie," *The New Republic*, 22 February 1939, p. 59. "Left v. Right Hand," *Time*, 6 March 1939, p. 22; "Hungary's Nazis," *Newsweek*, 6 March 1939, pp. 23-24.

[82]"Guardian," *Time*, 6 March 1939, pp. 17-20; "Pulse," *Time*, 13 March 1939, p. 19; "Beauty and Diplomacy," *Newsweek*, 20 March 1939, p. 21.

[83]"B.E.F.," *Time*, 20 March 1939, p. 21; "Britain: Preparing," *Newsweek*, 20 March 1939, pp. 22-23.

[84]"Babes in the Woods," *The New Republic*, 8 March 1939, p. 115; "Peekaboo," *Time*, 13 March 1939, p. 21; "Straws of Peace," *Newsweek*, 6 March 1939, pp. 22-23; "Rearm or Disarm?," *Newsweek*, 20 March 1939, pp. 21-22; "Peace Week," *Time* 20 March 1939, p. 18.

[85]Edwin Muller, "The Other Germans," *The Reader's Digest*, March 1939, p. 53; condensed from *The Commentator*, March 1939.

[86]"War This Spring?," *The New Republic*, 1 March 1939, pp. 87-88; *The Nation*, 11 March 1939, p. 278.

[87]*The Nation*, 18 March 1939, p. 305; "Shoulder to Shoulder," *Time*, 20 March 1939, p. 22; "Gouge No. 2," *Newsweek*, 20 March 1939, pp. 20-21; "Exit Czechoslovakia," *The New Republic*, 22 March 1939, p. 177.

[88]"Time Table," *Time*, 27 March 1939, pp. 17-18; "Nazi Caesar," *Newsweek*, 27 March 1939, pp. 19-22.

[89]"Tidbit," *Time*, 27 March 1939, p. 20; "Hungary's Share," *Newsweek*, 27 March 1939, pp. 21-22.

[90]"Surprise? Surprise?," *Time*, 27 March 1939, pp. 16-17; "Loot," *Time*, 27 March 1939, pp. 18-19; "Mehrer's Progress," *Time*, 27 March 1939, pp. 19-20.

[91]"Stop-Napoleon Tactics Revived in Power's Stop-Hitler Drive," *Newsweek*, 27 March 1939, pp. 17-19.

[92]"Hitler Takes a City," *The New Republic*, 29 March 1939, pp. 205-206; "Where Next?," *The New Republic*, 29 March 1939, p. 206; "The Bank Robbery at Prague," *The New Republic*, 29 March 1939, p. 206.

[93]Freda Kirchwey, "Munich: Act II," *The Nation*, 25 March 1939, pp. 335-338; Oswald G. Villard, "Issues and Men," *The Nation*, 25 March 1939, p. 350.

[94]"Temporary Extinguishment," *Time*, 27 March 1939, p. 11; "Stopping German-American Trade," *The New Republic*, 29 March 1939, pp. 206-207; "America's Czech," *Newsweek*, 27 March 1939, p. 22.

[95]"Surprise? Surprise?," *Time*, 27 March 1939, pp. 16-17; "Stop-Napoleon Tactics Revived in Power's Stop-Hitler Drive," *Newsweek*, 27 March 1939, pp. 17-19.

[96]"Surprise? Surprise?," *Time*, 27 March 1939, pp. 16-17.

[97]Freda Kirchwey, "Blood and Geography," *The Nation*, 1 April 1939, pp. 365-366; "Memel—and On," *Newsweek*, 3 April 1939, pp. 19-21; "Killing," *Time*, 3 April 1939, p. 17; "War Week," *Time*, 3 April 1939, pp. 17-18.

[98]"Memel—and On," *Newsweek*, 3 April 1939, pp. 19-21.

[99]"Coalition Coolness," *Newsweek*, 3 April 1939, p. 20; "Stop Hitler," *Time*, 3 April 1939, pp. 19-20; "Unstopping Hitler," *The New Republic*, 5 April 1939, pp. 236-237; Alymer Vallance, "The Grand Disillusion," *The Nation*, 8 April 1939, pp. 396-398.

[100]"Moral Warfare," *Newsweek*, 3 April 1939, pp. 13-14; "American Recognition of Franco Fits into 'Stop-Hitler' Drive," *Newsweek*, 10 April 1939, pp. 11-12.

[101]"Soured Thunderer," *Time*, 3 April 1939, pp. 21-22; "Stop Hitler," *Time*, 3 April 1939, pp. 19-20.

[102]"Watch on the Vistula," *Time*, 10 April 1939, p. 19; "Great Britain Finally Awakens to Reich Threat of Supremacy," *Newsweek*, 10 April 1939, pp. 19-23.

[103]"Great Britain Finally Awakens to Reich Threat of Supremacy," *Newsweek*, 10 April 1939, pp. 19-23.

[104]"Great Britain Finally Awakens to Reich Threat of Supremacy," *Newsweek*, 10 April 1939, pp. 19-23; "Watch on the Vistula," *Time*, 10 April 1939, p. 19; "The Turn of the Worm?," *the Nation*, 8 April 1939, pp. 391-392; "Chamberlain on Trial," *The New Republic*, 12 April 1939, pp. 264-265; H.N. Brailsford, "Will Chamberlain Stick It Out?," *The New Republic*, 19 April 1939, pp. 295-296.

[105]"Watch on the Vistula," *Time*, 10 April 1939, p. 19; "Great Britain Finally Awakens to Reich Threat of Supremacy," *Newsweek*, 10 April 1939, pp. 19-23.

[106]"Discomfited Duce," *Newsweek*, 27 March 1939, p. 19; "Theorist," *Time*, 3 April 1939, pp. 20-22; "Europe in Turmoil," *The Nation*, 15 April 1939, pp. 419-420.

[107]"Il Duce's Latest Conquest," *The New Republic*, 19 April 1939, p. 289.

[108]"Birth and Death," *Time*, 17 April 1939, pp. 26-27; "Duce's Threat to Sea Power Prods British into Action," *Newsweek*, 17 April 1939, pp. 19-22; "Spain: Axis Alliance," *Newsweek*, 17 April 1939, pp. 22-23.

[109]"Hitler Yardstick," *Newsweek*, 17 April 1939, p. 23; "Vatican Blackout," *Newsweek*, 17 April 1939, p. 24; "Madmen and Fools," *Time*, 17 April 1939, pp. 24-25.

[110]"Bewildered Congress Groping for Sound Neutrality Policy," *Newsweek*, 17 April 1939, pp. 13-14; "Defense Fever," *Newsweek*, 17 April 1939, pp. 14-15.

[111]"Spirit of Warm Springs," *Time*, 17 April 1939, pp. 17-18.

[112]"Worst Week," *Time*, 17 April 1939, pp. 19-20; "On the European Front," *The Nation*, 22 April 1939, pp. 247-248; "Old Custom," *Time*, 24 April 1939, p. 20.

[113]"Dynamite in the Dikes," *Time*, 24 April 1939, p. 21; "Birthday Present?," *Time*, 24 April 1939, p. 21.

[114]"Europe's Armies Match Size of Forces Mobilized in 1914," *Newsweek*, 24 April 1939, pp. 19-20; "Worst Week," Time, 24 April 1939, pp. 19-20.

[115]"Diplomacy," *Newsweek*, 24 April 1939, p. 20; "Worst Week," *Time*, 24 April 1939, pp. 19-20; "Aspirin," *Newsweek* 24 April 1939, pp. 20-21.

[116]"President's Plea to Dictators Hastens Showdown in Congress," *Newsweek*, 24 April 1939, pp. 11-13; "Will to Peace," *Time*, 24 April 1939, pp. 13-14.

[117]"President's Plea to Dictators Hastens Showdown in Congress," *Newsweek*, 24 April 1939, pp. 11-13; "Will to Peace," *Time*, 24 April 1939, pp. 13-14; Freda Kirchwey, "Roosevelt, Peace-Monger," *The Nation*, 22 April 1939, pp. 456-457.

[118]"The President to the Dictators," *The New Republic*, 26 April 1939, pp. 321-322.

[119]"President's Pleas to Dictators Hastens Showdown in Congress," *Newsweek*, 24 April 1939, pp. 11-13; "Contours," *Time*, 24 April 1939, pp. 16-17.

[120]"Secret Policeman," *Time*, 24 April 1939, pp. 24-26.

121"I Was Hitler's Buddy," *The New Republic*, 5 April 1939, pp. 239-242; "I Was Hitler's Buddy: II," *The New Republic*, 12 April 1939, pp. 270-272; "I Was Hitler's Buddy: III," *The New Republic*, 19 April 1939, pp. 297-300.

122Medicus, "A Psychiatrist Looks at Hitler," 26 April 1939, pp. 326-327.

123"Two Diagnoses," *Time*, 8 May 1939, p. 22.

124"Alliance and Axis Salesmen Stage Tug of War in Europe," *Newsweek*, 1 May 1939, pp. 17-19; "Chamberlain Says Please," *The New Republic*, 3 May 1939, p. 361; *The Nation*, 29 April 1939, p. 481.

125"Alliance and Axis Salesmen Stage Tug of War in Europe," *Newsweek*, 1 May 1939, pp. 17-19.

126 *The Nation*, 29 April 1939; p. 482; "Chamberlain Says Please," *The New Republic*, 3 May 1939, p. 361.

127"Alliance and Alliance," *Time*, 1 May 1939, pp. 22-23; *The Nation*, 29 April 1939, p. 481.

128Henry C. Wolfe, "Europe's Secret Nightmare," *Harper's*, 1939, pp. 10-18.

129*The Nation*, 6 May 1939, p. 514; "To Arms," *Time*, 8 May 1939, pp. 20-21; "Britain's Drift," *Newsweek*, 8 May 1939, pp. 18-19; "Hitler 'Enthroned,'" *Newsweek*, 1 May 1939, p. 21; "Aggrandizer's Birthday," *Time*, 1 May 1939, pp. 23-24; "Background for War," *Time*, 1 May 1939, pp. 30-34.

130"Plebiscite," *Time*, 1 May 1939, p. 22; "Who's Afraid of the B.B. Wolf?," *The New Republic*, 3 May 1939, p. 361.

131"Danger Spot," *Time*, 8 May 1939, p. 18; Freda Kirchwey, "Hitler Says No," *The Nation*, 6 May 1939, pp. 516-517; "Adolf to Franklin," *Time*, 8 May 1939, pp. 11-13; "Danger Spot Shifts to Poland in Wake of Hitler's Address," *Newsweek*, 8 May 1939, pp. 16-18.

132"Hitler Speech Splits Congress, Stiffens Isolationist Sentiment," *Newsweek*, 8 May 1939, pp. 11-12; "Hitler's Inning," *Time*, 8 May 1939, pp. 18-19; "Hitler Answers," *The New Republic*, 10 May 1939, pp. 4-5; Freda Kirchwey, "Hitler Says No," *The Nation*, 6 May 1939, pp. 516-517.

133Albert Vitron, "The Poles Are Ready," *The Nation*, 13 May 1939, pp. 551-552; "Innuendo," *Newsweek*, 15 May 1939, p. 18; "Soviet Retains the Whiphand in Europe's Diplomatic Race," *Newsweek*, 15 May 1939, pp. 17-19.

134"New Allies," *Time*, 15 May 1939, pp. 21-22; cf. "The New Munich," *The New Republic*, 17 May 1939, p. 29.

135"Soviet Retains the Whiphand in Europe's Diplomatic Race," *Newsweek*, 15 May 1939, pp. 17-19; "New Allies," *Time*, 15 May 1939, pp. 21-22; "What Will Russia Do?," *The New Republic*, 17 May 1939, pp. 32-33.

136"Hemisphere Defense Question Begins To Stir in the Nation," *Newsweek*, 15 May 1939, pp. 11-12; "Pulse," *Newsweek*, 15 May 1939, pp. 12-14.

137"Sleep on Haversacks!," *Time*, 22 May 1939, pp. 24—25; "Mussolini as Pacifier," *The New Republic*, 24 May 1939, p. 57; "Buntings and Icebergs," *Time*, 22 May 1939, p. 25.

138"Check to the Axis?," *The Nation* 20 May 1939, p. 575; "Friends and Foes," *Time*, 22 May 1939, pp. 26-27; "Russia and Mr. Chamberlain," *The New Republic*, 24 May 1939, pp. 60-61; "Does Chamberlain Mean Business," *The New Republic*, 24 May 1939, pp. 66-67; "Toward the New Munich," *The New Republic*, 31 May 1939, pp. 91-92.

139"Mixed," *Time*, 22 May 1939, p. 26; "Unfair Competition," *Time*, 22 May 1939, p. 27; "Totalitarian Tipples," *Time*, 22 May 1939, pp. 18-19.

140*The Nation*, 3 June 1939, p. 629; "That Russian Alliance," *The New Republic*, 7 June 1939, p. 113; "Britain Bows," *Newsweek*, 5 June 1939, pp. 18-19; "Boo!," *Time*, 5 June 1939, pp. 21-22.

[141]"Molotov's Terms," *The Nation*, 10 June 1939, p. 659; "Try, Try Again," *Time*, 12 June 1939, pp. 21-22; "Adolf Hitler Reshapes Policy To One of Outwaiting British," *Newsweek*, 12 June 1939, pp. 19-20.

[142]"Assurances," *Time*, 12 June 1939, p. 22; *The Nation*, 17 June 1939, p. 685: "Vatican v. Kremlin," *Time*, 19 June 1939, p. 22; "Pope of Peace," *Newsweek*, 19 June 1939, pp. 25-26; "Pelf," *Time*, 19 June 1939, p. 23.

[143]"Peace Plans," *Time*, 19 June 1939, p. 22; "Shell Game," *Newsweek*, 19 June 1939, pp. 24-25. "Spider and Fly," *Time*, 12 June 1939, pp. 23-24; "Appease Porridge Cold," *The New Republic*, 14 June 1939, p. 141; Freda Kirchwey, "Lull Before Appeasement," *The Nation*, 24 June 1939, pp. 717-718; "Immediately," *Time*, 26 June 1939, p. 26.

[144]"Woes of a Fuehrer," *Newsweek*, 5 June 1939, p. 12; Ray Tozier, "Moseley of the Fifth Column," *The New Republic*, 2 June 1939, pp. 119-121; "Who Is Behind Moseley?," *The New Republic*, 17 June 1939, pp. 114-115.

[145]Kenneth G. Crawford, "Moseley Loses His Horse," *The Nation*, 10 June 1939, pp. 662-663; "Moseley's Fears," *Newsweek*, 12 June 1939, p. 15.

[146]"The Catholics Fight Anti-Semitism," *The New Republic*, 28 June 1939, p. 198.

[147]"Endless Voyage," *Time*, 12 June 1939, p. 22; "Freight," *Newsweek*, 19 June 1939, pp. 24-25; "And Pilate Washed His Hands," *The New Republic*, 28 June 1939, p. 197.

[148]"In Search of a Country," *The New Republic*, 14 June 1939, p. 143.

[149]"Germany Drums Holiday Spot," *Time*, 10 July 1939, pp. 20-21; "That End of Summer Crisis," *The New Republic*, 5 July 1939, p. 233; Freda Kirchwey, "Appeasement or War?," *The Nation*, 8 July 1939, pp. 33-34; *The Nation*, 1 July 1939, p. 2; "Europe's Harvest," *Time*, 3 July 1939, pp. 18-19; Judith Gruenfield, "Exhausted Nazi Labor," *The Nation*, 8 July 1939, pp. 36-37.

[150]"Clouds Over Europe," *Newsweek*, 3 July 1939, pp. 17-18; "Crisis Clouds Over Danzig Gives Europe 'War of Nerves,' " *Newsweek*, 10 July 1939, pp. 17-18; "British Talk," *Time*, 10 July 1939, pp. 18-19.

[151]"Kind Words," *Time*, 3 July 1939, p. 21; Winston Churchill, "Let the Criminal Tyrants Bomb," *Collier's*, 14 January 1939, pp. 12-13, 36; Winston Churchill, "Now or Never," *Collier's*, 3 June 1939, pp. 9-10, 53-54; Winston Churchill, "Bombing Doesn't Scare Us Now," *Collier's*, 17 June 1939, pp. 11, 56-58; " 'Winnie' for Sea Lord?," *Time*, 17 July 1939, pp. 22-23.

[152]" 'We Have Guaranteed,' " *Time*, 17 July 1939, p. 20.

[153]"The Bill," *Time*, 24 July 1939, p. 16; " 'Brave Iron!' " *Time*, 13 July 1939, pp. 14-15; "Britain's Ironside," *Newsweek*, 31 July 1939, pp. 17-18.

[154]"The Paris Press," *Newsweek*, 24 July 1939, p. 20; "It Is Said," *Time*, 24 July 1939, pp. 15-16; Theodore Draper, "Nazi Spies in France," *The New Republic*, 23 August 1939, p. 72.

[155]"Europe Basks in Appeasement But Armies Continue To Prepare," *Newsweek*, 31 July 1939, pp. 15-16; "Smoke and Fire," *Time*, 31 July 1939, p. 14; "Back To Appeasement," *The New Republic*, 2 August 1939, p. 350.

[156]" 'Union of Jews,' " *Newsweek*, 17 July 1939, p. 20.

[157]"Shadow Over Palestine," *Time*, 4 September 1939, p. 25; "Jews at Sea," *Newsweek*, 31 July 1939, p. 19; "Supreme Right," *Time*, 24 July 1939, p. 21.

[158]Allan A. Michie, "The Jewish National Army," *The New Republic*, 9 August 1939, pp. 14-15.

[159]"Jewish Firebrands," *Newsweek*, 28 August 1939, pp. 19-20; "Shadow Over Promise," *Time*, 28 August 1939, p. 26; Freda Kirchwey, "Bargains in Refugees," *The Nation*, 5 August 1939, pp. 137-138.

[160]*The Nation*, 2 September 1939, p. 231; "Radio Does Its Bit," *The New Republic*, 6 September 1939, p. 113.

[161]*The Nation,* 9 September 1939, p. 257; "World War," *Time,* 11 September 1939, p. 13.

[162]"Ready for Signing," *Time,* 7 August 1939, pp. 20-21; "The War Nerves Goes On," *The New Republic,* 9 August 1939, p. 1; "Quo Vadis, Duce?," *Time,* 7 August 1939, p. 20; "Weird Week," Time, 21 August 1939, pp. 15-16.

[163]"Back To Appeasement," *The New Republic,* 2 August 1939, p. 350; "Awakening," *Time,* 7 August 1939, p. 17.

[164]"Washington Scraps a Treaty To Bring Japanese To Book," *Newsweek,* 7 August 1939, pp. 11-12; "Dead Hare, Weeping Fox," *Time,* 7 August 1939, pp. 11-12; "Awakening," *Time,* 7 August 1939, p. 17.

[165]*The Nation,* 3 June 1939, p. 630; "Road To Neutrality?," *Newsweek,* 5 June 1939, p. 13; "Mr. Hull on Neutrality," *The New Republic,* 7 June 1939, p. 113.

[166]*The Nation,* 17 June 1939, pp. 685-686; "Neutrality Fight," *Newsweek,* 26 June 1939, pp. 16-17; "Review of 76th Congress: A $13,400,000,000 Runaway," *Newsweek,* 14 August 1939, pp. 11-13.

[167]*The Nation,* 5 August 1939, p. 133; "Courting a Coy Russian Bear: Anglo-French Generals Try It," *Newsweek,* 7 August 1939, pp. 18-19; "Ready for Signing," *Time,* 7 August 1939, pp. 20-21; Edmund Stevens, "Not in the Cables," *The New Republic,* 1939, pp. 357-358; "The War of Nerves Goes On," *The New Republic,* 9 August 1939, p. 1.

[168]*The Nation,* 12 August 1939, p. 161; " 'Be Gone!,' " *Newsweek,* 14 August 1939, p. 19; "Reverse," *Time,* 14 August 1939, p. 18; Robert Dell, "Will There Be War?," *The Nation,* 19 August 1939, pp. 487-489.

[169]"Danzig Flare-Up," *Newsweek,* 14 August 1939, p. 20; "Sunrise," *Time,* 14 August 1939, p. 17; "War Anniversary Finds Europe Rehearsing an Encore," *Newsweek,* 14 August 1939, p. 18.

[170]"That Sleepy War of Nerves," *The New Republic,* 16 August 1939, p. 29; "British Blackout," *Newsweek,* 21 August 1939, pp. 18-19; "Eastland v. Westland," *Time,* 21 August 1939, pp. 16-17; "Humble Herrings and Magarine Set Nervous Europe a-Twitter," *Newsweek,* 21 August 1939, p. 17.

[171]"Army of the Po," *Time,* 14 August 1939, pp. 19-20; "'Burning Question,'" *Newsweek,* 21 August 1939, pp. 17-18; "Mussolini and His Partner," *The Nation,* 23 August 1939, p. 57; "Weird Week," *Time,* 21 August 1939, pp. 15-16; "Alliance or Bluff?," *The New Republic,* 23 August 1939, pp. 57-58; "Hitler's Danzig Plans," *The New Republic,* 23 August 1939, pp. 67-68.

[172]"Has Democracy Won Again?," *Collier's,* 6 September 1939, p. 54.

[173]"Red Star and Swastika," *The Nation,* 26 August 1939, pp. 211-212; "Roosevelt's Fight for Peace," *The Nation,* 2 September 1939, pp. 233-234; Freda Kirchwey, "Europe's Last Stand," *The Nation,* 26 August 1939, pp. 232-233.

[174]"Sudden German-Soviet Deal Leaves Europe Thunderstruck," *Newsweek,* 28 August 1939, pp. 16-17; "Bewildered British," *Newsweek,* 28 August 1939, pp. 18-19; "Statesmen Sitting Uncertainly on Europe's Rumbling Caissons," *Newsweek,* 4 September 1939, pp. 14-15.

[175]"Nightmare Shock," *Time,* 28 August 1939, pp. 20-21; "Nationalism," *Time,* 28 August 1939, pp. 23-24.

[176]"Stalin's Munich," *The New Republic,* 20 August 1939, pp. 88-89.

[177]" 'Not Since Napoleon,' " *Time,* 4 September 1939, p. 24; "Prologue," *Newsweek,* 4 September 1939, pp. 18-19; "In the Stomach," *Time,* 4 September 1939, p. 18; "Statesmen Sitting Uncertainly on Europe's Rumbling Caissons," *Newsweek,* 4 September 1939, p. 18.

[178]"Acts Before Words," *Time,* 4 September 1939, pp. 19-20; "Prologue," *Newsweek,* 4 September 1939, pp. 18-19.

[179] " 'War Is Very Near,' " *Time*, 4 September 1939, p. 20; "Measure for Measure," *Newsweek*, 4 September 1939, pp. 15-16; "Acts Before Words," *Time*, September 1939, pp. 19-20.

[180] "Vision, Vindication," *Time*, 4 September 1939, pp. 22-23; "Empire," *Time*, 4 September 1939, pp. 21-22.

[181] "Off-Base," *Time*, 4 September 1939, pp. 9-10. Cf. "One U.S. Eye Kept on Europe, Other on Our Neutrality Act," *Newsweek*, 4 September 1939, pp. 11-12; "Crisis," *Time*, 4 September 1939, pp. 11-12.

[182] "Revised Reds," *Time*, 4 September 1939, p. 11; "One U.S. Eye Kept on Europe, Other on Our Neutrality Act," Newsweek, 4 September 1939, pp. 11-12.

[183] "Revised Reds," *Time*, 4 September 1939, p. 11; "Blushing Leftists," *Newsweek*, 4 September 1939, pp. 12-14; "They Just Love Democracy," *The New Republic*, 6 September 1939, p. 114.

[184] "One U.S. Eye Kept on Europe, Other on Our Neutrality Act," *Newsweek*, 4 September 1939, pp. 11-12.

[185] "We Want To Stay Out," *The New Republic*, 6 September 1939, p. 114.

[186] *The Nation*, 6 September 1939, p. 257; "Grey Friday," *Time*, 11 September 1939, pp. 18-19; "Europe's Foes Unleash Forces After Slow Start of New War," *Newsweek*, 11 September 1939, pp. 11-14; "1914 Repeats Itself," *The New Republic*, 13 September 1939, p. 141.

Index